A-Z SOUTH WALES V

CONTENT

REFERENC

A Road	A467
Under Construction	
Proposed	
B Road	B4251
Dual Carriageway	
One Way Street Traffic flow on A Roads is also indicated by a heavy line on the driver's left.	→
Restricted Access	
Pedestrianized Road	
Track / Footpath	
Residential Walkway	
Railway	Station, Heritage Station, Level Crossing, Tunnel
Built Up Area	GWENT WAY
Local Authority Boundary	
Posttown Boundary	
Postcode Boundary within Posttown	
Map Continuation	32
Car Park selected	P
Church or Chapel	†
Cycleway selected	
Fire Station	■
Hospital	H
House Numbers A & B Roads only	13 8
Information Centre	i
National Grid Reference	320
Police Station	▲
Post Office	★
Toilet: without facilities for the Disabled with facilities for the Disabled	▽
Viewpoint	
Educational Establishment	
Hospital or Hospice	
Industrial Building	
Leisure or Recreational Facility	
Place of Interest	
Public Building	
Shopping Centre or Market	
Other Selected Buildings	

SCALE: 1:15,840 4 inches (10.16 cm) to 1 mile, 6.31 cm to 1 kilometre

0 ¼ ½ ¾ 1 Mile

0 250 500 750 1 Kilometre

Head Office:
Fairfield Road, Borough Green, Sevenoaks, Kent TN15 8PP
Telephone: 01732 781000 (General Enquiries & Trade Sales)

Showrooms:
44 Gray's Inn Road, London WC1X 8HX
Telephone: 020 7440 9500 (Retail Sales)
www.a-zmaps.co.uk

Ordnance Survey® This product includes mapping data licensed from Ordnance Survey® with the permission of the Controller of Her Majesty's Stationery Office.

Edition 1 2003

KEY TO MAP PAGES *Allwedd i Dudalennau'r Map*

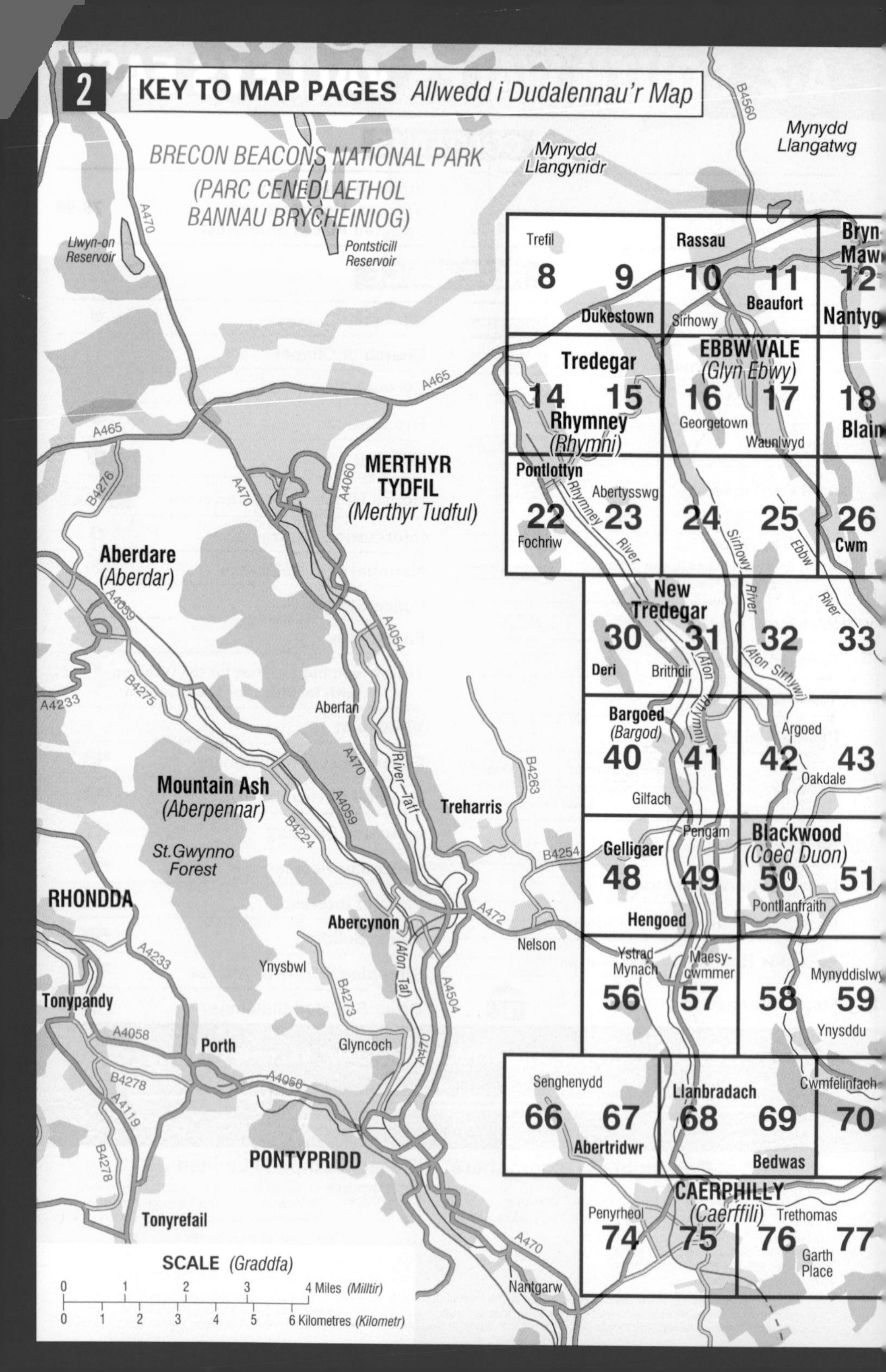

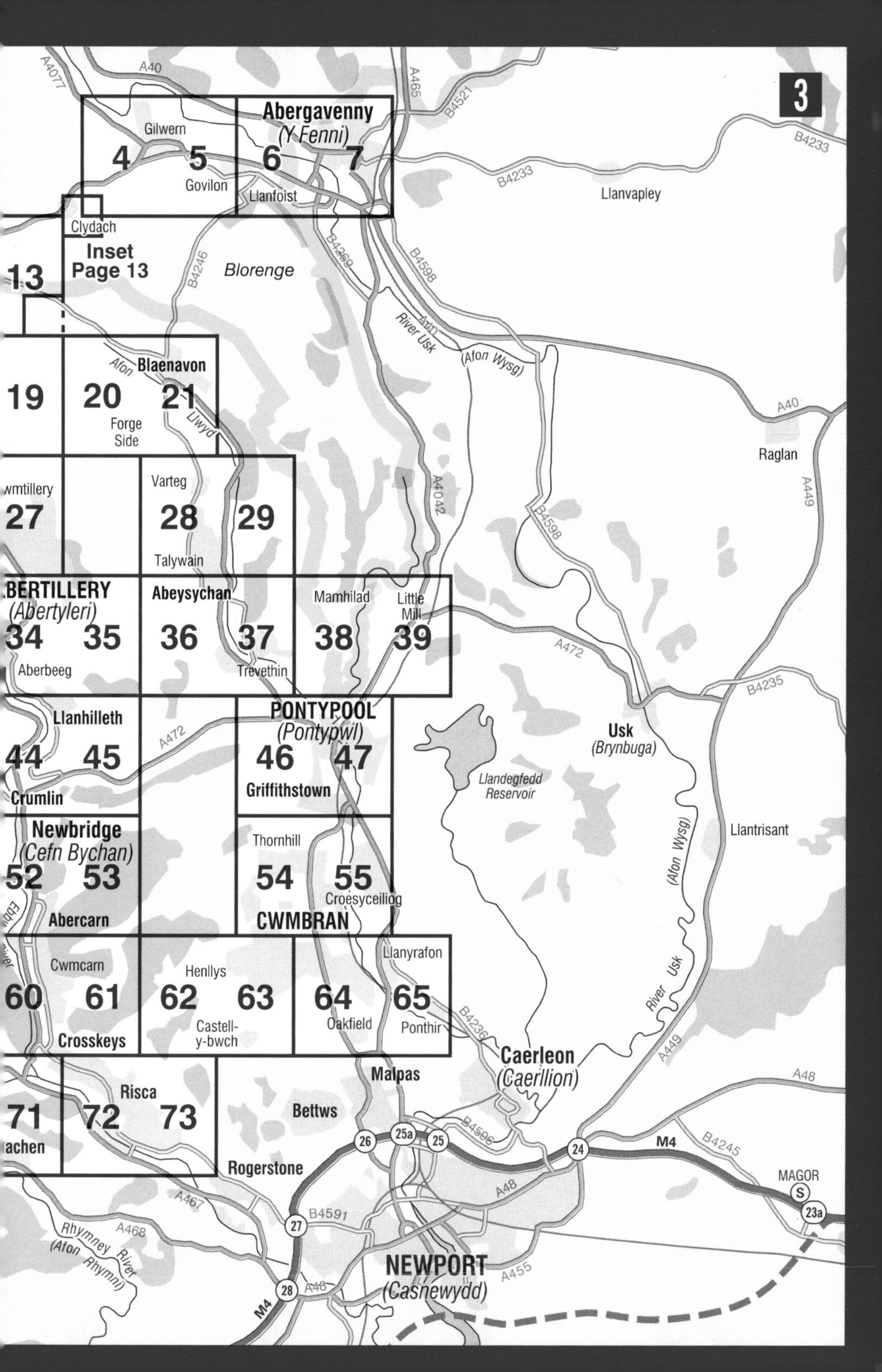
3
Abergavenny
(Y Fenni)
Gilwern
Govilon
Llanfoist
Clydach
Inset
Page 13
Blorenge
Llanvapley
River Usk
(Afon Wysg)
Afon
Llwyd
Blaenavon
Forge
Side
Varteg
Talywain
Raglan
wmtillery
BERTILLERY
(Abertyleri)
Aberbeeg
Abeysychan
Trevethin
Mamhilad
Little
Mill
PONTYPOOL
(Pontypwl)
Griffithstown
Llanhilleth
Crumlin
Usk
(Brynbuga)
Llandegfedd
Reservoir
Llantrisant
Newbridge
(Cefn Bychan)
Abercarn
Thornhill
Croesyceiliog
CWMBRAN
Llanyrafon
Cwmcarn
Crosskeys
Henllys
Castell-
y-bwch
Oakfield
Ponthir
Caerleon
(Caerllion)
Malpas
Risca
Bettws
achen
Rogerstone
MAGOR
NEWPORT
(Casnewydd)
Rhymney River
(Afon Rhymni)
A4077
A40
A465
B4521
B4233
B4246
B4269
B4598
A4042
A472
B4235
A449
B4236
A48
M4
B4245
B4596
A467
A468
B4591
A455
4
5
6
7
13
19
20
21
27
28
29
34
35
36
37
38
39
44
45
46
47
52
53
54
55
60
61
62
63
64
65
71
72
73
24
25
25a
26
27
28
23a
S

4
23
A
B
C
D
Coed-Perth-y-piod
The Paddocks
Llwyncytrych
Fawr
Forge House
Mill House
Glangrwyney
24
Glangrwyney Bridge
Lower Mill House
Grwyne
16
Crickhowell
NP8
RIVER USK
(AFON WYSG)
MONMOUTHSHIRE (SIR FYNWY)
POWYS
CRICKHOWELL
A4077
Dan-y-Warren
1
Pen-yr-adwy-wynt
Tir-Thomas Howell
Dan-y-graig
Glan-Wysg
The Ithon
Monmouthshire & Brecon Canal
Tir-Gunter
2
Glaslyn Court
Pwll Glaslyn
Ty Ffynon
Ffynnon-yr-eirin
RIVER CLYDACH
Maes-y-berllan
Lodge
Dan-y-coed
GLANGRWYNEY
THE SHIRES
THE HALFPENNYS
Dyffryn-Clydach
Lower Mill
CAE
FAIRHOME
TYR COMMON
THE GDNS.
HILL VIEW
ELM GRO.
MELDON
Upper Common
COMMON ROAD
Glaslyn Farm
Church Farm
215
BANK CRES.
Recreation Ground
Llanelly
(Llanelli)
OAKDENE WY.
AVENUE
MALFORD
GLANMOOR
BRYNGLAS
Weir
3
Grave Yard
Cross
LLANELLY
ROAD
Ysgubor-Edmund
ALLERFORD GRO.
EXFORD GRO.
GROVE
WINSFORD GRO.
Pen-y-bont
PEN-Y-BONT
DAN-Y-BONT
Reservoir (covered)
CHURCH
FOREST HILL
BACK RD.
Lib.
MAIN RD.
GLAN-RHYD
SCHOOL LA.
Coed Uchel
HIGH
ABERG
Ty'n-y-wern
Rec. Grd.
ORCHARD CLOSE
Pantybeiliau
VALL
Neuadd
Lion Ter.
Maesygwartha
4
CHURCH
Clydach Wood
OLD RECTORY CL.
CLYDACH
RIVER
Twyn yr Hebog
TRAP
OLD
ROAD
STATION ROAD
Ty-isaf
14
ROW
FORGE
OF THE
HEADS OF THE VALLEYS ROAD
MAESYGWARTHA
A465
Brunant
Dan-y-lan
Railway Terrace
Reservoir (covered)
BRECON BEACONS
(PARC CENEDLAETHOL
Saleyard
LLANELLY
5
Cwm Sion Mathew
LLANELLY HILL CARAVAN SITE
Wenallt
Ty-pwll
TY GWYN
Heol-fedw
Wenallt Fach
Twyn Wenallt
HEOL BEDD-DYN-HIR
Dan-y-lan
LLANELLY HILL ROAD
Sub.
P
Cabier Dyar
Draen
Troed-y-Wennol
Pant-glas
6
STATION ROAD
BRUNANT
Sports Field
Bath Row
Tanker's Row
13
Clydach
INSET
Page 13
A
B
GILWERN HILL
24
C
D
23

NP8
Gilwern
Abergavenny
NP7
Govilon
Twyn-Allws
NATIONAL PARK
BANNAU BRYCHEINIOG)
A40
A465
A4077
B4246
HEADS OF THE VALLEYS ROAD
MERTHYR ROAD
RIVER USK (AFON WYSG)
Monmouthshire & Brecon Canal
Mardy Cottage
Ashstead
Fair View
Tynewydd House
Ty Deri
Hall
Glenburnie
Roseville
Sewage Works
Talymaes
Grey Hall Cottage
Grey Hall
The Steps
Pyscodlyn Farm
Pant-yr-onen
Duffryn Farm
Lower House
Mardy Farm
The Grove
The Swamp
Ty Mawr Manor
Ty Mawr Site
Beiliau
Lodge
Cotswold Bungalow
Training Centre
Dyffryn-Bach
GILWERN PARK INDUSTRIAL SITE
Aberbaiden Farm
Sewage Farm
Hop-Yard Farm
Perthi Cottage
Canaan Bungalow
Boat Farm
War Memorial
King George's Field
Pav.
Rectory
Weir
Govilon Prim. Sch.
The Grange
The Elms Farm
Llanwenarth House
Ty-gwyn
Pentre Farm
Aqueduct House
Upper Mill Farm
Sunnybank
Pen-hoel-gerrigg
Red House Farm
The Nookfield
Coed-y-twyn
Pentwyn
White House
Heol-y-bwla
Cwm Llanwenarth
Ford
Cwm Farm
Pen-dovcae
OAK TREE LANE
PEN-Y-RHIW
LANCASTER DR.
BASILDENE CL.
USK DRIVE
ROAD
GREENWOOD PL.
CROSS ROADS
DAN-Y-BRYN CL.
GLANBAIDEN
Baiden Brook
Cwm-Shenkin Brook
MILL LANE
THE DRAGON
TY-CLYD CL.
MILL CR.
MAESHYFRYD AVENUE
CHURCH LA.
CHURCH RD.
LINDEN GRO.
PENYBONT
NTH.VW.
LLANWENARTH VW.
LLANWENARTH RD.
DERWEN DEG CL.
STEPHENS CRES.
USK VIEW
LANE
TWYN ALLWYS ROAD
PEN PADRIG
STATION ROAD
SCHOOL ROAD
CWM ROAD
PENTWYN LANE
Sub.
E
F
G
H
1
2
3
4
5
6
9
25
26
27
16
215
14
13

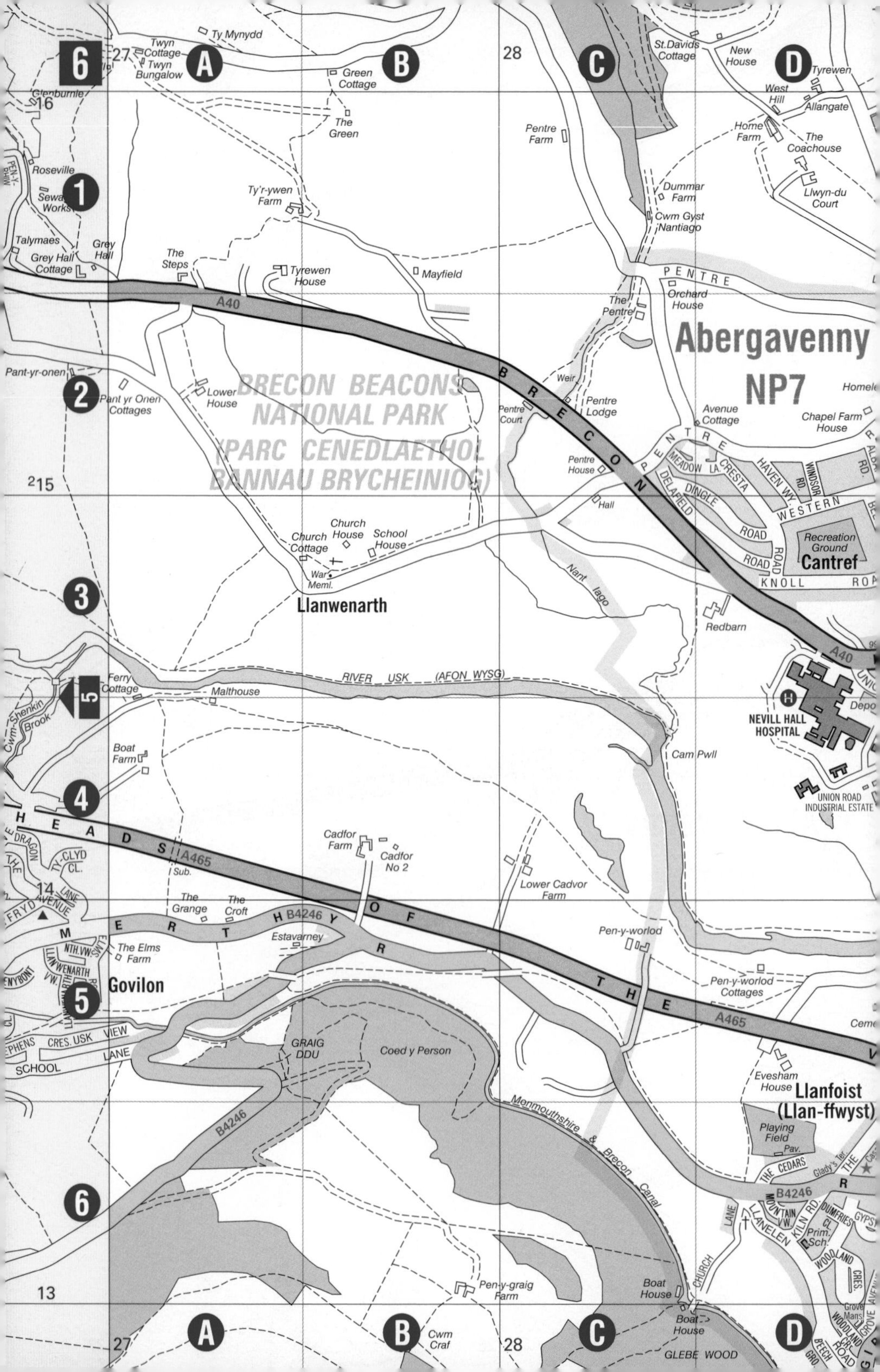
6
Abergavenny
NP7
BRECON BEACONS NATIONAL PARK (PARC CENEDLAETHOL BANNAU BRYCHEINIOG)
Llanwenarth
Govilon
Llanfoist (Llan-ffwyst)
Cantref
NEVILL HALL HOSPITAL
UNION ROAD INDUSTRIAL ESTATE
RIVER USK (AFON WYSG)
Monmouthshire & Brecon Canal
HEADS OF THE VALLEYS
A40
A465
B4246
Ty Mynydd
Twyn Cottage
Twyn Bungalow
Green Cottage
The Green
St.Davids Cottage
New House
Tyrewen
West Hill
Allangate
Home Farm
The Coachouse
Llwyn-du Court
Pentre Farm
Dummar Farm
Cwm Gyst
Nantiago
Glenburnie
Roseville
Sewage Works
Talymaes
Grey Hall
Grey Hall Cottage
Ty'r-ywen Farm
The Steps
Tyrewen House
Mayfield
PENTRE
Orchard House
The Pentre
Weir
Pentre Lodge
Pentre Court
Pentre House
Avenue Cottage
Chapel Farm House
Pant-yr-onen
Pant yr Onen Cottages
Lower House
Church House
Church Cottage
School House
War Meml.
Hall
Nant Iago
MEADOW LA.
CRESTA
HAVEN WY.
WINDSOR RD.
DELAFIELD
DINGLE ROAD
WESTERN ROAD
KNOLL ROAD
Recreation Ground
Redbarn
Ferry Cottage
Malthouse
Cwm-Shenkin Brook
Boat Farm
Cam Pwll
Depot
Cadfor Farm
Cadfor No 2
Lower Cadvor Farm
Sub.
The Grange
The Croft
Estavarney
The Elms Farm
Pen-y-worlod
Pen-y-worlod Cottages
MERTHYR
THE DRAGON
TY-CLYD CL.
AVENUE
LANE
NTH.VW.
ELMS
LLANWENARTH VW.
STEPHENS CRES.
USK VIEW
SCHOOL LANE
GRAIG DDU
Coed y Person
Evesham House
Playing Field
Pav.
THE CEDARS
Glady's Ter.
MOUNTAIN VW.
KILN RD
LLANELEN
DUMFRIES CL.
Prim. Sch.
WOODLAND CRES.
GROVE AVENUE
Grove Mans.
WOODLAND CR.
BEECH GRO.
CHURCH LANE
Pen-y-graig Farm
Boat House
Cwm Craf
GLEBE WOOD
A B C D
1 2 3 4 5 6
27 28
16 215 14 13
5

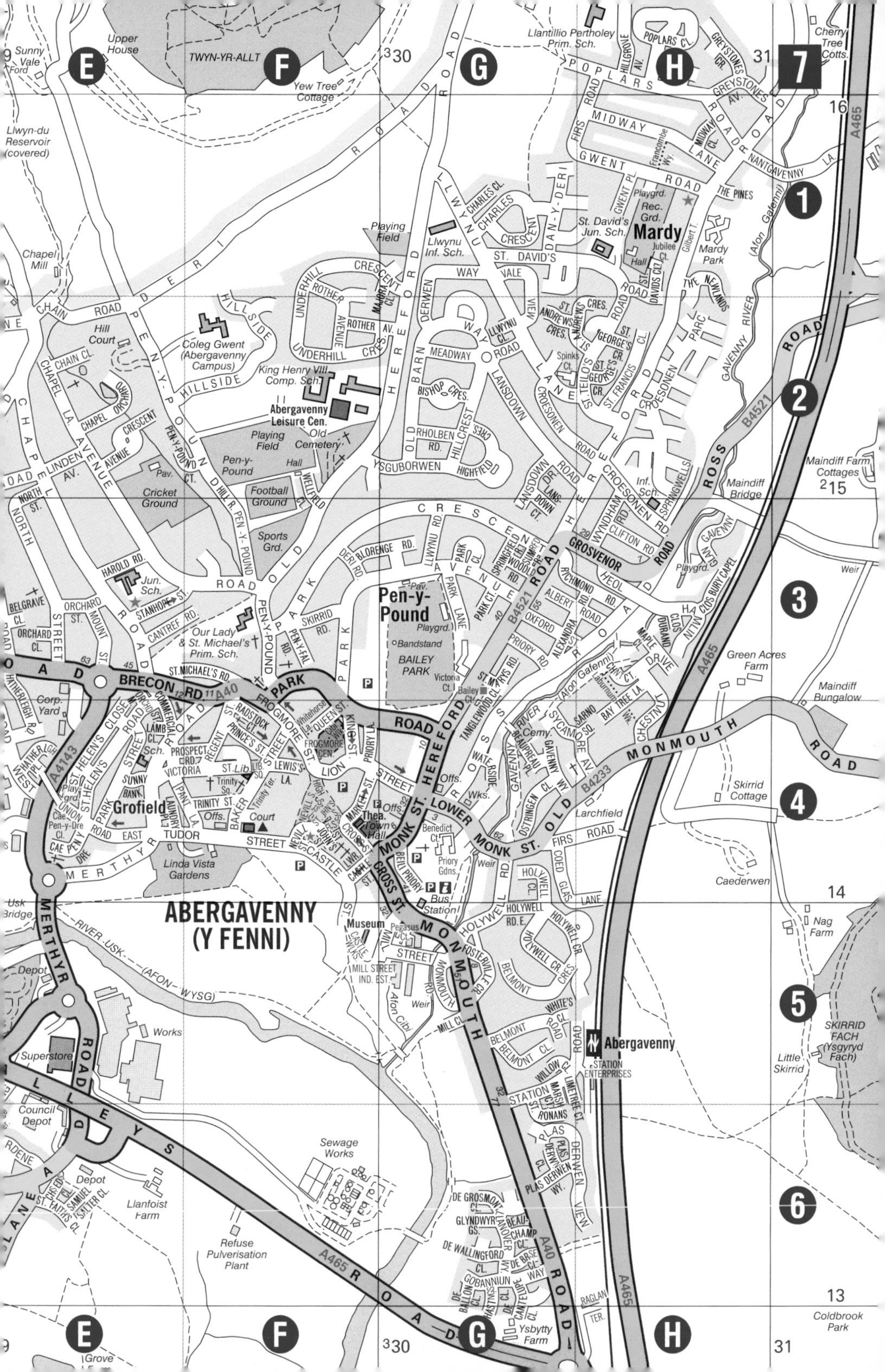

7
E
F
G
H
1
2
3
4
5
6
330
31
16
215
14
13
ABERGAVENNY
(Y FENNI)
Mardy
Grofield
Pen-y-Pound
Sunny Vale Ford
Upper House
TWYN-YR-ALLT
Yew Tree Cottage
Llantillio Pertholey Prim. Sch.
Cherry Tree Cotts.
Llwyn-du Reservoir (covered)
Chapel Mill
Hill Court
Coleg Gwent (Abergavenny Campus)
King Henry VIII Comp. Sch.
Abergavenny Leisure Cen.
Old Cemetery
Playing Field
Llwynu Inf. Sch.
St. David's Jun. Sch.
Rec. Grd.
Playgrd.
Hall
Mardy Park
Cricket Ground
Pen-y-Pound
Football Ground
Sports Grd.
Jun. Sch.
Our Lady & St. Michael's Prim. Sch.
Bandstand
BAILEY PARK
Victoria Ct.
Bailey Ct.
Inf. Sch.
Maindiff Bridge
Maindiff Farm Cottages
Green Acres Farm
Maindiff Bungalow
Weir
Corp. Yard
Cemy.
Skirrid Cottage
Larchfield
Caederwen
Nag Farm
SKIRRID FACH (Ysgyryd Fach)
Little Skirrid
Linda Vista Gardens
Thea.
Town Hall
Court
Offs.
Lib.
Wks.
Priory Gdns.
Bus Station
Museum
MILL STREET IND. EST.
Afon Cibi
Usk Bridge
RIVER USK (AFON WYSG)
Depot
Works
Superstore
Council Depot
Llanfoist Farm
Refuse Pulverisation Plant
Sewage Works
Abergavenny
STATION ENTERPRISES
Ysbytty Farm
Coldbrook Park
A465
A40
A4143
B4521
B4233
BRECON RD.
MONMOUTH ROAD
ROSS ROAD
HEREFORD ROAD
OLD HEREFORD ROAD
DERI ROAD
CHAIN ROAD
PEN-Y-POUND
PARK ROAD
PARK CRESCENT
AVENUE ROAD
GROSVENOR ROAD
MERTHYR ROAD
LLANFOIST
HOLYWELL RD.
CROESONEN ROAD
POPLARS ROAD
MIDWAY LANE
GWENT ROAD
NANTGAVENNY LA.
GREYSTONES AV.
THE PINES
LANSDOWN ROAD
MONK ST.
LOWER MONK ST.
OLD MONMOUTH ROAD
CROSS ST.
TUDOR STREET
FROGMORE ST.
LION STREET
FIRS ROAD
STATION RD.
PLAS DERWEN
RAGLAN TER.

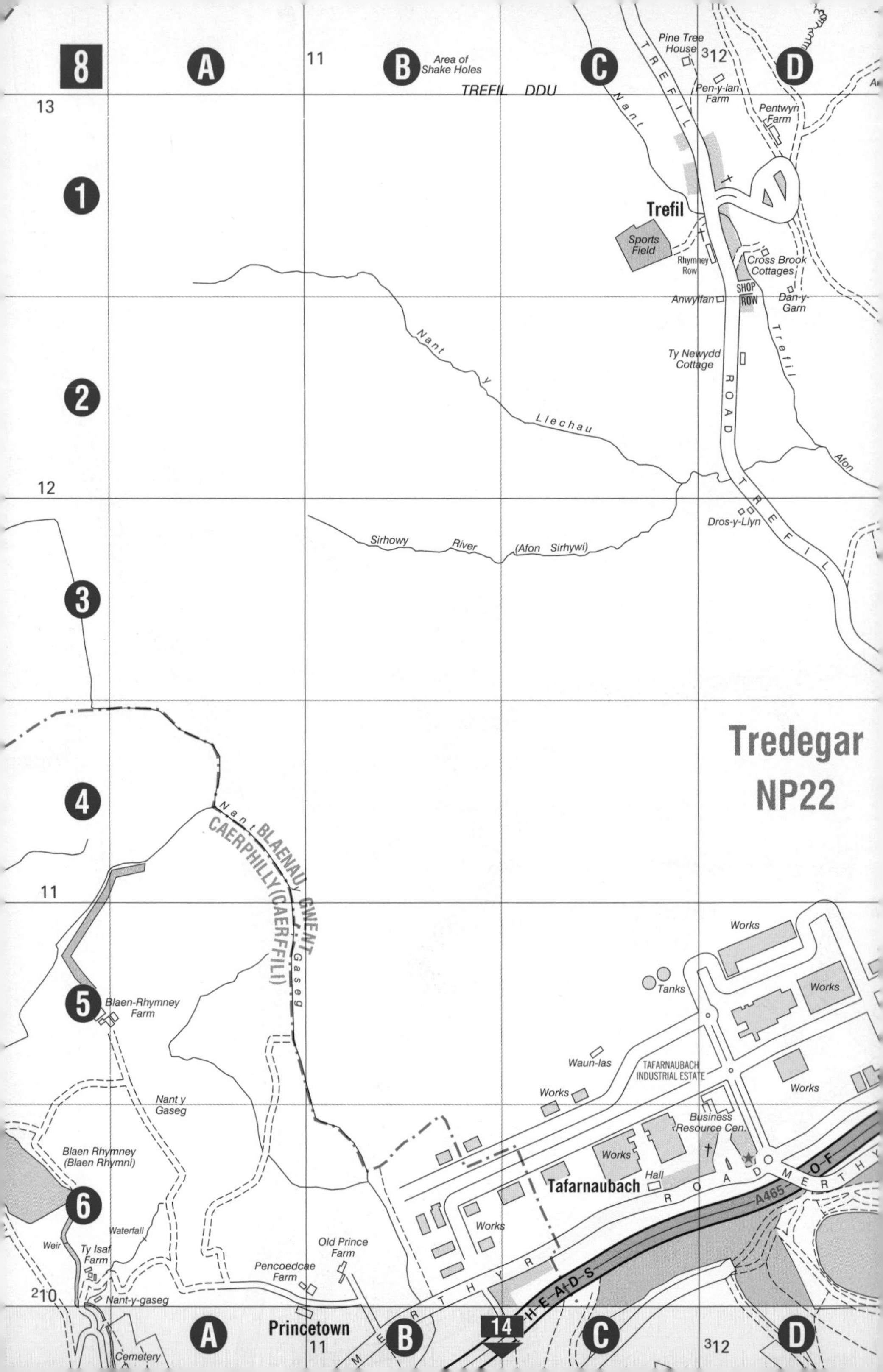
A
B
C
D
11
312
13
12
11
210
1
2
3
4
5
6
Area of Shake Holes
TREFIL DDU
Pine Tree House
Pen-y-lan Farm
Pentwyn Farm
Nant
TREFIL ROAD
Trefil
Sports Field
Rhymney Row
Cross Brook Cottages
SHOP ROW
Anwylfan
Dan-y-Garn
Ty Newydd Cottage
Trefil
Nant y Llechau
Afon
Dros-y-Llyn
Sirhowy River (Afon Sirhywi)
Tredegar
NP22
BLAENAU GWENT
CAERPHILLY (CAERFFILI)
Nant y Gaseg
Works
Tanks
Works
Blaen-Rhymney Farm
Waun-las
TAFARNAUBACH INDUSTRIAL ESTATE
Works
Works
Nant y Gaseg
Business Resource Cen.
Blaen Rhymney (Blaen Rhymni)
Works
Hall
Tafarnaubach
MERTHYR ROAD
A465
HEADS OF THE VALLEYS
Waterfall
Works
Weir
Ty Isaf Farm
Old Prince Farm
Pencoedcae Farm
Nant-y-gaseg
Princetown
14
Cemetery

E
F
G
H
13
14
Shake Holes
Milgatw
Nant
TWYN BRYN-MARCH
Ebbw
Vale
NP23
RASSAU
INDUSTRIAL ESTATE
Ffynnon Sion
Sieffre
Shon-Sheffrey's
Reservoir
Milgatw
Coates
Row
The Wells
Farm
Sub.
Garnddu
Farm
Water
Works
Blaen-y-
cwm
Hirgan
Penrhyn
Farm
Tynewydd
Golwg-y-
Mynydd
Afon
Tir Morgan-
Hywel
CROWN
BUSINESS
PARK
A465
ROAD
Waundeg
Cemetery
Works
Factory
Bryn Se
PEN-Y-BONT
BUSH BACH
Nant-y-
Bwch
Farm
VALLEYS
CROWN
Melyn
Works
Bus
Depot
Subway
Dukestown
Nant
THE
Nant-y-bwch
WILLOW CT.
ST. LUKE'S
STATION RD.
RODERICK HILL CT.
GLANHOWY
MEADOW CR.
SCWRFA
STAR
PICTON
DUKESTOWN
YSTRAD
DERI
SHEPHERDS CT.
HEATHER CL.
Hafod-Wen
Brynbach
Prim. Sch.
ROAD
A4048
Duke's
Meadow
Sch.
STREET
CROSS
FEEDER
Scwrfa
EBENEZER
CHARTIST
YSGUBOR
Sirhowy
Inf. Sch.
WEN
BRYN BACH PARK
LAKESIDE CL.
ST. MARTIN'S CR.
GREENWOOD AV.
BRYNBACH ST.
PEMBROKE ST.
CRESCENT
ASHVALE
COACH
BACH
LINDSAY GDNS
VARTEG PL.
Playground
BEVAN AV.
Griffiths Sq.
NORTH
AVENUE
SYCAMORE
CHARLES
ARNOLD
VICARAGE
Sch.
GRAHAM'S YARD
Ashvale
ASHVALE
IND. EST.
MAPLE AV.
LABURNAM AV.
AVENUE
PLACE
A4048
ROAD
A4047
Football
Grd.
VIEW
15
Factories
Deighton
Prim.
Sch.
STREET
DUKESTOWN
Sirhowy
(Sirhywi)
1
2
3
4
5
6
10
11
12
13
10

A
B
C
D
315
16
13
12
11
210
1
2
3
4
5
6
Reservoir (covered)
RASSAU INDUSTRIAL ESTATE
Rassau
Carmeltown
Recreation Ground
Carno Houses
Jun. & Inf. Sch.
Herrington Farm
Trevil Farm
Nant-y-croft
Coates Row
The Wells Farm
Beaufort Wells
Sub.
HEADS OF THE VALLEY
A465
A4046
A4047
B4478
CROWN BUSINESS PARK
Bryn Serth
Superstore
Rhyd -y-blew Pond
Small Rhyd-y-blew Pond
Ebbw Vale Comp. Sch.
YSBYTY'R TRI CHWM
Coleg Gwent (Ebbw Vale Campus)
Cemetery
Waun y Pound
WAUN-Y-POUND INDUSTRIAL ESTATE
Tredegar NP22
Sirhowy Inf. Sch.
Playground
Sirhowy (Sirhywi)
Willowtown
Factory
COLLEGE ROAD
WAUN-Y-POUND ROAD
BEAUFORT ROAD
RASSAU ROAD
MOUNTAIN RD. (WILLIAM MORRIS WY.)
BRYN-SERTH
MAN-MOEL ROAD
GWAUN HELYG ROAD
LETCHWORTH RD.
MOUNT PLEASANT AVENUE
CEMETERY
HONEYFIELD ROAD
GLYNDWR RD.
SUMMERFIELD RD.
CLYDACH AV.
MELYN CL.
FERNDALE CL.
PHILLIPS CL.
TUDOR CL.
RHONDDA CL.
RHYMNEY CL.
TAFF CL.
AVON CT.
ROWAN WAY
RESERVOIR ROAD
PRINCE CHARLES ROAD
ALDER GRO.
LABURNUM CL.
CEDAR CL.
HOLLY CL.
HAZEL CT.
USK PL.
MAPLE WY.
BRIAR CL.
ACORN CT.
CHESTNUT CL.
HONEYSUCKLE CL.
Pen-y-Crug
Tor-y-Crug
Gelli Crug
HOWY
NANT
STONEBRIDGE
IVY CL.
COEDCAE
CAE-Y-SCHOOL
SCHOOL LA.
RHYD MAES GLAS
MAES WAEN
HEOL WAEN
GRAIG WAUN FAWR
EBBW
CENDL CR.
MOOR VW.
ALANDALE RD.
BARNES CL.
MAES REG
Y-GAR
RUSSEL CL.
JAMES'S RW.
GREENFIELD
Cwrt Rhyd
Pav.
ALLOTMENT
PARTRIDGE ROW
BEVAN CRES.
BADMINTON
EMLYN
BRYN GLAS
TIR-Y-BERTH
PEN-Y-DRE
GLANFFRWD
Glyncoed Comp. Sch.
Carno Reservoir
Carno Cott.
Cwm Carno
Ebbw River
Hirgan
Melyn
DUKESTOWN
CHARTIST WAY
YSGUBOR
RHOSLAN
BRYN PICA
WEN
HEATHER CL.
SHEPHERDS CL.
SHEP-HERDS CT.
DERI
YSTRAD DERI
GRAIGY NOS
MDW.
GREEN
SIRHOWY CT.
KING ST.
BEAUFORT CT.
VARTEG PL.
FAIR-FIELD
WILLOW CL.
ANNES CT.
ELIZABETH CT.
ANDREWS CT.
EDWARDS CT.
BRENTWOOD P.
JOHN
ALFRED ST.
DAVIDS ST.
COUNCIL ST.
HUGHES
GARFIELD TER.
BRYNHEULOG
Sch.
Blaen Wern
Llwyn Celyn
Gwaun Helyg
ONNEN
PEN Y PARC
9
16

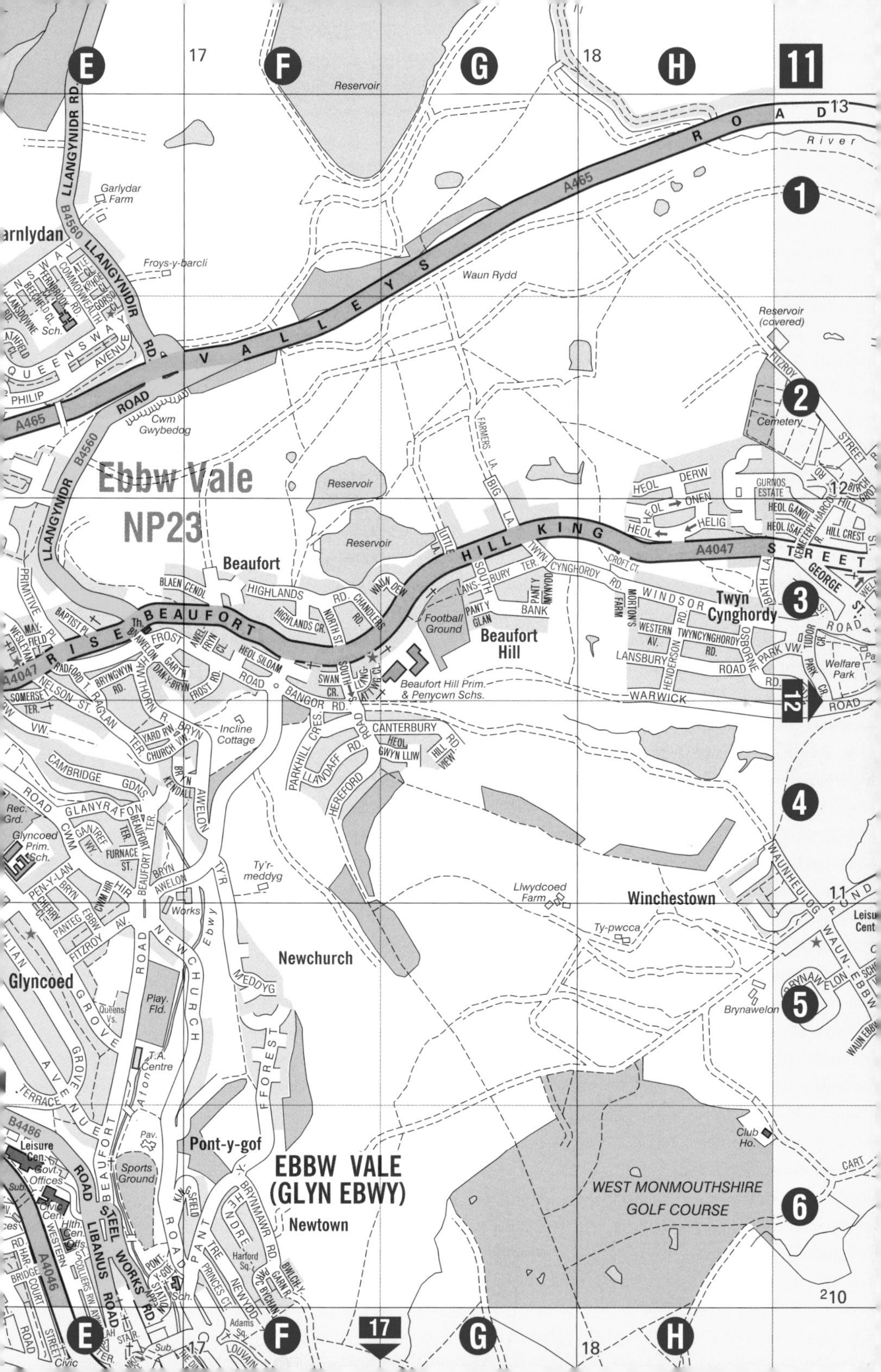
Ebbw Vale
NP23
EBBW VALE
(GLYN EBWY)
Beaufort
Beaufort Hill
Twyn Cynghordy
Winchestown
Newchurch
Glyncoed
Pont-y-gof
Newtown
Garnlydan
A465
HEADS OF THE VALLEYS ROAD
LLANGYNIDR RD.
B4560
A4047
BEAUFORT RISE
KING STREET
A4047
Reservoir
Reservoir (covered)
Cemetery
Football Ground
Beaufort Hill Prim. & Penycwn Schs.
Incline Cottage
Ty'r-meddyg
Llwydcoed Farm
Ty-pwcca
Brynawelon
Club Ho.
WEST MONMOUTHSHIRE GOLF COURSE
Welfare Park
Garlydar Farm
Froys-y-barcli
Waun Rydd
Cwm Gwybedog
Play. Fld.
T.A. Centre
Sports Ground
Works
Leisure Cen.
Govt. Offices
Civic Cen.
Hlth. Cen. Offs.
Harford Sq.
Adams Sq.
Glyncoed Prim. Sch.
Rec. Grd.
HIGHLANDS RD.
CHANDLERS RD.
WARWICK ROAD
WINDSOR RD.
LANSBURY ROAD
CANTERBURY RD.
PARKHILL CRES.
LLANDAFF RD.
HEREFORD
BANGOR RD.
NEWCHURCH ROAD
FFOREST
MEDDYG
BEAUFORT TER.
GROVE AVENUE
TERRACE
STEEL WORKS RD.
LIBANUS ROAD
B4486
A4046
WAUNHEULOG
WAUN-EBBW
FITZROY
GEORGE ST.
CAMBRIDGE GDNS.
GLANYRAFON
QUEENSWAY
PHILIP
SOMERSET TER.
NELSON ST.
FITZROY AV.
17
18
12
17

12
17

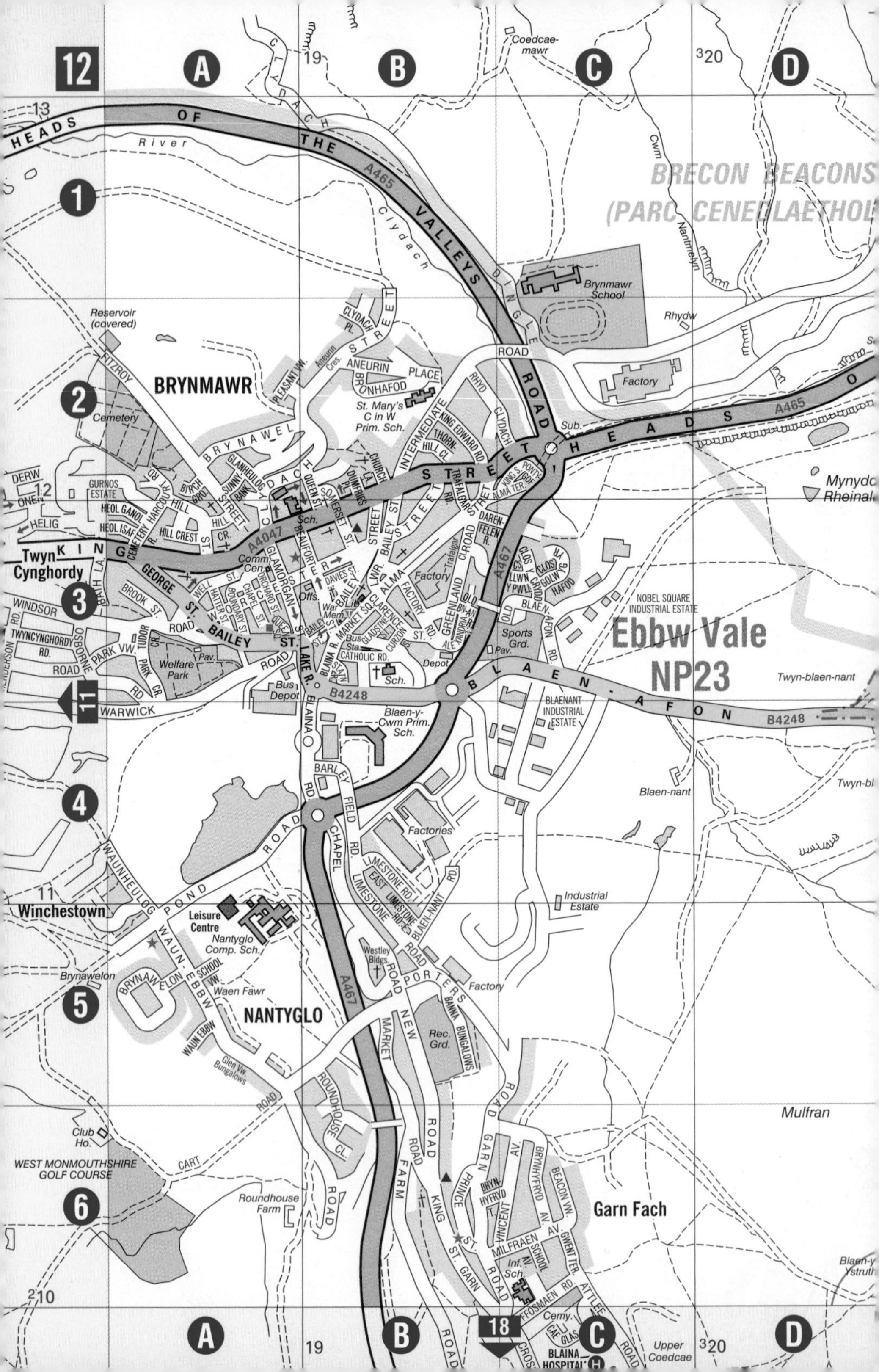

BRYNMAWR
Ebbw Vale
NP23
NANTYGLO
Twyn Cynghordy
Winchestown
Garn Fach
BRECON BEACONS
(PARC CENEDLAETHOL
HEADS OF THE VALLEYS
A465
A4047
A467
B4248
BLAEN-AFON
KING ST.
BAILEY ST.
Brynmawr School
Factory
Factories
Industrial Estate
NOBEL SQUARE INDUSTRIAL ESTATE
BLAENANT INDUSTRIAL ESTATE
Leisure Centre
Nantyglo Comp. Sch.
Blaen-y-Cwm Prim. Sch.
St. Mary's C in W Prim. Sch.
Welfare Park
Sports Grd.
Bus Depot
Cemetery
Reservoir (covered)
WEST MONMOUTHSHIRE GOLF COURSE
Club Ho.
Roundhouse Farm
Coedcae-mawr
Rhydw
Blaen-nant
Twyn-blaen-nant
Mulfran
Upper Coedcae
Mynydd Rheinal
Brynawelon
Waen Fawr
Rec. Grd.
BLAINA HOSPITAL

11
18

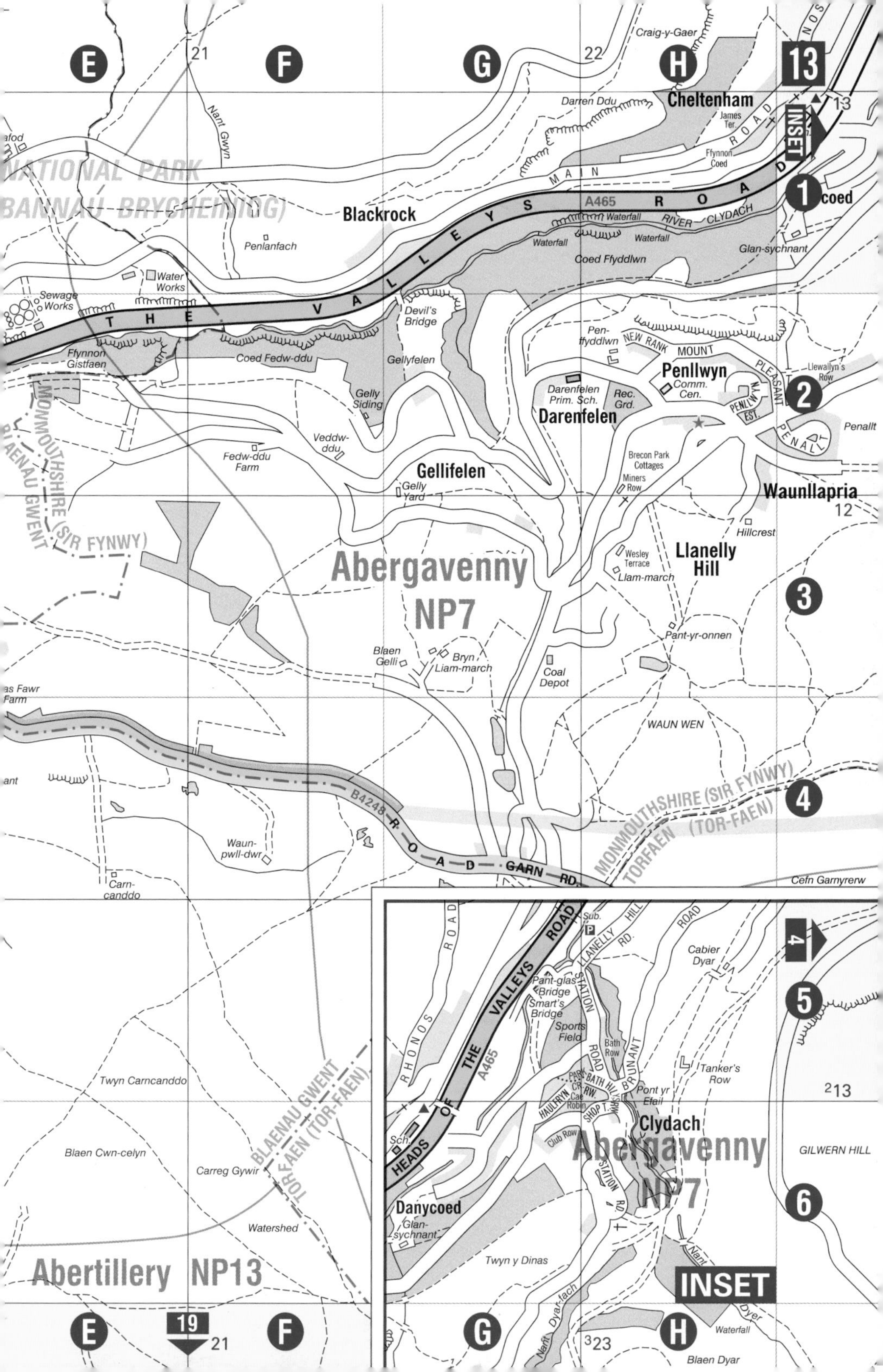

E
F
G
H
13
21
22
Craig-y-Gaer
Cheltenham
Darren Ddu
James Ter.
Ffynnon Coed
INSET
1
coed
NATIONAL PARK
(BANNAU BRYCHEINIOG)
Blackrock
MAIN ROAD
A465
THE VALLEYS ROAD
Waterfall
RIVER CLYDACH
Coed Ffyddlwn
Glan-sychnant
Penlanfach
Water Works
Sewage Works
Devil's Bridge
Ffynnon Gistfaen
Coed Fedw-ddu
Gellyfelen
Gelly Siding
Pen-ffyddlwn
NEW RANK
MOUNT PLEASANT
Penllwyn
Comm. Cen.
PENLLWYN EST.
Llewallyn's Row
2
Darenfelen Prim. Sch.
Rec. Grd.
Darenfelen
PENALLT
Penallt
MONMOUTHSHIRE (SIR FYNWY)
BLAENAU GWENT
Veddw-ddu
Fedw-ddu Farm
Gellifelen
Gelly Yard
Brecon Park Cottages
Miners Row
Waunllapria
12
Hillcrest
Abergavenny NP7
Llanelly Hill
Wesley Terrace
Llam-march
3
Pant-yr-onnen
Blaen Gelli
Bryn Llam-march
Coal Depot
WAUN WEN
MONMOUTHSHIRE (SIR FYNWY)
TORFAEN (TOR-FAEN)
4
B4248 ROAD
GARN RD.
Waun-pwll-dwr
Carn-canddo
Cefn Garnyrerw
HEADS OF THE VALLEYS ROAD
A465
RHONOS ROAD
Sub.
LLANELLY HILL RD.
ROAD
Cabier Dyar
Pant-glas Bridge
Smart's Bridge
STATION ROAD
Sports Field
Bath Row
BRUNANT
Tanker's Row
5
213
PARK CR.
BATH HILL
HAULFRYN
Cae Robin
SHOP T.
Club Row
Pont yr Efail
Clydach
GILWERN HILL
Sch.
STATION RD.
Danycoed
Glan-sychnant
6
Twyn Carncanddo
Blaen Cwn-celyn
Carreg Gywir
BLAENAU GWENT
TORFAEN (TOR-FAEN)
Watershed
Twyn y Dinas
Nant Dyar
Abertillery NP13
19
21
Nant Dyar-fach
323
Waterfall
Blaen Dyar

14
A
B
C
D
8
22
Works
Old Prince Farm
Weir
Waterfall
Ty Isaf
Nant-y-gaseg
Pencoedcae Farm
Princetown
HEADS OF THE VALLEYS ROAD
A465
Cemetery
Reservoir (covered)
Pleasant View
Reservoir (covered)
MERTHYR RD.
B4257
Llechryd
Pen-Twyn Farm
Rhymney Bridge
Old Furnace Farm
Comm. Cen.
Bute Town
Collins Rw.
Middle Row
Lwr. Row
Drenewydd Mus.
A469
Nant-melyn
Cwm Mawr
Nant-melyn Houses
Ras Bryn-oer
Bryn-oer Patch
Ffos-yr-hebog
HEOL UCHAF
PEN-Y-DRE
HEOL-Y-TWYN
IS-FRYN
ANEURIN
Comm. Cen.
UPPER HIGH STREET
TERRACE
TY-COCH
Cwm-carno
Nant Carno
Weirs
Cemetery
AFON RHYMNI (RHYMNEY RIVER)
CARNO ST.
CARNO STREET
STONE T.
BRYN SEION
GLAN-YR-AFON
GLAD. ST.
HARCOURT PL.
TWYN CARNO
PHILLIPS WALK
BRYN CARNO
CHURCH STREET
OAKLAND TER.
CAMBRIAN ST.
KING ST.
EDWARD TER.
CORONATION T.
Llys Joseph Parry
KINGS AV.
ROWAN PLACE
PRICE ST.
QUEEN'S CR.
TRE EDWARDS
GOLWYG-Y-MYNYDD
TAN-Y-LLAN TER.
Alexandra Pl.
COLENSO T.
CASTLE FLDS.
HIGH STREET
HEADS OF THE VALLEYS INDUSTRIAL ESTATE
Nant Llesg
OLD BREWERY LA.
Sports Grd.
ST.DAVIDS CL.
Playing Field
War Memorial Park
Pav.
GOSHEN ST.
CROSS ST.
MANEST
REDWOOD HOSP.
Sports Grd.
Hlth. Cen.
Gnoll
TERRACE
VICTORIA RD.
HAVARD'S ROW
THOMAS ROW
JENKINS
Field St.
Nant Celyn
Lib.
RAMSDEN ST.
LAWN TER.
Sch.
Depot
RHYMNEY (RHYMNI)
Rhymney
HEOL KLOCKNER
Tre York
THE LAWNS INDUSTRIAL ESTATE
Factory
BEULAH ST.
MOUNTBATTEN
CHURCHILL CT.
BRYNTEG CR.
LADY TYLER T.
Mertyr Tydfil
CF48
Lower Rhymney Primary Sch.
DUFFRYN VW. HILL
B4256
JERUSALEM
Eglwys Fan
HAFOD-Y-MYNYDD
Maes y Haf
Factory
FORGE CRES
STREET
BENJAMIN
210
09
08
07
11
312

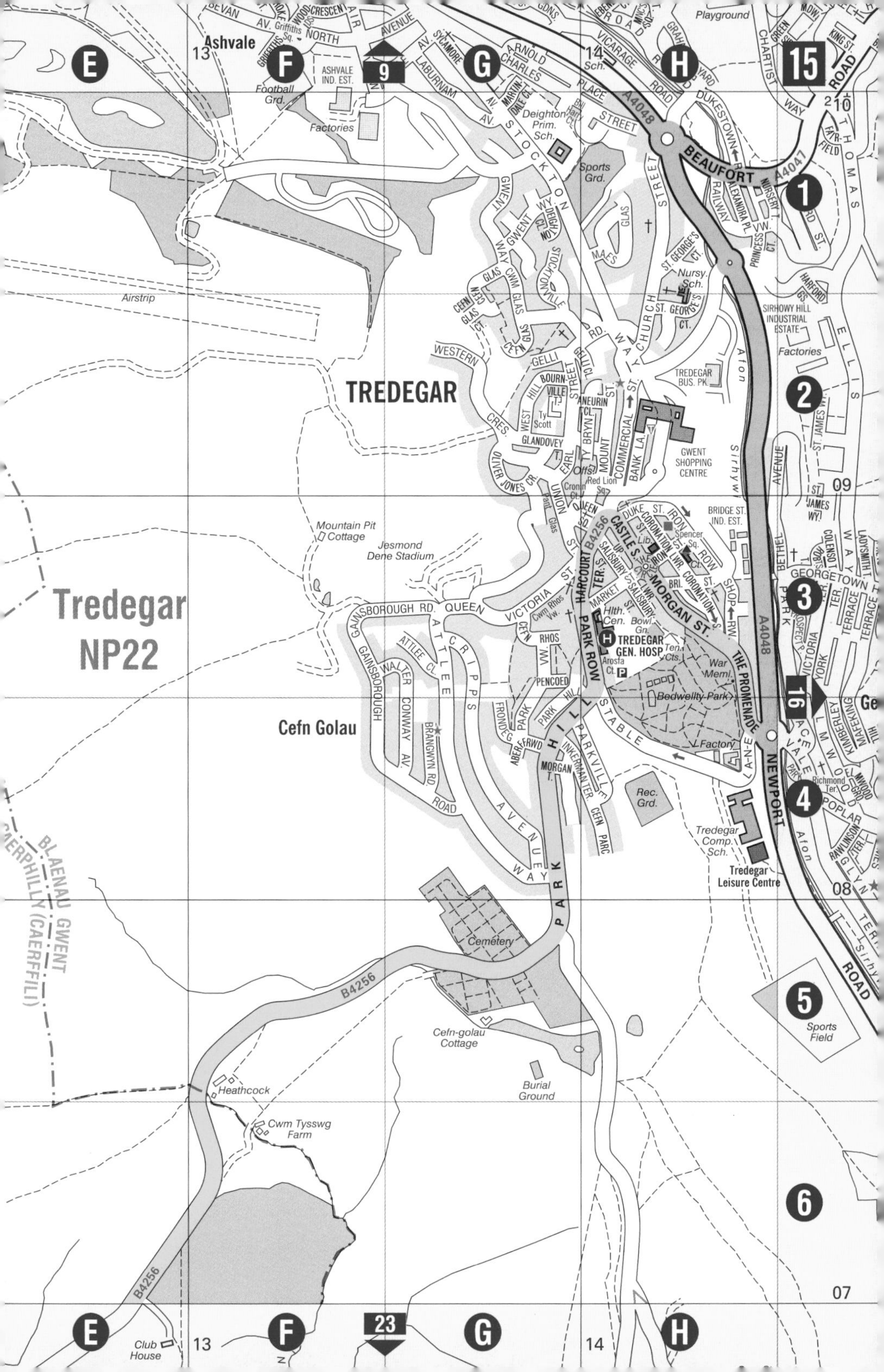

15
TREDEGAR
Tredegar
NP22
Ashvale
Cefn Golau
Airstrip
Mountain Pit Cottage
Jesmond Dene Stadium
Cemetery
Cefn-golau Cottage
Burial Ground
Heathcock
Cwm Tysswg Farm
Club House
Sports Field
Rec. Grd.
Tredegar Comp. Sch.
Tredegar Leisure Centre
Bedwellty Park
War Meml.
TREDEGAR GEN. HOSP
GWENT SHOPPING CENTRE
TREDEGAR BUS. PK.
SIRHOWY HILL INDUSTRIAL ESTATE
BRIDGE ST. IND. EST.
ASHVALE IND. EST.
Factories
Deighton Prim. Sch.
Sports Grd.
Football Grd.
Playground
BEAUFORT
NEWPORT ROAD
THE PROMENADE
PARK ROW
PARK HILL
MORGAN ST.
CASTLE ST.
QUEEN VICTORIA ST.
GAINSBOROUGH RD.
STOCKTON
CHURCH STREET
COMMERCIAL ST.
A4048
A4047
B4256
BLAENAU GWENT
CAERPHILLY (CAERFFILI)
9
16
23
E
F
G
H
1
2
3
4
5
6
13
14
07
08
09
10

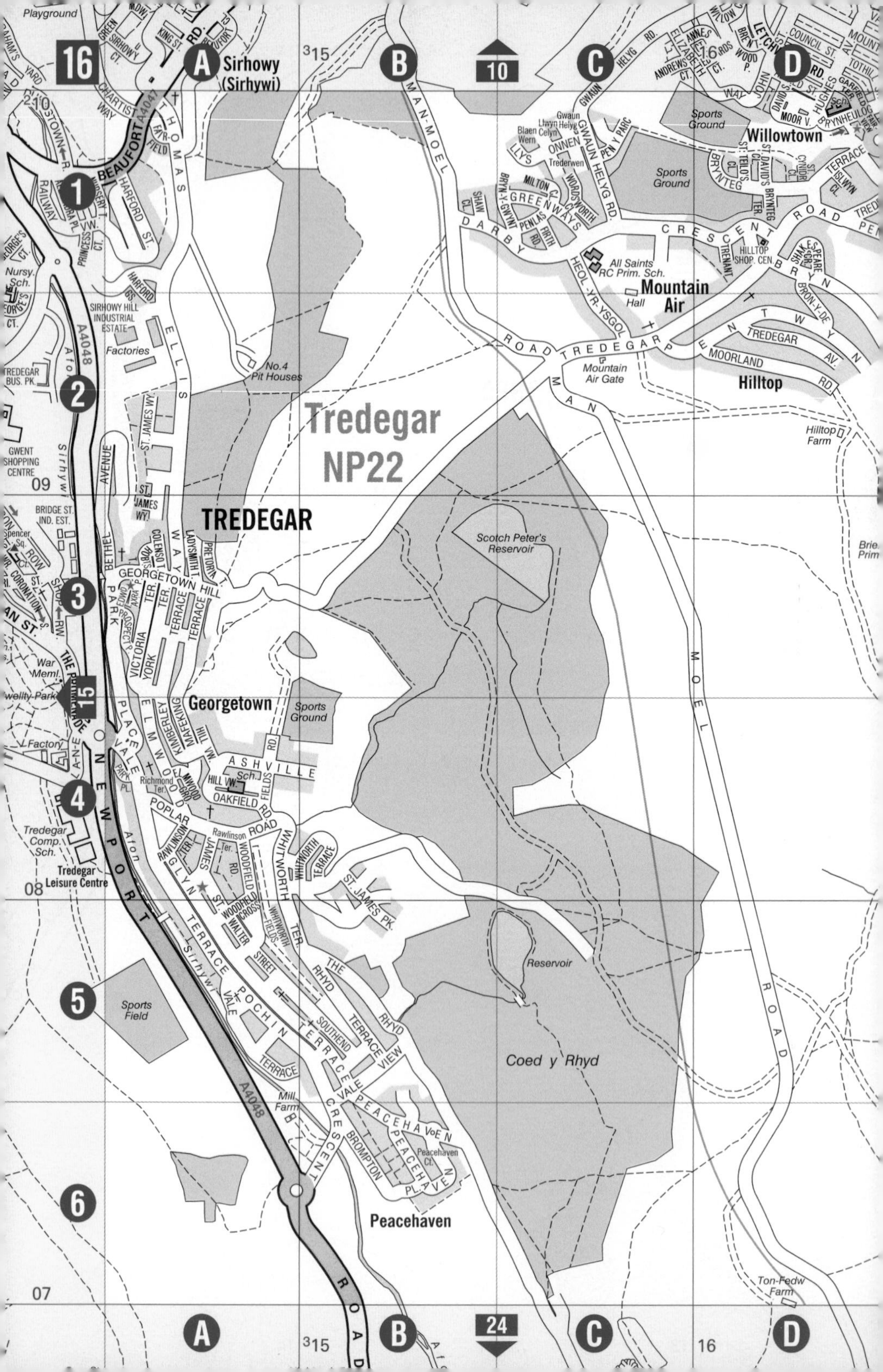
16
10
24
15
A
B
C
D
1
2
3
4
5
6
315
16
09
08
07
Sirhowy
(Sirhywi)
Playground
Tredegar
NP22
TREDEGAR
Georgetown
Willowtown
Mountain
Air
Hilltop
Peacehaven
Coed y Rhyd
Scotch Peter's
Reservoir
Reservoir
Sports Ground
Sports Field
Sports Ground
Sports Ground
Sports Ground
No.4
Pit Houses
Factories
SIRHOWY HILL
INDUSTRIAL
ESTATE
TREDEGAR
BUS. PK.
GWENT
SHOPPING
CENTRE
BRIDGE ST.
IND. EST.
Nursy.
Sch.
War
Meml.
Factory
Tredegar
Comp.
Sch.
Tredegar
Leisure Centre
Mill
Farm
All Saints
RC Prim. Sch.
Hall
HILLTOP
SHOP. CEN.
Mountain
Air Gate
Hilltop
Farm
Ton-Fedw
Farm
Peacehaven
Ct.
Richmond
Ter.
Rawlinson
Ter.
A4047
A4048
BEAUFORT
RD.
CHARTIST
WAY
THOMAS
ELLIS
WAY
HARFORD
ST.
RAILWAY
PRINCESS
CT.
AVENUE
ST. JAMES WY.
BETHEL
COLENSO
LADYSMITH
PRETORIA
GEORGETOWN HILL
PARK
VICTORIA
TER.
YORK
TER.
TERRACE
TERRACE
KIMBERLEY
MAFEKING
ELM WOOD
PLACE
VALE
ASHVILLE
FIELDS
RD.
OAKFIELD
RD.
HILL VW.
Sch.
POPLAR
ROAD
RAWLINSON
JAMES
WOODFIELD
RD.
WHITWORTH
TERRACE
ST. JAMES PK.
GLYN
TERRACE
WOODFIELD
CROSS
WALTER
STREET
TER.
THE
RHYD
TERRACE
RHYD
VIEW
POCHIN
TERRACE
SOUTHEND
VALE
CRESCENT
BROMPTON
PEACEHAVEN
PL.
NEW
PORT
ROAD
Afon
Sirhywi
MAN-MOEL
ROAD
MAN
MOEL
ROAD
TREDEGAR
ROAD
DARBY
CRESCENT
ROAD
PENTWYN
BRYN
HEOL-YR-YSGOL
TREDEGAR
AV.
MOORLAND
RD.
GWAUN HELYG RD.
GREENWAYS
WORDSWORTH
PENLAS
FIRTH
RD.
MILTON CL.
SHAW
CL.
BRYN-Y-GWYNT
LLYS
ONNEN
Trederwen
Blaen
Wern
Llwyn
Celyn
Gwaun
Helyg
PEN Y PARC
BRYNTEG
CL.
TRENANT
SHAKESPEARE
BRON-Y-DE
ISLWYN
CL.
TERRACE
HELYG
RD.
ELIZABETH
ANDREWS
CT.
BRENTWOOD
P.
COUNCIL ST.
JOHN
MOOR V.
BRYNHEULOG
Sch.
THE
CIRCLE
SPENCER
Sq.
ROW
CORONATION
SHOP
RW.
Bedwellty Park

EBBW VALE
(GLYN EBWY)
Ebbw Vale
NP23
Newtown
11
18
WEST MONMOUTHSHIRE
GOLF COURSE
BWLCH Y GARN
Bwlch
-y-garn
Castell-
coryn
Morning
Star Cotts.
Ty Llwyn
Mynydd Carn-y-cefn
Briery
Hill
EBBW
VALE HOSP.
Garden City
Victoria
Waun-Iwyd
Waunlwyd
Primary
School
Tarren y
Trwyn
Domen Fawr
Drysiog
Farm
CWM DRAW
IND. EST.
Factory
Depot
Works
WORKS ROAD
STEEL WORKS ROAD
PARK ROAD
STATION ROAD
VICTORIA RD.
CHURCH ST.
CHURCH CRES.
PLACE
EUREKA
A4046
B4478
B4486
25

Ebbw Vale
NP23
Garn Fach
Coedcae
BLAINA
BLAINA HOSPITAL
Upper Coedcae
Lower Coedcae
Newent House Farm
Ty'r-ywen
Ysgubor-fach
CH Y GARN
Coalbrookvale
Trostre Cottage
Chapelhouse
Llanerch -y-pant
RISING SUN INDUSTRIAL ESTATE
Central Park
Sports Grd.
Stone's Houses
Cae'r-Odyn
Offices
Offs.
Mynydd Carn-y-cefn
Tyn-y-berth Farm
Pilgrims Pk.
Glan Ebbw
Gwaelod-y-gelli
Duffryn Park
Tarren y Trwyn
Cemetery
Jun. Sch.
Pav.
Sch.
Riverside
Blaen-yr Ystruth
Blaina Junior Sc
A467
12
17
26

Watershed
E
13
21
F
G
22
H
19
210
1
Pontypool
NP4
Bryn-maen
TORFAEN (TOR-FAEN)
BLAENAU GWENT
Ystruth
Tir-
Andrew
Cwm
Celyn
2
Nant
Ty'r-gelli
09
Ty'n-y-
ffald
Cwm-celyn
ROAD
QUARRY RW.
3
20
Afon
Blaen-tillery
Cwm
Fm.
HAWTHORNE
GLADE
Pen-twyn
Mynydd James
TANGLEWOOD
DR.
4
Abertillery
NP13
Blaentillery
Farm
08
Glynmilwr
EAST PEN-TWYN
BUNGALOWS
Tyleri
5
Service
Reservoir
6
Cwmtillery
Reservoir
07
E
21
F
27
G
22
H

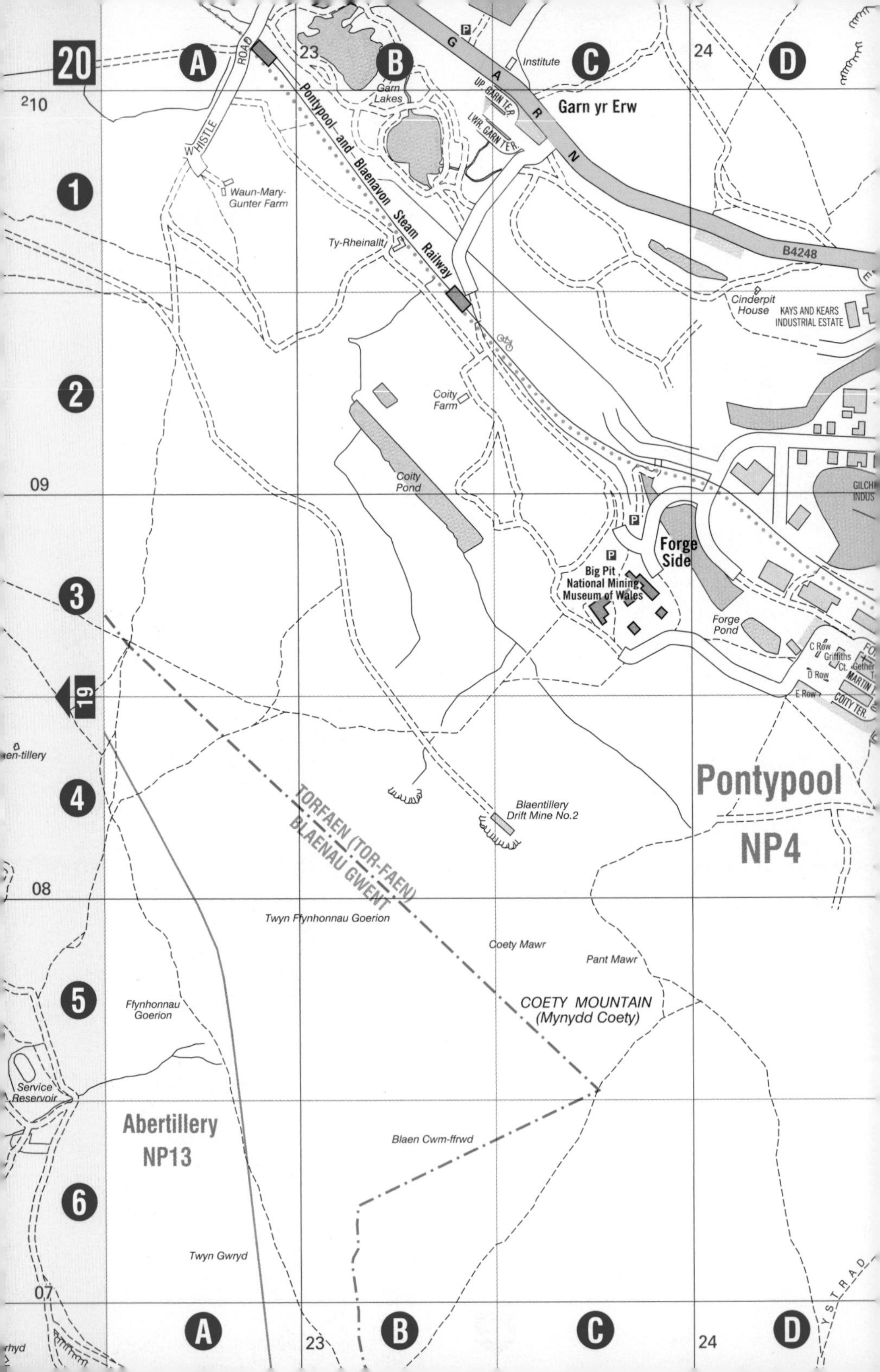

A
B
C
D
23
24
210
09
08
07
1
2
3
4
5
6
19
GARN
B4248
Institute
Garn yr Erw
UP. GARN TER.
LWR. GARN TER.
Garn Lakes
WHISTLE ROAD
Waun-Mary-Gunter Farm
Pontypool and Blaenavon Steam Railway
Ty-Rheinallt
Cinderpit House
KAYS AND KEARS INDUSTRIAL ESTATE
Coity Farm
Coity Pond
Forge Side
Big Pit National Mining Museum of Wales
Forge Pond
C Row
Griffiths Ct.
D Row
E Row
MARTIN
COITY TER.
en-tillery
Pontypool
NP4
Blaentillery Drift Mine No.2
TORFAEN (TOR-FAEN)
BLAENAU GWENT
Twyn Ffynhonnau Goerion
Coety Mawr
Pant Mawr
COETY MOUNTAIN
(Mynydd Coety)
Ffynhonnau Goerion
Service Reservoir
Abertillery
NP13
Blaen Cwm-ffrwd
Twyn Gwryd
YSTRAD
rhyd

E
F
G
H
325
26
210
NP7
1
2
3
4
5
6
09
08
07
Osborne Cottage
Upper Brick Yard
New House
Redhouse
Football Ground
Ball's Pond
Cwm Darrenfelen
Nant Llechan
Gwaun Felen
Mynydd y Garn-fawr
B4246 ROAD
ABERGAVENNY ROAD
Bunkers Hill
Football Field
Blaenavon Ironworks
Rifle Green
BLAENAVON
Hillside Avenue
Upper Coedcae
Middle Coedcae
Elgam Avenue
Neville Ter.
Blorenge Ter.
Llanfoist Cres.
Garndyrus Ter.
Court Ri.
Morris Ri.
Morgan Ri.
Gwaunfelin Wk.
Gilchrist Wk.
Caradoc Wk.
AEL-Y-BRYN
UPPER WOODLAND ST.
CASTLE ST.
KING STREET
NORTH ST.
CHURCH RD.
WAUN ST.
Nursy. Sch.
Hillside Prim. Sch.
Coun. Offs.
Hall
Lib.
Football Grd.
Pav.
Swim. Pool
Rec. Grd.
Blaenavon Rec. Cen.
MIDDLE COEDCAE RD.
UPPER COEDCAE ROAD
LLANOVER ROAD
Cemy.
Francis Morris Est.
TREM-Y-MYNYDD
CAPEL NEWYDD AV.
LLANOVER ROAD ESTATE
Brankleys Houses
THE FIRS
OAK VW.
ST. GILES ROAD
WEST VW. T.
Gilchrist Thomas Ct.
BLAENAVON HOSPITAL
THOMAS ESTATE
Kennard Cres.
Kennard Ct.
Llwyd
Brutes Row
War Mem.
PRINCE ST.
HIGH ST.
CWMAVON
A4043
VARTEG
BRYNAVON
Avondale
RIVERSIDE DR.
AVON ROAD
Afon Llwyd
Curwood
Barnfield Ter.
FORGE SIDE RD.
GLANTORVAEN TER.
ALLGOOD AV.
Playing Field
Mine
Works
Blaenavon Junction
Coed-avon
Cae-Dalwyn Farm
Cemetery
DRAIN
B4246
Waun Hoscyn
Tyr-hodd Farm
Glebeland Farm
CWM AFON
Ty Michael Farm
ROAD
Varteg

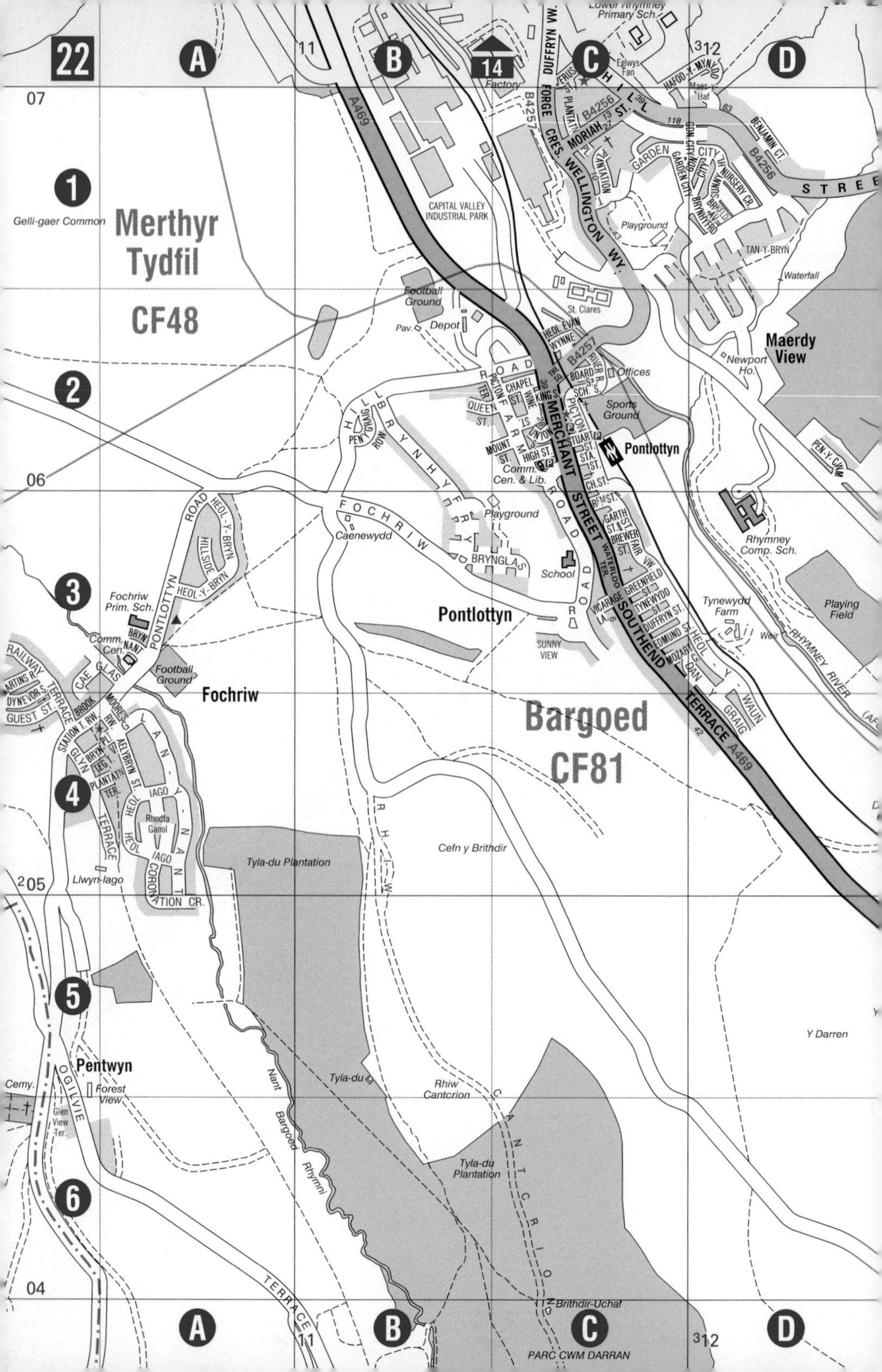

Merthyr Tydfil
CF48
Bargoed
CF81
Gelli-gaer Common
Pontlottyn
Fochriw
Pentwyn
Maerdy View
Lower Rhymney Primary Sch.
Eglwys Fan
Factory
CAPITAL VALLEY INDUSTRIAL PARK
Football Ground
Depot
Pav.
St. Clares
Playground
Offices
Sports Ground
Comm. Cen. & Lib.
School
Caenewydd
Fochriw Prim. Sch.
Comm. Cen.
Rhymney Comp. Sch.
Tynewydd Farm
Playing Field
Weir
RHYMNEY RIVER
Newport Ho.
Waterfall
TAN-Y-BRYN
Maes-y-Haf
Rhodfa Ganol
Llwyn-Iago
Tyla-du Plantation
Cefn y Brithdir
Tyla-du
Rhiw Cantcrion
Nant Bargoed Rhymni
Brithdir-Uchaf
PARC CWM DARRAN
Y Darren
Cemy.
Forest View
Glen View Ter.
SUNNY VIEW
A469
B4257
B4256
MERCHANT STREET
SOUTHEND TERRACE
WELLINGTON WY.
FOCHRIW ROAD
PONTLOTTYN ROAD
HEOL-Y-BRYN
HILLSIDE
FARM ROAD
BRYNHYFRYD
BRYNGLAS
RHIW
CANTCRION
TERRACE
OGILVIE
CORONATION CR.
HEOL IAGO
LAN-Y-NANT
RAILWAY TERRACE
GUEST ST.
DYNEVOR S.
MARTINS R.
CAE GLAS
BROOK
STATION T.
GLYN TERRACE
PEN-Y-CWM
HEOL-Y-WAUN
DAN-Y-GRAIG
GARDEN CITY
BENJAMIN CT.
NURSERY CR.
HAFOD-Y-MYNYDD
DUFFRYN VW.
FORGE CRES.
MORIAH ST.
PLANTATION
HEOL EVAN WYNNE
RIVER R.
BOARD S.
SCH. S.
PICTON
KING S.
CHAPEL ST.
QUEEN ST.
MOUNT ST.
HIGH ST.
UNION ST.
STUART ST.
STA. ST.
CH. ST.
GARTH ST.
BREWER ST.
FAIR VW.
GREENFIELD ST.
TYNEWYDD
DUFFRYN ST.
EDMUND ST.
MOZART
VICARAGE LA.
WATERLOO TER.
PENYGRAIG ROW
BRYN
NANT
MOORES RW.
AELYBRYN ST.
PLANTATN TER.
TEG T.
STREET
A B C D
1 2 3 4 5 6
07 06 205 04
11 312
14

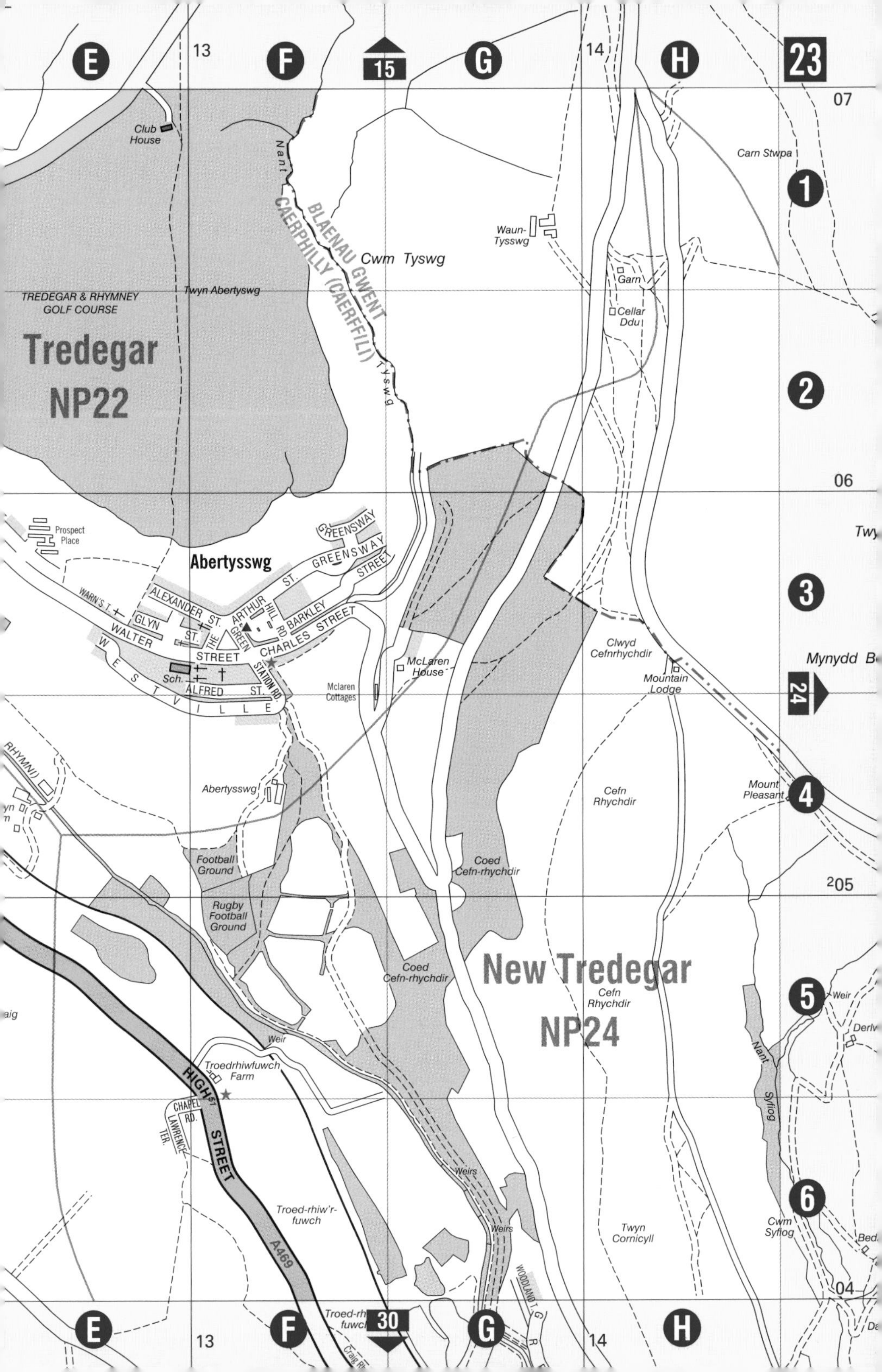

E
F
G
H
13
14
15
07
06
205
04
1
2
3
4
5
6
24
30
Club House
Nant
BLAENAU GWENT
CAERPHILLY (CAERFFILI)
Cwm Tyswg
Tyswg
Waun-Tysswg
Garn
Cellar Ddu
Carn Stwpa
TREDEGAR & RHYMNEY GOLF COURSE
Twyn Abertyswg
Tredegar
NP22
Prospect Place
Abertysswg
GREENSWAY
GREENSWAY ST.
STREET
ALEXANDER ST.
ARTHUR ST.
HILL RD.
BARKLEY STREET
CHARLES STREET
WARN'S T.
GLYN ST.
THE GREEN
WALTER STREET
WESTVILLE
Sch.
ALFRED ST.
STATION RD.
McLaren House
Mclaren Cottages
Clwyd Cefnrhychdir
Mountain Lodge
Mynydd B
RHYMNI
Abertysswg
Mount Pleasant
Cefn Rhychdir
Football Ground
Rugby Football Ground
Coed Cefn-rhychdir
Coed Cefn-rhychdir
New Tredegar
NP24
Cefn Rhychdir
Weir
Nant Syfiog
Derlw
Troedrhiwfuwch Farm
Weir
HIGH ST
STREET
CHAPEL RD.
LAWRENCE TER.
A469
Troed-rhiw'r-fuwch
Weirs
Weirs
Twyn Cornicyll
Cwm Syfiog
WOODLAND T.
Troed-rh fuwc
Craig R

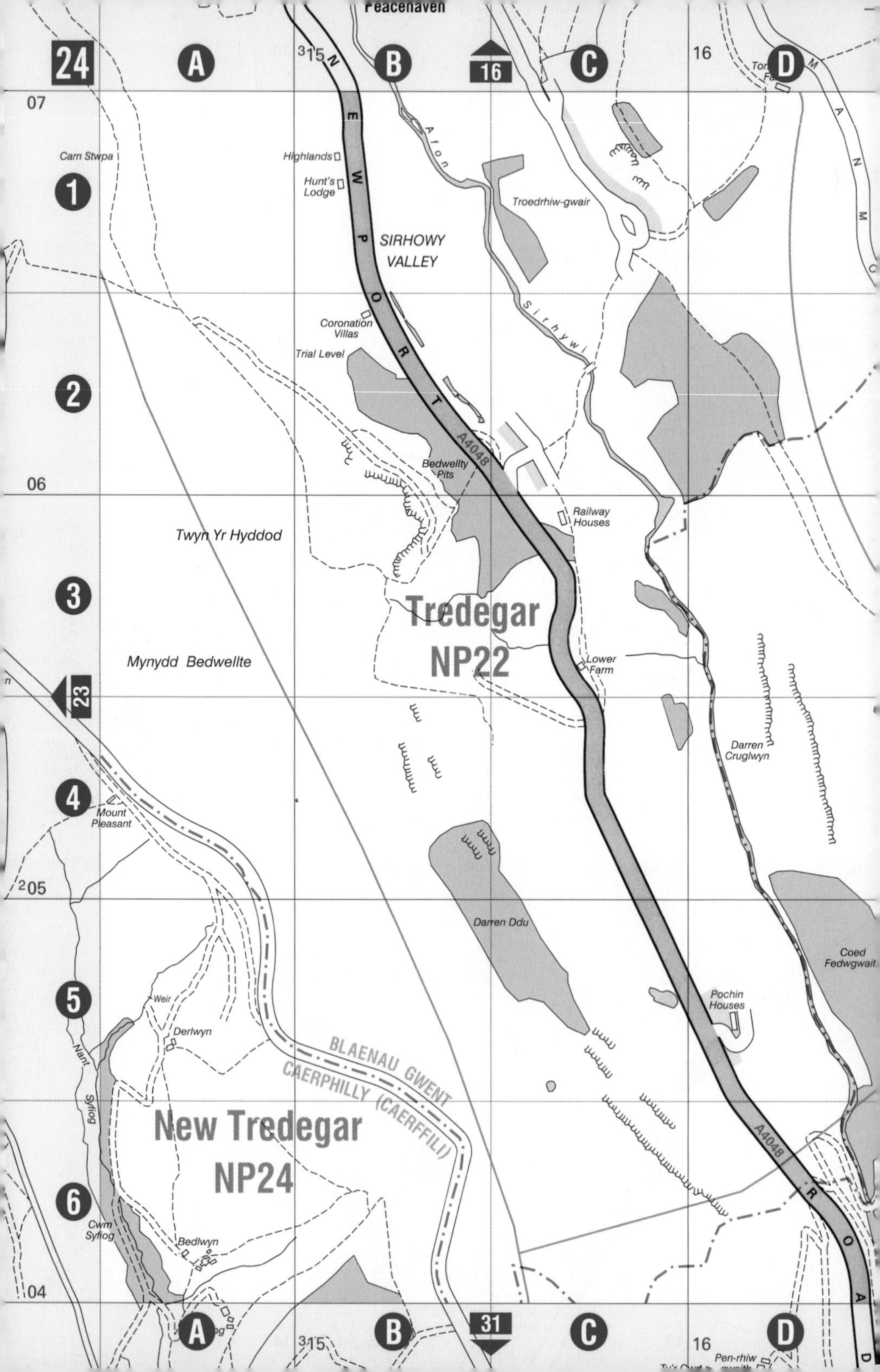
Peacehaven
A
B
C
D
16
315
NEWPORT ROAD
A4048
07
06
205
04
1
2
3
4
5
6
Carn Stwpa
Highlands
Hunt's Lodge
Afon
Troedrhiw-gwair
SIRHOWY VALLEY
Sirhywi
Coronation Villas
Trial Level
Bedwellty Pits
Railway Houses
Twyn Yr Hyddod
Tredegar NP22
Lower Farm
Mynydd Bedwellte
Darren Cruglwyn
Mount Pleasant
Darren Ddu
Coed Fedwgwait
Pochin Houses
Weir
Derlwyn
Nant Syfiog
BLAENAU GWENT
CAERPHILLY (CAERFFILI)
New Tredegar NP24
Cwm Syfiog
Bedlwyn
Pen-rhiw

16
23
31

Waun-lwyd
Waunlwyd Primary School
Coed y Garn
Cwm Merddog
Garn-Cam-Isaf
Cefn Manmoel
Troed-rhiw'r-clawdd
Festival Park
FACTORY PARK FACTORY SHOPPING VILLAGE
Ebbw Vale
NP23
The Croft
Cemetery
Rec. Grd.
Cwm Prim Sch.
Lower Woods
Craig Rhiwargan
BLAENAU GWENT
CAERPHILLY (CAERFFILI)
Maes-yr-onn-fach
Nant Maes-yr-onn
Craig Gyngi
Maes Mawr
Health Cen.
Lib.
CWM
Tallistown
MARINE IND. EST.
Coed Waun-bleiddian
Nant yr Helyg
Blackwood
NP12
Coed y Llanerch
Pont Gwaithyrhaearn
CWM-ABERBEEG BY-PASS (Est. Comp. late 2004)
A4046
B4486
STATION RD.
DYFFRYN RD.
PARK PL.
CWM RD.
CEMETERY ROAD
TERRACE
MARINE STREET
COED-Y-GARN TERRACE
PARK GREEN ST.
BRECON HEIGHTS
AUGUSTA ST.
QUEEN STREET
HALL ST.
BEECH GRO.
BRYNHYFRYD
CANNING STREET
CURRE STREET
ELM ST.
ASH ST.
CARNE ST.
OAK ST.
BROOK PL.
RIVER RD.
WILLIAM ST.
AUBREY TER.
YORK TER.
STANFIELD
KING ST.
STEWART ST.
DYFFRYN PL.
FALCON TER.
RAILWAY TER.
EMLYN
WOODFIELD
BAILEY
SCHOOL L.
HILLSIDE
EXCELSIOR
Ebbw River
ROAD
E F G H
1 2 3 4 5 6
17 18
07 06 05 04

17
26
32

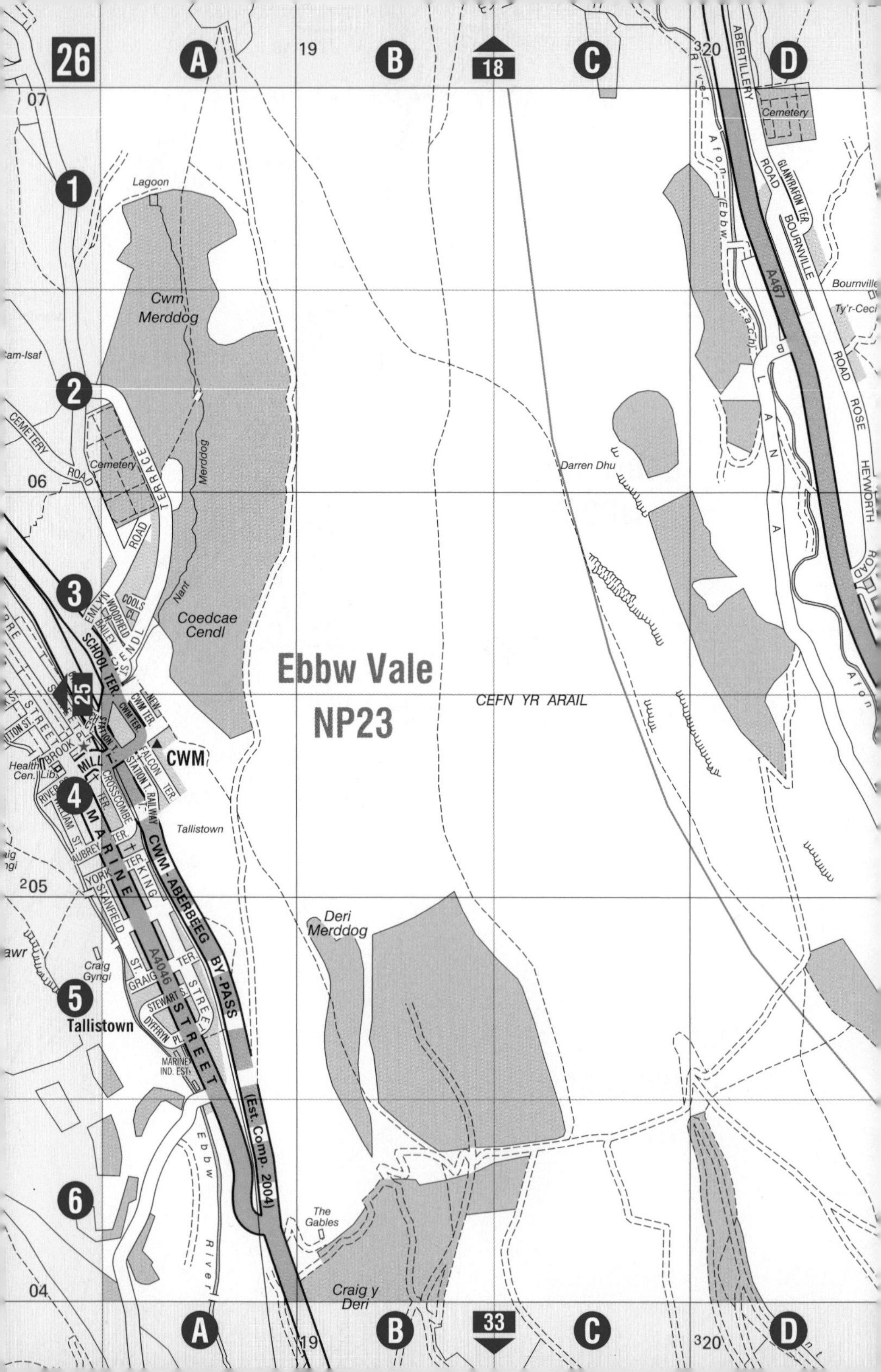

A
B
C
D
19
320
18
07
06
205
04
1
2
3
4
5
6
25
33
Ebbw Vale
NP23
Lagoon
Cwm Merddog
Nant Merddog
Coedcae Cendl
Cemetery
CEMETERY ROAD
TERRACE ROAD
CWM
Tallistown
Deri Merddog
The Gables
Craig y Deri
Craig Gyngi
Darren Dhu
CEFN YR ARAIL
ABERTILLERY ROAD
GLANYRAFON TER.
BOURNVILLE ROAD
Bournville
Ty'r-Ceci
ROSE HEYWORTH ROAD
A467
LLANIA
Afon Ebbw Fach
River Ebbw
Afon
MARINE STREET
A4046
CWM - ABERBEEG BY-PASS
(Est. Comp. 2004)
SCHOOL TER.
EMLYN
WOODFIELD
BAILEY
COOLS CL.
CENDL
NEW
CWM TER.
STATION T.
FALCON TER.
RAILWAY
CROSSCOMBE TER.
MILL
BROOK PL.
RIVER
WILLIAM ST.
AUBREY TER.
YORK TER.
KING
STANFIELD
GRAIG TER.
ST.
STREET
STEWART S.
DYFFRYN PL.
MARINE IND. EST.
Health Cen.
Lib.
Cam-Isaf

E
F
G
H
19
21
22
07
06
05
04
1
2
3
4
5
6
Cwmtillery Reservoir
Gwrhyd
Gwrhyd-bach
Cwm Tyleri
Coedcae Tillery
Abertillery NP13
Cefn Crib
Coedcae Tyle
Coed Castellau
West Bank
East Bank
Gwastad Fm.
Blaentillery Prim. Sch.
Twyn Pentre
Sports Grd.
Cwmtillery (Cwmtyleri)
CWMTILLERY INDUSTRIAL ESTATE
Ty Pwdr
Hillcrest View
White House Ct.
Pen-y-Bont
Green-meadow Ter.
Gwern Las
ROSE HEYWORTH ESTATE
Prim. Sch.
Rec. Grd.
Rugby Football Ground
Cricket Grd.
Cyril Place
Blaenau Gwent
BLAENAU GWENT ROWS
Comp. School
Prim. School
Rec. Grd.
The Pines
Rec.Gd.
Cemy.
Hlth. Cen.
Lib. & Mus.
Rhiw-Park (Rhiw-Parc)
ABERTILLERY (ABERTYLERI)
Cefn Bach
Works
34
ABERBEEG ROAD
A467
Pant-y-p

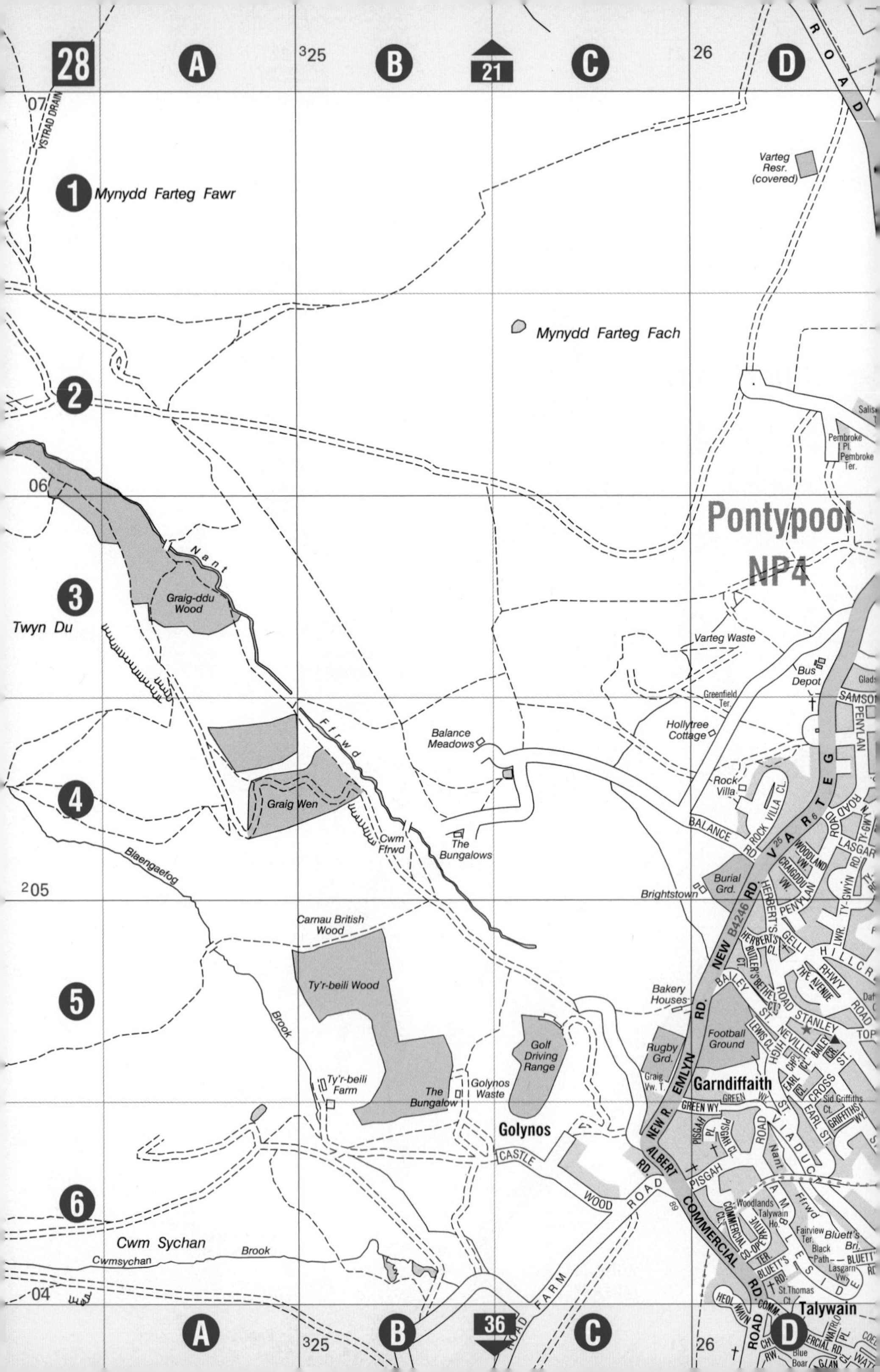

A
B
C
D
21
36
325
26
07
06
205
04
1
2
3
4
5
6
Mynydd Farteg Fawr
Mynydd Farteg Fach
Varteg Resr. (covered)
Pontypool
NP4
Twyn Du
Graig-ddu Wood
Nant Ffrwd
Graig Wen
Cwm Ffrwd
Balance Meadows
The Bungalows
Varteg Waste
Bus Depot
Greenfield Ter.
Hollytree Cottage
Rock Villa
Brightstown
Burial Grd.
Blaengaefog
Carnau British Wood
Ty'r-beili Wood
Ty'r-beili Farm
The Bungalow
Golynos Waste
Golf Driving Range
Golynos
Bakery Houses
Rugby Grd.
Football Ground
Garndiffaith
Cwm Sychan
Cwmsychan Brook
Brook
CASTLE WOOD ROAD
FARM ROAD
NEW R.
ALBERT RD.
COMMERCIAL RD.
NEW EMLYN RD.
B4246
VARTEG RD.
BALANCE RD.
ROCK VILLA CL.
Pembroke Pl.
Pembroke Ter.
YSTRAD DRAIN
PISGAH
GREEN WY.
Talywain
Woodlands Talywain Ho.
Fairview Ter.
Black Path
Bluett's Bri.
Lasgarn Vw.
St.Thomas Ct.
Sid Griffiths Ct.
Blue Boar

NP7
BRECON BEACONS NATIONAL PARK
(PARC CENEDLAETHOL BANNAU BRYCHEINIOG)
MONMOUTHSHIRE (SIR FYNWY)
TORFAEN (TOR-FAEN)
Ty Michael Farm
Cwmavon Reservoir
Gallowsgreen
FURLONG WOOD
Cwmavon Ho.
Forge Row
Works
Cwmavon
CWMAVON ROAD
A4043
LLANOVER R.
Pistyll-gwyn
Penrhoel-Medwyn
Beili-glas
Craig y Felin
Pwll Gwyn
Garn-llech
Mynydd Garnclochdy
Garn Clochdy
B4246
Kear's Row
SNAIL CREEP
SHOP
Varteg
Ysgol Bryn Onnen
Hafod-wenog
Little Beili-glas
Lower Little Beili-glas
Beili-glas
Ty Dda Farm
Bryn-glas
Mill Farm
Hen-felin
Pen-y-lan Wood
Rugby Grd.
Rec. Grd.
Coedcae Sal
Cwmavon Farm
Pen-y-ddoyga
Pant-y-gelli
Pant-yr-heol
Severn View
Garnteg Primary Sch.
Greenmeadow Farm
Maelor
Nant
Cwm Lasgarn
Nant-yr-mailor Reservoir
WATERWORKS
Rising Sun Bridge
LASGARN WOOD
Garn-wen
ABERSYCHAN
STATION STREET
Victoria Village
LASGARN LANE
37

A
B
C
D
13
14
23
40
04
03
02
01
1
2
3
4
5
6
Bargoed
CF81
Tir-Phil
Deri
Troed-rhiw'r-fuwch
Craig-Rhymney Farm
Cefn y Brithdir
Grove Park
Rec. Grd.
New Tredegar Sports Hall
Twyn Cornicyll
Coed-Cefn-rhychdir
Cefnrhychdir
ORCHARD
FIELD T.
CROFT ST.
Schools
BEDLWYN
DERLWYN
FOTHERGILLS
POWELL'S
TER.
TREDEGAR
GREENFIELD
WOODLAND T.
SCHOOL
RAILWAY TER.
BIRCHGROVE
Greenwood Ct.
Sch.
Comm. Cen.
STREET
RUPERRA
SUNNYBANK
CHAPEL ST.
COMMERCIAL ST.
THOMAS ST.
MORGAN ST.
GEORGE ST.
JAMES STREET
DUFFRYN
WHITE
CHURCH T.
Lib.
Health Cen.
RHYMNEY RIVER
PLEASANT VIEW
A469
A4049
COLLIERS ROW
STATION ROW
Coed Cae
Dan-y-Graig
Capel y Brithdir (Monument)
Pen-y-fid Fedw
Tyr-capel
Cefn Bach Farm
Plas Milfre
Nant Lan
Coed Groes-faen
Groes-faen Farm
Waterfall
Troed-y-rhiw Jestyn
PARC CWM DARRAN
OGILVIE
HILLSIDE
TERRACE
Craig Ysgwydd-gwyn
BAILEY STREET
Nant Bargod Rhymni
Coed Deri-Newydd
CWM DARRAN
GLYN DERI
Is-y-coed
Rugby Football Ground
Morgan Ter.
DERI-NEWYDD
CROSS ST.
CHAPEL
CEFN RD.
Deri Prim. Sch.
Lib.
GLYNMARCH ST.
Ysgwydd-gwyn-uchaf
Ysgwyddgwyn
Jenkins Row
ROAD
SCHOOL ST.
CAMBRIAN ST.
Hall
Wks.
NEW HILL ST.
CEFN ROAD
Coed Cefn-bach
MILL
Mill House
Craig y Felin
EDWARDS RW.
Rugby Grd.
Tarren yr Ysgwydd-gwyn
Mill Top Bungalow
Cwm Ysgwydd-gwyn
ROAD
Nant y Twpa
Ysgwydd-gwyn-

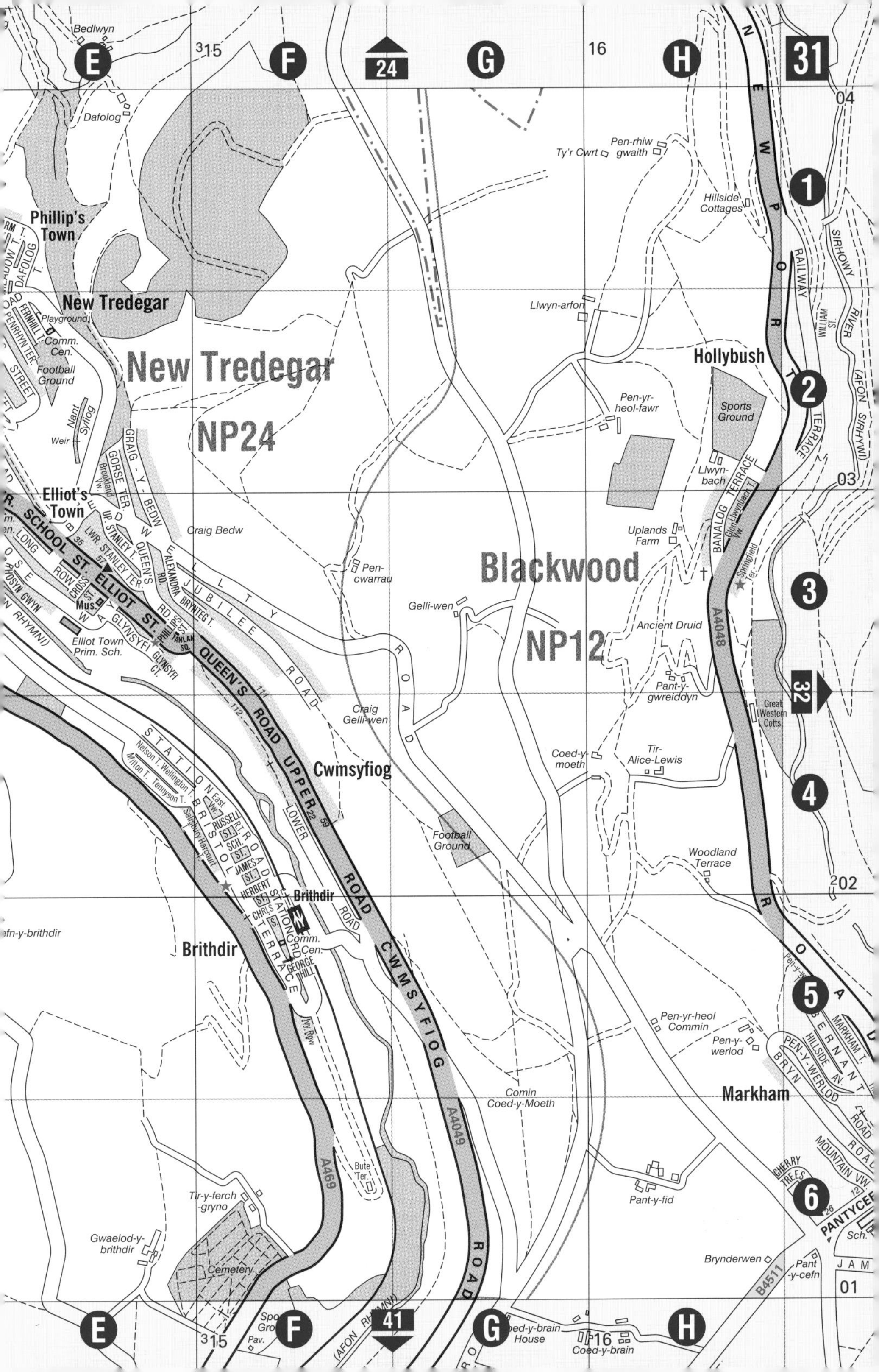
New Tredegar
NP24
Blackwood
NP12
Phillip's Town
Elliot's Town
Hollybush
Cwmsyfiog
Brithdir
Markham
Bedlwyn
Dafolog
Ty'r Cwrt
Pen-rhiw gwaith
Hillside Cottages
Llwyn-arfon
Pen-yr-heol-fawr
Sports Ground
Llwyn-bach
Uplands Farm
Craig Bedw
Pen-cwarrau
Gelli-wen
Ancient Druid
Pant-y-gwreiddyn
Great Western Cotts.
Craig Gelli-wen
Coed-y-moeth
Tir-Alice-Lewis
Football Ground
Woodland Terrace
Pen-yr-heol Commin
Pen-y-werlod
Comin Coed-y-Moeth
Pant-y-fid
Brynderwen
Pant-y-cefn
Tir-y-ferch-gryno
Gwaelod-y-brithdir
Cemetery
Bute Ter.
Ivy Row
Comm. Cen.
Playground
Football Ground
Nant Syfiog
Weir
Elliot Town Prim. Sch.
Mus.
Coed-y-brain House
Coed-y-brain
Pav.
NEWPORT ROAD
RAILWAY TERRACE
WILLIAM ST.
SIRHOWY RIVER (AFON SIRHYWI)
BANALOG TERRACE
Glen Llwynbach T.
Springfield Ter.
A4048
A4049
A469
B4511
SCHOOL ST.
ELLIOT ST.
QUEEN'S ROAD UPPER
JUBILEE ROAD
ALEXANDRA RD.
BRYNTEG T.
GRAIG-Y-BEDW
GORSE TER.
Brookland Vw.
UP. STANLEY T.
LWR. STANLEY TER.
CROSS ST.
ROW
GLYNSYFI CT.
TANLAN SQ.
PHILLIPS ST.
STATION ROAD
STATION TERRACE
BRISTOL
Nelson T. Wellington T.
Milton T. Tennyson T.
Salisbury Harcourt
RUSSELL ST.
SCH. ST.
JAMES ST.
HERBERT ST.
CHRLS S.
GEORGE HILL
East Vw.
LOWER CWMSYFIOG ROAD
CWMSYFIOG ROAD
ROAD
BERNANT
MARKHAM T.
HILLSIDE AV.
PEN-Y-WERLOD
BRYN
ROAD
MOUNTAIN VW.
CHERRY TREES
PANTYCEF
Sch.
JAM
Pen-y-w
PENRHYN TER.
FERNHILL T.
DAFOLOG T.
LONG
PHOSYN GWYN
(AFON RHYMNI)
(AFON RHYMNI)
Sport Gro
efn-y-brithdir
E
F
G
H
24
32
41
1
2
3
4
5
6
315
16
04
03
202
01

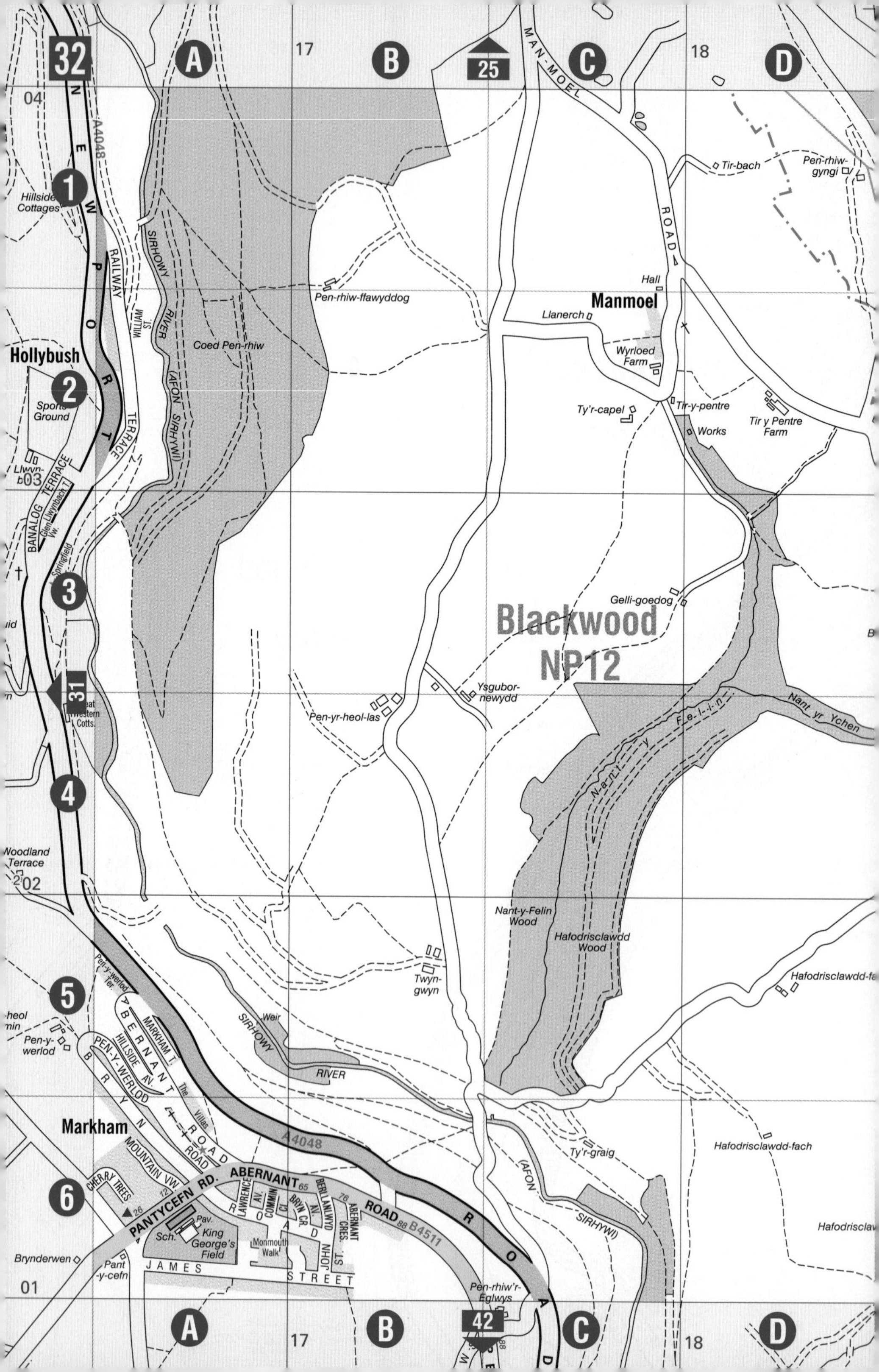

A
B
C
D
17
18
25
42
31
04
03
02
01
1
2
3
4
5
6
A4048
NEWPORT ROAD
Hillside Cottages
Hollybush
Sports Ground
RAILWAY TERRACE
WILLIAM ST.
SIRHOWY RIVER (AFON SIRHYWI)
Coed Pen-rhiw
BANALOG TERRACE
Glen Llwynbach T.
Vw.
Springfield
Great Western Cotts.
Woodland Terrace
Pen-y-werlod Ter.
Pen-y-werlod
ABERNANT
MARKHAM T.
HILLSIDE AV.
PEN-Y-WERLOD
BRYN ROAD
The Villas
Markham
MOUNTAIN VW.
CHERRY TREES
PANTYCEFN RD.
ABERNANT ROAD
B4511
LAWRENCE AV.
COMMIN CL.
BRYN CR.
BERLLANLWYD AV.
ABERNANT CRES.
JOHN ST.
Sch.
Pav.
King George's Field
Monmouth Walk
JAMES STREET
Brynderwen
Pant-y-cefn
Pen-rhiw'r-Eglwys
Weir
SIRHOWY RIVER
(AFON SIRHYWI)
Ty'r-graig
MAN-MOEL ROAD
Tir-bach
Pen-rhiw-gyngi
Hall
Manmoel
Llanerch
Wyrloed Farm
Ty'r-capel
Tir-y-pentre
Works
Tir y Pentre Farm
Pen-rhiw-ffawyddog
Gelli-goedog
Blackwood
NP12
Ysgubor-newydd
Pen-yr-heol-las
Nant-y-Felin
Nant yr Ychen
Nant-y-Felin Wood
Hafodrisclawdd Wood
Twyn-gwyn
Hafodrisclawdd-fach

Gables
E
F
26
G
H
19
320
04
Ebbw Vale
NP23
Craig y Deri
Nant
1
Hafod-y-dafal
The Plantation
A4046
Cwm Big
Abertillery
NP13
2
Big
Ton-yr-efail-Fach
Ebbw
03
Craig Fawr
Penrhiw-lech
3
River
34
BLAENAU GWENT
CAERPHILLY (CAERFFILI)
A4046
Pen-y-fan-ganol
4
Mynydd Pen-y-fan
202
Twyn-Coc-y-north
ABERTILLERY & DISTRICT HOSP.
5
Graig Fawr
PENDARREN RD.
Pen-y-fan
Pen-y-fan-isaf
MAN-MOEL
Pen-y-fan-fach
6
Brunant
PENYFAN CARAVAN AND LEISURE PARK
Pentrapeod
Glencoe Cottages
Windsor
Cwm-nant-gwynt
Windsor Pl.
Pen-y-fan Pond Country Park
01
ROAD
PARKWAY
43
Bungalow
Bute Pl.
Nant
Ter.

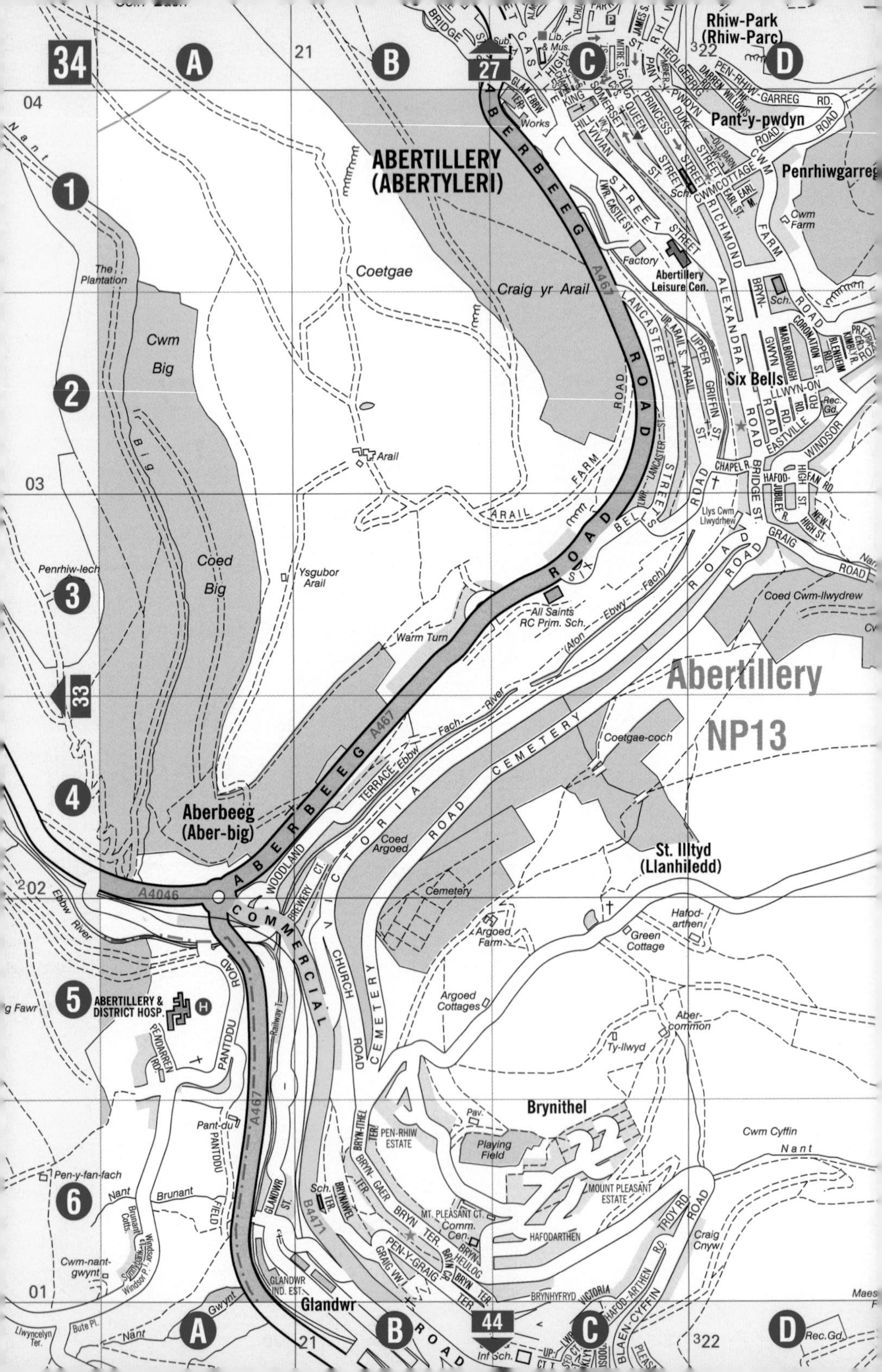
ABERTILLERY
(ABERTYLERI)
Abertillery
NP13
Aberbeeg
(Aber-big)
St. Illtyd
(Llanhiledd)
Six Bells
Rhiw-Park
(Rhiw-Parc)
Pant-y-pwdyn
Penrhiwgarreg
Brynithel
Glandwr
ABERTILLERY &
DISTRICT HOSP.
ABERBEEG ROAD
A467
A4046
B4471
COMMERCIAL
VICTORIA ROAD
CEMETERY ROAD
CHURCH ROAD
SIX BELLS ROAD
ALEXANDRA ROAD
Coetgae
Craig yr Arail
Cwm Big
Coed Big
The Plantation
Penrhiw-lech
Coed Argoed
Cemetery
Coetgae-coch
All Saints
RC Prim. Sch.
Abertillery
Leisure Cen.
Factory
Warm Turn
Ysgubor
Arail
Argoed
Farm
Argoed
Cottages
Green
Cottage
Hafod-
arthen
Aber-
common
Ty-llwyd
Cwm Cyffin
Playing
Field
MOUNT PLEASANT
ESTATE
PEN-RHIW
ESTATE
HAFODARTHEN
Craig
Cnyw
Pant-du
Pen-y-fan-fach
Brunant
Cwm-nant-
gwynt
GLANDWR
IND. EST.
Coed Cwm-llwydrew
Llys Cwm
Llwydrhew
Cwm
Farm
Rec.Gd.
Inf.Sch.
27
33
44
A B C D
21
322
04
03
02
01

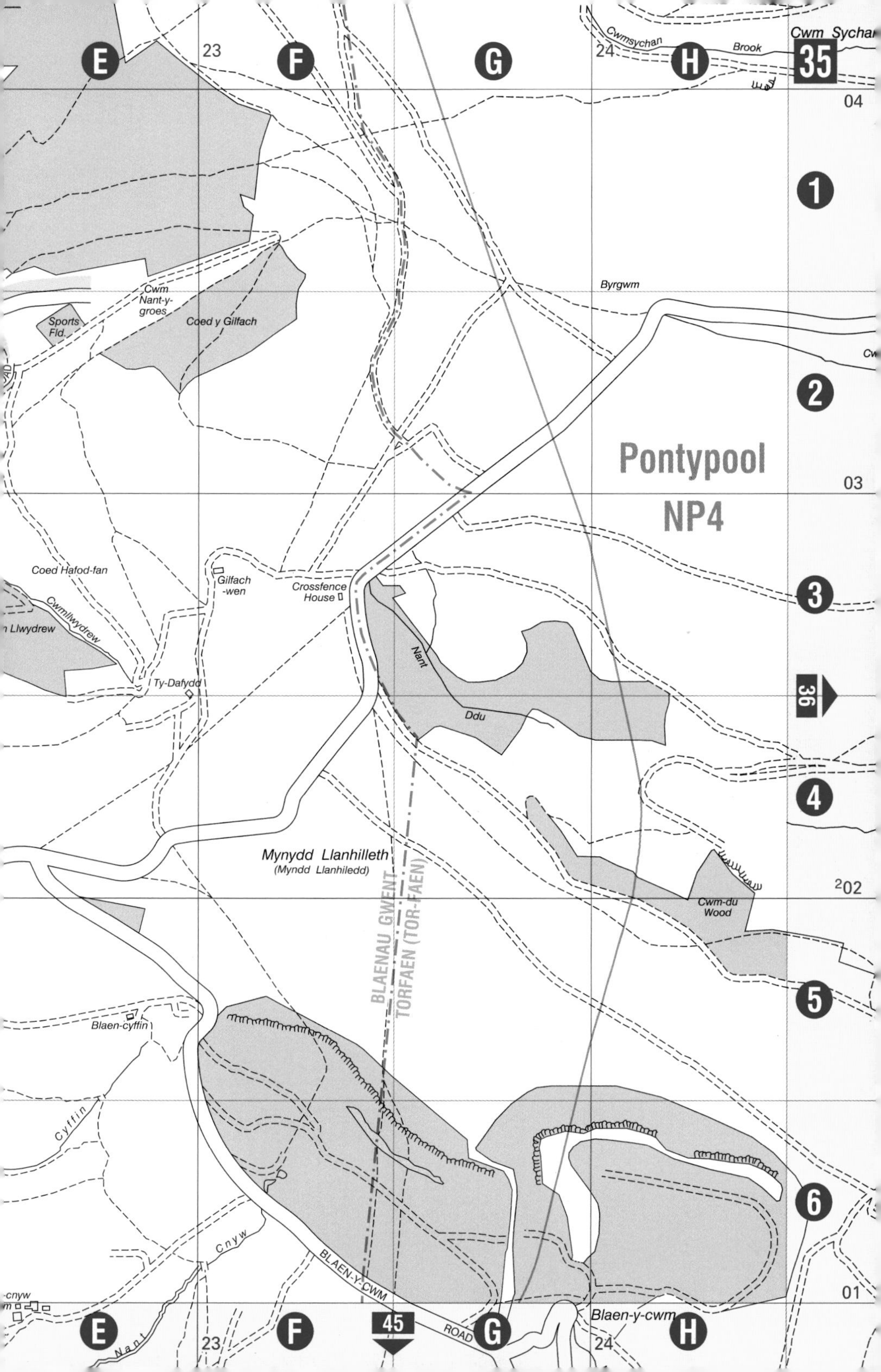
35
Cwm Sychan
Cwmsychan
Brook
23
24
E
F
G
H
04
1
Byrgwm
Cwm
Nant-y-
groes
Sports
Fld.
Coed y Gilfach
2
Pontypool
NP4
03
Coed Hafod-fan
Gilfach
-wen
Crossfence
House
3
Cwmllwydrew
Llwydrew
Nant
Ty-Dafydd
Ddu
36
4
Mynydd Llanhilleth
(Myndd Llanhiledd)
BLAENAU GWENT
TORFAEN (TOR-FAEN)
202
Cwm-du
Wood
5
Blaen-cyffin
Cyffin
6
Cnyw
-cnyw
BLAEN-Y-CWM
ROAD
01
Blaen-y-cwm
Nant
45

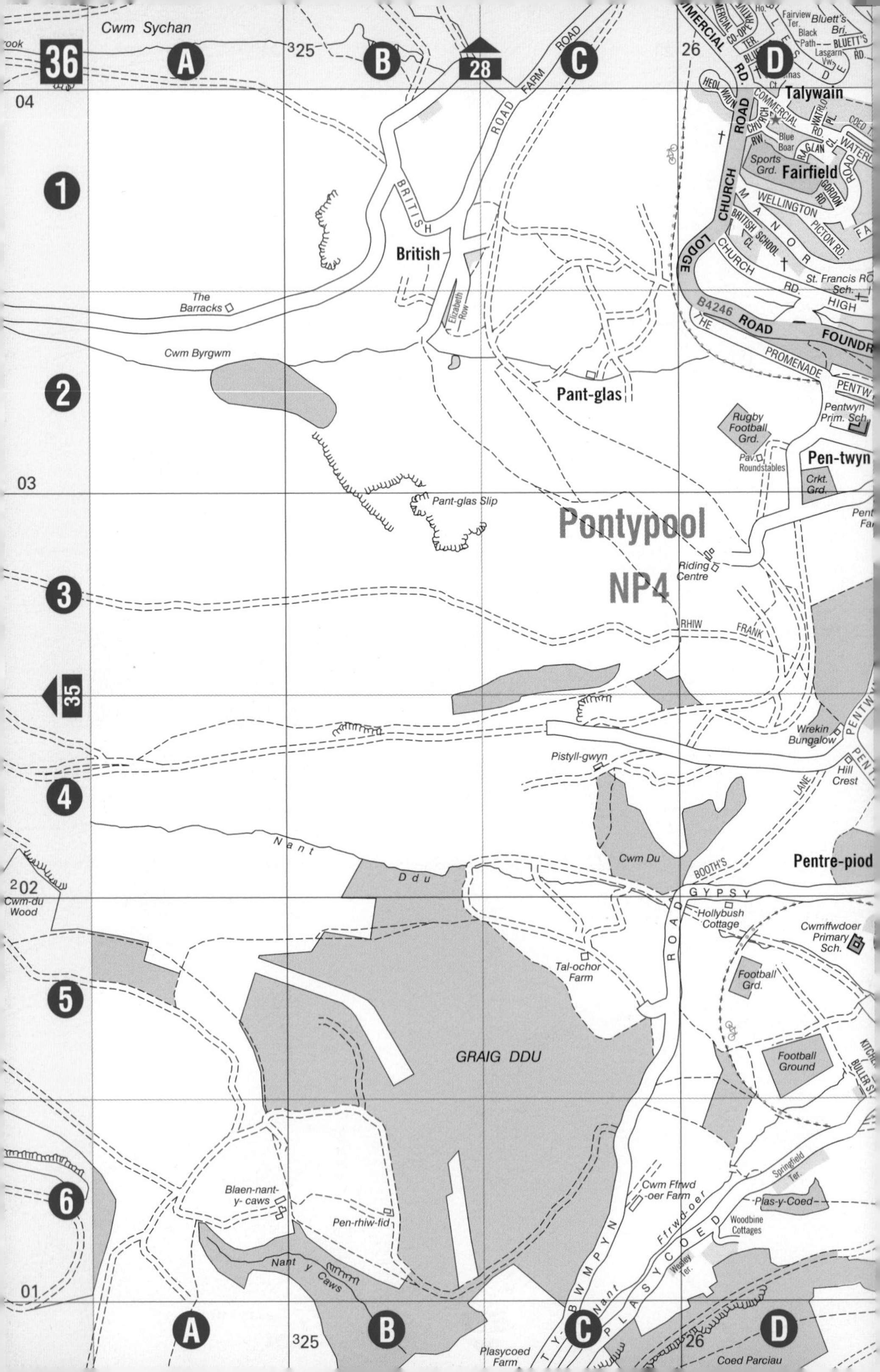

Cwm Sychan
36
A
B
C
D
28
325
26
04
03
02
01
1
2
3
4
5
6
35
FARM ROAD
ROAD
BRITISH
British
The Barracks
Elizabeth Row
Cwm Byrgwm
Pant-glas
Pant-glas Slip
Pontypool
NP4
Riding Centre
RHIW
FRANK
Talywain
Fairfield
Sports Grd.
Blue Boar
COMMERCIAL RD.
CHURCH ROAD
LODGE ROAD
CHURCH RD.
WELLINGTON
MANOR
PICTON RD.
GORDON RD.
RAGLAN CL.
BRITISH SCHOOL CL.
St. Francis RC Sch.
HIGH
B4246
ROAD
FOUNDR
THE PROMENADE
PENTW
Pentwyn Prim. Sch.
Rugby Football Grd.
Pav.
Roundstables
Pen-twyn
Crkt. Grd.
Fairview Ter.
Bluett's Bri.
BLUETT'S RD.
Black Path
Lasgarn Vw.
Wrekin Bungalow
Hill Crest
Pistyll-gwyn
LANE
Cwm Du
Nant Ddu
Pentre-piod
BOOTH'S
GYPSY
ROAD
Hollybush Cottage
Cwmffwdoer Primary Sch.
Football Grd.
Football Ground
BULLER ST
Tal-ochor Farm
GRAIG DDU
Cwm-du Wood
Blaen-nant-y-caws
Pen-rhiw-fid
Nant y Caws
Cwm Ffrwd-oer Farm
Ffrwd-oer
Nant
TY BWMPYN
PLASYCOED
Plas-y-Coed
Springfield Ter.
Woodbine Cottages
Wesley Ter.
Plasycoed Farm
Coed Parciau

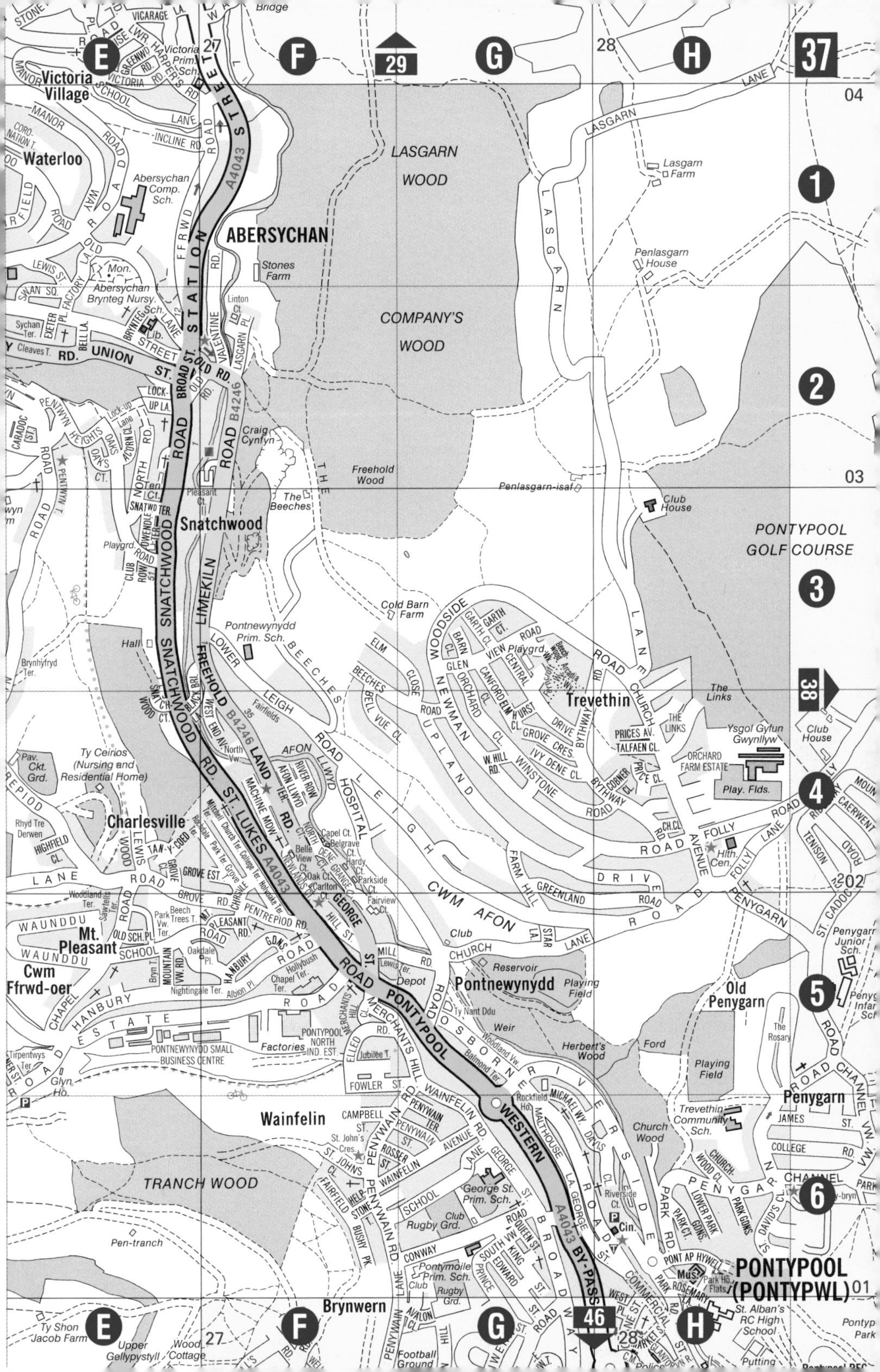

29
38
46
E
F
G
H
1
2
3
4
5
6
27
28
04
03
02
01
Victoria Village
Waterloo
Abersychan Comp. Sch.
ABERSYCHAN
Stones Farm
LASGARN WOOD
COMPANY'S WOOD
Lasgarn Farm
Penlasgarn House
Penlasgarn-isaf
Club House
PONTYPOOL GOLF COURSE
Freehold Wood
The Beeches
Craig Cynfyn
Snatchwood
Cold Barn Farm
Pontnewynydd Prim. Sch.
Trevethin
The Links
Ysgol Gyfun Gwynllyw
ORCHARD FARM ESTATE
Play. Flds.
Hlth. Cen.
Ty Ceirios (Nursing and Residential Home)
Charlesville
Mt. Pleasant
Cwm Ffrwd-oer
PONTNEWYNYDD SMALL BUSINESS CENTRE
Factories
PONTYPOOL NORTH IND. EST.
Pontnewynydd
Reservoir
Playing Field
Weir
Herbert's Wood
Ford
Old Penygarn
Penygarn Junior Sch.
Penygarn
Trevethin Community Sch.
Church Wood
Wainfelin
TRANCH WOOD
Pen-tranch
George St. Prim. Sch.
Rugby Grd.
Pontymoile Prim. Sch.
PONTYPOOL (PONTYPWL)
St. Alban's RC High School
Brynwern
Ty Shon Jacob Farm
Upper Gellypystyll
Wood Cottage
Football Ground
A4043
B4246
STATION STREET
SNATCHWOOD ROAD
LIMEKILN ROAD
FREEHOLD LAND RD.
ST. LUKES RD.
PONTYPOOL ROAD
WESTERN BY-PASS
UNION ST.
BROAD ST.
LASGARN LANE
CHURCH LANE
FOLLY ROAD
PENYGARN ROAD
CWM AFON ROAD
HANBURY ROAD
ESTATE ROAD
CHANNEL VIEW
RIVERSIDE
COMMERCIAL ST.

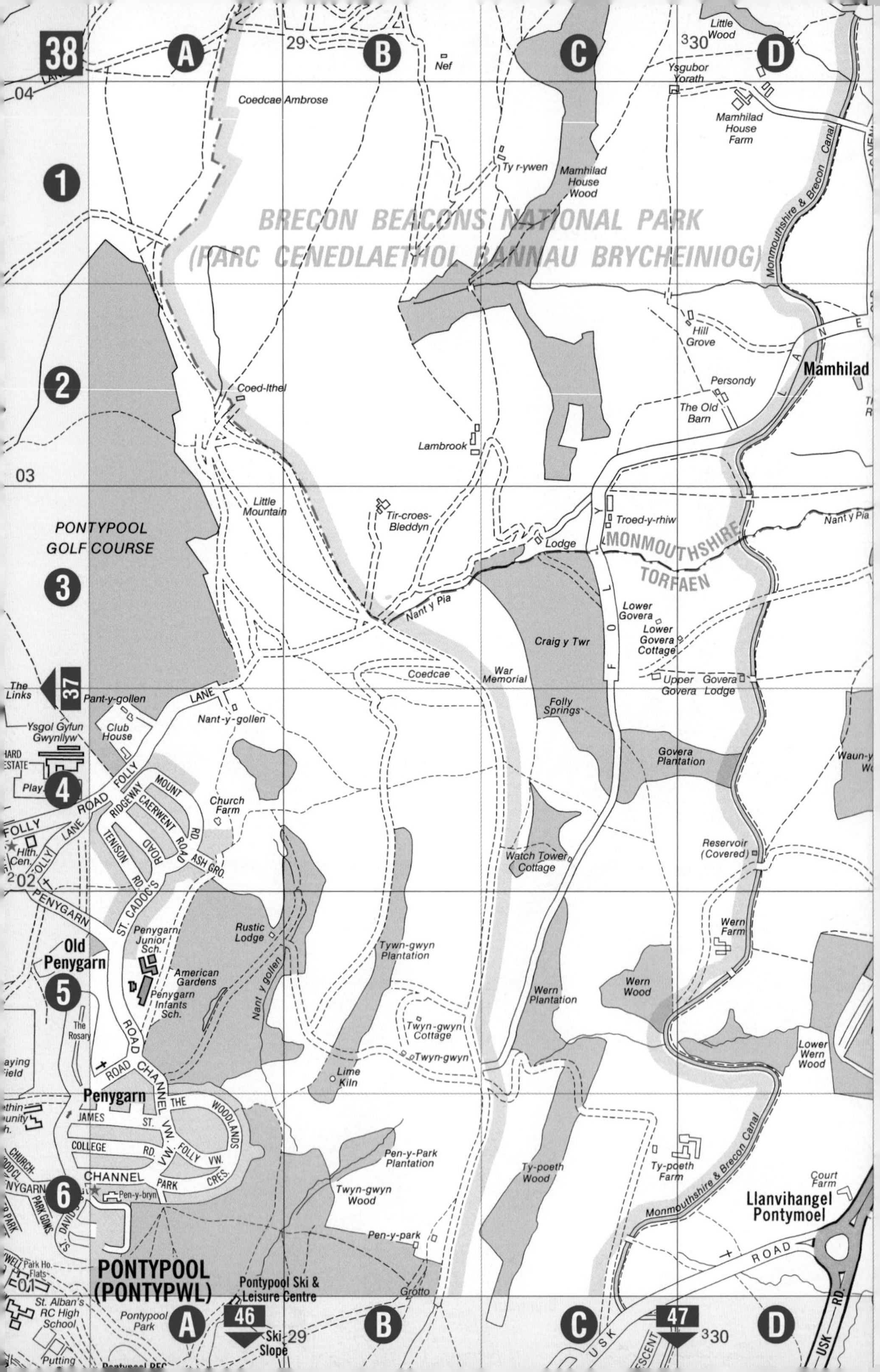
A
B
C
D
1
2
3
4
5
6
04
03
02
01
29
330
Little Wood
Nef
Coedcae Ambrose
Ysgubor Yorath
Mamhilad House Farm
Ty r-ywen
Mamhilad House Wood
Monmouthshire & Brecon Canal
BRECON BEACONS NATIONAL PARK
(PARC CENEDLAETHOL BANNAU BRYCHEINIOG)
Hill Grove
Mamhilad
Persondy
The Old Barn
Coed-Ithel
Lambrook
PONTYPOOL GOLF COURSE
Little Mountain
Tir-croes-Bleddyn
Troed-y-rhiw
Nant y Pia
Lodge
MONMOUTHSHIRE
TORFAEN
FOLLY LANE
Lower Govera
Lower Govera Cottage
Craig y Twr
War Memorial
Coedcae
Upper Govera
Govera Lodge
The Links
37
Pant-y-gollen
Nant-y-gollen
Ysgol Gyfun Gwynllyw
Club House
Folly Springs
Govera Plantation
Play
FOLLY ROAD
RIDGEWAY
MOUNT RD
CAERWENT ROAD
Church Farm
LANE
TENISON RD.
ROAD
ASH GRO.
Hlth. Cen.
FOLLY
Reservoir (Covered)
Watch Tower Cottage
PENYGARN
ST. CADOC'S
Rustic Lodge
Penygarn Junior Sch.
Old Penygarn
Tywn-gwyn Plantation
Wern Farm
American Gardens
Penygarn Infants Sch.
Nant y gollen
Wern Plantation
Wern Wood
The Rosary
Twyn-gwyn Cottage
Twyn-gwyn
Lower Wern Wood
Lime Kiln
Penygarn
CHANNEL VW.
THE WOODLANDS
JAMES ST.
COLLEGE RD.
FOLLY VW.
CHANNEL
PARK CRES.
Pen-y-Park Plantation
Ty-poeth Wood
Ty-poeth Farm
Court Farm
Pen-y-bryn
Twyn-gwyn Wood
Llanvihangel Pontymoel
PARK GDNS
ST DAVIDS
Pen-y-park
Park Ho. Flats
PONTYPOOL (PONTYPWL)
Pontypool Ski & Leisure Centre
Grotto
St. Alban's RC High School
Pontypool Park
46
Ski Slope
USK
47
USK RD.
Putting

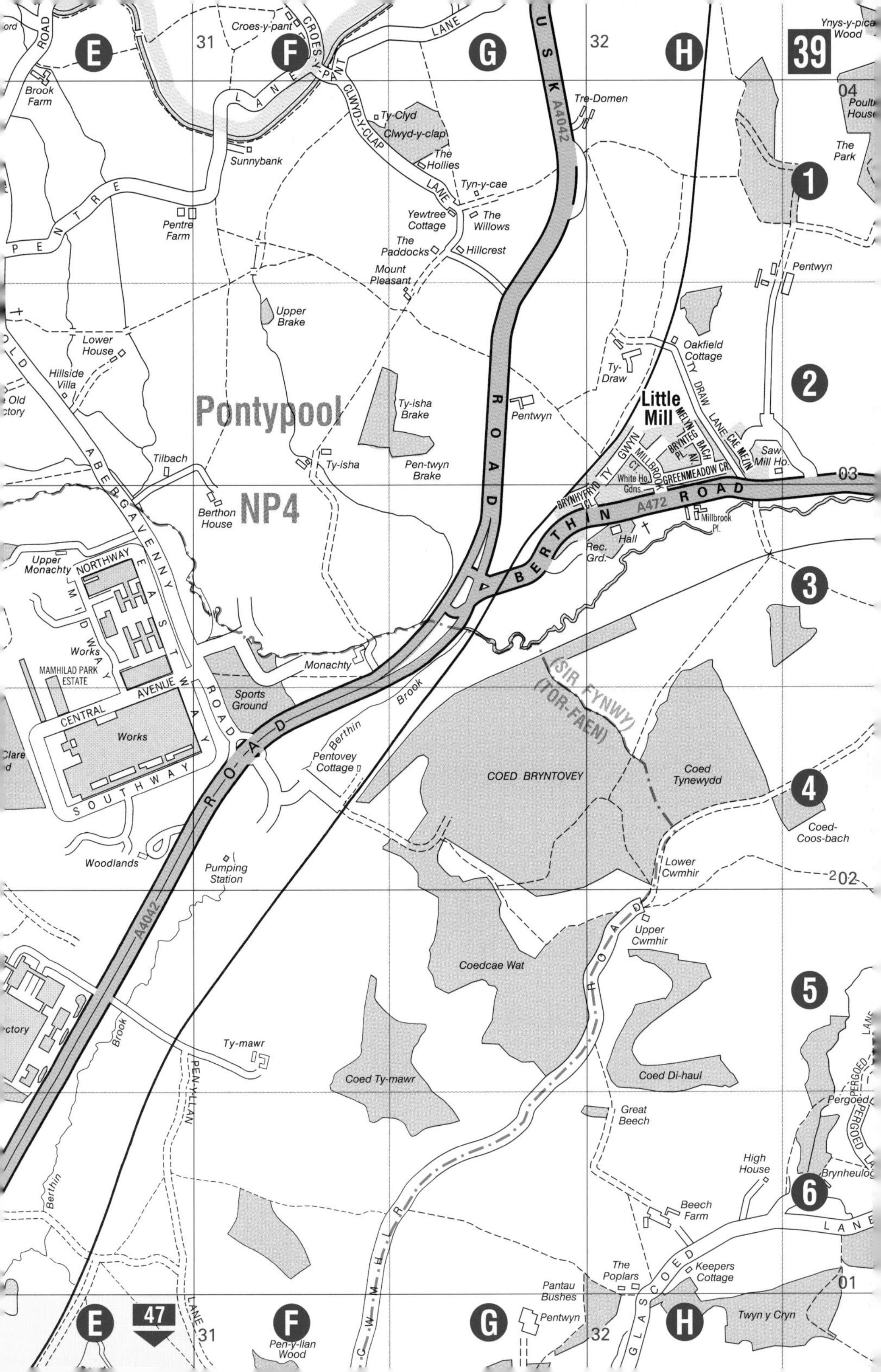

Pontypool
NP4
Little Mill
Croes-y-pant
Brook Farm
Sunnybank
Pentre Farm
Ty-Clyd
Clwyd-y-clap
The Hollies
Tyn-y-cae
Yewtree Cottage
The Willows
The Paddocks
Hillcrest
Mount Pleasant
Tre-Domen
Upper Brake
Lower House
Hillside Villa
Ty-isha Brake
Pen-twyn Brake
Ty-isha
Tilbach
Berthon House
Pentwyn
Oakfield Cottage
Ty-Draw
Saw Mill Ho.
White Ho. Gdns.
Millbrook Pl.
Hall
Rec. Grd.
Upper Monachty
Monachty
Works
MAMHILAD PARK ESTATE
Sports Ground
Pentovey Cottage
COED BRYNTOVEY
Coed Tynewydd
Coed-Coos-bach
(SIR FYNWY)
(TOR-FAEN)
Lower Cwmhir
Upper Cwmhir
Woodlands
Pumping Station
Coedcae Wat
Ty-mawr
Coed Ty-mawr
Coed Di-haul
Great Beech
High House
Beech Farm
Brynheulog
Pergoed
The Poplars
Keepers Cottage
Pantau Bushes
Pentwyn
Twyn y Cryn
Pen-y-llan Wood
The Park
Ynys-y-pica Wood
USK ROAD A4042
BERTHIN ROAD A472
PENTRE LANE
CROES-Y-PANT LANE
CLWYD-Y-CLAP LANE
ABERGAVENNY ROAD
EAST WAY
NORTHWAY
MID WAY
CENTRAL AVENUE
SOUTHWAY
TY DRAW LANE
CAE MELIN
GREENMEADOW CR.
BRYNHYFRYD CL.
TY GWYN CT.
MILLBROOK
BRYNTEG PL.
MELYN BACH AV.
CWMHIR ROAD
PEN-Y-LLAN LANE
GLASCOED LANE
PERGOED LANE
Brook
Berthin
Berthin Brook
E
F
G
H
1
2
3
4
5
6
31
32
04
03
02
01
47

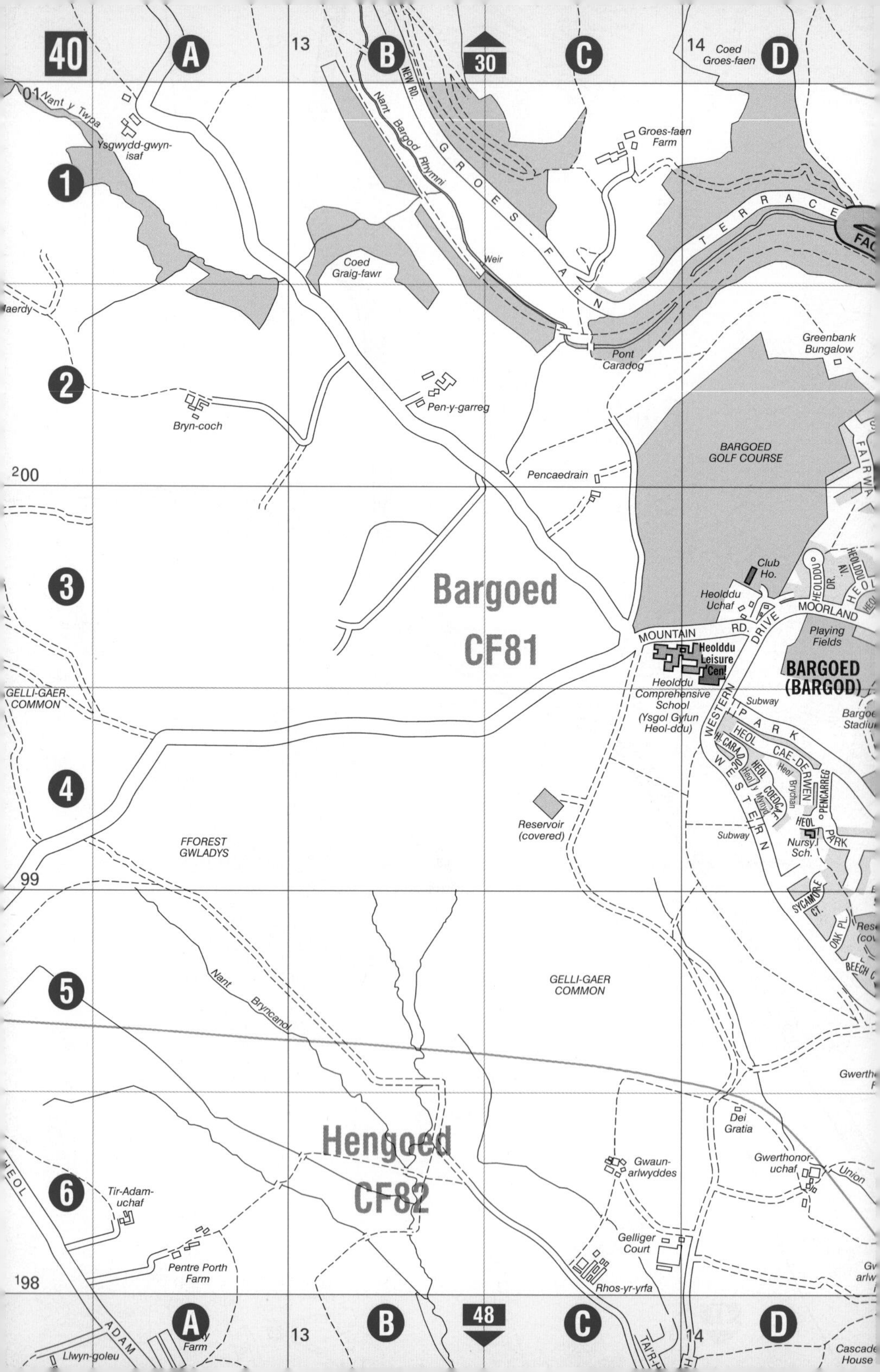
A
13
B
30
C
14
D
Coed Groes-faen
01
Nant y Twpa
Ysgwydd-gwyn-isaf
NEW RD.
Nant Bargod Rhymni
GROES-FAEN
TERRACE
Groes-faen Farm
Coed Graig-fawr
Weir
Pont Caradog
Greenbank Bungalow
Pen-y-garreg
Bryn-coch
BARGOED GOLF COURSE
Pencaedrain
200
Bargoed
CF81
Club Ho.
Heolddu Uchaf
MOORLAND
MOUNTAIN RD.
DRIVE
Playing Fields
Heolddu Leisure Cen.
Heolddu Comprehensive School (Ysgol Gyfun Heol-ddu)
BARGOED (BARGOD)
GELLI-GAER COMMON
WESTERN
PARK
HEOL CAE-DERWEN
PENCARREG
Subway
Reservoir (covered)
Nursy. Sch.
FFOREST GWLADYS
99
SYCAMORE CT.
OAK PL.
BEECH
Nant Bryncanol
GELLI-GAER COMMON
Dei Gratia
Hengoed
CF82
Gwaun-arlwyddes
Gwerthonor-uchaf
Union
Tir-Adam-uchaf
Gelliger Court
Pentre Porth Farm
198
Rhos-yr-yrfa
HEOL
ADAM
48
Farm
Llwyn-goleu
Cascade House

41
31
42
49
E
F
G
H
315
16
01
00
99
98
Gwaelod-y-brithdir
Cemetery
Sports Ground
Pav.
Brynderwen
Coed-y-brain House
Coed-y-brain
Pen-y-Waun
RHYMNEY RIVER (AFON RHYMNI)
CWMSYFIOG ROAD
A4049
A469
B4511
Bedwellty Stadium
Tir-Neuaddwen
BEDWELLTY ROAD
Weir
William Forbes Bungs.
Aberbargoed Sports Hall
Recreation Grd.
Playground
Lib.
HOSP
The Laurels
Adult Educ. Cen.
Aberbargoed Jun. Sch.
Bargoed
STATION RD.
HIGH ST.
HANBURY RD.
COMMERCIAL STREET
West View Villas
TREDEGAR TER.
HEOL TIR-Y-LLAN
Ysgol Gyfun Cwm Rhymni (Lwr. Sch.)
Reservoir
Rectory
Aberbargoed (Aberbargod)
PENGAM ROAD
Foundry
Sports Field
Factory
Library
Offices
Bargoed Park
War Mem.
Ysgol Gyfun Cwm Rhymni (Upper School)
Football Ground
Sports Ground
Gilfach Fargoed
GILFACH ST.
PARK PLACE
BOWEN INDUSTRIAL ESTATE
Penycoed-fach
Bedwellty Comp. Sch.
Ffynnon-wen
Coed Ty'n-y-pwll
Blackwood
NP12
Sports Ground
Cefn Fforest
Playing Fields
BRITANNIA CENTRE FOR ENTERPRISE
Rhymney Valley
Gwerthonor-isaf
Gwerthonor-isaf Wood
Gilfach
School
Sch.
Pav.
GWERTHONOR PL.
CARDIFF RD.
Playing Field
HEOL PIT-Y-CEILIOGOD

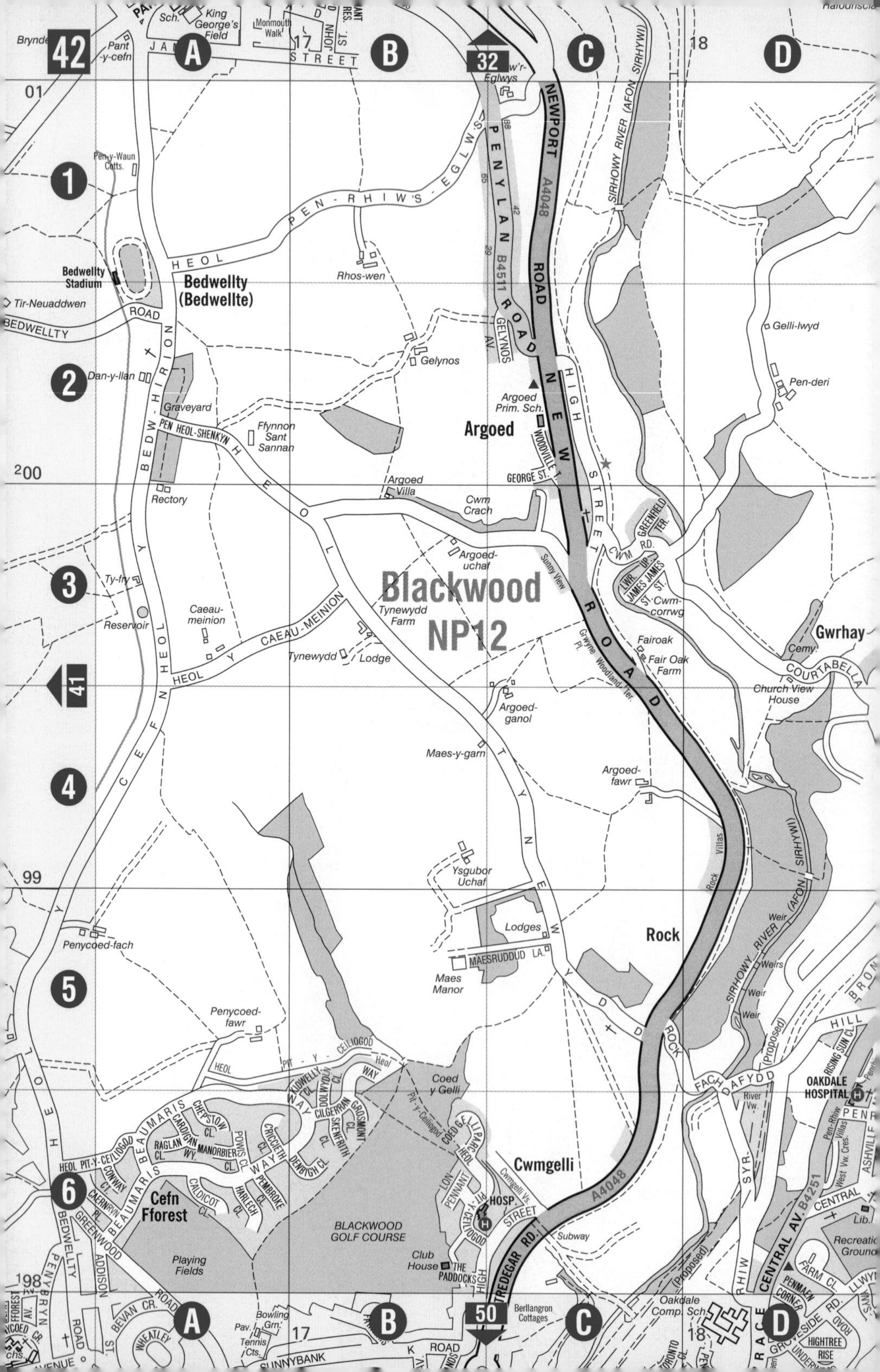

42
32
41
50
A
B
C
D
1
2
3
4
5
6
Blackwood
NP12
Bedwellty
(Bedwellte)
Bedwellty Stadium
Argoed
Argoed Prim. Sch.
Gwrhay
Rock
Cwmgelli
Cefn Fforest
OAKDALE HOSPITAL
BLACKWOOD GOLF COURSE
Playing Fields
Club House
THE PADDOCKS
NEWPORT ROAD
A4048
PENYLAN ROAD
B4511
HIGH STREET
NEW ROAD
HEOL PEN-RHIW'S-EGLWYS
HEOL Y BEDW-HIRION
HEOL Y CAEAU-MEINION
HEOL PIT-Y-CEILIOGOD
CEFN HEOL
PEN HEOL-SHENKYN
HEOL TYNEWYDD
BEDWELLTY ROAD
SIRHOWY RIVER (AFON SIRHYWI)
Rhos-wen
Gelynos
Gelli-lwyd
Pen-deri
Ffynnon Sant Sannan
Graveyard
Rectory
Dan-y-llan
Tir-Neuaddwen
Pen-y-Waun Cotts.
Ty-fry
Reservoir
Caeau-meinion
Tynewydd
Tynewydd Farm
Lodge
Argoed Villa
Cwm Crach
Argoed-uchaf
Argoed-ganol
Maes-y-garn
Argoed-fawr
Ysgubor Uchaf
Lodges
Maes Manor
MAESRUDDUD LA.
Penycoed-fach
Penycoed-fawr
Coed y Gelli
Fairoak
Fair Oak Farm
Cemy.
COURTABELLA
Church View House
Cwm-corrwg
GREENFIELD TER.
CWM RD.
JAMES ST.
GEORGE ST.
WOODVILLE T.
GELYNOS AV.
Sunny View
Grwyne Woodland Ter.
Rock Villas
Weir
Weirs
(Proposed)
River Vw.
CENTRAL AV.
B4251
Lib.
Recreation Ground
FARM CL.
PENMAEN CORNER
GROVESIDE RD.
HIGHTREE RISE
Oakdale Comp. Sch.
Berllangron Cottages
Subway
TREDEGAR RD.
HOSP.
COED GELLI PARC
LON PENNANT
Cwmgelli Vs.
BEAUMARIS WAY
CHEPSTOW CL.
CARDIGAN CL.
RAGLAN CL.
MANORBIER WY.
POWIS CL.
CRICCIETH CL.
DENBIGH CL.
PEMBROKE CL.
HARLECH CL.
CALDICOT CL.
CONWAY CT.
CAERNRYN PL.
KIDWELLY CL.
DOLWYDDLAN CL.
CILGERRAN CL.
SKENFRITH CL.
GROSMONT CL.
GREENWOOD ROAD
ADDISON ROAD
PENYBRYN AVENUE
BEVAN CR.
WHEATLEY
SUNNYBANK
Bowling Grn.
Pav.
Tennis Cts.
King George's Field
Monmouth Walk
JAMES STREET
Pant-y-cefn
Sch.
01
200
99
198
17
18

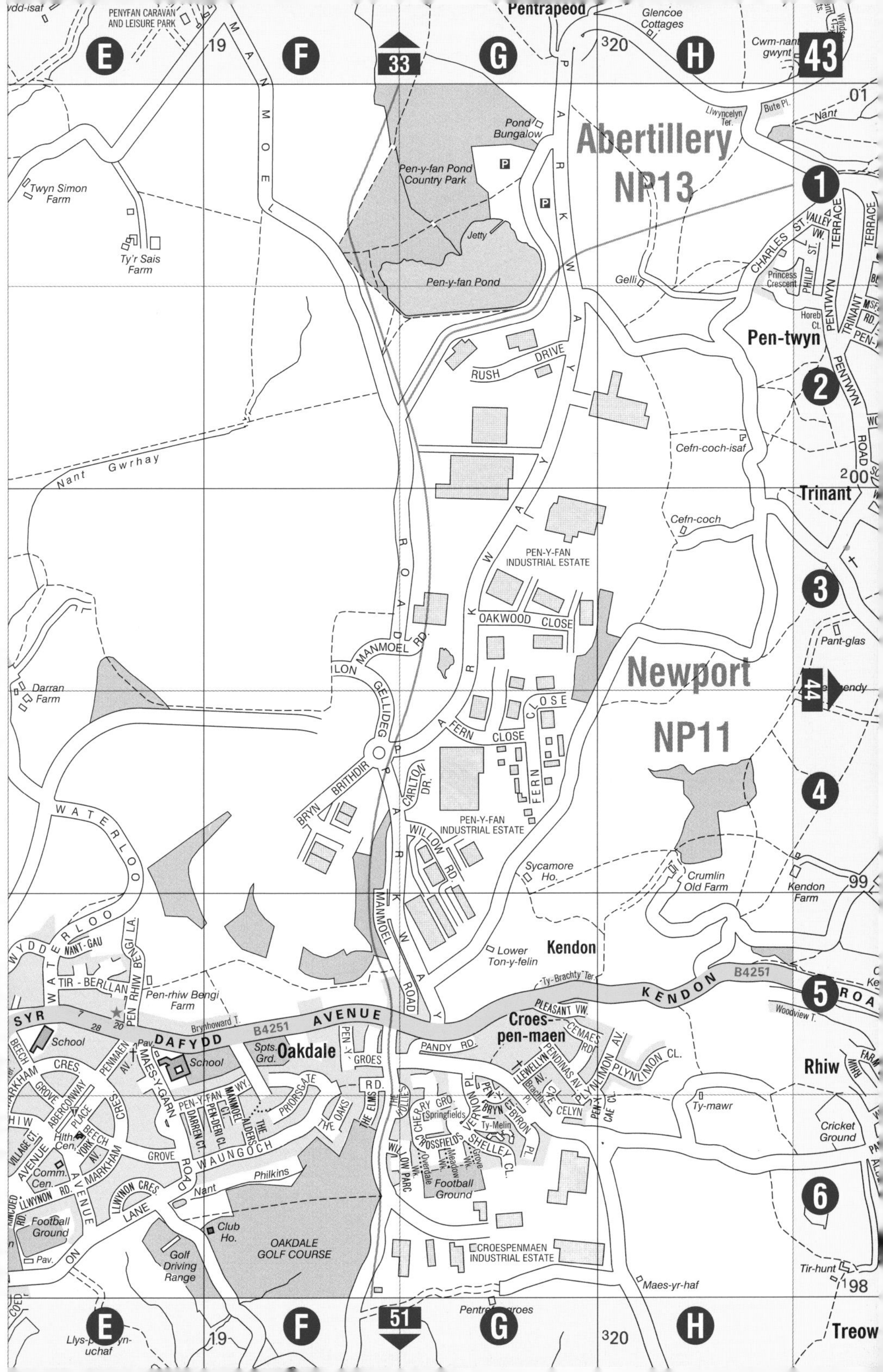

43
33
51
44
Abertillery
NP13
Newport
NP11
Pentrapeod
Glencoe Cottages
Cwm-nant gwynt
PENYFAN CARAVAN AND LEISURE PARK
Twyn Simon Farm
Ty'r Sais Farm
Pond Bungalow
Pen-y-fan Pond Country Park
Jetty
Pen-y-fan Pond
Gelli
Pen-twyn
Trinant
Cefn-coch-isaf
Cefn-coch
PEN-Y-FAN INDUSTRIAL ESTATE
OAKWOOD CLOSE
FERN CLOSE
Pant-glas
Darran Farm
Nant Gwrhay
Crumlin Old Farm
Kendon Farm
Sycamore Ho.
Lower Ton-y-felin
Kendon
KENDON ROAD
B4251
SYR DAFYDD AVENUE
Croes-pen-maen
Oakdale
Pen-rhiw Bengi Farm
Rhiw
Ty-mawr
Cricket Ground
Football Ground
OAKDALE GOLF COURSE
Golf Driving Range
Club Ho.
CROESPENMAEN INDUSTRIAL ESTATE
Maes-yr-haf
Tir-hunt
Pentref-y-groes
Llys-pentwyn-uchaf
Treow

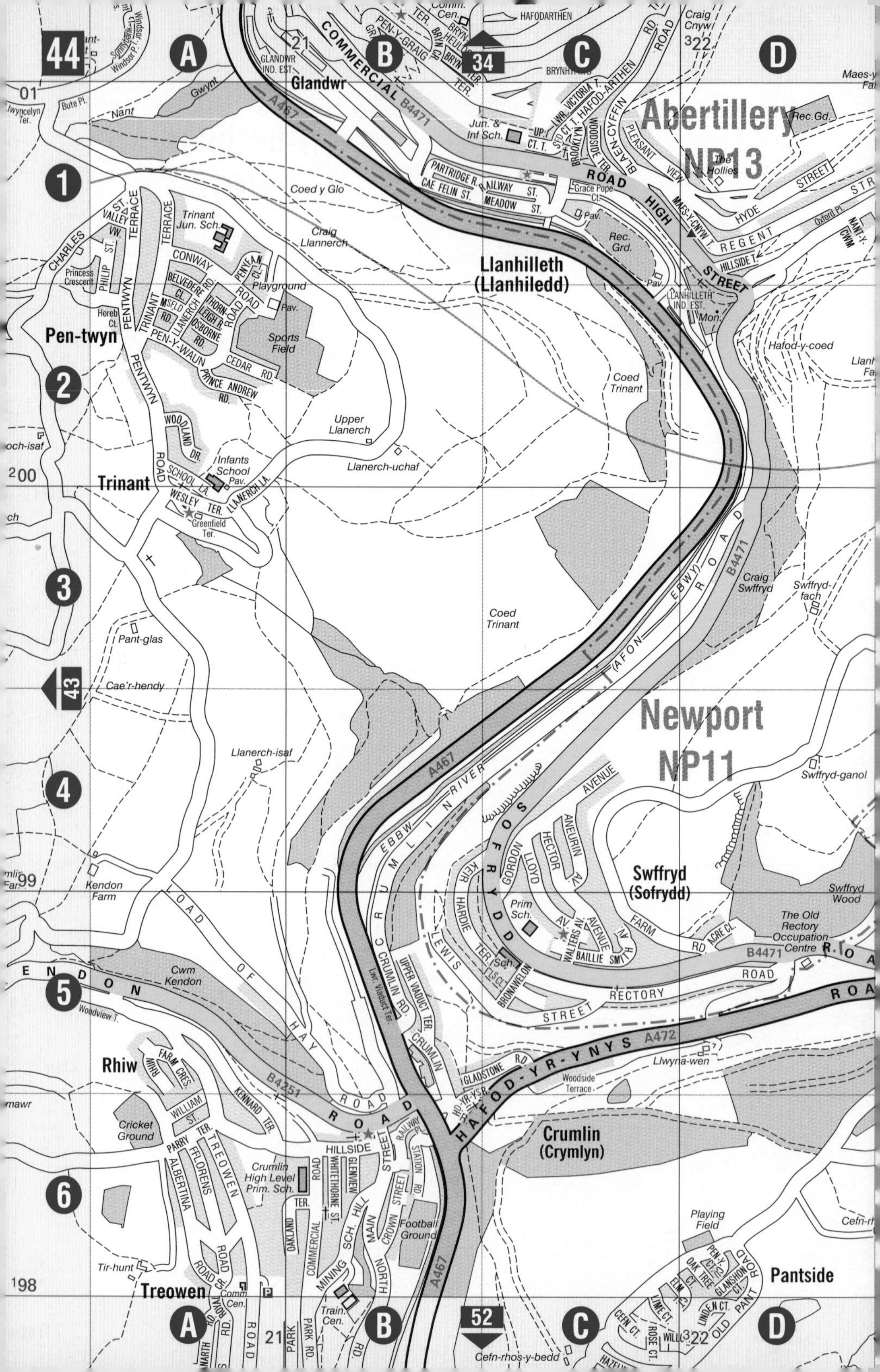

Glandwr
Abertillery NP13
Llanhilleth (Llanhiledd)
Pen-twyn
Trinant
Newport NP11
Swffryd (Sofrydd)
Rhiw
Crumlin (Crymlyn)
Treowen
Pantside
Coed y Glo
Craig Llannerch
Coed Trinant
Upper Llanerch
Llanerch-uchaf
Llanerch-isaf
Pant-glas
Cae'r-hendy
Kendon Farm
Cwm Kendon
Hafod-y-coed
Craig Swffryd
Swffryd-fach
Swffryd-ganol
Swffryd Wood
The Old Rectory Occupation Centre
Llwyna-wen
Woodside Terrace
Playing Field
Cricket Ground
Football Ground
Sports Field
Trinant Jun. Sch.
Infants School
Crumlin High Level Prim. Sch.
Prim. Sch.
Jun. & Inf Sch.
Train. Cen.
Tir-hunt
Cefn-rhos-y-bedd
COMMERCIAL ROAD
HIGH STREET
ROAD OF HAY
HAFOD-YR-YNYS
RECTORY ROAD
SOFRYDD
EBBW RIVER
KENDON
A467
A472
B4471
B4251
34
43
52

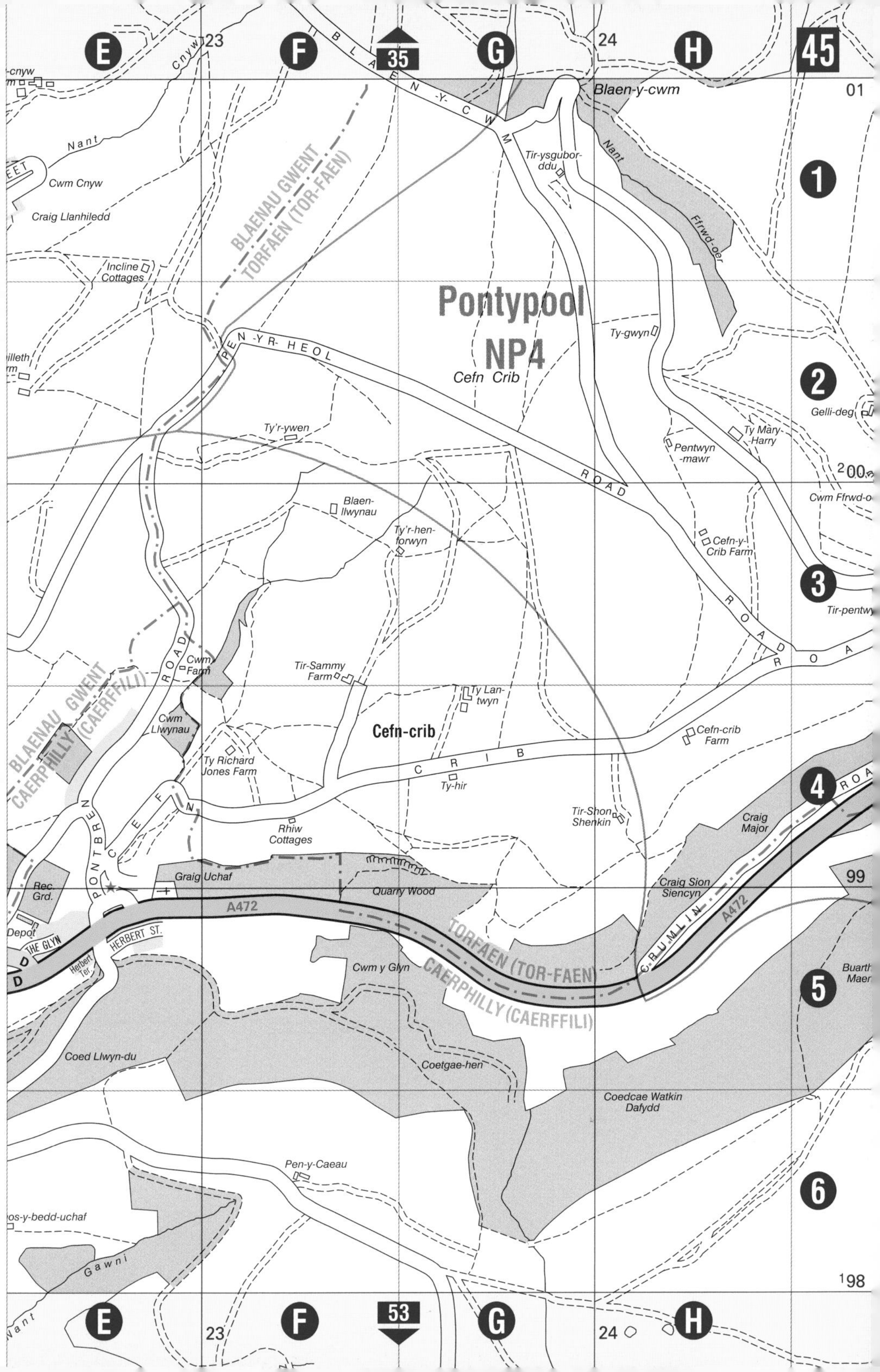
E
F
G
H
23
24
35
53
01
00
99
98
1
2
3
4
5
6
Blaen-y-cwm
BLAEN-Y-CWM
Nant Ffrwd-oer
Tir-ysgubor-ddu
Cwm Cnyw
Nant
Craig Llanhiledd
Incline Cottages
BLAENAU GWENT
TORFAEN (TOR-FAEN)
Pontypool
NP4
Cefn Crib
PEN-YR-HEOL ROAD
Ty-gwyn
Gelli-deg
Ty Mary-Harry
Pentwyn-mawr
Ty'r-ywen
Blaen-llwynau
Ty'r-hen-forwyn
Cwm Ffrwd-oer
Cefn-y-Crib Farm
Tir-pentwy
ROAD
Cwm Farm
Tir-Sammy Farm
Ty Lan-twyn
Cefn-crib
Cefn-crib Farm
CRIB
Cwm Llwynau
Ty Richard Jones Farm
Ty-hir
BLAENAU GWENT
CAERPHILLY (CAERFFILI)
CEFN
PONTBREN
Rhiw Cottages
Tir-Shon Shenkin
Craig Major
Rec. Grd.
Graig Uchaf
Quarry Wood
A472
Craig Sion Siencyn
CRUMLIN
Depot
THE GLYN
HERBERT ST.
Herbert Ter.
TORFAEN (TOR-FAEN)
CAERPHILLY (CAERFFILI)
Cwm y Glyn
Buarth Maen
Coed Llwyn-du
Coetgae-hen
Coedcae Watkin Dafydd
Pen-y-Caeau
Gawni
Nant

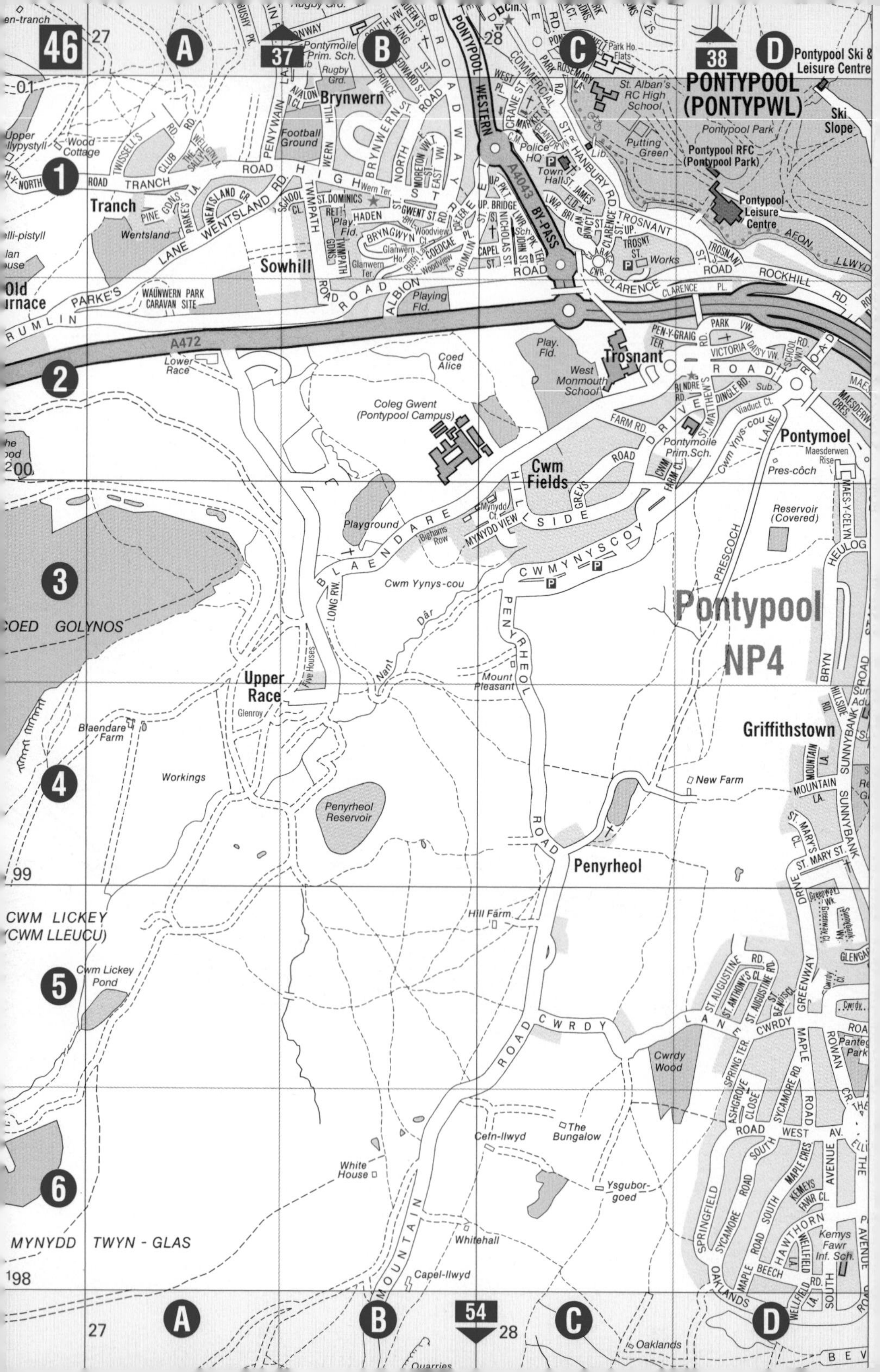

PONTYPOOL
(PONTYPWL)
Pontypool Ski & Leisure Centre
Ski Slope
Pontypool Park
Pontypool RFC (Pontypool Park)
Pontypool Leisure Centre
St. Alban's RC High School
Putting Green
Brynwern
Football Ground
Tranch
Sowhill
Wentsland
Old Furnace
WAUNWERN PARK CARAVAN SITE
Playing Fld.
Trosnant
West Monmouth School
Coleg Gwent (Pontypool Campus)
Coed Alice
Lower Race
Cwm Fields
Pontymoel
Pontymoile Prim. Sch.
Reservoir (Covered)
Playground
Cwm Ynys-cou
COED GOLYNOS
Upper Race
Mount Pleasant
Pontypool
NP4
Griffithstown
Blaendare Farm
Workings
Penyrheol Reservoir
New Farm
Penyrheol
Hill Farm
CWM LICKEY (CWM LLEUCU)
Cwm Lickey Pond
Cwrdy Wood
The Bungalow
Cefn-llwyd
White House
Ysgubor-goed
Whitehall
Capel-llwyd
MYNYDD TWYN - GLAS
Kemys Fawr Inf. Sch.
Oaklands
Quarries
A472
A4043
PONTYPOOL WESTERN BY-PASS
BLAENDARE ROAD
CWMYNYSCOY ROAD
PENYRHEOL ROAD
CWRDY ROAD
CWRDY LANE
MOUNTAIN ROAD
PRESCOCH LANE
ALBION ROAD
CLARENCE ROAD
ROCKHILL RD.
TROSNANT ROAD
HANBURY RD.
COMMERCIAL ST.
HIGH STREET
BROADWAY
TRANCH ROAD
WENTSLAND RD.
SUNNYBANK
GREENWAY
SPRINGFIELD
OAKLANDS

37 38 54

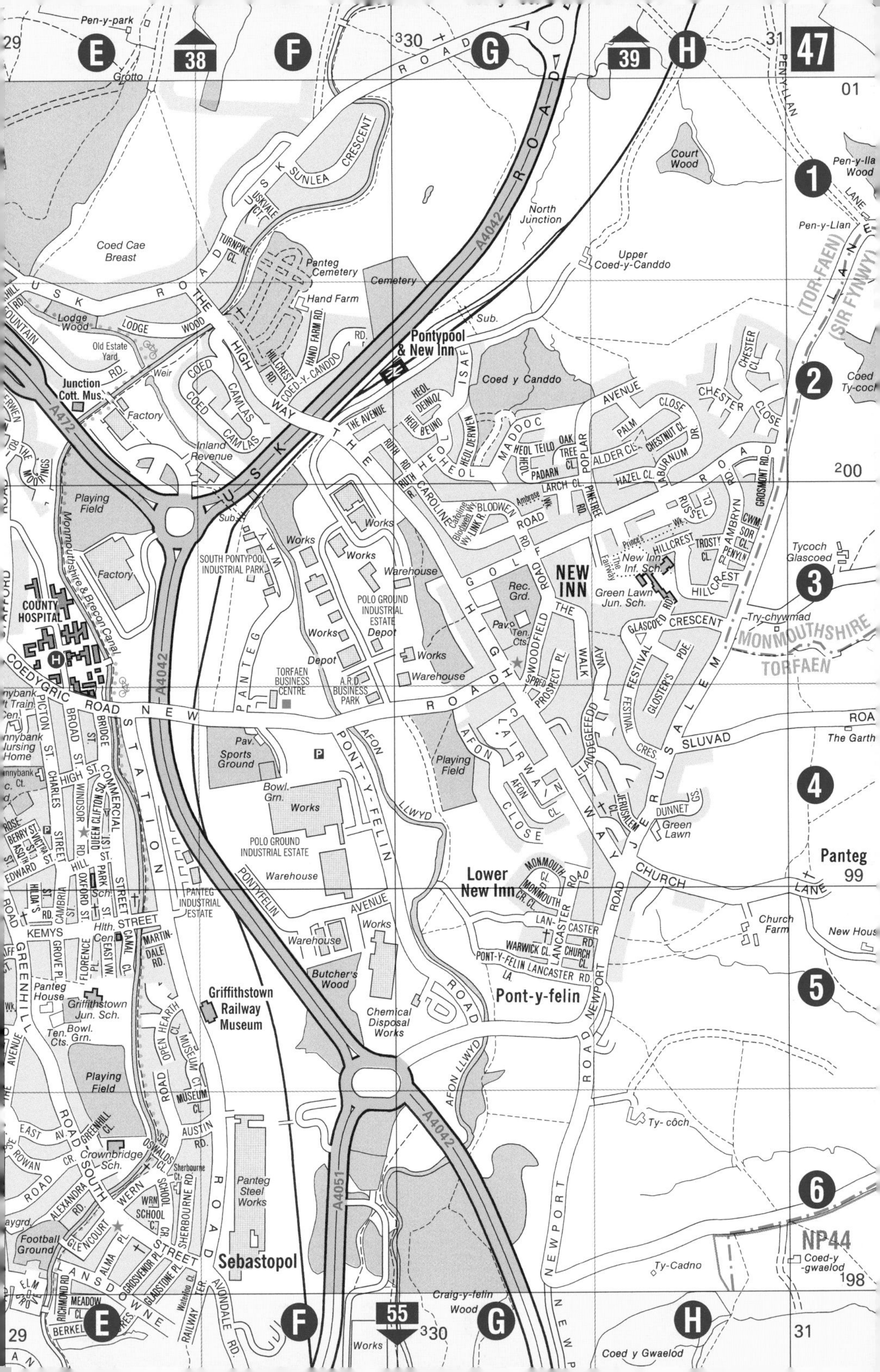

38
39
55
Pen-y-park
Grotto
Coed Cae Breast
Lodge Wood
Old Estate Yard
Junction Cott. Mus.
Factory
Weir
Inland Revenue
Playing Field
COUNTY HOSPITAL
Monmouthshire & Brecon Canal
USK ROAD
USK WAY
THE HIGHWAY
SUNLEA CRESCENT
USKVALE CT.
TURNPIKE CL.
Panteg Cemetery
Hand Farm
HAND FARM RD.
HILLCREST RD.
COED-Y-CANDDO RD.
Cemetery
Pontypool & New Inn
A4042
A472
A4051
North Junction
Upper Coed-y-Canddo
Court Wood
Pen-y-Llan
Pen-y-lla Wood
PENYLLAN LANE
(TOR-FAEN)
(SIR FYNWY)
Coed Ty-coch
Coed y Canddo
HEOL ISAF
HEOL DEINIOL
HEOL BEUNO
HEOL DERWEN
HEOL MADDOC
HEOL TEILO
HEOL PADARN
OAK TREE CL.
POPLAR AVENUE
ALDER CL.
PALM CLOSE
CHESTNUT CL.
LABURNUM DR.
HAZEL CL.
CHESTER CLOSE
CHESTER CL.
LARCH CL.
PINETREE RD.
RUSSEL CL.
GROSMONT RD.
AMBRYN RD.
CWM SOR CL.
PENYLYN CL.
TROSTY CL.
HILLCREST
THE AVENUE
RUTH RD.
CAROLINE RD.
BLODWEN ROAD
LINK R.
Ambrose Wk.
Prince's Wk.
The Fairway
New Inn Inf. Sch.
Green Lawn Jun. Sch.
NEW INN
GOLF ROAD
Rec. Grd.
Pav.
Ten. Cts.
THE WOODFIELD
THE WALK
WAY
PROSPECT PL.
GLASCOED RD.
GLASCOED CRESCENT
FESTIVAL CRES.
GLOSTER'S PDE.
JERUSALEM LANE
JERUSALEM CL.
SLUVAD ROAD
Tycoch Glascoed
Try-chywmad
MONMOUTHSHIRE
TORFAEN
The Garth
DUNNET GS.
Green Lawn
Panteg
CHURCH LANE
Church Farm
New House
Sub.
Works
Warehouse
Depot
SOUTH PONTYPOOL INDUSTRIAL PARK
POLO GROUND INDUSTRIAL ESTATE
TORFAEN BUSINESS CENTRE
A.R.D. BUSINESS PARK
PANTEG WAY
COEDYGRIC ROAD
NEW ROAD
AFON LLWYD
PONT-Y-FELIN ROAD
CLAIRWAIN
AFON CLOSE
LLANDEGFEDD WAY
Playing Field
Pav. Sports Ground
Bowl. Grn.
Lower New Inn
MONMOUTH CL.
MONMOUTH CR. CL.
MONMOUTH ROAD
LANCASTER
LANCASTER RD.
WARWICK CL.
CHURCH CL.
PONT-Y-FELIN LA.
Pont-y-felin
NEWPORT ROAD
PONTYFELIN AVENUE
Butcher's Wood
Chemical Disposal Works
PANTEG INDUSTRIAL ESTATE
Griffithstown Railway Museum
STATION ROAD
PICTON ST.
BROAD ST.
BRIDGE ST.
HIGH ST.
CHARLES ST.
WINDSOR RD.
QUEEN CLIFTON SQ.
COMMERCIAL ST.
ROSEBERY ST.
VICTORIA ST.
ASQUITH ST.
EDWARD ST.
HILDA'S ST.
CAMBRIA ST.
OXFORD ST.
PARK ST.
HILL ST.
KEMYS STREET
CANAL CL.
MARTINDALE RD.
GREENHILL ROAD
GROVE PL.
FLORENCE PL.
EAST VW.
Hlth. Cen.
Panteg House
Griffithstown Jun. Sch.
Bowl. Grn.
Ten. Cts.
OPEN HEARTH CL.
MUSEUM CT.
MUSEUM CL.
AUSTIN RD.
Playing Field
GREENHILL CL.
EAST AV.
ROWAN CR.
SOUTH ROAD
Crownbridge Sch.
ALEXANDRA RD.
WERN
GLENCOURT
ALMA PL.
ST. OSWALDS
Sherbourne Ct.
SHERBOURNE RD.
SCHOOL GR.
SCHOOL C.
GROSVENOR PL.
GLADSTONE PL.
Waterloo Cl.
RAILWAY TER.
AVONDALE RD.
Panteg Steel Works
Sebastopol
Football Ground
LANSDOWNE
RICHMOND RD.
ELM GRO.
MEADOW CL.
BERKELEY CRES.
Ty-coch
Ty-Cadno
Coed-y-gwaelod
NP44
Craig-y-felin Wood
Coed y Gwaelod
Works
E
F
G
H
1
2
3
4
5
6
29
330
31
01
200
99
198

A
B
C
D
13
14
40
56
98
97
96
195
1
2
3
4
5
6
Pentre Porth Farm
Gelliger Court
Rhos-yr-yrfa
HEOL
Poulty Farm
Llwyn-goleu
Cwrtevan House
Llwyngoleu Cottage
Tir-y-rhen Farm
TAI'R-HEOL
HOSPITAL
GARREG WEN
GELLI-RON
TYLA-GWYN
PEN-Y-BONT
GWAUN-FRO
TY-NANT
WILLOW PL.
MAES-Y-DDERWEN
SWN-YR-NANT
RHOS-Y-BETWS
NANT-FFYDDLON
GWAUN-FRO
DUFFRYN CL.
RHOS AV.
AMBLESIDE CT.
ROAD
THE SQUARE
BRYNCOED TER.
BERLLANLWYD
BRYNHYFRYD TER.
HAULWEN ROAD
PENDARREN ST.
PENGAM
Comm. Cen.
LLWYN ONN
Playing Field
HENGOED AVENUE
BRON-Y-GARTH
GLAS FRYN
PEN-Y-
BRYN
Cas
Ho
ADAM
ROMAN CAMP
Rec. Grd.
Pav.
Hall
B4254
NEWTON CL.
WALLIS DR.
ROLLS
FARRADAY DR.
BRUNEL CL.
ST. DAVID'S CL.
OAKS END CL.
ROYCE CL.
BARRY CL.
TELFORD CL.
PAXTON CL.
SORREL
GELLIGAER ROAD CHURCH
B4254
LEGION'S WY.
PENYWRLOD
GEORGE
ST. JULIAN'S CL.
ANUERIN BEVAN AV.
RECTORY RD.
The Old Rectory
ROMAN FORT
Graveyard
Greenhill Prim. Sch.
HEOL EDWARD
GREENHILL
PLACE
ROAD
CASTLE HILL
CH. MDW.
COMMERCIAL ST.
Sq.
Leicester
OXFORD ST.
GLYN-GAER
Gelligaer Village Primary School
Nant Cylla
TANSY CL.
RAMSON CL.
DRIVE
BURNET DR.
GRO
DOMNEY
Green Acres
CLAERWEN
Comm. Cen.
CLAERWEN
DAN-Y-GAER RD.
GAER PL.
HAMAN PL.
LEWIS
Sch.
RHINAMOTH ST.
PENALLTA CL.
HMTN
South View Houses
Hengoed
ROAD POTTERY
NORTH
ANUERIN BEVAN AV.
ST. CATTWG'S AV.
HEOL-Y-WAUN
HEOL
Waun Rhydd
HEOL CATTWG
Gelligaer
CF82
Ford
Coed Gelliau'r-gwellt
Gelliargwellt Uchaf Farm
Brynheulog
FFYNNON CAE
CRESCENT
GELLIWEN ST.
CYLLA ST.
Penybryn T.
Tir Trosnant
PENALLTA INDUSTRIAL ESTATE
Waun Rydd
Penybryn
BRYNHEULOG ST.
CYLLA ST.
GELLIAR GWELLT RD.
Terrace
ROAD
EAST
ROAD
SOUTH RD.
Penrhiwfelin Farm
GELLIARGWELLT RD.
CEFN LLWYNAU ST.
TROSNANT
Penybryn
Football Ground
WEST
Cefn-llwynau
Waun Rydd
Cefn-llwynau Bungalow
PENALLTA COMMUNITY PARK
P
ROAD PENALLTA
Cefn Duffryn
CLOS BRYN CELYN
DUFFRYN ST.
Treharris CF46
A472
HEOL PONT Y SESON
Coed Penalltau
Penalltau-fawr
Penalltau-isaf
Tai-Fforest Cottages
Penalltau

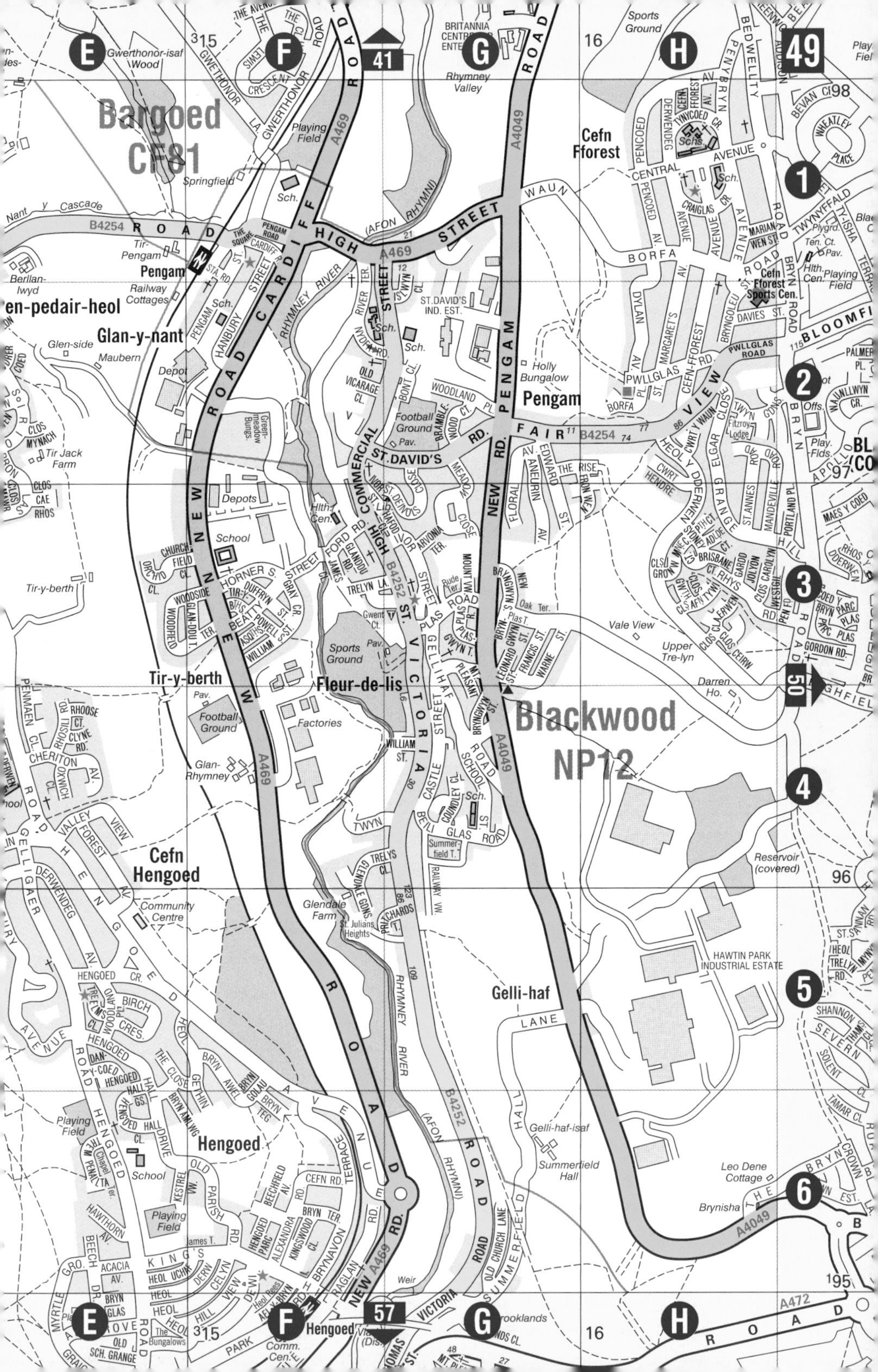

49
41
50
57
E
F
G
H
1
2
3
4
5
6
Bargoed
CF81
Blackwood
NP12
Pengam
Glan-y-nant
Cefn Fforest
Fleur-de-lis
Tir-y-berth
Cefn Hengoed
Hengoed
Gelli-haf
Upper Tre-lyn
Gwerthonor-isaf Wood
Rhymney Valley
Sports Ground
Playing Field
Football Ground
Factories
Reservoir (covered)
HAWTIN PARK INDUSTRIAL ESTATE
ST.DAVID'S IND. EST.
Community Centre
Gelli-haf-isaf
Summerfield Hall
Leo Dene Cottage
Brynisha
Glendale Farm
Holly Bungalow
Vale View
Darren Ho.
Tir Jack Farm
Glen-side
Maubern
Springfield
Railway Cottages
NEW ROAD
CARDIFF ROAD
HIGH STREET
PENGAM ROAD
NEW RD.
FAIR VIEW
PWLLGLAS ROAD
ST. DAVID'S RD.
COMMERCIAL STREET
ST. VICTORIA ROAD
BLOOMFIELD
A469
A4049
B4254
B4252
A472
315
16
98
97
96
195

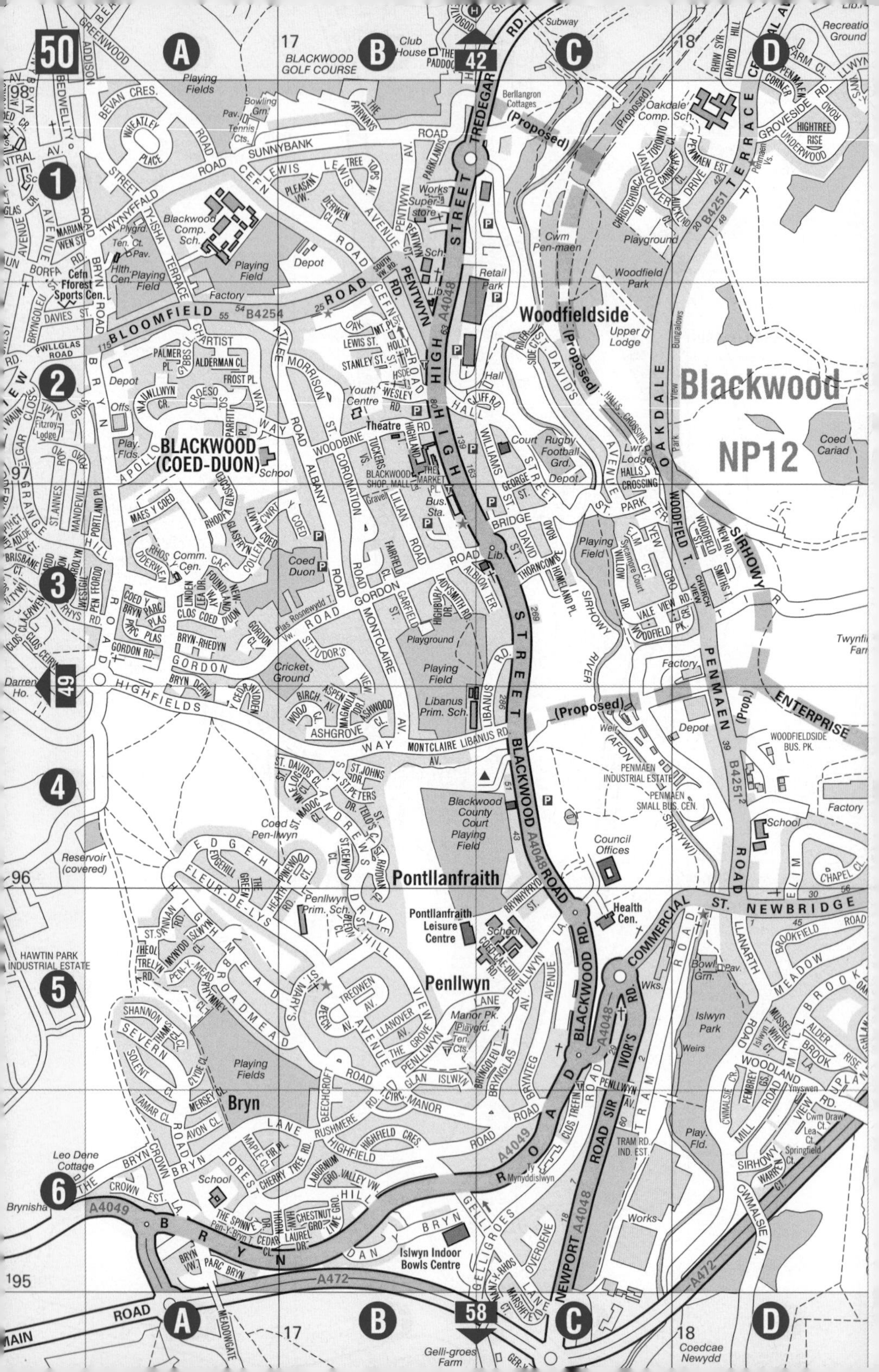
A
B
C
D
17
18
1
2
3
4
5
6
98
97
96
195
42
49
58
Club House
BLACKWOOD GOLF COURSE
THE PADDOCK
Playing Fields
Bowling Grn.
Pav.
Tennis Cts.
THE FAIRWAYS
BEVAN CRES.
WHEATLEY PLACE
SUNNYBANK ROAD
CEFN ROAD
LEWIS TREE TOPS AV.
PLEASANT VW.
DERWEN CL.
LEWIS AVENUE
PENTWYN AV.
PARKLANDS
TREDEGAR RD.
Subway
Berllangron Cottages
(Proposed)
Oakdale Comp. Sch.
RHIW SYR DAFYDD HILL
FARM CL.
CORNER
PENMAEN
GROVESIDE RD.
HIGHTREE RISE
UNDERWOOD
Recreation Ground
CRESCENT
TORONTO
VANCOUVER
CANBERRA CL.
CHRISTCHURCH RD.
PENMAEN EST.
DRIVE
B4251
TERRACE
Penmaen Vs.
Playground
Woodfield Park
Upper Lodge
Blackwood
NP12
Coed Cariad
GREENWOOD
ADDISON
BEDWELLTY
CENTRAL AV.
AVENUE
GLAS CR.
MARIAN WEN ST.
BORFA RD.
Cefn Fforest Sports Cen.
DAVIES ST.
BRYNGOLEU
PWLLGLAS ROAD
TWYNYFFALD STREET
TY-ISHA TERRACE
Plygrd.
Ten. Ct. Pav.
Hlth. Cen.
Playing Field
Blackwood Comp. Sch.
Factory
BLOOMFIELD ROAD
B4254
Depot
SOUTH VW. RD.
CEFN RD.
PENTWYN RD.
PENTWYN CT.
Works
Super-store
Sch.
Lib.
HIGH STREET
A4048
Retail Park
Cwm Pen-maen
Woodfieldside
RIVERSIDE CT.
ST. DAVID'S AVENUE
HALLS CROSSING
OAKDALE
Park View
Bungalows
CHARTIST
PALMER PL.
GIBBS CL.
ALDERMAN CL.
FROST PL.
WAUNLLWYN CR.
CROESO
PARFITT PL.
ATTLEE WAY
MORRISON ROAD
OAK
MT. PL.
LEWIS ST.
HOLLY
STANLEY ST.
HSDE
WESLEY RD.
Youth Centre
Theatre
HIGHLAND RD.
HALL
CLIFF RD.
WILLIAMS STREET
Court
Rugby Football Grd.
Depot
Lwr. Lodge
TWYN GDNS.
Fitzroy Lodge
Offs.
Play. Flds.
APOLLO WAY
BLACKWOOD (COED-DUON)
School
WOODBINE
ALBANY
CORONATION
TUCKERS VS.
BLACKWOOD SHOP. MALL
THE MARKET PL.
Bus. Sta.
GEORGE ST.
BRIDGE
DAVID ST.
PARK TER.
WOODFIELD T.
SIRHOWY
MANDEVILLE
PORTLAND PL.
ST. ANNES
GRANGE
HILL
MAES Y COED
RHODFA
GLASFRYN
LLWYN COED
COLLEN
Y COED
Gravel
LILIAN ROAD
FAIRFIELD CL.
ROAD
ALBION TER.
THORNCOMBE
HOMELAND PL.
Playing Field
ELM CT.
Sycamore Court
WILLOW DR.
YEW GRO.
NEW RD.
SMITHS T.
CHURCH VIEW
RHOS DDERWEN
Comm. Cen.
LINDEN
LEA DR.
FOUNDLAND WAY
NEW-DUON
Coed Duon
GORDON ROAD
GARFIELD ST.
LADYSMITH RD.
HIGHBURY DR.
BRISBANE CT.
CAROLYN
WESTGIL
PEN FFORDD
RHYS RD.
COED Y BRYN
PARC PLAS
CLOS COED DUON
BRYN-RHEDYN
GORDON CL.
Plas Rosnewydd T.
MONTCLAIRE
VALE VIEW RD.
WOODFIELD PK.
Playground
Playing Field
Twynffi Farm
GORDON RD.
GORDON
ST. TUDOR'S
Cricket Ground
Libanus Prim. Sch.
LIBANUS RD.
Factory
Darren Ho.
HIGHFIELDS
BRYN DERW
Y CEDRWYDDEN
BIRCH AV.
ASPEN AV.
MAGNOLIA DR.
ASHWOOD CL.
VIEW
WOOD CL.
ASHGROVE
WAY
MONTCLAIRE AV.
LIBANUS RD.
BLACKWOOD STREET
(Proposed)
Weir
(AFON SIRHYWI)
Depot
PENMAEN INDUSTRIAL ESTATE
PENMAEN ROAD
(Prop.)
ENTERPRISE
WOODFIELDSIDE BUS. PK.
ST. DAVIDS CL.
ST. JOHNS DR.
ST. PETERS
MAELOG
ST. MADOC CL.
ANDREWS
TEILO'S CT.
Blackwood County Court Playing Field
PENMAEN SMALL BUS. CEN.
Factory
School
Coed Pen-llwyn
EDGEHILL
ST. CENYDD CL.
ST. RHIDIAN
Council Offices
Reservoir (covered)
Pontllanfraith
CHAPEL CL.
ELM
PINEWOOD
THE GREEN
HEATH
FLEUR-DE-LYS
DRIVE
BRYNHYFRYD ST.
Health Cen.
COMMERCIAL ST.
NEWBRIDGE
ROAD
HAWTIN PARK INDUSTRIAL ESTATE
ST. SANNAN RD.
ISLWYN CL.
HEOL TRELYN
MYNYDD
PEN-Y-MEAD
RHYMNEY CL.
HIGH MEAD
BROADMEAD
Penllwyn Prim. Sch.
BLEDDYN CL.
HILL
Pontllanfraith Leisure Centre
School
COED-CAE-DDU RD.
BLACKWOOD RD.
LLANARTH
BROOKFIELD
MEADOW
ST. MARY'S
TREOWEN AV.
BEECH AV.
AVENUE
LLANOVER AV.
Penllwyn
LANE
PENLLWYN AV.
Manor Pk. (Playgrd.)
Ten. Cts.
Wks.
ROAD
Bowl. Grn.
Pav.
Islwyn Park
Weirs
MILLBROOK
MUSSEL
WHITE
ALDER
BROOK LA.
RISE
UPLAND
SHANNON
SEVERN
THAMES CL.
SOLENT
CLYDE CL.
Playing Fields
Bryn
MERSEY CL.
TAMAR CL.
AVON CL.
THE GROVE
PENLLWYN
ROAD
GLAN ISLWYN
MANOR
CIRC.
BRYNGOLEU T.
BRYNGLAS
BRYNTEG
ROAD
A4048
IVOR'S RD.
SIR IVOR'S ROAD
TRAM ROAD
TRAM RD. IND. EST.
CLOS TREFIN
PENLLWYN
Play. Fld.
WOODLAND
CWMALSIE CR.
PEMBREY
MILL ROAD
VIEW RD.
Ynyswen
Cwm Draw Ct.
Lea Ct.
Springfield Ct.
BEECHCROFT
RUSHMERE RD.
HIGHFIELD CRES.
HIGHFIELD
LANE
A4049
Leo Dene Cottage
THE BRYN
CROWN
BRYN ROAD
FOREST
MAPLE CL.
FIR PL.
CHERRY TREE RD.
LABURNUM GRO.
VALLEY VW.
ROAD
Ty Mynyddislwyn
SIRHOWY
WARREN CT.
CWMALSIE LA.
Brynisha
CROWN EST.
School
THE SPINNEY
Pen-Y-Bryn T.
CEDAR CL.
THORN
HAW.
CHESTNUT GRO.
LAUREL DR.
LIME GRO.
DAN Y BRYN
Islwyn Indoor Bowls Centre
GELLI
GELLIGROES
OVERDENE
NANT-Y-RHOS
MARSHFIELD CT.
LANE
NEWPORT ROAD
A4048
Works
A472
BRYN VW.
PARC BRYN
MAIN ROAD
MEADOWGATE
Gelli-groes Farm
GER-Y
Coedcae Newydd

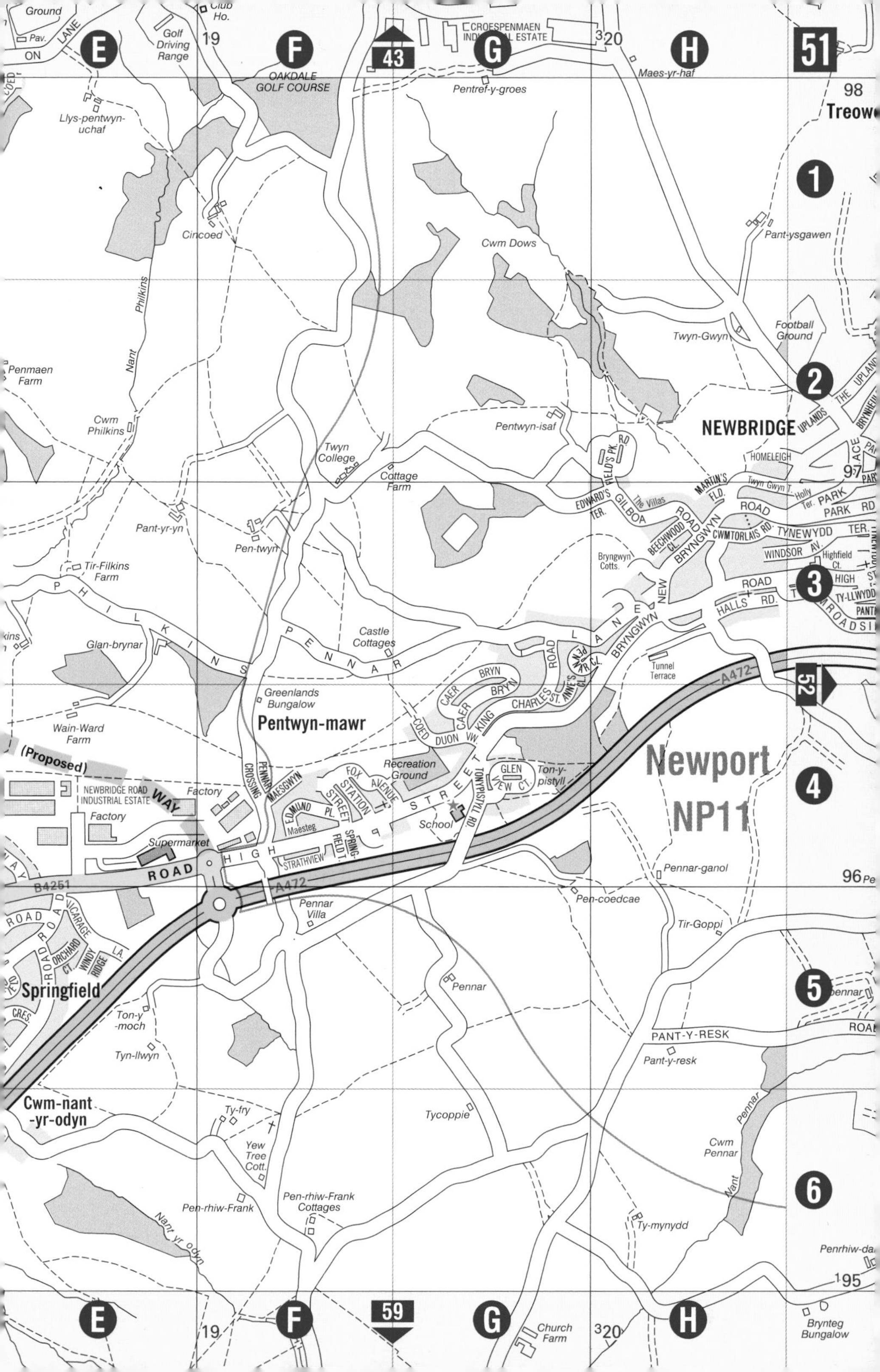

E
F
G
H
43
59
52
19
320
98
97
96
95
1
2
3
4
5
6
OAKDALE GOLF COURSE
Golf Driving Range
CROESPENMAEN INDUSTRIAL ESTATE
Pentref-y-groes
Maes-yr-haf
Treow
Llys-pentwyn-uchaf
Cincoed
Cwm Dows
Pant-ysgawen
Twyn-Gwyn
Football Ground
NEWBRIDGE
Penmaen Farm
Cwm Philkins
Nant Philkins
Twyn College
Cottage Farm
Pentwyn-isaf
Pant-yr-yn
Pen-twyn
Tir-Filkins Farm
PHILKINS PENNAR LANE
Glan-brynar
Castle Cottages
Bryngwyn Cotts.
Tunnel Terrace
Greenlands Bungalow
Pentwyn-mawr
Wain-Ward Farm
(Proposed) WAY
NEWBRIDGE ROAD INDUSTRIAL ESTATE
Factory
Supermarket
Recreation Ground
School
Ton-y-pistyll
Newport NP11
HIGH ROAD
B4251
A472
Pennar Villa
Pen-coedcae
Pennar-ganol
Tir-Goppi
Springfield
Ton-y-moch
Tyn-llwyn
Pennar
PANT-Y-RESK
Pant-y-resk
Cwm-nant-yr-odyn
Ty-fry
Yew Tree Cott.
Tycoppie
Cwm Pennar
Nant Pennar
Pen-rhiw-Frank
Pen-rhiw-Frank Cottages
Nant yr odyn
Ty-mynydd
Penrhiw-da
Church Farm
Brynteg Bungalow

Treowen
Tir-hunt
Pant-ysgawen
Football Ground
NEWBRIDGE
Train. Cen.
Comm. Cen.
AIWA TECHNOLOGY PARK
Pantside Primary School
Cefn-rhos-y-bedd
Pantside
Coed Goferau
Playing Field
Coed Cil-lonydd
Coed Rhiw-defaid
Coed yr Ellyn
Newport
Twyn-gnol
NP11
Coed Poeth
Pant Farm Estate
Caetwmpyn Park
Newbridge Leisure Centre
Sports Ground
Monmouthshire & Brecon Canals
Craig y Chain
Craig Glan-sion
High Meadows
Pennar-fach
Tyle-coch Wood
Pen-graig-pennar
Cefn-pennar
Playing Field
School
Cemetery
Persondy
Lodge
West End
Rec. Grd.
Craig y Darren
Penrhiw-darren
NP12
Cwm Pennar
Coed Ffordd-fawr
ABERCARN
Llanfach
Twyn Plas
Clytha Sq.
Brynteg Bungalow
Craig y Darren
Playground
Weir
A467
A472
B4591
PANT RD.
EBBW RIVER
NORTH ROAD
BRIDGE STREET
HIGH STREET
CEMETERY ROAD
CELYNEN ROAD
LLANFACH
GWYDDON ROAD
44
51
60
A
B
C
D
1
2
3
4
5
6
98
97
96
195
21
322

E
F
G
H
45
61
23
24
98
97
96
95
1
2
3
4
5
6
Gawni
Blaengwrney Farm
P
Cil-Lonydd
Coed Prysg
Hafod-fach
Cwm Hafod-fach
Pwllgwinau
Coed Sara
Craig y Trwyn
Cwm Gwyddon-fach
Tirwyn
Craig Pant-glas
Ysgubor Wen
Hafod-Owen
Craig Hafodowen
Ford
Craig Furnace
CWM GWYDDON
Twyn Llysganol
Graig Wen
Nant Gwyddon
Ford
Graig Ddu
Craig y Glyn
EBBW FOREST

MYNYDD TWYN - GLAS
Whitehall
46
Capel-llwyd
Pontypool
NP4
Oaklands
Uplands
Quarries (dis.)
Wain Hywel
Little Greenmeadow Farm
Mountain Farm
Kemys Fawr Inf. Sch.
Monmouthshire & Breco
Bryn
Tunnel
Wren's Nest Farm
Weir
PONTNEWYDD GOLF COURSE
Maes-gwyn
COED GWAUN-Y-FFEIRIAD
Glyn Bran Cottage
Yewtree
Blaen Bran Reservoirs
Mine Slope Cottages
MOUNTAIN ROAD
Upper Cwmbran
Pencoed Cwm Bran
Upper Cwmbran Inf. Sch.
Five Locks
Club House
Cwmbran House
Coed Gwern-Esgob
The Square
Works
UPPER CWMBRAN ROAD
TY PWCA ROAD
FIVE LOCKS ROAD
Playing Field
The Hawthorns
Penywaun Farm
Resr. (covered)
Woodlands Junior & Infants Schools
Lowlands
Football Ground
Rec. Grd.
Bellevue
Gorse House
Gelli-gravog
The Graigs
West Pontnewydd
Pontnewydd Prim. Sch.
Church Wood
Football Ground
Garn-Wen
Park House Farm
Cwmbran
NP44
Cwm-bran
Graig Fawr
Thornhill
Subway
Works
Church Wood
Brook
Forge Hammer
FORGE HAMMER INDUSTRIAL ESTATE
Hillside Cottage
SPRINGVALE WAY
SPRINGVALE INDUSTRIAL ESTATE
Greenmeadow Wood
Greenmeadow Community Farm
Factory
Pen-llan-gwyn
Greenmeadow
Subway
GREENFORGE WAY
ST. DIALS
Playing Field
Hodges Terr.
Police Training Centre
CWMBRAN (CWMBRÂN)
Maes y Rhiw
Dowlais
Greenmeadow Primary Sch.
Brook
The Twinings
LITTLEDENE
Blenheim Square Shops
Maes-y-Rhiw Resr. covered
Subway
63
Fairwater High School
Comm. Cen.
Subways
Fairwater Jun. & Inf. Schs
64
Tranch
A
B
C
D
1
2
3
4
5
6
27
28
98
97
96
195

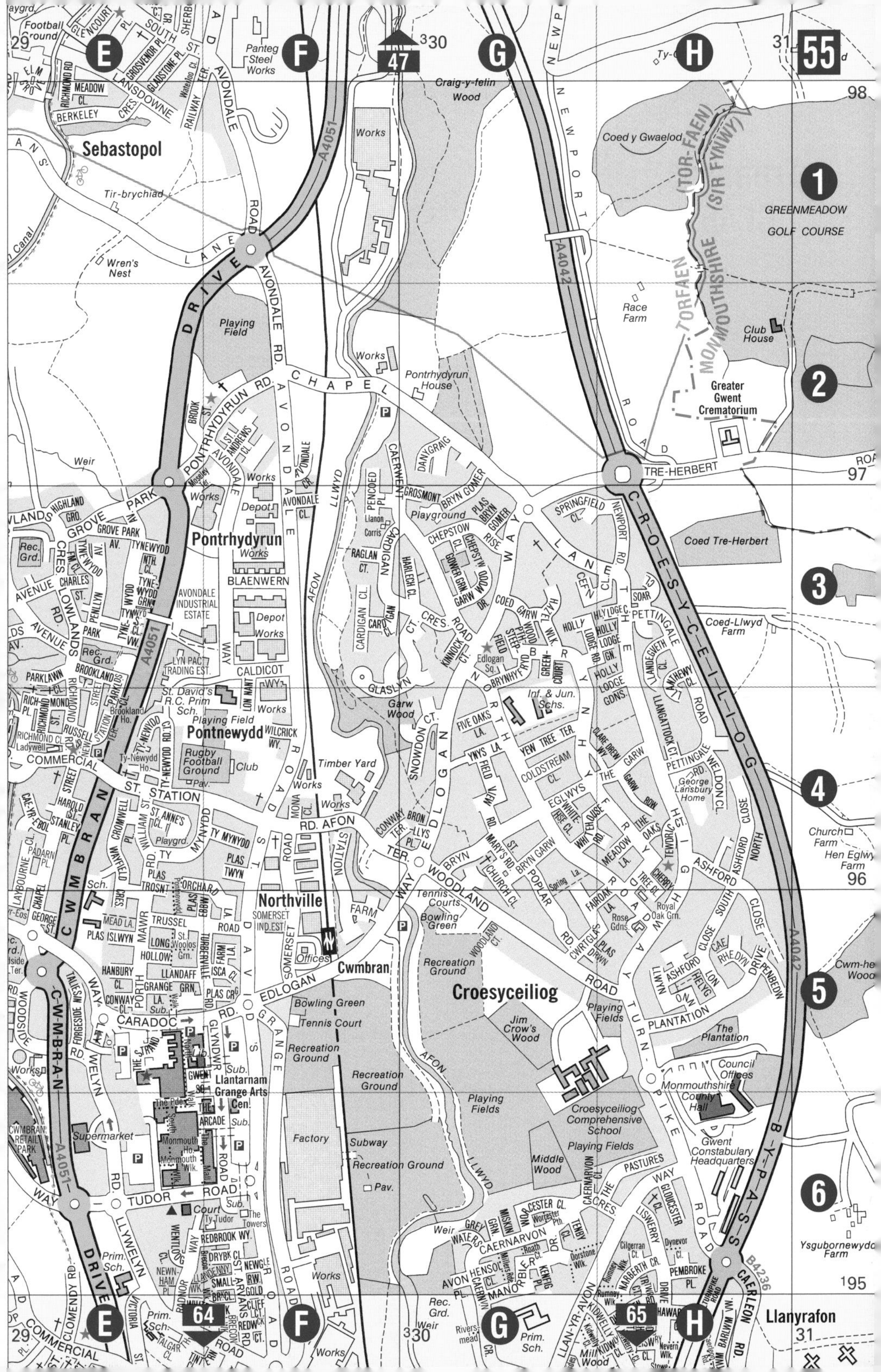
E
F
G
H
47
64
65
29
330
31
98
97
96
195
1
2
3
4
5
6
Sebastopol
Pontrhydyrun
Pontnewydd
Northville
Cwmbran
Croesyceiliog
Llanyrafon
Panteg Steel Works
Craig-y-felin Wood
Coed y Gwaelod
GREENMEADOW GOLF COURSE
TORFAEN
MONMOUTHSHIRE
(TOR-FAEN)
(SIR FYNWY)
Race Farm
Club House
Greater Gwent Crematorium
Coed Tre-Herbert
Coed-Llwyd Farm
Church Farm
Hen Eglwys Farm
Cwm-hen Wood
Ysgubornewydd Farm
Tir-brychiad
Wren's Nest
Playing Field
Pontrhydyrun House
Works
Depot
AVONDALE INDUSTRIAL ESTATE
LYN PAC TRADING EST.
St. David's R.C. Prim Sch.
Rugby Football Ground
Club
Timber Yard
Garw Wood
Edlogan Sq.
Inf. & Jun. Schs.
George Lansbury Home
Royal Oak Grn.
Tennis Courts
Bowling Green
Recreation Ground
Jim Crow's Wood
Playing Fields
Croesyceiliog Comprehensive School
Middle Wood
The Plantation
Council Offices
Monmouthshire County Hall
Gwent Constabulary Headquarters
SOMERSET IND.EST.
Offices
Llantarnam Grange Arts Cen.
Supermarket
CWMBRAN RETAIL PARK
Court
Ty-Tudor
The Towers
Factory
Subway
Recreation Ground
Pav.
Prim. Sch.
Rec. Grd.
Weir
Riversmead
A4051
A4042
B4236
CWMBRAN DRIVE
CROESYCEILIOG BY-PASS
NEWPORT ROAD
TRE-HERBERT ROAD
CHAPEL LANE
AVONDALE ROAD
PONTRHYDYRUN RD.
EDLOGAN WAY
WOODLAND ROAD
TURNPIKE ROAD
NORTH ROAD
CAERLEON RD.
AFON LLWYD
COMMERCIAL ST.
STATION RD.
GRANGE RD.
TUDOR ROAD
PLANTATION

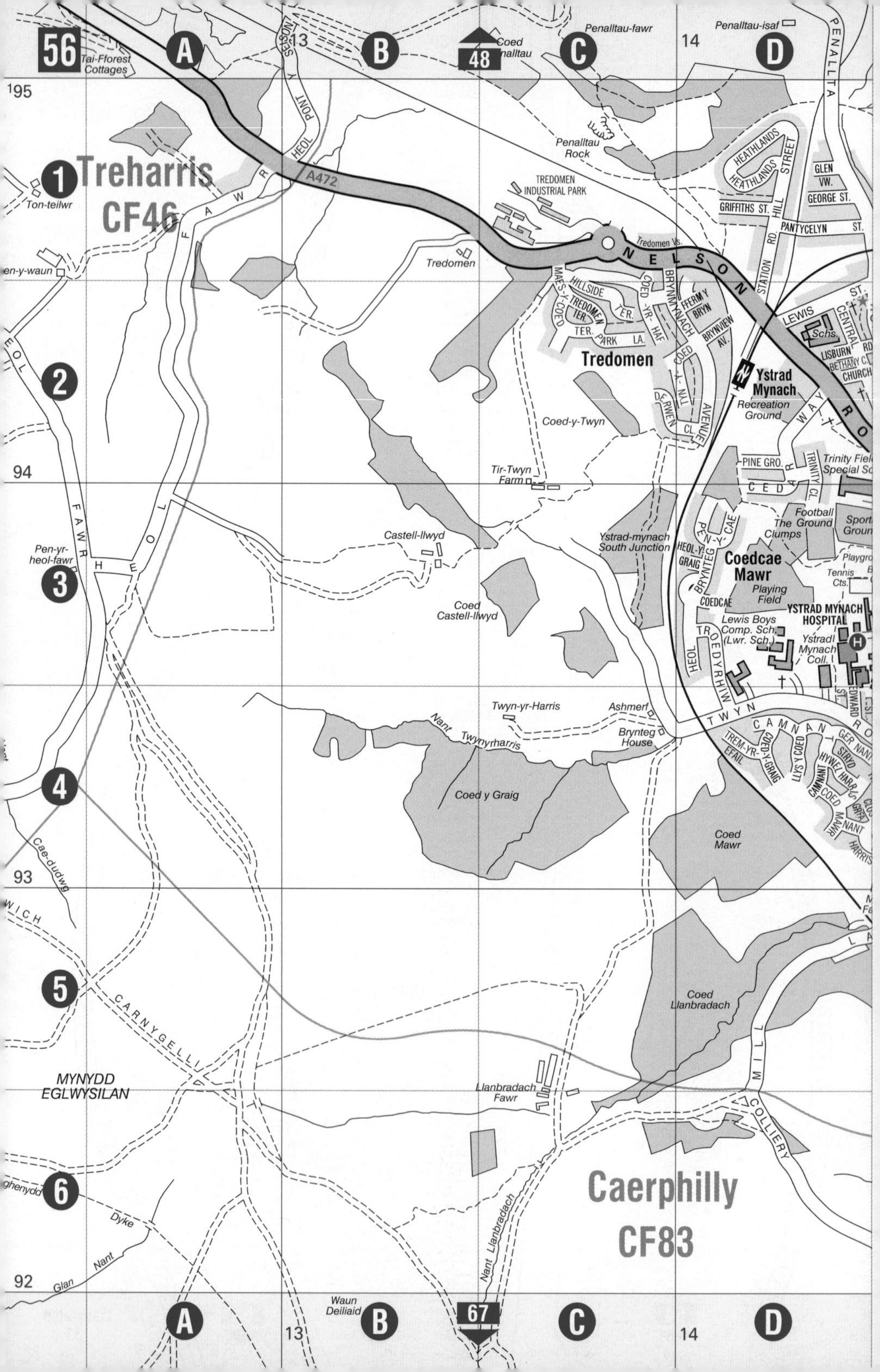
Treharris
CF46
Tai-Fforest Cottages
Ton-teilwr
Pen-y-waun
Penalltau-fawr
Penalltau-isaf
Coed Penalltau
Penalltau Rock
A472
TREDOMEN INDUSTRIAL PARK
Tredomen
NELSON RD
HEATHLANDS
GRIFFITHS ST.
GEORGE ST.
PANTYCELYN ST.
GLEN VW.
LEWIS ST.
Ystrad Mynach
Recreation Ground
Coed-y-Twyn
Tir-Twyn Farm
Castell-llwyd
Coed Castell-llwyd
Ystrad-mynach South Junction
Coedcae Mawr
Playing Field
YSTRAD MYNACH HOSPITAL
Ystradl Mynach Coll.
Lewis Boys Comp. Sch. (Lwr. Sch.)
Trinity Field Special Sch.
Football Ground
The Clumps
Sports Ground
Tennis Cts.
Pen-yr-heol-fawr
HEOL FAWR
Twyn-yr-Harris
Ashmerf
Brynteg House
Nant Twynyrharris
Coed y Graig
Coed Mawr
Cae-dudwg
CARNYGELLI
MYNYDD EGLWYSILAN
Llanbradach Fawr
Coed Llanbradach
COLLIERY
MILL
Caerphilly
CF83
Nant Llanbradach
Dyke
Glan Nant
Waun Deiliaid
48
67
195
94
93
92
13
14
A
B
C
D
1
2
3
4
5
6

Hengoed
Ystrad Mynach
YSTRAD MYNACH
Maesycwmmer
Hengoed
CF82
A472
A469
A4049
B4252
NEW ROAD
MAIN ROAD
THOMAS ST.
VICTORIA RD
SUMMERFIELD HALL LA.
Brooklands
BROOKLANDS CL.
MT. PLEASANT
GELLIDEG CT.
GELLIDEG CLOSE
GELLIDEG HEIGHTS
GELLIDEG INDUSTRIAL ESTATE
BRYN MEADOWS GOLF COURSE
Gelli-deg uchaf
Special School
Ystrad Mynach Sports Hall
Lewis Girls' Comp. Sch.
Coed Gwernau
Playing Fields
Comm. Cen.
Viaduct (Dis.)
Ystrad-mynach Bridge
Cwm-du Wood
Cwm-du
Gwernau-fawr
Nant y Twyn
Gwernau Reservoir (covered)
Gwernau-ganol
Gwernau Hall
Mount Pleasant
Twyn-Shon-Ifan
Pontprencrwca House
Sports Field
Offices
Tredomen Athletic Stadium
Factory
DUFFRYN BUSINESS PARK
Malt House
Superstore
Riverbank House
Coed Mawr
Ty'r-ywen
Gwernydd
Pant-y-ffawydden
Coed Graddfa
Ty-isaf
The Brakes
Ty'n-y-coed
Cae-brith
Nant y Ffrwd
Wern Cae-brith
Ffrwd
Graddfa
Coed Ochr-ddu
49
58
68

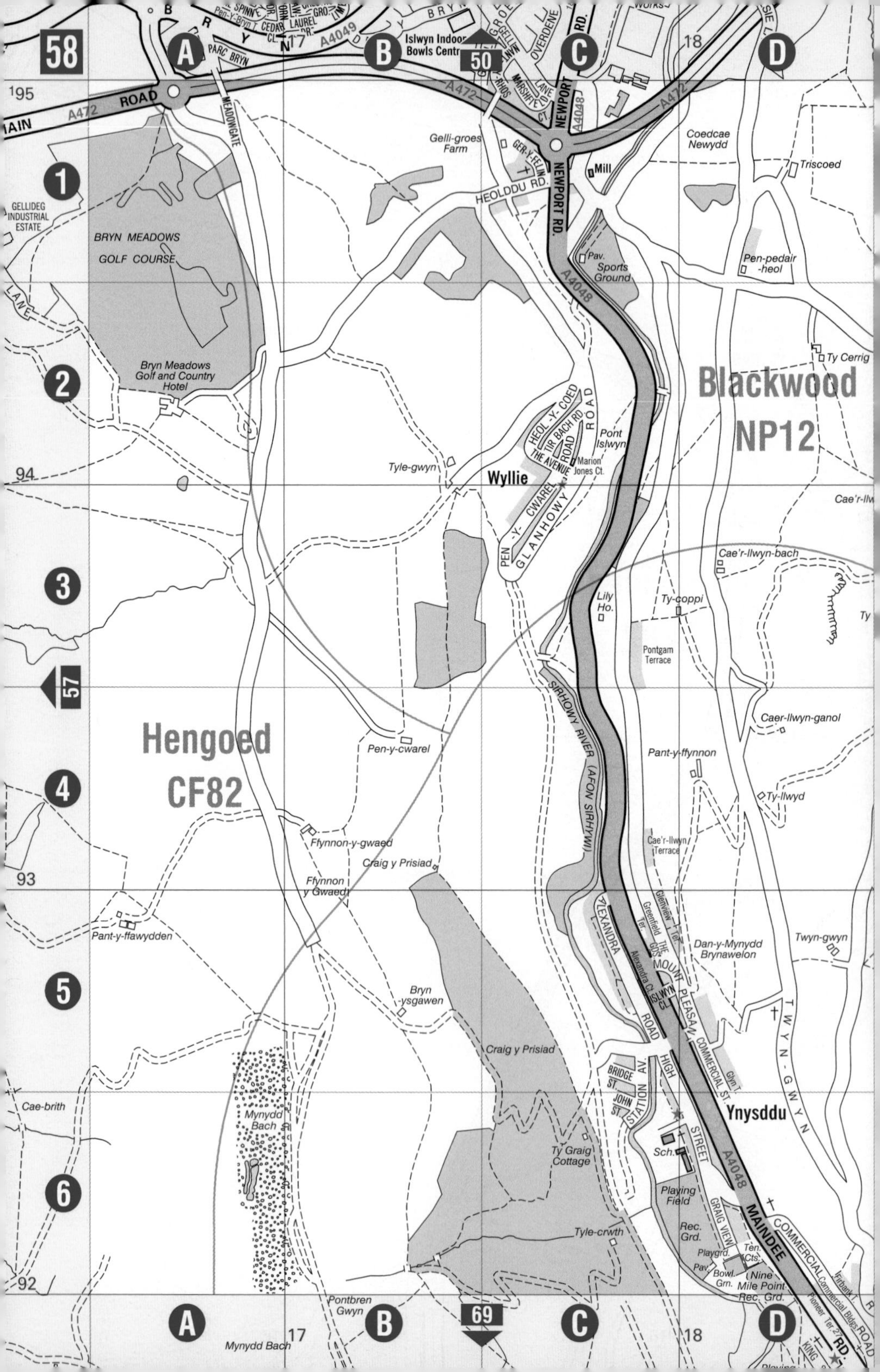

A
B
C
D
1
2
3
4
5
6
195
94
93
92
17
18
50
57
69
A472
A4049
A4048
ROAD
MAIN
PARC BRYN
MEADOWGATE
Islwyn Indoor Bowls Centre
NEWPORT RD.
NEWPORT
OVERDENE
LANE
Works
Gelli-groes Farm
GER-Y-FELIN
Mill
HEOLDDU RD.
Coedcae Newydd
Triscoed
GELLIDEG INDUSTRIAL ESTATE
BRYN MEADOWS GOLF COURSE
Bryn Meadows Golf and Country Hotel
Pav.
Sports Ground
Pen-pedair -heol
Ty Cerrig
Blackwood NP12
HEOL-Y-COED
TIR BACH RD
ROAD
THE AVENUE
Marion Jones Ct.
Pont Islwyn
Tyle-gwyn
Wyllie
PEN-Y-CWAREL
GLANHOWY
Cae'r-llwyn-bach
Lily Ho.
Ty-coppi
Pontgam Terrace
SIRHOWY RIVER (AFON SIRHWY)
Caer-llwyn-ganol
Hengoed CF82
Pen-y-cwarel
Pant-y-ffynnon
Ty-llwyd
Ffynnon-y-gwaed
Craig y Prisiad
Cae'r-llwyn Terrace
Ffynnon y Gwaed
Pant-y-ffawydden
ALEXANDRA
Alexandra Ct.
Greenfield Ter.
Glenview Ter.
MOUNT PLEASANT
ISLWYN CL.
Dan-y-Mynydd
Brynawelon
Twyn-gwyn
Bryn -ysgawen
COMMERCIAL ST.
TWYN-GWYN
Craig y Prisiad
BRIDGE ST.
JOHN ST.
STATION AV.
HIGH STREET
Ynysddu
Cae-brith
Mynydd Bach
Ty Graig Cottage
Sch.
Playing Field
Rec. Grd.
GRAIG VIEW
MAINDEE
COMMERCIAL ROAD
Tyle-crwth
Playgrd.
Ten. Cts.
Pav.
Bowl. Grn.
Nine Mile Point Rec. Grd.
Commercial Bldgs.
Pioneer Ter.
KING
RD.
Pontbren Gwyn
Mynydd Bach

E
F
G
H
51
Nant yr odyn
19
320
Ty-mynydd
Brynteg
Bungalow
195
Church
Farm
1
Graig
Farm
2
Reservoir
(covered)
Sychpant
Farm
Pen-heol
-cae'r-llwyn
Ty-pentre
Mynyddislwyn
94
Rifle Shooting
Range
Twyn
Tudor
3
Cwm-cae
-singrug
Nant-y-draenog
Reservoir
(dis.)
60
Mynydd y Lan
Cae'r-llwyn-isaf
4
Pant-glas
93
Newport
NP11
Glebe
Farm
Ton-eithin
MYNYDD Y LAN
5
Hafod-tudur
Ty-cae-brith
Pant-y-trwyn
Mynydd y Lan
Ty'r-waun
Nant y Draenog
Nant
6
Hafod-tudur-ganol
92
Pen-rhiw-arwydd
70
19
Pen-y-trwyn
Cwmfelinfach
Cottage

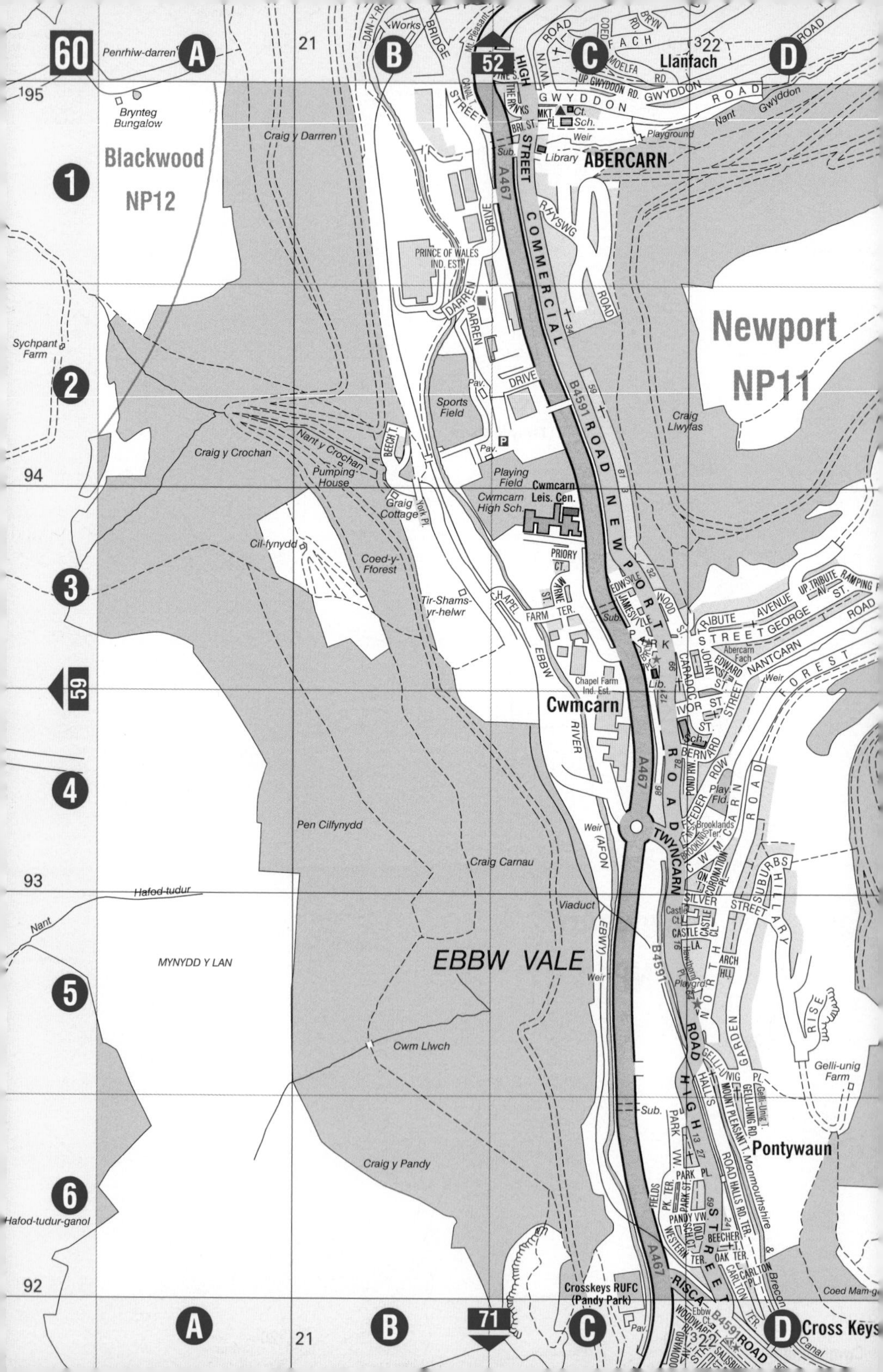

60
A
B
C
D
21
22
52
59
71
95
94
93
92
1
2
3
4
5
6
Blackwood
NP12
Newport
NP11
ABERCARN
Llanfach
Cwmcarn
Pontywaun
Cross Keys
EBBW VALE
Penrhiw-darren
Brynteg Bungalow
Craig y Darrren
Sychpant Farm
Craig y Crochan
Nant y Crochan
Pumping House
Graig Cottage
Cil-fynydd
Coed-y-Fforest
Tir-Shams-yr-helwr
Pen Cilfynydd
Craig Carnau
Hafod-tudur
MYNYDD Y LAN
Cwm Llwch
Craig y Pandy
Hafod-tudur-ganol
Crosskeys RUFC (Pandy Park)
PRINCE OF WALES IND. EST.
Sports Field
Playing Field
Cwmcarn Leis. Cen.
Cwmcarn High Sch.
Chapel Farm Ind. Est.
Craig Llwyfas
Abercarn Fach
Gelli-unig Farm
Coed Mam-gu
Library
Playground
Nant Gwyddon
GWYDDON ROAD
COMMERCIAL STREET
HIGH STREET
NEWPORT ROAD
TWYNCARN ROAD
HIGH STREET
RISCA ROAD
A467
B4591
Viaduct
Weir
Monmouthshire & Brecon Canal

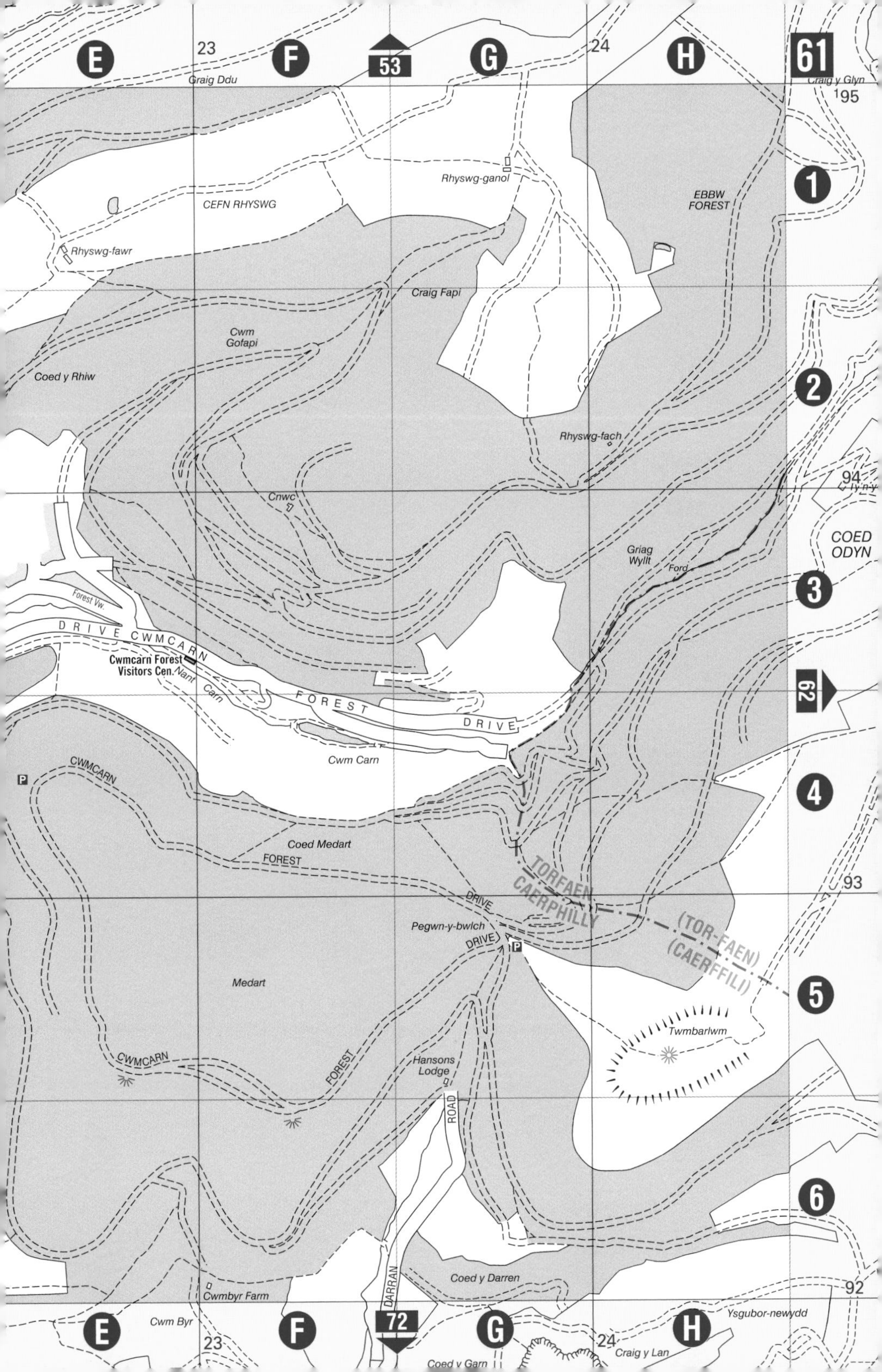

E
23
F
53
G
24
H
61
Craig Ddu
Craig y Glyn
95
Rhyswg-ganol
CEFN RHYSWG
EBBW FOREST
Rhyswg-fawr
Craig Fapi
Cwm Gofapi
Coed y Rhiw
Rhyswg-fach
94
Cnwc
COED ODYN
Griag Wyllt
Ford
Forest Vw.
DRIVE CWMCARN
Cwmcarn Forest Visitors Cen.
Nant Carn
FOREST DRIVE
62
Cwm Carn
CWMCARN
Coed Medart
FOREST
TORFAEN
CAERPHILLY
93
DRIVE
Pegwn-y-bwlch
(TOR-FAEN)
(CAERFFILI)
Medart
Twmbarlwm
CWMCARN
FOREST
Hansons Lodge
ROAD
DARRAN
Coed y Darren
92
Cwmbyr Farm
Cwm Byr
72
Ysgubor-newydd
Craig y Lan
Coed y Garn
1
2
3
4
5
6

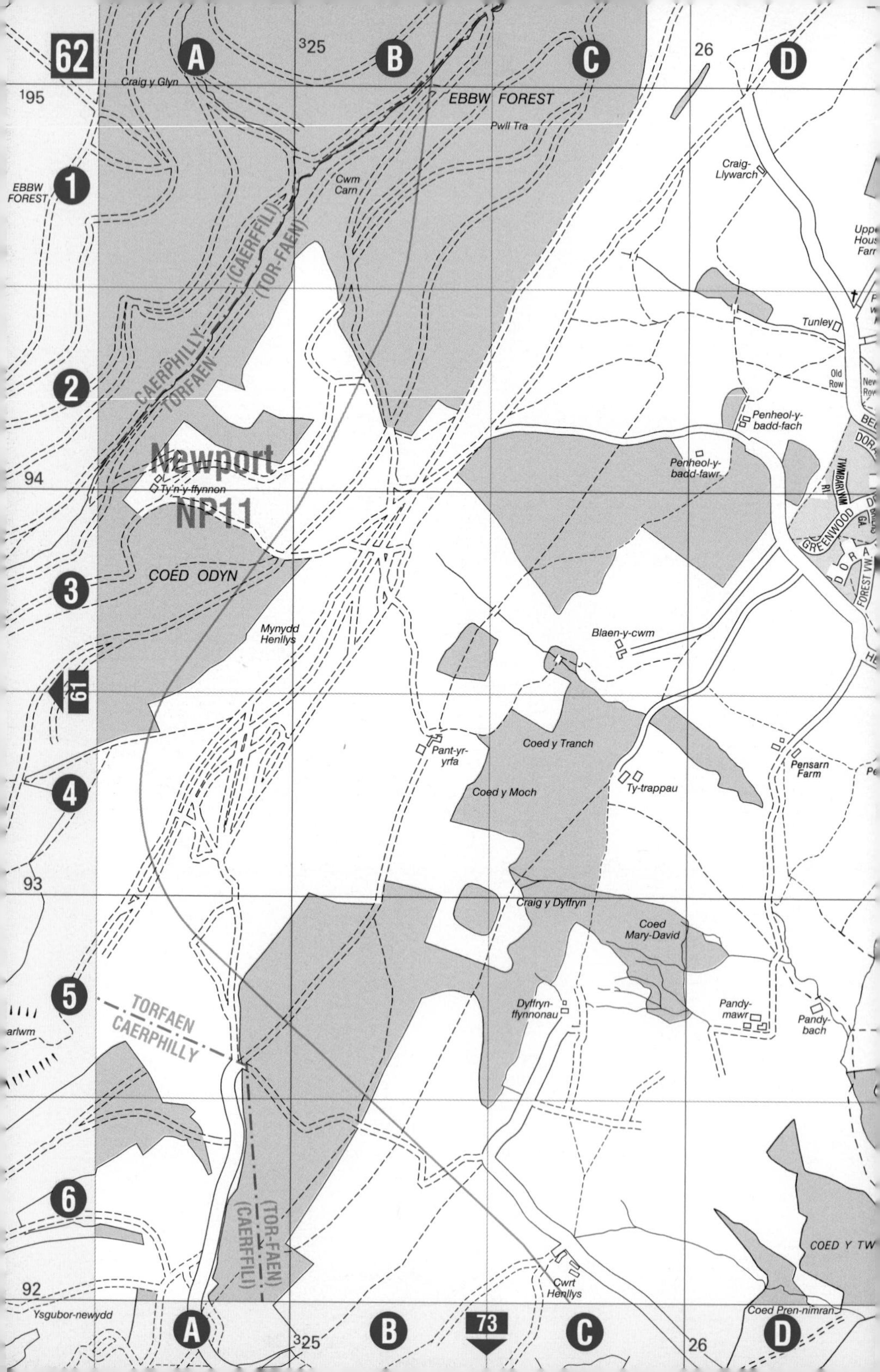
A
B
C
D
325
26
195
Craig y Glyn
EBBW FOREST
Pwll Tra
Craig-Llywarch
EBBW FOREST
1
Cwm Carn
CAERPHILLY (CAERFFILI)
TORFAEN (TOR-FAEN)
Upper House Farm
Tunley
2
Old Row
New Row
Penheol-y-badd-fach
Newport NP11
94
Ty'n-y-ffynnon
Penheol-y-badd-fawr
TWMBARLWM RI
GREENWOOD DR
DORA
FOREST VW
3
COED ODYN
Mynydd Henllys
Blaen-y-cwm
61
Pant-yr-yrfa
Coed y Tranch
Pensarn Farm
4
Coed y Moch
Ty-trappau
93
Craig y Dyffryn
Coed Mary-David
5
TORFAEN
CAERPHILLY
Dyffryn-ffynnonau
Pandy-mawr
Pandy-bach
arlwm
6
(TOR-FAEN)
(CAERFFILI)
COED Y TW
92
Cwrt Henllys
Ysgubor-newydd
Coed Pren-nimran
73

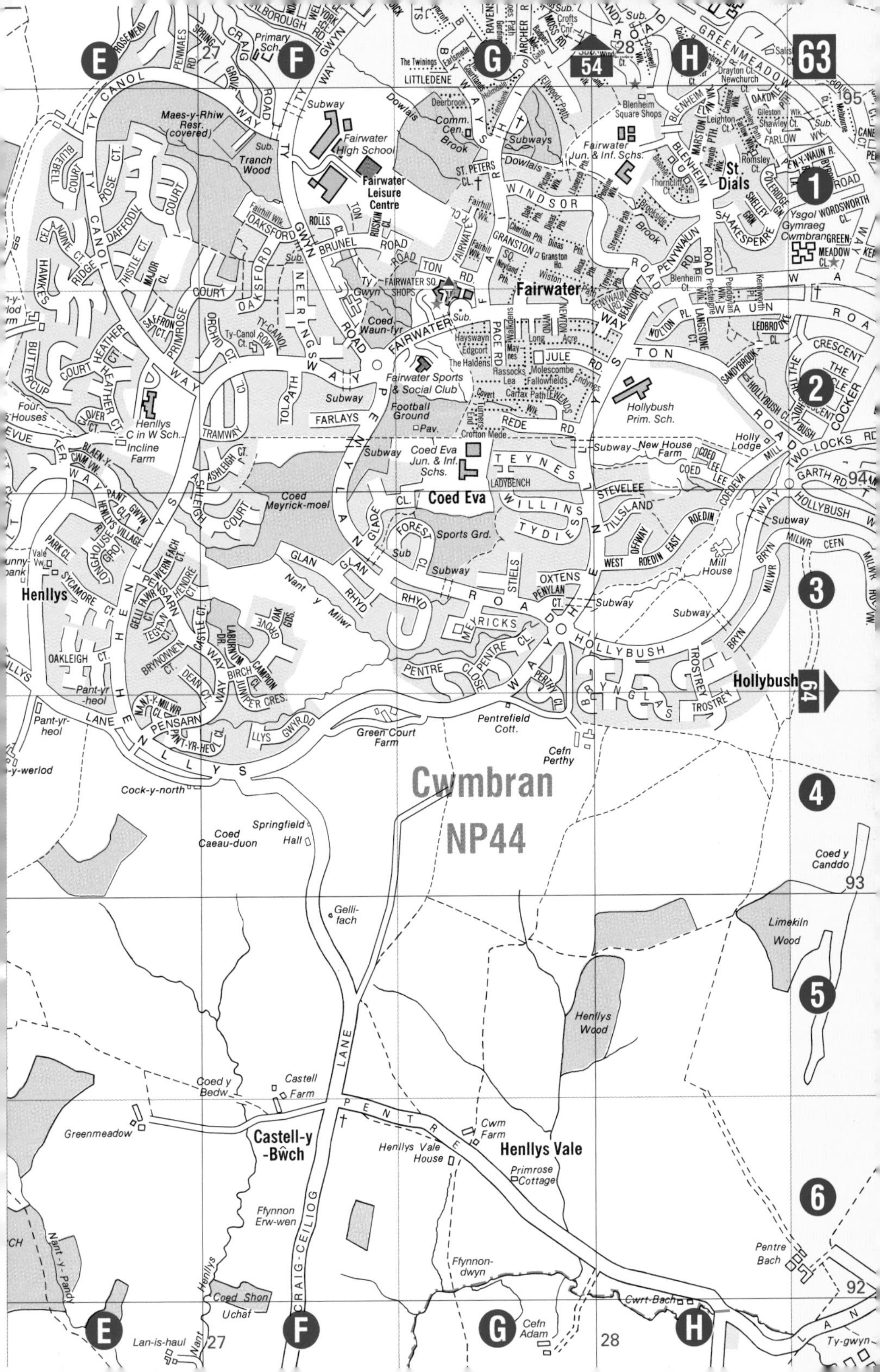

63
54
64
E
F
G
H
1
2
3
4
5
6
27
28
95
94
93
92
Fairwater
St. Dials
Coed Eva
Henllys
Hollybush
Cwmbran
NP44
Castell-y
-Bŵch
Henllys Vale
Fairwater High School
Fairwater Leisure Centre
Maes-y-Rhiw Resr. (covered)
Tranch Wood
Comm. Cen.
Fairwater Jun. & Inf. Schs.
Blenheim Square Shops
Ysgol Gymraeg Cwmbran
Fairwater Sports & Social Club
Football Ground
Coed Eva Jun. & Inf. Schs.
Coed Meyrick-moel
Sports Grd.
Henllys C in W Sch.
Incline Farm
Hollybush Prim. Sch.
New House Farm
Holly Lodge
Mill House
Pentrefield Cott.
Green Court Farm
Cefn Perthy
Cock-y-north
Coed Caeau-duon
Springfield Hall
Gelli-fach
Coed y Canddo
Limekiln Wood
Henllys Wood
Coed y Bedw
Castell Farm
Greenmeadow
Cwm Farm
Henllys Vale House
Primrose Cottage
Ffynnon Erw-wen
Ffynnon-dwyn
Pentre Bach
Cwrt-Bach
Coed Shon Uchaf
Cefn Adam
Lan-is-haul
Ty-gwyn
Nant-y-Pandy
Nant y Milwr
Nant Henllys
Pant-yr-heol
TY CANOL WAY
GREENMEADOW WAY
TY GWYN WAY
FAIRWATER WAY
WINDSOR ROAD
PENYWAUN ROAD
TON ROAD
PENYLAN ROAD
HENLLYS WAY
HENLLYS LANE
HOLLYBUSH WAY
PENTRE LANE
CRAIG-CEILIOG
TWO-LOCKS RD.

A
54
29
B
C
55
330
D
195
94
93
92
1
2
3
4
5
6
Southville
St. Dials
Two Locks
Ty-Coch
Oakfield
Hollybush
63
Croes-y-mwyalch
Llanyrafon Mill
Llanyrafon Prim. Sch.
Llanyrafon Farm Museum
LLANYRAFON GOLF COURSE
Club House
Recreation Ground
Cwmbran FC (Cwmbran Stadium)
Cemetery
Oakfield Prim. Sch.
Llantarnam Comprehensive School
LLANTARNAM INDUSTRIAL ESTATE
LLANTARNAM INDUSTRIAL PARK
Llantarnam House
GRANGE INDUSTRIAL ESTATE
COURT ROAD INDUSTRIAL ESTATE
TY-COCH DISTRIBUTION CENTRE
Refuse Destructor
Cwmbran Park
Tennis Courts
Ysgol Gymraeg Cwmbran
Cwmbran Two Locks Nursy. Sch.
Comm. Cen. Depot
The Cold Store
Boat House
Sports Grd.
Monmouthshire & Brecon Canal
Monmouthshire & Brecon Towing Path
Top Lock
Rachels Lock
Brake Lock
Shop Lock
Bottom Lock
Tredeger Lock
Draper's Lock
Tamplin Lock
Pentre-basket
Pentre-basket Cottage
Coed y Canddo
Limekiln Wood
Ty Coch Wood
Pantglas
Cidermill
Wheatsheaf Cottage
Eureka House
Pentre Bach
Ty-gwyn
Grove Farm
Lodge Farm
Cottage Farm
Croes-y-mwyalch Farm
Reservoir (covered)
Brooklands Farm
Mill House
Holly Lodge
Fair View
Baltic Terrace
Plas Newydd
A4051
CWMBRAN DRIVE
LLANFRECHFA WAY
HENLLYS WAY
TWO-LOCKS ROAD
HOLLYBUSH WAY
LLANTARNAM WAY
TY-COCH LANE
PENTRE LANE
GLAS PANT ROAD
MALPAS ROAD
NEWPORT ROAD
LAKESIDE
LAKEVIEW
OAKFIELD ROAD
COURT ROAD
ST. DIALS RD.
COMMERCIAL ST.
VICTORIA ST.
AVENUE WESLEY
GREENMEADOW WAY
TRAWS MAWR LA.
NP20
BRYNGLAS TUNNELS & MALPAS ROAD RELIEF RD.
Afon Llwyd
Dowlais Brook
Cwmbran Brook

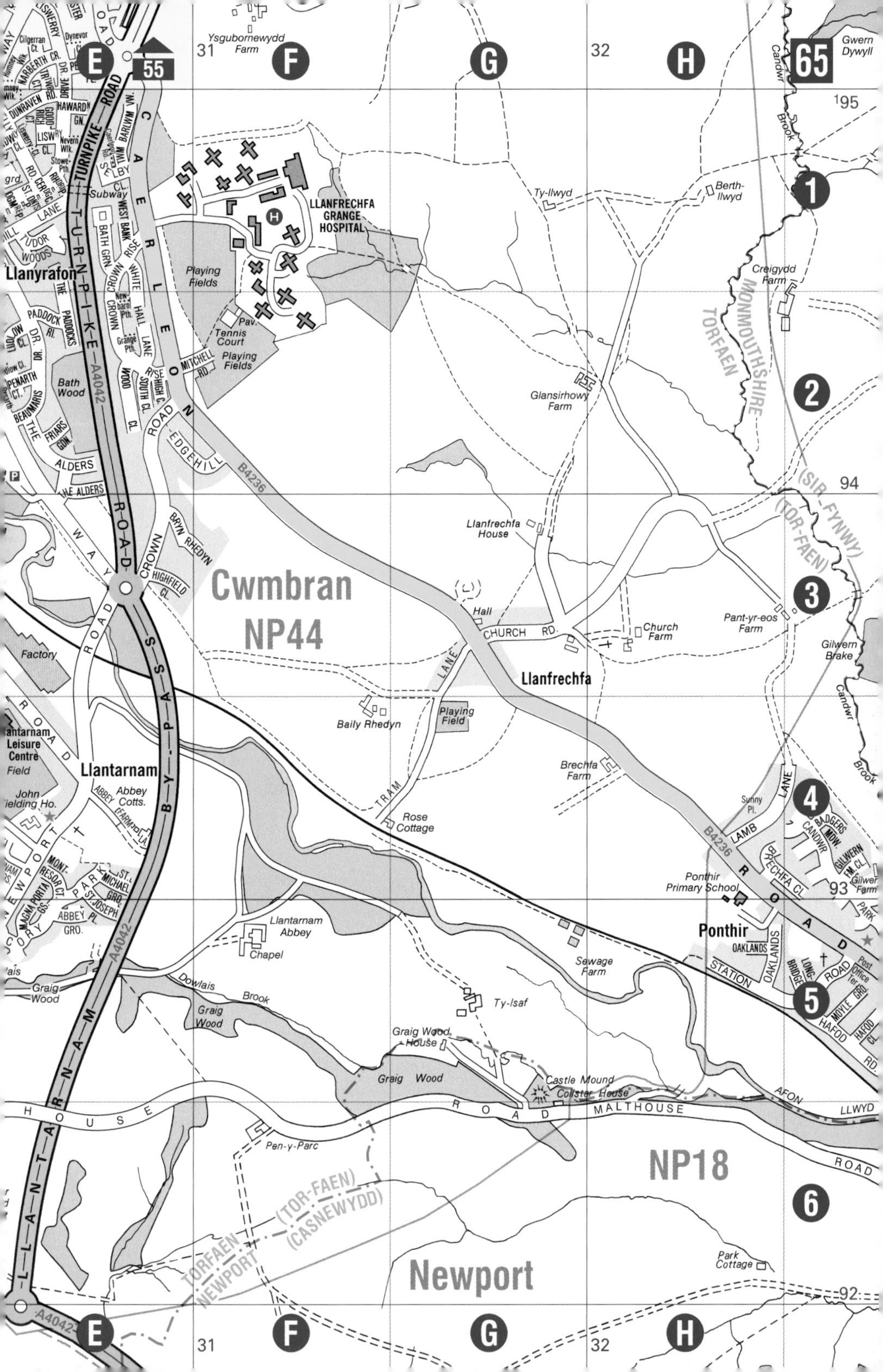
55
E
F
G
H
31
32
Ysgubornewydd Farm
Gwern Dywyll
Candwr Brook
195
1
2
3
4
5
6
94
93
92
Ty-llwyd
Berth-llwyd
LLANFRECHFA GRANGE HOSPITAL
Playing Fields
Pav.
Tennis Court
Creigydd Farm
MONMOUTHSHIRE
TORFAEN
Glansirhowy Farm
(SIR FYNWY)
(TOR-FAEN)
Llanfrechfa House
Hall
CHURCH RD.
Church Farm
Pant-yr-eos Farm
Gilwern Brake
Llanfrechfa
Cwmbran
NP44
B4236
CAERLEON ROAD
EDGEHILL
MITCHELL RD.
BRYN RHEDYN
HIGHFIELD CL.
CROWN ROAD
TURNPIKE ROAD
A4042
BY-PASS
Llanyrafon
TUDOR WOODS
Bath Wood
ALDERS
THE ALDERS
WAY
Subway
Factory
Llantarnam Leisure Centre
Llantarnam
Abbey Cotts.
John Fielding Ho.
Baily Rhedyn
Playing Field
TRAM LANE
Rose Cottage
Brechfa Farm
Sunny Pl.
LAMB LANE
BADGERS MDW.
CANDWR
GILWERN FM. CL.
BRECHFA CL.
Ponthir Primary School
Ponthir
OAKLANDS
STATION ROAD
LONG-BRIDGE
Post Office
HAFOD
MOYLE GRO.
Llantarnam Abbey
Chapel
Sewage Farm
Ty-Isaf
Dowlais Brook
Graig Wood
Graig Wood House
Castle Mound
Collstar House
MALTHOUSE ROAD
AFON LLWYD
Pen-y-Parc
NP18
(TOR-FAEN)
(CASNEWYDD)
TORFAEN
NEWPORT
Newport
Park Cottage
LLANTARNAM ROAD

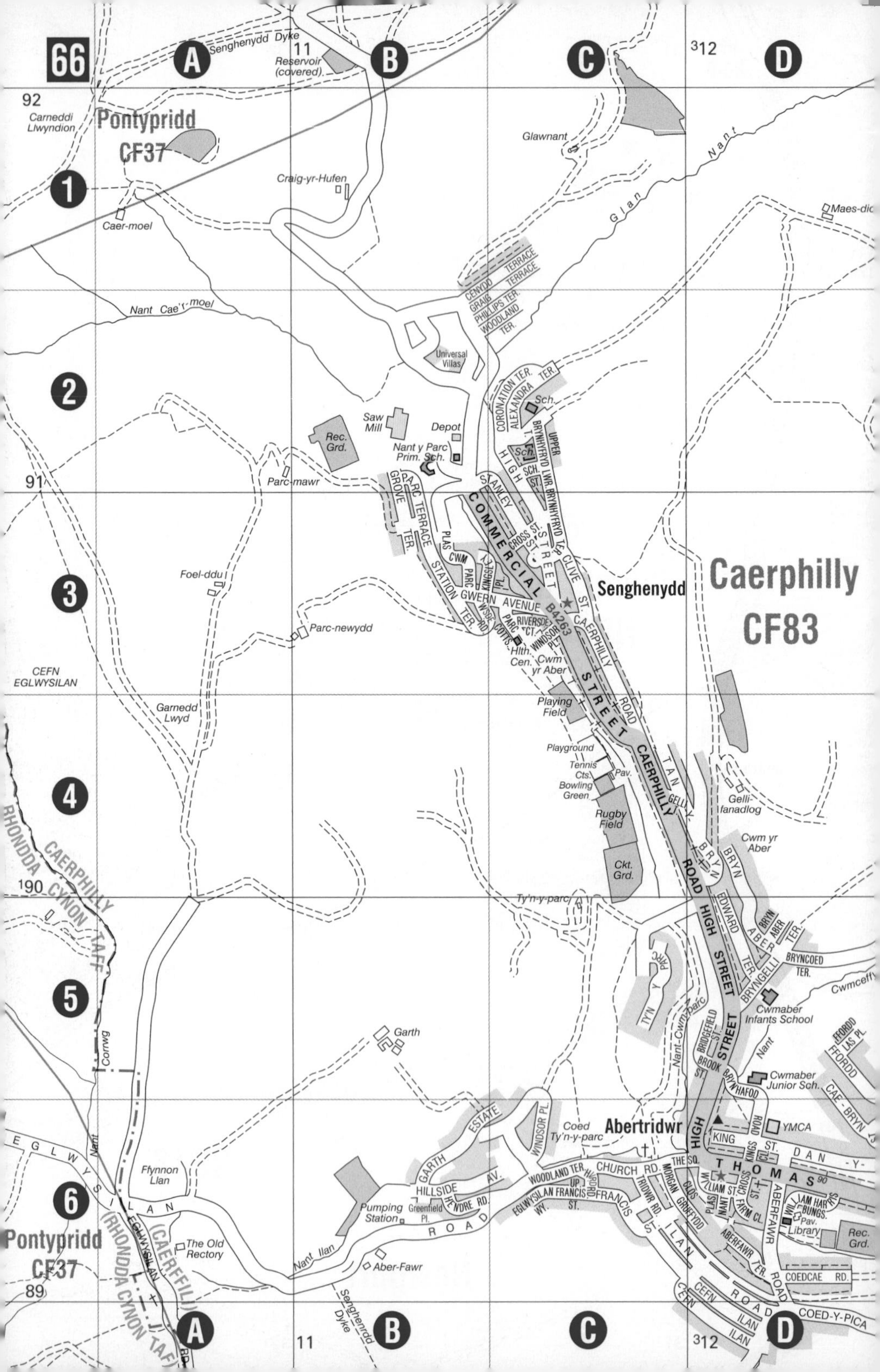

Pontypridd
CF37
Caerphilly
CF83
Senghenydd
Abertridwr
Senghenydd Dyke
Reservoir (covered)
Carneddi Llwyndion
Caer-moel
Craig-yr-Hufen
Glawnant
Glan Nant
Maes-dic
Nant Cae'r-moel
Universal Villas
Saw Mill
Rec. Grd.
Depot
Nant y Parc Prim. Sch.
Parc-mawr
Foel-ddu
Parc-newydd
CEFN EGLWYSILAN
Garnedd Llwyd
COMMERCIAL STREET
CAERPHILLY ROAD
HIGH STREET
B4263
Playing Field
Playground
Tennis Cts.
Bowling Green
Rugby Field
Ckt. Grd.
Hlth. Cen.
Cwm yr Aber
Gelli-fanadlog
Ty'n-y-parc
Cwmaber Infants School
Cwmaber Junior Sch.
YMCA
Library
Pav.
Garth
Ffynnon Llan
The Old Rectory
Pumping Station
Aber-Fawr
Nant Ilan
Coed Ty'n-y-parc
EGLWYSILAN ROAD
CHURCH RD.
THOMAS ST.
CEFN ILAN ROAD
COED-Y-PICA
COEDCAE RD.
RHONDDA CYNON TAF
CAERPHILLY
(CAERFFILI)
Corwg
Nant

E
13
F
56
G
14
H
Waun
Deiliaid
92
1
Nant
Llanbradach
Llanbradach
Isaf
2
Nant
Owen
91
Ford
The Bryn
Blaen-y-fforch
Cefn-llwyd
Cwm-sarn
Nant
3
89
Senghenydd
Dyke
4
Cae'r-llwyn
Llanbradach
PLAS CAE LLWYD
90
Waterfall
Coed y Brain
5
COED-Y-BRAIN CT.
Pen yr Heol
Las Farm
Graig-wen
Cwm-Ifor
Craigyfedw
UNDERWOOD TER.
GRAIGWEN
CRESCENT
Sunnybank Mountain Vw.
B4263
STREET
178
Pont y
Felin
6
BOWLS
LANE
Cwarrau-mawr
HEOL
CWARREL
CLARK
HEOL
PEN-Y-DRE
HENFRON
BLAEN
IFOR
BRYN OWAIN
CAE PEN-Y-GRAIG
CAE YSGUBOR
PANT
89
Waterfall
74
Pen-twyn

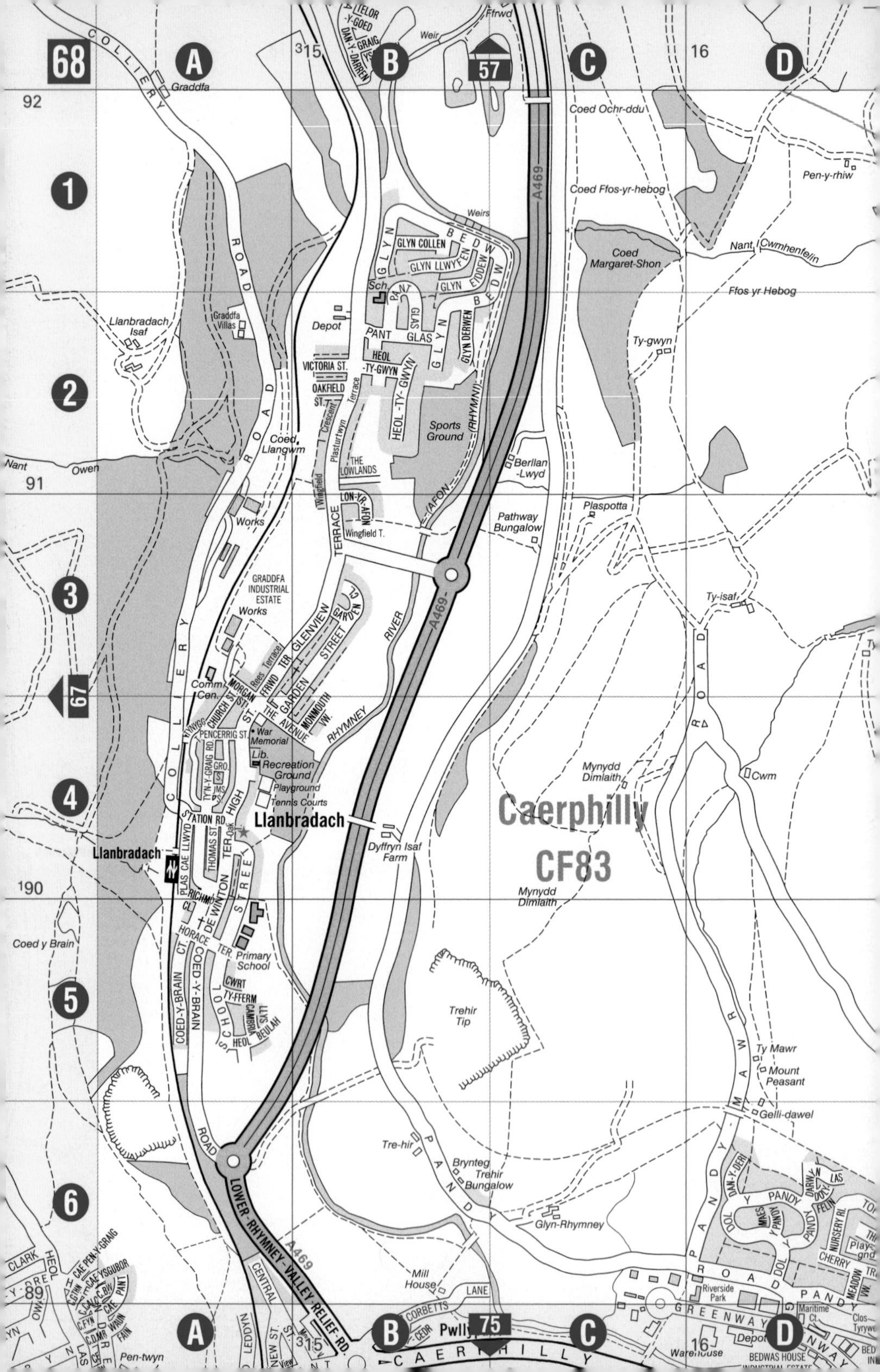

A
B
C
D
1
2
3
4
5
6
92
91
190
89
315
16
57
67
75
COLLIERY ROAD
Graddfa
TELOR-Y-GOED
DAN-Y-DARREN
Weir
Ffrwd
Coed Ochr-ddu
Coed Ffos-yr-hebog
A469
Pen-y-rhiw
Weirs
GLYN BEDW
GLYN COLLEN
GLYN LLWYFEN
GLYN EDDEW
GLYN DERWEN
Coed Margaret-Shon
Nant Cwmhenfelin
Ffos yr Hebog
Sch.
PANT GLAS
Depot
HEOL-TY-GWYN
VICTORIA ST.
OAKFIELD ST.
Crescent
Plasturtwyn Terrace
Sports Ground
AFON (RHYMNI)
Llanbradach Isaf
Graddfa Villas
Ty-gwyn
Coed Llangwm
Nant Owen
THE LOWLANDS
Berllan-Lwyd
Wingfield
LON-YR-AFON
Works
Plaspotta
Pathway Bungalow
TERRACE
Wingfield T.
GRADDFA INDUSTRIAL ESTATE
Works
GLENVIEW TER
GARDEN STREET
GARDEN CL.
RIVER
Ty-isaf
Rees Terrace
FFRWD TER
MORGAN ST.
Comm. Cen.
CHURCH ST.
THE AVENUE
MONMOUTH VW.
RHYMNEY
ROAD
PENCERRIG ST.
War Memorial
Lib.
Recreation Ground
Playground
Tennis Courts
Mynydd Dimlaith
Cwm
Llanbradach
Caerphilly
CF83
STATION RD.
HIGH STREET
THOMAS ST.
DE WINTON TER.
PLAS CAE LLWYD
Dyffryn Isaf Farm
Llanbradach
Mynydd Dimlaith
Coed y Brain
HORACE TER.
Primary School
COED-Y-BRAIN CT.
COED-Y-BRAIN
CWRT TY-FFERM
CAMBRIA ST.
BEULAH ST.
SCHOOL
HEOL
Trehir Tip
Ty Mawr
Mount Peasant
Gelli-dawel
Tre-hir
PANDY
Brynteg
Trehir Bungalow
Glyn-Rhymney
LOWER-RHYMNEY-VALLEY-RELIEF-RD.
DAN-Y-DERI
DOL-Y-PANDY
MAES Y PANDY
NURSERY RI.
CHERRY
Play-gnd
MEADOW VW.
CLARK
HEOL
CAE PEN-Y-GRAIG
CAE YSGUBOR
CAE PANT
Mill House
LANE
CENTRAL
CORBETTS
Riverside Park
GREENWAY
Maritime Ct.
Clos Tyrywen
Depot
Warehouse
BEDWAS HOUSE INDUSTRIAL ESTATE
Pen-twyn
LEDDYN
NEW ST.
Pwllypant
CAERPHILLY

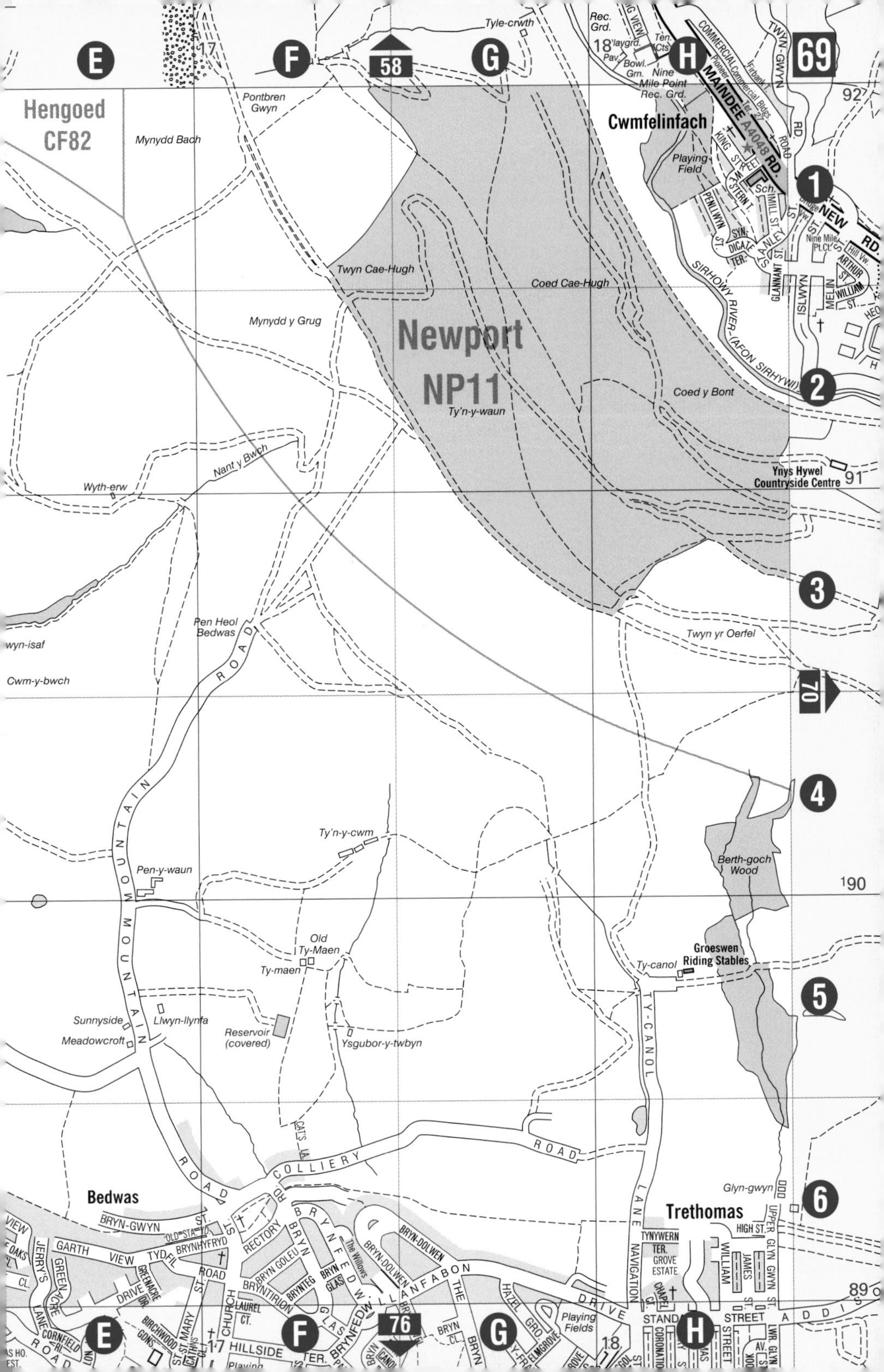
E
F
58
G
H
Tyle-crwth
Hengoed
CF82
Pontbren
Gwyn
Mynydd Bach
Cwmfelinfach
Playing
Field
Nine
Mile Point
Rec. Grd.
MAINDEE
A4048
RD.
COMMERCIAL
KING STREET
Sch.
PENLLWYN
MILL ST.
NEW
RD.
Nine Mile
Pt.Ct.
Hill Vw.
ARTHUR
ST.
WILLIAM
GLANNANT
ISLWYN
MELIN
TWYN-GWYN
RD.
92
Twyn Cae-Hugh
Coed Cae-Hugh
Mynydd y Grug
Newport
NP11
Ty'n-y-waun
SIRHOWY RIVER (AFON SIRHYWI)
Coed y Bont
Nant y Bwch
Wyth-erw
Ynys Hywel
Countryside Centre
91
1
2
3
4
5
6
Pen Heol
Bedwas
wyn-isaf
Cwm-y-bwch
Twyn yr Oerfel
70
MOUNTAIN ROAD
Ty'n-y-cwm
Pen-y-waun
Berth-goch
Wood
190
Old
Ty-Maen
Ty-maen
Groeswen
Riding Stables
Ty-canol
TY-CANOL LANE
Sunnyside
Llwyn-llynfa
Meadowcroft
Reservoir
(covered)
Ysgubor-y-twbyn
CATS LA.
COLLIERY ROAD
Glyn-gwyn
Bedwas
BRYN-GWYN ST.
Trethomas
HIGH ST.
UPPER GLYN GWYN ST.
TYNYWERN TER.
GROVE ESTATE
NAVIGATION
WILLIAM
JAMES
GARTH VIEW
TYDFIL
BRYNHYFRYD
RECTORY
BRYN
BRYNFEDW
BRYN GOLEU
BRYNTEG
BRYNTIRION
The Willows
BRYN-DOLWEN
LLANFABON
DRIVE
JERRY'S LANE
GREEN ACRE
GREENACRE DR.
ROAD
ST. MARY
CHURCH
LAUREL CT.
HILLSIDE TER.
HAZEL GRO.
ELMGROVE
Playing Fields
CHAPEL
STAND
STREET
ADDI
89
CORNFIELD
BIRCHWOOD GDNS.
76
17
18

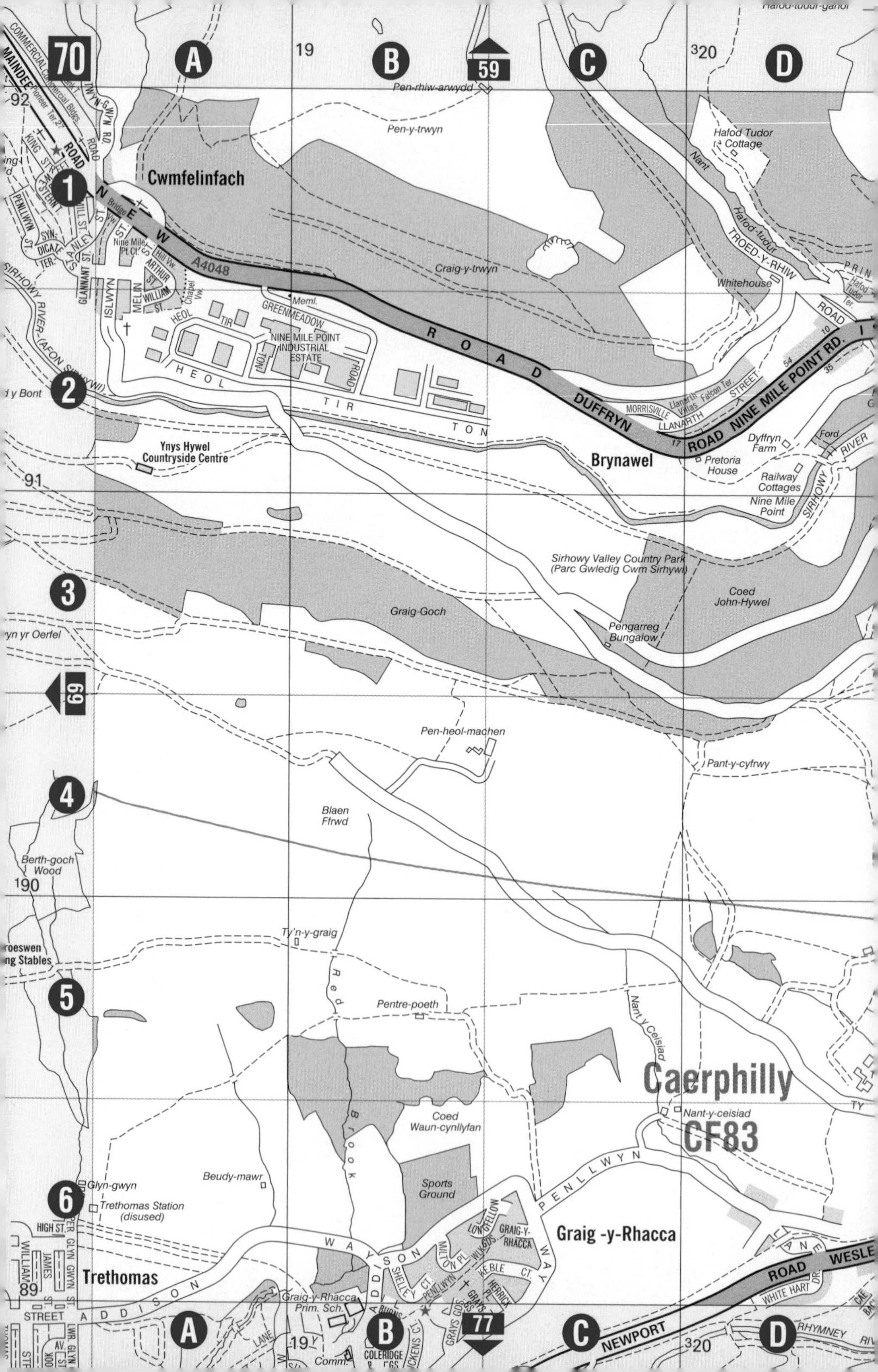

A
B
C
D
19
320
59
Pen-rhiw-arwydd
Pen-y-trwyn
Hafod Tudor Cottage
Cwmfelinfach
Nant
Hafod-tudur
TROED-Y-RHIW
A4048
Craig-y-trwyn
Whitehouse
NEW ROAD
DUFFRYN ROAD
NINE MILE POINT RD.
NINE MILE POINT INDUSTRIAL ESTATE
GREENMEADOW
HEOL TIR TON
Meml.
MORRISVILLE
LLANARTH STREET
Falcon Ter.
Llanarth Villas
Brynawel
Dyffryn Farm
Pretoria House
Railway Cottages
Nine Mile Point
Ford
SIRHOWY RIVER
SIRHOWY RIVER (AFON SIRHYWI)
Ynys Hywel Countryside Centre
91
92
Sirhowy Valley Country Park (Parc Gwledig Cwm Sirhywl)
Coed John-Hywel
Graig-Goch
Pengarreg Bungalow
69
Pen-heol-machen
Pant-y-cyfrwy
Blaen Ffrwd
Berth-goch Wood
190
Ty'n-y-graig
Red Brook
Pentre-poeth
Nant y Ceisiad
Caerphilly CF83
Nant-y-ceisiad
Coed Waun-cynllyfan
Sports Ground
Beudy-mawr
Glyn-gwyn
Trethomas Station (disused)
PENLLWYN
Graig -y-Rhacca
Trethomas
ADDISON WAY
89
HIGH ST.
Graig-y-Rhacca Prim. Sch.
77
NEWPORT ROAD
WESLEY
WHITE HART DR.
RHYMNEY RIVER
MAINDEE
COMMERCIAL
KING STREET
Cwmfelinfach
Nine Mile Pt.Ct.
Hill Vw.
ARTHUR ST.
WILLIAM ST.
Chapel Vw.
GLANNANT ST.
STANLEY ST.
ISLWYN
MELIN
PENLLWYN ST.
DICAZE TER.
LONGFELLOW
GRAIG-Y-RHACCA
MILTON PL.
KEBLE CT.
HERRICK PL.
SHELLEY CT.
PENLLWYN
COLERIDGE GS.
Comm.
1
2
3
4
5
6

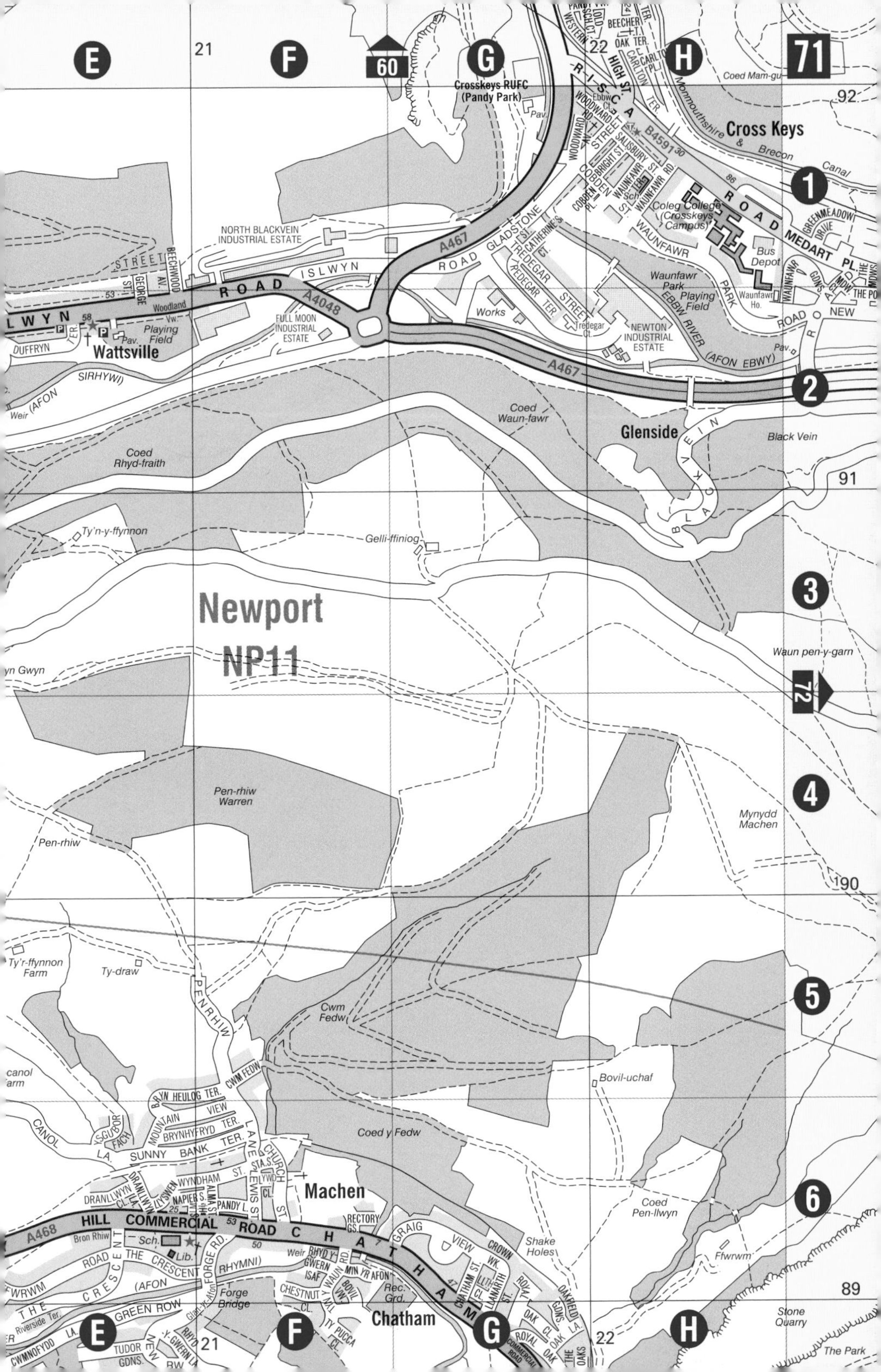
E
F
G
H
60
72
21
22
92
91
190
89
1
2
3
4
5
6
Crosskeys RUFC
(Pandy Park)
Cross Keys
Coed Mam-gu
Monmouthshire & Brecon Canal
RISCA ROAD
B4591
HIGH ST.
MEDART PL.
Coleg College
(Crosskeys Campus)
Bus Depot
Waunfawr Park
Playing Field
EBBW RIVER (AFON EBWY)
NEWTON INDUSTRIAL ESTATE
NORTH BLACKVEIN INDUSTRIAL ESTATE
FULL MOON INDUSTRIAL ESTATE
ISLWYN ROAD
A4048
A467
GLADSTONE ROAD
Works
Wattsville
Playing Field
SIRHYWI (AFON
Coed Waun-fawr
Glenside
BLACKVEIN
Black Vein
Coed Rhyd-fraith
Ty'n-y-ffynnon
Gelli-ffiniog
Newport
NP11
Waun pen-y-garn
Pen-rhiw Warren
Pen-rhiw
Mynydd Machen
Ty'r-ffynnon Farm
Ty-draw
PENRHIW
Cwm Fedw
Bovil-uchaf
Coed y Fedw
Machen
Coed Pen-llwyn
Shake Holes
Ffwrwm
A468
HILL COMMERCIAL ROAD
CHATHAM
Chatham
Forge Bridge
GREEN ROW
Stone Quarry
The Park

A
23
B
Cwmbyr Farm
61
C
24
D
92
Cross Keys
Cwm Byr
Coed y Garn
Craig y Lan
Monmouthshire & Brecon Canal
Cwm-byr-isaf
1
RISCA RD.
MEDART
GREENMEADOW DRIVE
MEDART ST.
Hall's Road Junction
Bus Depot
Cromwell Rd. Bungalows
Cemetery
RISCA (RHISGA)
Risca Quarries
PL. CROMWELL
B4591
THE POPLARS
Waunfawr Ho.
NEW PARK ROAD
RAGLAN ST.
ROAD ST. MARY
CRESCENT
EBBW RIVER (AFON EBWY)
Fernlea
Cwm-y-nant
2
A467
BLACKVEIN
Black Vein
Ty Darren
RISCA DAY HOSP
CHURCH ST.
RAILWAY ST.
American Villas
NAVIGATION RD
YORK PL.
TAYLOR ST.
SANSOM ST.
Play Fld.
Penrhiw
91
Buck Farm
NP11
Sub.
EXCHANGE RD.
St. Mary's Ct.
RIFLEMAN ST.
TRINITY CT.
GROVE ROAD
LEYDNE CL.
HIGHFIELD CL.
PENRHIW RD.
FAIRVIEW
BIRCH GRO.
PINE CL.
ROSEMONT AV.
Ty-Sign Jun. & Inf. Schs.
3
Sports Ground
Danygraig
Dan y Graig
Craig y Neuadd
DAN Y GRAIG
PHILLIP ST.
CLARENCE PL.
BRIDGE STREET
MACHEN ST.
TREDEGAR STREET
DAN-Y-GRAIG RD.
GWENDOLINE RD.
Schs.
Wks.
STATION RD.
MOUNT PLEASANT RD.
PARK ROAD IND. EST.
Hillside
PRIORY ST.
HILL ST.
LLWYNN GELLI CR.
GELLI WOOD
WOOD VIEW
Waun pen-y-garn
71
4
Mynydd Machen
Dan y Graig Bungalows
TIR-Y-CWM RD.
Tredegar Gds.
Rugby Football Ground
Cemetery
Coed y Mochyn
MALVERN TER.
PARK PLACE
LYNE RD.
Youth Cen.
Lib.
BROOKLAND RD.
CLYDE ST.
WELLSPRING
Works
Pontymister
Weir
COMMERCIAL STREET
190
PONTYMISTER INDUSTRIAL ESTATE
COMMERCIAL ST. CARAVAN SITE
BIRDS IND. EST.
ISLWYN WORKSHOPS
5
Castle Farm
Cwm-y-Nant
Lower Ochrwyth
Upper Ochrwyth
Caerphilly
6
CF83
Hedda Farm
Llan-danglws
Heollas Farm
Ffwrwm
89
Stone Quarry
Pen-y-parc
Upper Park Cottage
The Park
Twyn Pant-teg

E
F
G
H
325
26
62
73
1
2
3
4
5
6
92
91
190
89
COED Y TWRCH
Nant-y-Pandy
Cwm Henllys
Coed Pren-nimran
Cwmbran
NP44
Coed y Cwrt
Coed Pant-yr-eos
TORFAEN
NEWPORT
(TOR-FAEN)
(CASNEWYDD)
Pant-yr-eos Reservoir
Upper Grippath
Pantyreos Farm
Pantyreos Brook
Pen-twyn
Little Pentwyn
Lower Pen-twyn Farm
MOUNTAIN
NEWPORT
CAERPHILLY
(CASNEWYDD)
(CAERFFILI)
Upper Wenallt
Tregwillym House
Newport
Craig y Wenallt
Lower Wenallt Farm
Ty'n-y-pwll
Ty-Sign
Manor Ct.
Play-grd.
ROWAN RD.
SNOWDON CL.
EPPYNT CL.
PRESCELI CL.
CADER IDRIS CL.
TWM BARLWM CL.
TWM BARLWM CT.
CHEVIOT CL.
PENNINE CL.
QUANTOCK CL.
BRIERLEY CL.
CLEVELAND DR.
BREDON CL.
MENDIP CL.
PENTLAND CL.
MALVERN CL.
WAY
Golynos
Golynos Fach Farm
Golynos Fawr Farm
Golynos Cottage
ALMOND
MAPLE AVENUE
THISTLE WAY
WYNDHAM T.
WYNDHAM TER.
MNR. CL.
Factory Cotts.
MANOR ROAD
AVENUE
DRIVE
FORSYTHIA CL.
SYCAMORE
CHARTIST CT.
SEVERN
MACHEN
CHANNEL
CARRAN CL.
COTSWOLD
CHILTERN CL.
MOUNTSIDE
WENTWOOD PL.
Play-grd.
CRES.
MANOR WY.
WAY
PONTYMASON
Ty-Sign
Sch.
Risca Leisure Centre
Tennis Cts.
Ysgubor-wen
Heol-fawr
ROAD
Inf. Sch.
CLOSE
Monmouthshire & Brecon Canal
Graig
STREET
ISAF RD.
Recreation Ground
Bowl. Grn.
Pav.
SPRINGFIELD RD.
SPRING FIELD RD.
TY-ISAF
VIEW HERBERT
Works
CLIFTON ST.
Playing Field
NEWPORT GOLF COURSE
Pen y van
Upper Mount Pleasant
Lower Mount Pleasant
Llwyni Wood
MILL
SPRINGFIELD RD.
TY-ISAF CR.
TY-ISAF PK.
CIRCLE
PARK
AVENUE
ROAD
NEWPORT ROAD
RISCA
B4591
MEADOW CR.
Ten. Cts.
Pav.
Bowl. Grn.
Recreation Ground
SUFFLEX ESTATE
MAPLE GDNS.
TANYBRYN
NP10
FIELDS ROAD
FIELDS RD
Old Pontymister Farm
Tam-y-coed
Factory
DEWBERRY GRO.
SNOWDROP LA.
CAMELLIA DR.
BURBERRY CL.
DELPHINIUM RD.
JASMINE CL.
CAMPANULA DR.
AFON EBBW RD.
LILAC GRO.
MEADOWLAND DR.
DAFFODIL LA.
AZALEA ROAD
WOODLAND DR.
RIVERMEAD
Oaktree Cottage
CEDAR WOOD
CEDAR WOOD CL.
TREE
LABURNUM CL.
MULBERRY DRIVE
WILLOW WK.
OAK
BLUEBELL DRIVE
BUTTCP. WY.
GERBERA DR.
RIVERMEAD WAY
PRIMROSE WAY
LAVENDER
VIOLET WK.
ROSE WK.
POPPY PL.
AFON
RIVERMEAD WAY
LILY WY.
PONTYMASON CT.
PONTYMASON CLOSE
PONTYMASON LANE
ROAD
THORNHILL GDNS.
THORNHILL WAY
THORN HILL WY.
The Uplands
GREAT OAKS PK.
CEFN RD.
VICARAGE GS.
COURT GDS.
ST. JOHN'S CR.
BIRCHGRO.
COED MAWR
Coed-mawr Cottage
Coed y Squire
A467
Llwyn-deri
IRIS RD.
FUSCIA
TULIP WK.
MARGLD CL.
caddon

74
Abertridwr
67
A
B
C
D
13
14
1
2
3
4
5
6
89
88
87
186
Pav.
Library
Rec. Grd.
Pont y Felin
Mountain Vw.
CRESCENT
COEDCAE RD.
COED-Y-PICA
BRON-MYNNYD
THOMAS STREET
B4263
Coed Cae pica
Cwm yr Aber
Nant yr Aber
Waterfall
CWM FFOR
Cwarrau-mawr
HEOL CWARREL
PEN-Y-DRE
HENFRON
BLAEN
IFOR
OWAIN
BRYN
BOWLS LA.
BRYN AWEL
PEN-Y-BRYN
HEOL FAWR
HEOL FER
HEOL-Y-GOGLEDD
PENTWYN
ANEURIN
Play-ground
FFRWD
GLAN
CEFN-Y-LON
LANE
HEOL TIR BACH
PEN-Y-GROES
WEN
GRAIG
BRYNGLAS
HEULOG
BRYN-TIRION
TROED-Y-RHIW
RHIW FACH
TIR COED
TIR
GIBE
PLEKSANT
Cemetery
CWM IFOR
FFORDD EVANS
CALEDFRYN
BRYN NANT
BRYN-YR-YSGOL
CAE CARADOG
CLOS CYNCOED
MOEL FRYN
HEOL SERTH
BRYN
CLYD
SIRIOL
BRYN IFOR
Cwn Ifor Primary Sch.
WAY
Ty-isaf
BRYN SIRIOL
Penyrheol
Play-ground
Tennis Cts.
Pav.
Bowl. Grn.
Aneurin Park
PL.
Hall
Bowls Terrace
BOWLS CL.
BRYNHYFRYD
Energlyn Ter.
Ty Isaf Bungalows
TY-ISAF
STATION TER.
THOMASVILLE
TY NANT
Hendredenny-uchaf Farm
Plymouth House
Hendredenny-ganol
Hendredenny Park
RHUDDLAN CT.
CHESTER CT.
GOLWG Y COED
BUNHAVEN CT.
HENDREDENNY DRIVE
TENBY CT.
CAERNARVON CT.
KIDWELLY CT.
CLOS GWERNYDD
BROOKSIDE
CL.
Orchards Poultry Farm
Works
BRIGHAM CT.
CAERLEON CT.
NARBERTH CT.
DENBIGH CT.
OGMORE CT.
MORLAIS CT.
HARLECH CT.
CONWAY CT.
CARMARTHEN CT.
CALDICOT CT.
RAGLAN CT.
MONMOUTH CT.
GROESWEN
WHITE CROSS LA.
ST. CENYDD ROAD
CENYDD CL.
Sch.
CAERPHILLY ROAD
CRESC.
HEOL FACH
Rec. Grd.
HOLYHEAD CT.
PEMBROKE CT.
ROAD
Hendredenny Park Primary Sch.
St. Cenydd Comprehensive Sch.
Hendre Jun. Sch.
Playing Fields
Ty-newydd
BY-PASS
ST. CENYDD
THE WEST
TEGFAN
THIRD AV.
WEST
SECOND
FIRST AV.
TRECENYDD IND. EST.
Tai Cae bryn
Ty-llwyd
Cartref
Bryngolau
Y Groes-wen
Groes-wen Farm
GROESWEN
Cefn Brith
Cardiff CF15
GYPSY LANE
Gledyr
Nant
A468
CAERPHILLY ROAD
CLOS CWM GARW
HEOL Y-HWYAD
HEOL-Y-PIA
LON-Y-FRAN
MAES-Y-SGLEN
LON Y TRESGLEN
CAE NANT
CLOS GWAUN
RHOS GLEDYR
FFORDD PENRHOS
GLEDYR
COED-YR-EOS
CAE'R FFERM
GLENFIELDS ESTATE
LON ROBIN GOCH
COED-Y-WENNOL
DOL-Y-PAUN
DRUDWEN
GRAIG-Y-WYLAN
LLWYD-Y-BERTH
SUNNINGDALE
LON-Y-RHEDYN
Gledyr Bungalow
B4600
NANTGARW ROAD
Fac.
WESTERN
WESTERN INDUSTRIAL ES.
Depot
EGLWYSILAN ROAD
RHONDDA CYNON TAFF
CAERPHILLY
Gwaun-gleclyr-uchaf
Gwaun-gledyr-isaf
Penrhos House
(CAERFFILI)
NANTGARW ROAD
(RHONDDA CYNON TAF)
Coed Caedyrys
Ty-fry
Works
Tŷ-hen
OLD
Llusern
Graig Cottages
EMANUEL CL.
TRAWS CWM
FFORDD
MEILLION
CAE
Sch.
COOPERS PL.
WAY
BEECH
BADHAM
MEADOW
COGGINS CL.
WESLEY RD.
ASHMAN CL.
CORBETT
HYNES CL.
WARE RD.
HERONS WAY
CLOS GWASTIR
FFORDD TRAWS CWM
CLOS
ENFYS
HEOL WAUN FAWR
CAE ROWLAND DR.
HEOL-Y-BERTH
HEOL TYDDYN
TREM Y CASTELL
GWAUN Y CWRT
CAE NANTGCH
CAE CROES
CWRT NANT Y FELIN
HEOL DAN YR ARDD
CLOS-Y-PANT

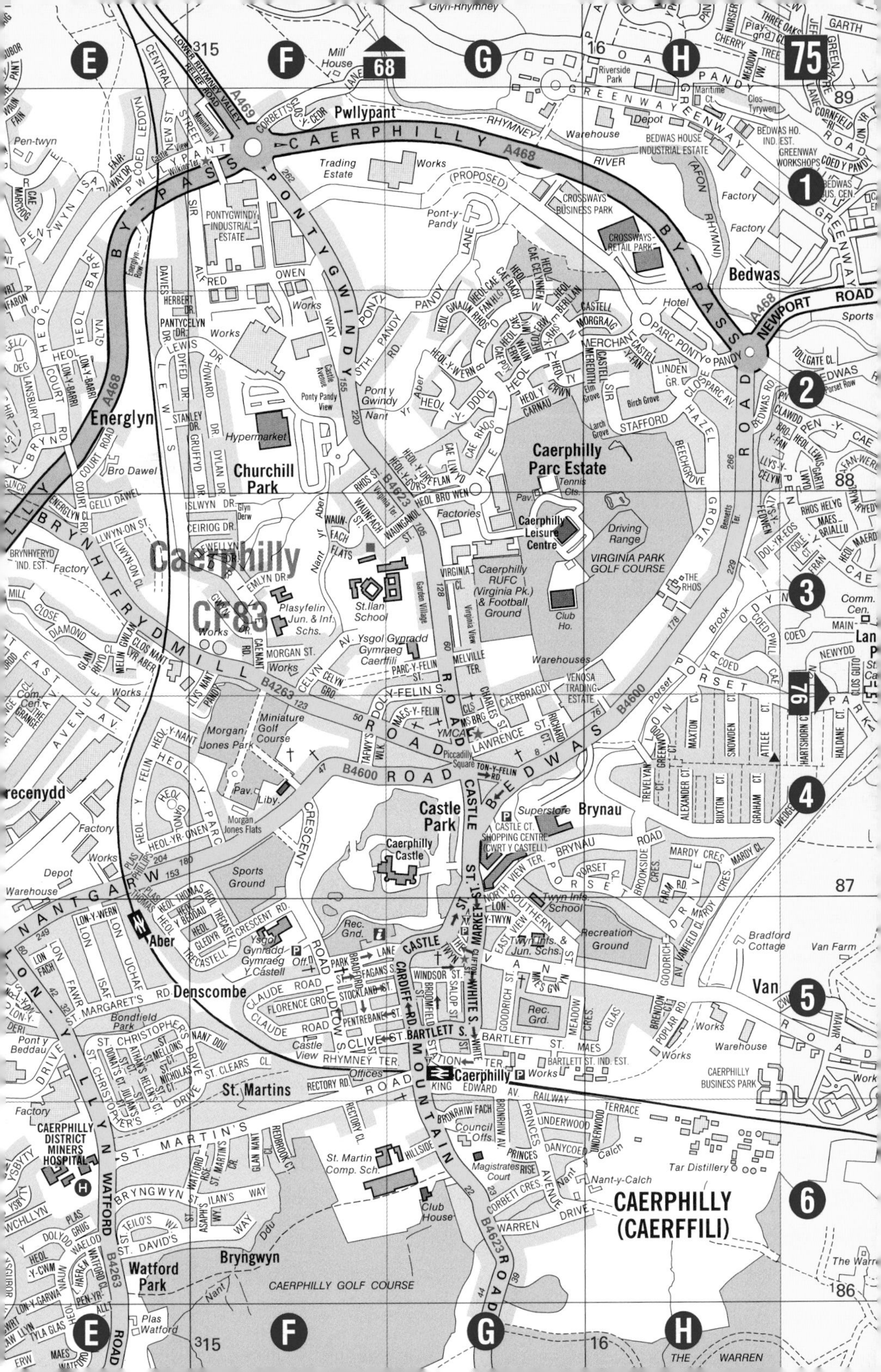

75
68
76
E
F
G
H
1
2
3
4
5
6
315
16
89
88
87
186
Glyn-Rhymney
Mill House
Pwllypant
CAERPHILLY
A469
A468
LOWER RHYMNEY VALLEY RELIEF ROAD
BY-PASS
PONTYGWINDY
Trading Estate
Works
(PROPOSED)
RHYMNEY RIVER
Riverside Park
GREENWAY
Depot
Warehouse
BEDWAS HOUSE INDUSTRIAL ESTATE
BEDWAS HO. IND. EST.
GREENWAY WORKSHOPS
COED Y PANDY
Factory
Bedwas
NEWPORT ROAD
Sports
TOLLGATE CL.
BEDWAS RD.
Pen-twyn
PONTYGWINDY INDUSTRIAL ESTATE
CROSSWAYS BUSINESS PARK
CROSSWAYS RETAIL PARK
Pont-y-Pandy
Energlyn
HEOL BARRI
Hypermarket
Churchill Park
Bro Dawel
Caerphilly
CF83
Caerphilly Parc Estate
Tennis Cts.
Pav.
Caerphilly Leisure Centre
Driving Range
VIRGINIA PARK GOLF COURSE
Factories
Caerphilly RUFC (Virginia Pk.) & Football Ground
Club Ho.
THE RHOS
Warehouses
VENOSA TRADING ESTATE
BRYNHYFRYD IND. EST.
Factory
St.Ilan School
Plasyfelin Jun. & Inf. Schs.
Ysgol Gynradd Gymraeg Caerffili
Garden Village
MORGAN ST.
Works
PARC-Y-FELIN ST.
MELVILLE TER.
DOL-Y-FELIN ST.
CAERBRAGDY
LAWRENCE ST.
YMCA
Piccadilly Square
TON-Y-FELIN RD.
B4263
B4600
B4623
Morgan Jones Park
Miniature Golf Course
Liby.
Morgan Jones Flats
Castle Park
Caerphilly Castle
Superstore
Brynau
CASTLE CT. SHOPPING CENTRE (CWRT Y CASTELL)
recenydd
Factory
Works
Depot
Warehouse
Sports Ground
NANTGARW RD.
Aber
Ysgol Gynradd Gymraeg Y Castell
Rec. Gnd.
Twyn Infs. School
Recreation Ground
Twyn Infs. & Jun. Schs.
Bradford Cottage
Van Farm
Van
Denscombe
Bondfield Park
CLAUDE ROAD
CASTLE ST.
CARDIFF RD.
MOUNTAIN RD.
Rec. Grd.
Castle View
RHYMNEY TER.
Offices
Caerphilly
KING EDWARD AV.
RAILWAY TERRACE
BARTLETT ST. IND. EST.
Works
Warehouse
CAERPHILLY BUSINESS PARK
St. Martins
ST. MARTIN'S RD.
Factory
CAERPHILLY DISTRICT MINERS HOSPITAL
Council Offs.
Magistrates Court
St. Martin Comp. Sch.
Club House
Nant-y-Calch
Tar Distillery
CAERPHILLY (CAERFFILI)
WARREN DRIVE
Watford Park
Bryngwyn
CAERPHILLY GOLF COURSE
Plas Watford
The Warren
THE WARREN

76
A
B
C
D
69
18
17
1
2
3
4
5
6
75
89
88
87
186
Bedwas
Trethomas
Mornington Meadows
Lansbury Park
Van
Wern Ddu
BRYN-GWYN
GARTH VIEW
TYDFIL
BRYNHYFRYD
RECTORY
BRYN GOLEU
BRYNTIRION
BRYN-DOLWEN
LLANFABON
THE BRYN
NAVIGATION
TYNYWERN TER.
GROVE ESTATE
WILLIAM
JAMES
HIGH ST.
DRIVE
Playing Fields
STANDARD STREET
CORONATION ST.
MARY STREET
THOMAS ST.
REDBROOK AV.
HEOL YR YSGOL
ASHGROVE
ELMGROVE
BRYN-Y-FRAN
BIRCHGROVE
BEVAN CL.
BEVAN RI.
HAZEL GRO.
Playground
Tennis Ct.
Club
Bowl. Grn.
Bedwas Comp. Sch.
BEDWAS CENTRE
Comm. Cen.
Lib.
HILLSIDE TER.
Playing Field
THE CRESCENT
CROSS ST.
EAST AVENUE
GLEBE ST.
CELTIC WY.
Jun. Sch.
PARK AV.
BRYNFEDW
The Willows
LAUREL CT.
ST. MARY STREET
CHURCH ROAD
NEWPORT ROAD
A468
Offices
The Square
Bedwas Inf. Sch.
BIRCHWOOD GDNS.
CORNFIELD RI.
LON YR YSGOL
GREENACRE DR.
JERRY'S LANE
GREEN ACRE
THREE OAKS CL.
NURSERY
Play CL.
Clos Tyrywen
BEDWAS HO. IND. EST.
GREENWAY WORKSHOPS
COED Y PANDY
BEDWAS BUS. CEN.
CAERPHILLY ENTERPRISE CENTRE
Factory
Sports Ground
Pav.
Pont Bedwas
Cemetery
PANT GLAS INDUSTRIAL ESTATE
Works
CLOS PANT GLAS
ST. MARGARET'S CL.
THE AV.
GLEBE RD.
RHYMNEY RIVER (AFON RHYMNI)
RHYD-Y-GWERN
LLANFEDW CL.
RUDRY CL.
ST. JAMES CL.
DARREN CL.
TRAP WELL
Maes-yr-Afon
Westview Ter.
Porset Row
BEDWAS RUDRY ROAD
TOLLGATE CL.
PANDY
BYPASS
PEN-TWYN-GWYN
Plas-newydd
Sunnybank
Halt Farm
Branch Cottages
Gwaun-y-Cottage
Nant Arian
Ty-yr-efail
Gwern-y-domen
Garth
PEN-Y-CAE
HEOL LEWIS
LLYS-Y-FAN
LLYS-Y-CELYN
BRO-Y-FAN
PEN CLAWDD
HAFAN-WERDD
BRYN-RHEDYN
LLWYN EITHAM
HYFRYD
RHOS HELYG
MAES BRIALLU
HEOL MAERDY
GWAUN
DOL-YR-EOS
COLE CT.
DOL FRAN
LLYS-Y-FEDWEN
Comm. Cen.
Lansbury Park Jun. & Inf. Schs.
St.Helen's Catholic Prim. Sch.
ODYN
COED YR PWLL
MAIN
NEWYDD
CLOS GUTO
PARK
PORSET
LON COED
BEDWAS ROAD
Brook
HAZEL
PARC AV.
THE RHOS
Bennetts Ter.
MAXTON
SNOWDEN
ATTLEE
HARTSHORN CT.
HALDANE CT.
ALEXANDER CT.
BUXTON CT.
WEDGEWOOD CT.
MARDY CRES.
MARDY CL.
Coed y Maerdy
Nant Gwaunybara
Coed Parc-y-van
Mynydd Rudry
RUDRY CO
Parc-y-Van
Coed Parc-y-Van
Bradford Cottage
Van Farm
VAN
CWRT TY MAWR
Van Terrace
Works
Warehouse
CAERPHILLY BUSINESS PARK
WERN DDU CT.
ROAD
Tar Distillery
Tenafly
Wern-ddu Row
The Warren
THE WARREN

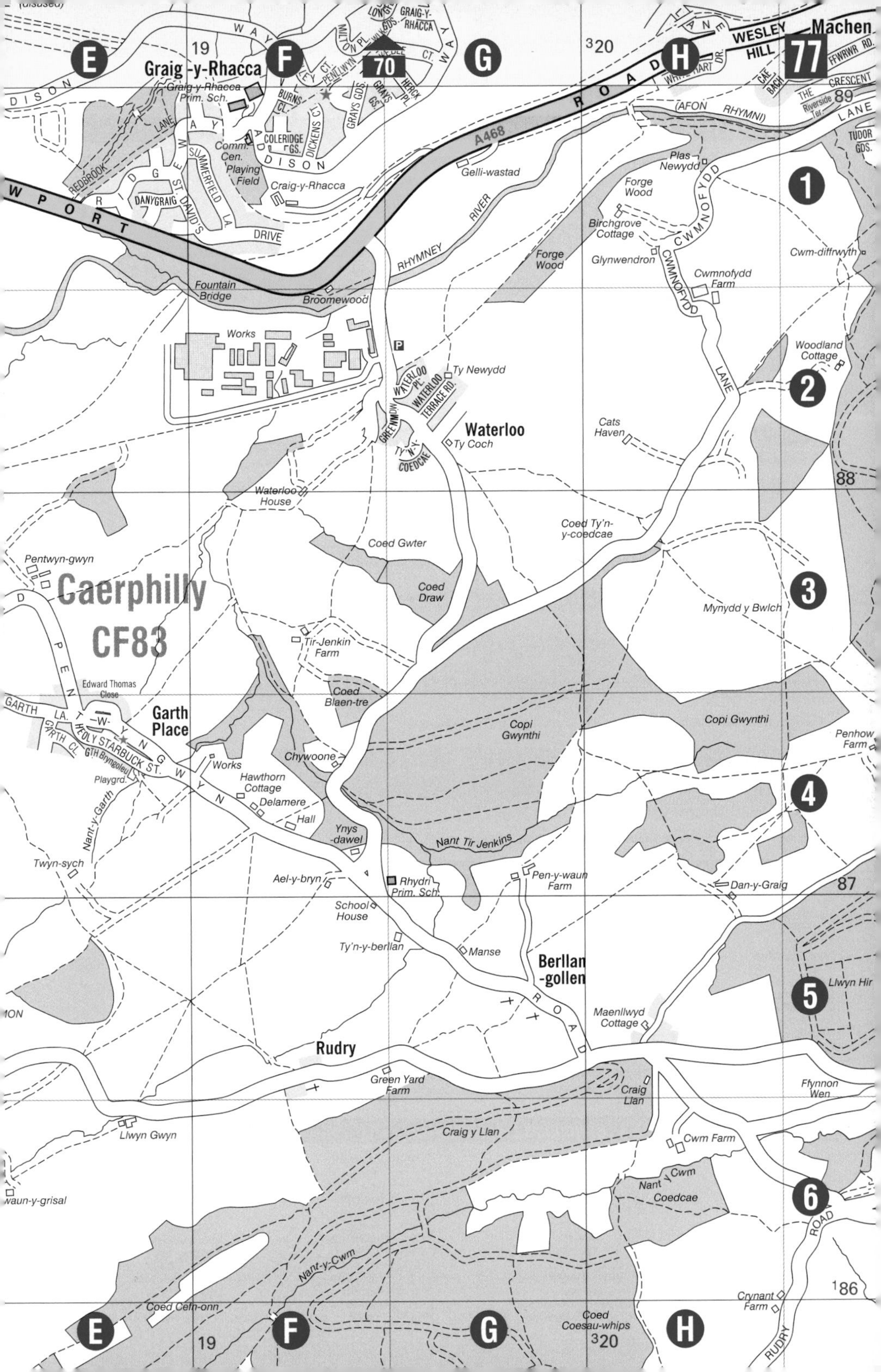

70
77
Machen
Graig-y-Rhacca
Graig-y-Rhacca Prim. Sch.
Comm. Cen.
Playing Field
Craig-y-Rhacca
ADDISON WAY
RHYMNEY RIVER
A468
NEWPORT ROAD
WESLEY HILL
Gelli-wastad
Forge Wood
Plas Newydd
Birchgrove Cottage
Glynwendron
CWMNOFYDD LANE
Cwmnofydd Farm
Cwm-diffrwyth
Woodland Cottage
(AFON RHYMNI)
Fountain Bridge
Broomewood
Works
Ty Newydd
Waterloo
Ty Coch
Cats Haven
Waterloo House
Coed Gwter
Coed Draw
Coed Ty'n-y-coedcae
Pentwyn-gwyn
Caerphilly
CF83
Mynydd y Bwlch
Tir-Jenkin Farm
Coed Blaen-tre
Edward Thomas Close
Garth Place
Copi Gwynthi
Penhow Farm
Chywoone
Hawthorn Cottage
Delamere
Hall
Playgrd.
Nant-y-Garth
Twyn-sych
Ynys-dawel
Nant Tir Jenkins
Ael-y-bryn
Rhydri Prim. Sch.
Pen-y-waun Farm
Dan-y-Graig
School House
Ty'n-y-berllan
Manse
Berllan-gollen
Llwyn Hir
Maenllwyd Cottage
Rudry
Green Yard Farm
Craig Llan
Ffynnon Wen
Llwyn Gwyn
Craig y Llan
Cwm Farm
Nant y Cwm Coedcae
waun-y-grisal
Nant-y-Cwm
Coed Cefn-onn
Coed Coesau-whips
Crynant Farm
RUDRY ROAD
E
F
G
H
1
2
3
4
5
6
19
320
89
88
87
86

INDEX

Including Streets, Places & Areas, Hospitals & Hospices, Industrial Estates, Selected Flats & Walkways, Stations and Selected Places of Interest.

HOW TO USE THIS INDEX

1. Each street name is followed by its Postcode District and then by its Locality abbreviation(s) and then by its map reference; e.g. **Abbey Rd.** NP44: C'brn . . . .1B **64** is in the NP44 Postcode District and the Cwmbran Locality and is to be found in square 1B on page **64**. The page number is shown in bold type.
2. A strict alphabetical order is followed in which Av., Rd., St., etc. (though abbreviated) are read in full and as part of the street name; e.g. **Alderman Cl.** appears after **Alder Gro.** but before **Alder Ri.**
3. Streets and a selection of flats and walkways too small to be shown on the maps, appear in the index with the thoroughfare to which it is connected shown in brackets; e.g. **Afon Ct.** *NP4: Abers. . . .2F **37** (off Valentine Rd.)*
4. Addresses that are in more than one part are referred to as not continuous.
5. Places and areas are shown in the index in **BLUE TYPE** and the map reference is to the actual map square in which the town centre or area is located and not to the place name shown on the map; e.g. **ABERBARGOED. . . . 3G 41**
6. An example of a selected place of interest is **Abergavenny Mus. & Castle. . . . 5F 7**
7. An example of a station is **Abergavenny Station (Rail) 5H 7**
8. An example of a hospital or hospice is **ABERTILLERY & DISTRICT HOSPITAL. . . . 5A 34**

MYNEGAI

Yn cynnwys Strydoedd, Lleoedd ac Ardaloedd, Ysbytai a Hosbisys, Stadau Diwydiannol, Fflatiau a Llwybrau Troed dethol, Gorsafoedd a Detholiad o Fannau Diddorol.

SUD I DDEFNYDDIO'R MYNEGAI HWN

1. Dilynir pob enw stryd gan ei Ardal Cod Post ac wedyn gan fyrfodd(au) ei Leoliad ac wedyn gan ei gyfeirnod map; e.e. mae **Abbey Rd.** NP44: C'brn . . . .1B **64** yn Ardal Cod Post NP44 a Lleoliad Cwmbran a gellir dod o hyd iddi yn sgwâr 1B ar dudalen **64**. Dangosir Rhif y Dudalen mewn teip trwm.
2. Glynir yn gaeth wrth drefn y wyddor, gyda Av., Rd., St., ayb (er eu bod wedi eu talfyrru) yn cael eu darllen yn llawn ac fel rhan o enw'r stryd; e.e. mae **Alderman Cl.** yn ymddangos ar ôl **Alder Gro.** ond cyn **Alder Ri.**
3. Mae strydoedd a detholiad o fflatiau a llwybrau troed sy'n rhy fychan i'w dangos ar y mapiau, yn ymddangos yn y mynegai gyda'r dramwyfa y mae'n gysylltiedig â hi wedi'i dangos mewn cromfachau; e.e. **Afon Ct.** *NP4: Abers. . . .2F **37** (off Valentine Rd.)*
4. Cyfeirir at gyfeiriadau sydd mewn mwy nag un rhan fel cyfeiriadau nan ydynt yn barhaus.
5. Dangosir ardaloedd a lleoedd yn y mynegai mewn **TEIP GLAS** ac mae'r cyfeirnod map yn cyfeirio at y sgwâr ar y map lle mae lleoliad canol y dref neu'r ardal ac nid at yr enw lle a ddangosir ar y map; e.e. **ABERBARGOD. . . . 3G 41**
6. Enghraifft o fan diddorol dethol yw **Abergavenny Mus. & Castle. . . . 5F 7**
7. Enghraifft o orsaf yw **Abergavenny Station (Rail) 5H 7**
8. Enghraifft o Ysbyty neu Hosbis yw **ABERTILLERY & DISTRICT HOSPITAL. . . . 5A 34**

GENERAL ABBREVIATIONS *Talfyriadau Cyffredinol*

App. : Approach
Arc. : Arcade
Av. : Avenue
Bri. : Bridge
Bldgs. : Buildings
Bungs. : Bungalows
Bus. : Business
Cvn. : Caravan
Cen. : Centre
Chu. : Church
Circ. : Circle
Cl. : Close
Comn. : Common
Cnr. : Corner
Cotts. : Cottages
Ct. : Court
Cres. : Crescent
Dr. : Drive
E. : East
Emb. : Embankment
Ent. : Enterprise
Est. : Estate
Fld. : Field
Flds. : Fields
Gdn. : Garden
Gdns. : Gardens
Ga. : Gate
Gt. : Great
Grn. : Green
Gro. : Grove
Hgts. : Heights
Ho. : House
Ho's. : Houses
Ind. : Industrial
Info. : Information
La. : Lane
Lwr. : Lower
Mans. : Mansions
Mdw. : Meadow
Mdws. : Meadows
M. : Mews
Mt. : Mount
Mus. : Museum
Nth. : North
Pde. : Parade
Pk. : Park
Pl. : Place
Ri. : Rise
Rd. : Road
Shop. : Shopping
Sth. : South
Sq. : Square
St. : Street
Ter. : Terrace
Trad. : Trading
Up. : Upper
Vw. : View
Vs. : Villas
Vis. : Visitors
Wlk. : Walk
W. : West
Yd. : Yard

LOCALITY ABBREVIATIONS *Byrfoddau Lleoliadau*

A'goed : **Aberbargoed**
A'beeg : **Aberbeeg**
Aberc : **Abercarn**
A'gvnny : **Abergavenny**
Abers : **Abersychan**
A'lery : **Abertillery**
Abert : **Abertridwr**
A'swg : **Abertysswg**
Argoed : **Argoed**
Barg : **Bargoed**
B'fort : **Beaufort**
B'ws : **Bedwas**
Bet : **Bettws**
B'wood : **Blackwood**
B'avn : **Blaenavon**
Blai : **Blaina**
Brith : **Brithdir**
B'thel : **Brynithel**
B mawr : **Bryn-mawr**
C'ln : **Caerleon**
Caer : **Caerphilly**
Cefn F : **Cefn Fforest**
Cefn H : **Cefn Hengoed**
Cly : **Clydach**
C'maen : **Croespenmaen**
C'iog : **Croesyceiliog**
C'keys : **Crosskeys**
Crum : **Crumlin**
Cwm : **Cwm**
C'avn : **Cwmavon**
C'brn : **Cwmbran**
C'crn : **Cwmcarn**
C'fch : **Cwmfelinfach**
C'lery : **Cwmtillery**
Deri : **Deri**
E Vale : **Ebbw Vale**
F'wtr : **Fairwater**
Fleur : **Fleur-de-lis**
Foch : **Fochriw**
G lydan : **Garn-lydan**
G Erw : **Garn Yr Erw**
G'gaer : **Gelligaer**
Gilf : **Gilfach**
Gilw : **Gilwern**
Glas : **Glascoed**
Gov : **Govilon**
G'mdw : **Greenmeadow**
Grif : **Griffithstown**
Heng : **Hengoed**
H'lys : **Henllys**
Holly B : **Holly Bush**
Lit M : **Little Mill**

L'brad : **Llanbradach**
L Hill : **Llanelly Hill**
L'fst : **Llanfoist**
Llanf : **Llanfrechfa**
L'hth : **Llanhilleth**
L'narth : **Llanwenarth**
Llan : **Llanyravon**
Mac : **Machen**
Maes C : **Maes-y-cwmmer**
Malp : **Malpas**
Mamh : **Mamhilad**
Man M : **Man-moel**
Mardy : **Mardy**
Mark : **Markham**
Myn : **Mynyddislwyn**
N'grw : **Nantgarw**
N'glo : **Nantyglo**
Nels : **Nelson**
Newb : **Newbridge**
New I : **New Inn**
New T : **New Tredegar**
Oakd : **Oakdale**
Oakf : **Oakfield**
P'seg : **Pantygasseg**
Peng : **Pengam**
P'heol : **Penpedairheol**
Pent C : **Pentwyn Crumlin**
P'hir : **Ponthir**
P'fraith : **Pontllanfraith**
P'tyn : **Pontlottyn**
Pnwd : **Pontnewydd**
P'nydd : **Pontnewynydd**
P'pool : **Pontypool**
P'prdd : **Pontypridd**
P'waun : **Pontywaun**
Rassa : **Rassau**
R'fln : **Rhydyfelin**
Rhym : **Rhymney**
Ris : **Risca**
Roger : **Rogerstone**
Rud : **Rudry**
Sen : **Senghenydd**
S Bells : **Six Bells**
Tal : **Talywain**
Tir B : **Tir-y-Berth**
Tred : **Tredegar**
Tref : **Trefil**
T'lewis : **Trelewis**
Tret : **Trethomas**
Trev : **Trevethin**
Up Cwm : **Upper Cwmbran**
Up R : **Upper Race**
Var : **Varteg**
W'vle : **Wattsville**
W lwyd : **Waun-lwyd**
Yny : **Ynysddu**
Ystrad : **Ystrad**

A

Abbey Farm La. NP44: Oakf 4E 65
Abbey Grn. NP44: Oakf 3C 64
Abbey Gro. NP44: Oakf 5E 65
Abbey Rd. NP44: C'brn 1B 64
ABERBARGOD 3G 41
ABERBARGOED 3G 41
Aberbargoed Sports Hall 2G 41
ABERBEEG 4B 34
Aberbeeg Rd.
NP13: A'lery, S Bells 1C 34
ABER-BIG 4B 34
ABERCARN 6C 52
Abercarn Fach NP11: C'crn 3D 60
Aberconway Pl. NP12: Oakd 6E 43
Aberfawr Rd. CF83: Abert 6D 66
Aberfawr Ter. CF83: Abert 6D 66
Aberffrwd NP22: Tred 4G 15
ABERGAVENNY 4F 7
Abergavenny Leisure Cen. 2F 7
Abergavenny Mus. & Castle 5F 7
Abergavenny Rd. NP4: B'avn 2F 21
NP7: Gilw 3D 4
Abergavenny Station (Rail) 5H 7
Abernant Cres. NP12: Mark 6B 32
Abernant Rd. NP12: Mark 5A 32
Aber Station (Rail) 5E 75
ABERSYCHAN 2D 36
ABERTILLERY 1C 34
ABERTILLERY & DISTRICT HOSPITAL 5A 34
Abertillery Community Theatre 5G 27
Abertillery Leisure Cen. 1C 34
Abertillery Rd. NP13: Blai 5D 18
ABERTRIDWR 6D 66
ABERTYLERI 1C 34
ABERTYSSWG 3F 23
Acacia Av. CF82: Heng 6E 49
Acacia Ter. NP11: Aberc 5C 52
Acorn Cl. NP4: Abers 2E 37
NP23: Rassa 2D 10
Acorn Vs. NP23: W lwyd 6F 17
Acre Cl. NP11: Crum 5D 44
Adams Sq. NP23: E Vale 1F 17
Adam St. NP13: A'lery 6H 27
Addison St. NP12: B'wood 6A 42
Addison Way CF83: Mac, Tret . . .1E 77
Adelaide Ct. NP12: Cefn F 3H 49
Adit Wlk. NP44: Pnwd 4C 54
(not continuous)
Ael-y-Bryn CF82: Heng 1F 57
CF83: Caer 2D 74
CF83: Tret 1C 76
NP4: B'avn 2G 21
NP11: Newb 2A 52
NP22: Rhym 3A 14
Aelybryn St. CF81: Foch 4A 22
Aeron Ct. CF81: Gilf 5F 41
Aeron Pl. CF81: Gilf 5F 41
Afon Cl. NP4: New I 4G 47
Afon Ct. *NP4: Abers 2F 37*
(off Valentine Rd.)
Afon Ebbw Rd. NP10: Roger 6F 73
Afon Llwyd Ter. NP4: P'nydd 4F 37
Afon Mead NP10: Roger 6G 73
Afon Ter. NP44: C'iog 4F 55
Aiwa Technology Pk.
NP11: Newb 2B 52
Alandale Rd. NP23: Rassa 3B 10
Albany Rd. NP7: A'gvnny 2D 6
NP12: B'wood 2B 50
Albertina Rd. NP11: Newb 6A 44
Albert Rd. NP4: Tal 6C 28
NP7: A'gvnny 3G 7
Albion Pl. NP4: P'nydd 5F 37
Albion Rd. NP4: P'pool 2B 46
Albion Ter. NP12: B'wood 3B 50
Alder Cl. NP4: New I 2H 47
Alder Gro. NP23: Rassa 2D 10
Alderman Cl. NP12: B'wood 2A 50
Alder Ri. NP12: P'fraith 5D 50
Alders, The NP12: Oakd 6F 43
NP44: Llan 2E 65
Alexander Ct. CF83: Caer 4H 75
Alexander St. NP22: A'swg 3E 23
Alexandra Ct. NP11: Yny 5C 58
Alexandra Pl. NP11: Newb 2A 52
NP22: Rhym 4B 14
NP22: Tred 1H 15
(Beaufort Rd.)
NP22: Tred 3A 16
(Georgetown Hill)
Alexandra Rd. CF82: Heng 6F 49
NP4: Grif 6E 47
NP7: A'gvnny 3G 7
NP11: Yny 5C 58
NP13: S Bells 2D 34
NP24: New T 3E 31
Alexandra St. NP13: Blai 5D 18
NP23: E Vale 2E 17
Alexandra Ter. CF83: Sen 2C 66
NP23: B mawr 3B 12
Alfred St. CF81: Gilf 5F 41
NP22: A'swg 3F 23
NP23: E Vale 6D 10
Allerford Gro. NP7: Gilw 3C 4
Allgood Av. NP4: B'avn 3E 21
Allotment Rd. NP23: B'fort 3D 10
Alma Pl. NP4: Grif 6E 47
Alma St. CF83: Mac 6F 71
NP4: B'avn 2F 21
NP13: A'lery 5G 27
(not continuous)
NP23: B mawr 3B 12
Alma Ter. NP23: B mawr 2C 12
Almond Av. NP11: Ris 3E 73
Ambleside NP4: Tal 6D 28
Ambleside Ct. CF82: P'heol 2D 48
Ambrose Wlk. NP4: New I 3G 47
Ambryn Rd. NP4: New I 3H 47
American Vs. NP11: Ris 2C 72
Amroth Wlk. NP44: G'mdw 1H 63
Andrews Cl. CF81: Gilf 5F 41
Andrews Ct. NP23: E Vale 6C 10
Aneurin Av. NP11: Crum 4C 44
NP12: Cefn F 2G 49
Aneurin Bevan Ct.
NP4: P'pool 1C 46
Aneurin Cl. NP22: Tred 2H 15
Aneurin Cres. NP23: B mawr 2B 12
Aneurin Pl. NP23: B mawr 2B 12
Aneurin Ter. NP22: Rhym 3B 14
Angel Cl. NP23: E Vale 3E 17
Angel La. CF81: A'goed 5G 41
CF81: Gilf 5F 41
Angel Sq. NP23: E Vale 3E 17
Annes Ct. NP23: E Vale 6D 10
Anne St. NP4: B'avn 3F 21
Anuerin Bevan Av.
CF82: G'gaer 3B 48
Apollo Way NP12: B'wood 2A 50
Arael Vw. NP13: A'lery 3E 27
(not continuous)
Arail Farm Rd. NP13: S Bells . . .3C 34
Arail St. NP13: S Bells 2C 34
Aran Ct. NP44: G'mdw 4B 54
Arcade, The *NP13: A'lery 6G 27*
(off High St.)
NP44: C'brn 6F 55
Arcadia Way NP4: C'avn 3G 37
Archer Rd. NP44: G'mdw 6B 54
Arch Hill NP11: P'waun 5D 60
A.R.D. Bus. Pk. NP4: New I 3F 47
ARGOED 2C 42
Argyle St. NP13: A'lery 6G 27
Armoury Ter. NP23: E Vale 2E 17
Arnold Pl. NP22: Tred 6G 9
Arosfa Ct. NP22: Tred 3H 15
Arran Cl. NP11: Ris 4F 73
Arthur St. NP11: C'fch 1A 70
NP22: A'swg 3F 23
Arundel Cl. NP44: G'mdw 6A 54
Arvonia Ter. NP12: Fleur 3G 49
Ash Ct. *NP12: Oakd 3D 50*
(off Vale Vw. Rd.)
Ashfield Rd. NP11: Newb 2A 52
NP13: A'lery 6G 27
Ashford Cl. NP44: C'iog 4H 55
Ashford Cl. Nth. NP44: C'iog 4H 55
Ashford Cl. Sth. NP44: C'iog 5H 55
Ash Grn. NP44: Oakf 3C 64
Ashgrove CF82: Heng 1E 57
CF83: Tret 1C 76
Ash Gro. NP4: C'avn 4A 38
Ashgrove NP12: B'wood 4B 50
Ash Gro. NP23: E Vale 3F 17
Ashgrove Cl. NP4: Grif 6D 46
Ashleigh Ct. NP44: H'lys 2E 63
Ashman Cl. CF83: Caer 6C 74
Ash Pl. CF81: Barg 5E 41
Ash St. NP23: Cwm 3H 25
ASHVALE 6F 9
Ashvale NP22: Tred 6F 9
Ashvale Ind. Est. NP22: Tred 6F 9
Ashville NP12: Oakd 6D 42
NP22: Tred 4A 16
Ashwood Cl. NP12: B'wood 4B 50
Aspen Av. NP12: B'wood 4B 50
Asquith St. CF82: Tir B 3F 49
NP4: Grif 4E 47
Aster Cl. NP11: Ris 3E 73
Atlee Cl. NP22: Tred 3G 15
NP23: G lydan 1E 11
Atlee Rd. NP12: B'wood 2B 50
Atlee Way NP22: Tred 3G 15
Attlee Av. NP13: A'lery 4E 27
Attlee Ct. CF83: Caer 4H 75
Attlee Rd. NP23: N'glo 6C 12
Aubrey Ter. NP23: Cwm 4H 25
Auckland Cl. NP12: Oakd 1D 50
Augusta Pk. NP23: W lwyd 1F 25
Augusta St. NP23: W lwyd 6F 17
Austin Rd. NP4: Grif 6E 47
Avalon Cl. NP4: P'pool 1B 46
Avalon Ter. *NP22: Tred 6H 9*
(off Dukestown Rd.)
Avenue Cl. CF82: Ystrad 1E 57
Avenue Cres. NP7: A'gvnny 2E 7
Avenue Rd. NP7: A'gvnny 2E 7
Avenue, The CF81: Gilf 6F 41
CF82: Heng, Ystrad 1E 57
CF83: L'brad 4A 68
CF83: Tret 1D 76
NP4: Grif 5E 47
NP4: New I 2F 47
NP4: Var 5D 28
NP7: Gov 4H 5
NP12: Yny 2C 58
Avon Cl. NP12: P'fraith 6A 50
Avon Ct. NP23: Rassa 2D 10
Avondale NP4: B'avn 3F 21
Avondale Cl. NP44: Pnwd 3F 55
Avondale Cres. NP44: Pnwd 2F 55
Avondale Ind. Est.
NP44: Pnwd 3E 55
Avondale Rd. NP4: Grif, Pnwd . . .6F 47
NP44: Pnwd 1F 55
Avondale Way NP44: Pnwd 2F 55
Avon Pl. NP44: Llan 6G 55
Avon Rd. NP4: B'avn 3F 21
Awelfryn Cl. NP23: B'fort 3F 11
Aynho Pl. NP23: E Vale 1E 17
Azalea Rd. NP10: Roger 6F 73

B

Back Rd. NP7: Gilw 3D 4
Badgers Mdw. NP18: P'hir 4H 65
Badgers Mede NP44: G'mdw 6B 54
Badham Cl. CF83: Caer 6C 74
Badminton Gro.
NP23: E Vale 4D 10
Bagley Ct. NP44: G'mdw 4B 54
Bailey Ct. NP7: A'gvnny 3G 7
Bailey Cres. NP4: Var 5D 28
Bailey St NP23: B mawr 3A 12
Baileys Ter. *NP4: P'nydd 5E 37*
(off Hanbury Rd.)
Bailey St. CF81: Deri 4A 30
NP4: Var 5D 28
NP23: Cwm 3A 26
Baillie Smith Av.
NP11: Crum 5C 44
Baker St. NP7: A'gvnny 4F 7
Balance Rd. NP4: Var 4D 28
Baldwin St. CF81: Barg 3E 41
Balmond Ter. NP4: P'pool 5G 37
Baltic Ter. NP44: Oakf 4B 64
Banalog Ter. NP12: Holly B 3H 31
Bangor Rd. NP23: B'fort 3F 11
Bank Cres. NP7: Gilw 2C 4
Bank La. NP22: Tred 2H 15
Banna Bungs. NP23: N'glo 5B 12
Banwell Ct. NP44: G'mdw 4B 54
Baptist Pl. NP23: B'fort 3E 11
Barce Av. NP13: A'lery 4E 27
BARGOD 3E 41
BARGOED 3E 41
Bargoed Station (Rail) 2F 41
Bargoed Ter. CF81: Deri 3A 30
Barker Av. NP13: A'lery 5F 27
Barkley St. NP22: A'swg 3F 23
Barley Fld. Rd.
NP23: B mawr, N'glo 4B 12
Barn Cl. NP4: C'avn 3G 37
Barnes Cl. NP23: Rassa 3B 10
Barnets NP44: G'mdw 6B 54
Barnfield Pl. NP44: Pnwd 3C 54
Barnfield Ter. NP4: B'avn 3E 21
Barry Cl. CF82: P'heol 2D 48
Bartlett St. CF83: Caer 5G 75
Bartlett St. Ind. Est.
CF83: Caer 5G 75
Basildene Cl. NP7: Gilw 3E 5
Bath Grn. NP44: Llanf 1E 65
Bath La. NP23: B mawr 3H 11
Bath Row NP7: Cly 6A 4
(Hileys Row)
NP7: Cly 6A 4
(Station Rd.)
Bay Tree La. NP7: A'gvnny 4H 7
Beacon Vw. NP23: N'glo 6C 12
Beatty St. CF82: Tir B 3F 49
Beauchamp Cl. NP7: A'gvnny 6G 7
BEAUFORT 3F 11
Beaufort Cl. NP44: F'wtr 2H 63
Beaufort Theatre 3E 11
BEAUFORT HILL 3G 11
Beaufort Hill NP23: B'fort 3E 11
Beaufort Ri. NP23: B'fort 3D 10
Beaufort Rd. NP22: Tred 1H 15
NP23: E Vale 6E 11
NP23: E Vale 6A 10

Beaufort St. NP23: B mawr 3B 12
Beaufort Ter. NP23: B'fort 4E 11
Beaumaris Dr. NP44: Llan 1D 64
Beaumaris Way
NP12: B'wood 6A 42
Beaumont Cl. NP23: N'glo 1C 18
Beaupreau Pl. NP7: A'gvnny 4G 7
Beddick NP44: G'mdw 6A 54
Bedford Cl. NP44: G'mdw 6A 54
Bedlwyn Rd. NP24: New T 2D 30
BEDWAS 1B 76
Bedwas Bus. Cen.
CF83: B'ws 1A 76
Bedwas Cen. CF83: B'ws 1B 76
Bedwas Ho. Ind. Est.
CF83: B'ws 1H 75
(not continuous)
Bedwas Rd. CF83: Caer 4G 75
(not continuous)
BEDWELLTE 2A 42
BEDWELLTY 2A 42
Bedwellty Rd. CF81: A'goed 2F 41
NP12: Cefn F 6H 41
NP12: Mark 3E 31
NP24: New T 3E 31
Bedwellty Stadium 1A 42
Bedwlwyn Cl. CF82: Heng 1E 57
Bedwlwyn St. CF82: Ystrad 2E 57
Bedwlwynx Rd. CF82: Ystrad 2E 57
Beech Av. NP12: P'fraith 5B 50
Beech Cl. CF83: Caer 6C 74
NP44: Pnwd 3D 54
Beech Ct. CF81: Barg 5D 40
Beechcroft NP12: P'fraith 6B 50
Beech Dr. CF82: Heng 6E 49
Beech Emb. CF82: Ystrad 1E 57
Beecher Ter. NP11: C'keys 6D 60
Beeches Rd. NP4: C'avn 3F 37
Beeches, The NP4: C'avn 2F 37
NP44: C'brn 1A 64
Beechfield Av. CF82: Heng 6F 49
Beechfield Cl. NP23: G lydan . . .1E 11
Beechgrove CF83: Caer 2H 75
Beech Gro. NP7: L'fst 6D 6
NP12: Oakd 5E 43
NP23: W lwyd 1F 25
Beechleigh Cl.
NP44: G'mdw 6A 54
Beech Rd. NP4: Grif 6D 46
Beech Ter. NP11: C'crn 2B 60
Beech Trees Ter.
NP4: P'nydd 5E 37
Beechwood Av. NP11: W'vle 1E 71
Beechwood Cl. NP11: Newb 3H 51
Beechwood Wlk. NP4: C'avn 3G 37
Beili Glas Rd. NP12: Fleur 4G 49
Beili Priory NP7: A'gvnny 4G 7
Belgrave Cl. NP7: A'gvnny 3E 7
Belgrave Ct. NP4: P'nydd 4F 37
Belgrave Rd. NP7: A'gvnny 3D 6
Belle Vw. Ct. NP4: P'nydd 4F 37
Bellevue NP23: E Vale 5E 17
Bellevue Cl. NP44: C'brn 1B 64
Bellevue Rd. NP44: C'brn 2B 64
Bellevue Ter. NP44: H'lys 2D 62
Bell La. NP4: Abers 2E 37
Bell Vue Cl. NP4: C'avn 4F 37
Belmont Cl. NP7: A'gvnny 5G 7
Belmont Cres. NP7: A'gvnny 5G 7
Belmont Rd. NP7: A'gvnny 5G 7
Belvedere Cl. NP11: Pent C 1A 44
Belvedere Ter. NP11: Ris 2C 72
Benedict Ct. NP7: A'gvnny 4G 7
Bengi La. NP12: Oakd 5E 43
Benjamin Ct. NP22: Rhym 1D 22
Bennetts Ter. CF83: Caer 3H 75
Bennett St. NP13: Blai 5D 18
Berea Cl. NP13: Blai, N'glo 2C 18
Berkeley Ct. NP44: G'mdw 4B 54
Berkeley Cres. NP4: Grif 1E 55
BERLLAN-GOLLEN 5G 77
Berllangron Cotts.
NP12: B'wood 1C 50
Berllanlwyd Av. NP12: Mark 6B 32
Berllanlwyd St. CF82: P'heol 1D 48
Bernard St. NP11: C'crn 4D 60
Berthin NP44: G'mdw 6B 54
Berthin Rd. NP4: Lit M 3G 39
Bethany Cl. CF82: Ystrad 2D 56
Bethcar St. NP23: E Vale 1E 17
Bethel Av. NP22: Tred 3A 16
Bethel Ct. NP4: Var 5D 28
Bethel La. NP4: B'avn 2F 21
NP44: Up Cwm 3B 54
Bethlehem Sq. *NP4: B'avn 3F 21*
(off Broad St.)
Betwyns *NP44: F'wtr 2H 63*
(off Henllys Way)
Beufort Cl. NP22: Tred 6A 10
Beulah Pl. NP23: E Vale 1E 17
Beulah St. NP22: Rhym 6C 14
Bevan Av. NP22: Tred 6F 9
Bevan Cl. CF83: Tret 1C 76
Bevan Cres. NP12: B'wood 1A 50
NP23: E Vale 4D 10
Bevan Ri. CF83: Tret 1C 76
Bevans' La. NP44: Pnwd 1D 54
Beynon St. NP11: Newb 3A 52
Bighams Row NP4: P'pool 3B 46
Big La. NP23: B'fort 2G 11
Big Pit, National Mining Mus.
of Wales 3C 20
Bill Harry Ct. NP22: Tred 1G 15
Birch Cres. CF82: Cefn H 5E 49
Birches, The NP44: Pnwd 4C 54
Birch Gro. CF83: Caer 2H 75
Birchgrove CF83: Tret 1C 76
NP10: Roger 6H 73
Birch Gro. NP11: Ris 3D 72
NP23: B mawr 2A 12
Birchgrove NP24: New T 1C 30
Birch Gro. NP44: H'lys 3F 63
Birchwood Cl. NP12: B'wood 4B 50
Birchwood Gdns. CF83: B'ws 1A 76
Birds Ind. Est. NP11: Ris 5D 72
Bishop Cres. NP7: A'gvnny 2G 7
Bishop's Pl. NP23: E Vale 1E 17
Bishop St. NP13: A'lery 6H 27
Blackbirds Cl. NP44: Oakf 6D 64
Black Bri. La. NP4: P'nydd 4E 37
Black Path NP4: Tal 6D 28
BLACKROCK 1F 13
Blackvein Rd.
NP11: C'keys, Ris 3H 71
BLACKWOOD 2B 50
Blackwood Little Theatre 2B 50
Blackwood Rd. NP12: P'fraith . . .4C 50
Blackwood Shop. Mall
NP12: B'wood 2B 50
Blaen-Afon Rd.
NP23: B mawr 3B 12
Blaenant Ind.Est.
NP23: B mawr 4C 12
BLAENAU GWENT 5F 27
Blaenau Gwent Rows
NP13: A'lery 5F 27
BLAENAVON 3F 21
BLAENAVON HOSPITAL 2E 21
Blaenavon Ironworks 2E 21
Blaenavon Recreation Cen. 3G 21
Blaenavon Workmens Hall 3F 21
Blaen-Blodau St.
NP11: Newb 3A 52
Blaen Cendl NP23: B'fort 3E 11
Blaen-Cyffin Rd. NP13: L'hth 1C 44
Blaendare Rd.
NP4: P'pool, Up R 3B 46
(not continuous)
Blaen Ifor CF83: Caer 1D 74
Blaen-Nant Rd. NP23: N'glo 5B 12
Blaen Wern NP23: E Vale 1C 16
Blaenwern NP44: Pnwd 3F 55
Blaen-y-Cwm *CF81: A'goed 2F 41*
(off Mt. Pleasant St.)
Blaen-y-Cwm Rd. NP4: P'seg 6F 35
Blaen-y-Cwm Vw.
NP44: H'lys 2E 63
BLAINA 4D 18
BLAINA & DISTRICT HOSPITAL
. . . . .1C 18
Blaina Rd. NP23: B mawr 3B 12
Blania Rd. NP13: A'lery 2D 26
Blenheim Ct. NP44: G'mdw 1H 63
Blenheim Rd. NP13: S Bells 2D 34
NP44: G'mdw 1H 63
Blenheim Sq. Shops
NP44: G'mdw 1H 63
Blodwen Rd. NP4: New I 3G 47
Blodwen Way NP4: New I 3G 47
Bloomfield Rd
NP12: B'wood 2A 50
Blorenge Rd. NP7: A'gvnny 3F 7
Blorenge Ter. NP4: B'avn 2G 21
NP7: L'fst 6E 7
Bluebell Ct. NP44: F'wtr 1E 63
Bluebell Way NP10: Roger 6G 73
Blue Boar NP4: Tal 1D 36
Bluett's Rd. NP4: Tal 6D 28
(not continuous)
Blythe St. NP13: A'lery 6G 27
Board St. CF81: P'tyn 2C 22
Bont Cl. NP12: Peng 2G 49
Booth's La.
NP4: Abers, P'nydd 4D 36
Boot La. NP4: B'avn 3F 21
Boot, The CF82: Maes C 2F 57
Borfa Pl. NP12: Cefn F 2H 49
Borough Theatre, The 4F 7
Boundary St. NP23: B mawr 3A 12
Bournville Rd. NP13: Blai 1D 26
Bournville Ter. NP22: Tred 2G 15
Bovil Cl. CF83: Mac 6F 71
Bowen Cl. NP4: B'avn 2F 21
Bowen Ind. Est. CF81: A'goed . . .5H 41
Bowleaze NP44: G'mdw 6B 54
Bowls Cl. CF83: Caer 2C 74
Bowls La. CF83: Caer 6G 67
(not continuous)
Bowls Ter. CF83: Caer 2D 74
Brachty Pl. NP11: C'maen 5G 43
Bradford St. CF83: Caer 5F 75
Bramblewood Ct. NP12: Peng . . .2G 49
Brangwyn Av. NP44: Oakf 3C 64
Brangwyn Rd. NP22: Tred 4G 15
Brechfa Cl. NP18: P'hir 4H 65
Brecon Beacons National Pk.
NP7 . . . . .5C 4
NP23 . . . . .1D 12
NP4 . . . . .1B 38
Brecon Heights
NP23: W lwyd 1F 25
Brecon Pk. Cotts. NP7: L Hill 2H 13
Brecon Rd.
NP7: A'gvnny, L'narth 2C 6
Brecon Ter. CF81: Deri 5A 30
Brecon Wlk. NP44: C'brn 6E 55
Bredon Cl. NP11: Ris 4F 73
Brendon Ct. CF83: Caer 5H 75
Brentwood Pl. NP23: E Vale 6D 10
Brett Rd. NP11: Aberc 6C 52
Brewer St. CF81: P'tyn 3C 22
Brewery Ct. NP13: A'beeg 5B 34
Briar Cl. NP23: Rassa 2D 10
Briardene NP7: L'fst 6E 7
Bridgefield St. CF83: Abert 5D 66
Bridge St.
CF81: A'goed, Barg 2F 41
NP4: Grif 4E 47
NP11: Aberc 6B 52
(not continuous)
NP11: Newb 3B 52
NP11: Ris 3C 72
NP11: Yny 5C 58
NP12: B'wood, Oakd 3C 50
NP13: A'lery 6F 27
NP13: S Bells 2D 34
NP22: Tred 3H 15
NP23: E Vale 6E 11
Bridge St. Ind. Est.
NP22: Tred 3H 15
Bridge Ter. NP11: Newb 3B 52
Bridge Vw. NP11: C'fch 1A 70
Brierley Cl. NP11: Ris 4F 73
Brierly Pl. NP11: C'crn 3C 60
Briers Ga. NP44: H'lys 3D 62
Briery Hill NP23: E Vale 3E 17
Brigham Ct. CF83: Caer 3B 74
Bright St. NP11: C'keys 1H 71
Brisbane Ct. NP12: Cefn F 3H 49
Bristol Ter. CF81: Barg 2E 41
NP24: Brith 4F 31
Bristol Vw. Cl. NP44: G'mdw 5A 54
Britannia Cen. For Ent.
NP12: Peng 6G 41
Britannia Ter. NP12: Peng 6G 41
Britannia Wlk. NP12: Peng 5G 41
BRITHDIR 4F 31
Brithdir Station (Rail) 5F 31
BRITISH 1B 36
British Rd. NP4: Tal 1B 36
British School Cl.
NP4: Abers, Tal 1D 36
Brittania Cl. NP11: Ris 4D 72
Broadmead NP7: Gilw 3D 4
NP12: P'fraith 5A 50
Broad St. NP4: Abers 2E 37
NP4: B'avn 3F 21
NP4: Grif 4E 47
Broad Vw. NP44: Pnwd 4C 54
Broadway NP4: P'pool 6G 37
Broadweir Rd. NP44: C'brn 1B 64
Brompton Pl. NP22: Tred 6B 16
Bronawelon NP11: Crum 5C 44
Bronhafod NP23: B mawr 2B 12
Bron Las CF82: P'heol 2E 49
Bronllys Pl. NP44: C'iog 4G 55
Bronmynydd CF83: Abert 1A 74
Bron Rhiw CF83: Mac 6E 71
Bronrhiw Av. CF83: Caer 6G 75
Bronrhiw Fach CF83: Caer 6G 75
Bronwydd NP12: Oakd 5D 42
Bron-y-De NP23: E Vale 2D 16
Bron-y-Garth CF82: P'heol 2D 48
Brookfield Av. NP22: Rhym 1D 22
Brookfield Rd.
NP12: P'fraith 5D 50
Brookland Ho. NP44: Pnwd 4E 55
Brookland Rd. NP11: Ris 4D 72
Brooklands NP11: C'crn 4D 60
Brooklands Cl. CF82: Maes C 1G 57
Brooklands Ter. NP11: C'crn 4D 60
Brookland Ter. NP44: Pnwd 3E 55
Brookland Vw. NP24: New T 2E 31
Brook La. NP12: P'fraith 5D 50
Brooklyn Ter. NP13: L'hth 1C 44
Brook Pl. NP23: Cwm 4H 25
Brook Row CF81: Foch 4A 22
Brookside NP4: B'avn 3G 21
NP44: G'mdw 1H 63
Brookside Cl. CF83: Caer 3C 74
Brookside Cres. CF83: Caer 4H 75
Brookside Row NP13: C'lery 3G 27
Brook St. CF83: Abert 5D 66
NP11: Aberc 5C 52
(not continuous)
NP23: B mawr 3A 12
NP44: Pnwd 2E 55
Broom Cl. NP10: Roger 6H 73
Broome Path NP44: G'mdw 1H 63
Broomfield St. CF83: Caer 5G 75
Bro-y-Fan CF83: Caer 2H 75
Brunant Cotts. NP13: A'beeg 6A 34
Brunant Rd. NP7: Cly, Gilw 6A 4
Brunel Cl. CF82: P'heol 2D 48
Brunel Rd. NP44: F'wtr 1F 63
Brutes Row NP4: B'avn 3E 21
BRYN 6A 50
Bryn Aber CF83: Abert 4D 66
Bryn Aber Ter. CF83: Abert 5D 66
Bryn Amlwg CF82: Cefn H 6E 49
BRYNAU 4H 75
Brynau Rd. CF83: Caer 4G 75
Brynavon NP4: B'avn 3F 21
Brynavon Ter. CF82: Heng 6F 49
BRYNAWEL 2C 70
Bryn Awel CF82: Cefn H 5F 49
CF83: B'ws 1C 76
Brynawel CF83: Caer 1C 74
Bryn Awelon CF82: P'heol 2D 48
NP23: B'fort 3E 11
(not continuous)
Brynawelon NP23: N'glo 5A 12
Brynawel St. NP23: B mawr 2A 12
Brynawel Ter. NP13: B'thel 6B 34
Brynbach St. NP22: Tred 6F 9
Bryn Brithdir NP12: Oakd 4F 43
Bryn Canol CF82: Cefn H 4D 48
CF83: B'ws 1B 76
Bryn Carno NP22: Rhym 3B 14
Bryncelyn NP13: Blai 3D 18
Bryncelyn Pl. NP44: Pnwd 4D 54
Bryn Celyn Rd. NP44: Pnwd 4C 54
Bryn Cl. CF83: Tret 1C 76
BRYN COCH 2D 10
Bryncoed Ter. CF82: P'heol 1D 48
CF83: Abert 5D 66
Bryn Cr NP12: Mark 6B 32
Bryn Cres. NP13: B'thel 6B 34
Bryn Deri Drysiog St.
NP23: E Vale 1D 16
Bryn-Deri Ter. NP11: Newb 2A 52
Bryn Derw NP12: B'wood 3A 50
Bryn-Dolwen CF83: B'ws 6F 69
Bryn Ebbw NP23: E Vale 4E 11
Bryn Eglwys NP44: C'iog 4G 55
Bryn Eglwys Ct. *NP23: E Vale 3E 17*
(off Commercial St.)
Brynfedw CF83: B'ws 6F 69
Bryn-Gaer Ter. NP13: B'thel 6B 34
Bryn-Garreg NP4: Var 6E 29
Bryn Garw NP44: C'iog 4G 55
Bryngelli Ter. CF83: Abert 5D 66
Bryngas CF81: P'tyn 3B 22
Bryn Glas CF82: Heng 1E 57
CF83: B'ws 6F 69
Brynglas CF83: Caer 1D 74
NP7: Gilw 3D 4
Bryn Glas NP23: E Vale 4D 10
Brynglas NP44: F'wtr 3H 63
Brynglas Av. NP12: P'fraith 5C 50
Brynglas Cl. NP7: Gilw 3D 4
Brynglas Tunnels & Malpas Rd.
Relief Rd. NP20: Oakf 6D 64
Bryn Golau CF82: Cefn H 5F 49

Bryn Goleu CF83: B'ws 6F 69
Bryngoleu CF83: Rud 4E 77
Bryngoleu St. NP12: Cefn F 2H 49
Bryngoleu Ter.
NP12: P'fraith 5C 50
Bryn Gomer NP44: C'iog 3G 55
Bryng-Wennol CF83: L'brad 6F 57
BRYNGWYN 6F 75
Bryngwyn CF83: Caer 6E 75
Bryngwyn Cotts. NP11: Newb . . .3H 51
Bryngwyn Rd. NP4: P'pool 1B 46
NP11: Newb 3H 51
Bryn-Gwyn Rd. NP13: S Bells . . .1D 34
Bryngwyn Rd. NP23: B'fort 3E 11
Bryn-Gwyn St. CF83: B'ws 6E 69
Bryngwyn St. NP12: Fleur 4G 49
(not continuous)
Brynhafod Rd. CF83: Abert 5D 66
Bryn Heol CF83: B'ws 1B 76
Bryn Heulog CF83: Caer 2D 74
NP4: Grif, P'pool 3D 46
Brynheulog NP13: B'thel 6B 34
NP13: Blai 4D 18
Brynheulog Rd. NP11: Newb 2A 52
Brynheulog St. CF82: G'gaer 4C 48
NP23: E Vale 1D 16
Bryn Heulog Ter. CF83: Mac 5E 71
Brynhoward Ter. NP12: Oakd 5E 43
Brynhyfrd NP22: Rhym 1D 22
Brynhyfryd CF81: P'tyn 2B 22
CF83: B'ws 6E 69
CF83: Caer 2D 74
NP13: B'thel 6C 34
NP44: C'iog 3G 55
Brynhyfryd Av. NP23: N'glo 6C 12
Brynhyfryd Cl. NP4: Lit M 3G 39
Brynhyfryd Ind. Est.
CF83: Caer 3E 75
Brynhyfryd St. NP12: P'fraith 5C 50
Brynhyfryd Ter CF82: P'heol 1D 48
Brynhyfryd Ter. CF83: Mac 6E 71
NP4: Abers 3E 37
Bryn-Hyfryd Ter. NP11: Ris 3C 72
Brynhyfryd Ter. NP23: N'glo 6B 12
NP23: W Iwyd 1G 25
Bryn Ifor CF83: Caer 2C 74
Brynithel NP13: B'thel 6C 34
Bryn-Ithel Ter. NP13: B'thel 6B 34
Bryn Kendall NP23: B'fort 4E 11
Bryn La. NP12: P'fraith 6A 50
BRYNMAWR 3A 12
Brynmawr Rd. NP23: E Vale 6F 11
Bryn Meadow Cl. NP22: Tred 6F 9
Bryn Milwr NP44: F'wtr 3H 63
Brynm y Nach Av.
CF82: Ystrad 2C 56
Bryn Nant CF81: Foch 3A 22
CF83: Caer 1C 74
Brynonnen Ct. NP44: H'lys 3E 63
Bryn Owain CF83: Caer 1D 74
Bryn Pica NP22: Tred 6A 10
Bryn-Rhedyn CF83: Caer 3A 76
NP12: B'wood 3A 50
Bryn Rhedyn NP44: Llanf 3E 65
Bryn Rhosyn NP22: Tred 5E 9
Bryn Rd. NP11: Aberc 6C 52
NP12: Cefn F 1A 50
NP12: Mark 5H 31
NP12: P'fraith 6A 50
Bryn Seion St. NP22: Rhym 4A 14
Bryn-Serth Rd. NP23: Rassa 3A 10
Bryn Siriol CF82: P'heol 2D 48
CF83: Caer 2C 74
Bryn Teg CF81: Barg 5E 41
CF82: Cefn H 6F 49
Brynteg CF83: B'ws 6F 69
Bryn Teg CF83: Caer 2D 74
Brynteg NP4: Abers 2E 37
Brynteg Av. NP12: P'fraith 5C 50
Brynteg Cres. NP22: Rhym 6C 14
Brynteg Pl. NP4: Lit M 2H 39
Brynteg Rd. NP13: Blai 5D 18
Brynteg Ter. CF81: Foch 4A 22
NP23: E Vale 1D 16
NP24: New T 3E 31
Bryn Ter. CF82: Heng 6F 49
NP4: B'avn 3G 21
NP4: P'nydd 5E 37
NP13: B'thel 6B 34
(not continuous)
NP23: W Iwyd 6G 17
Bryn, The CF83: Tret 6G 69
NP12: P'fraith 6H 49
Bryntirion CF83: B'ws 6F 69
CF83: Caer 2D 74
Bryn Vw. NP12: P'fraith 6A 50
Brynview Av. CF82: Ystrad 2D 56
Bryn-Welon Cl. NP4: B'avn 3H 21
BRYNWERN 1B 46
Brynwern NP4: P'pool 1B 46
Bryn-y-Fran Av. CF83: Tret 1C 76
Bryn-y-Gwynt NP23: E Vale 1C 16
Bryn-y-Pwll CF81: A'goed 3G 41
Bryn-yr-Ysgol CF83: Caer 1C 74
Bude Ter. NP12: Fleur 3G 49
Buller St. NP4: P'nydd 5D 36
Bungalows, The CF82: Heng 1E 57
Burberry Cl. NP10: Roger 6G 73
Burford St. NP4: B'avn 3F 21
Burnet Dr. CF82: P'heol 3D 48
Burns Cl. CF83: Mac 1F 77
Burns La. NP44: G'mdw 1A 64
Bush Bach NP22: Tred 5F 9
Bush La. NP4: P'pool 1B 46
(not continuous)
Bushy Pk. NP4: P'pool 6F 37
Bute Pl. NP13: A'beeg 1H 43
Bute Ter. NP24: Brith 6F 31
BUTE TOWN 2A 14
Butleigh Ter. *NP22: Tred 6H 9*
(off Carmel St.)
Butler's Ct. NP4: Var 5D 28
Buttercup Cl. NP10: Roger 6G 73
Buttercup Ct. NP44: F'wtr 2E 63
Buttry Ter. *NP12: Fleur 4G 49*
(off Gellihaf Rd.)
Buxton Ct. CF83: Caer 4H 75
Bwich Carnygelli
CF46: Ystrad 5A 56
Bwlch-y-Garn Rd.
NP23: E Vale 6F 11
Byron Pl. NP11: C'maen 6G 43
NP44: G'mdw 1A 64
Byron Rd. CF81: A'goed 4G 41
Bythway Rd. NP4: C'avn 4G 37
Byways NP44: G'mdw 6B 54

C

Caddick's Row NP13: Blai 3D 18
Cader Idris Cl. NP11: Ris 4F 73
Cadoc Rd. NP44: Pnwd 3C 54
Cae Bach CF83: Mac 6D 70
Cae Bedw CF83: Caer 6A 68
Cae-Bryn CF83: Abert 5D 66
Cae Calch CF83: Caer 1D 74
Cae Caradog CF83: Caer 1B 74
Cae Celyn NP11: C'maen 6G 43
Cae Collen NP12: B'wood 3A 50
Cae Croes Heol CF83: Caer 6C 74
Cae Derw NP7: Gilw 3E 5
Cae Derwen NP44: C'brn 2A 64
Cae Du Mawr CF83: Caer 1D 74
Cae Felin St. NP13: L'hth 1B 44
Cae Ffynnon CF82: G'gaer 4C 48
CF83: Caer 1D 74
Cae Gethin CF83: Caer 6H 67
Cae Glas CF81: Foch 3A 22
CF83: Caer 2D 74
NP23: N'glo 1C 18
Cae Gorlan Ct. NP11: Aberc 6B 52
Cae Gorlan St. NP11: Aberc 6B 52
Cae Llwyd CF83: Caer 2G 75
Cae Maen Llwy CF82: Cefn H . . .4D 48
Cae Marchog CF83: Caer 1E 75
Cae Meillion CF83: Caer 6D 74
Cae Meldon NP7: Gilw 2D 4
Cae Melin NP4: Lit M 2H 39
Cae Nant Gledyr CF83: Caer 4C 74
Cae Nant Gogh CF83: Caer 6C 74
Caenant Rd. CF83: Caer 3F 75
Caepalish *NP4: P'nydd 5F 37*
(off Pentrepiod Rd.)
Caepalish Pl. *NP4: P'nydd 5F 37*
(off Pentrepiod Rd.)
Cae Pandy CF83: Caer 2G 75
Cae Pant CF83: Caer 1E 75
Cae Pen y Dre NP7: A'gvnny 4E 7
Cae Pen-y-Dre Cl.
NP7: A'gvnny 4E 7
Cae Pen-y-Graig CF83: Caer 6H 67
Caerbragdy CF83: Caer 4G 75
Caer Bryn NP11: Newb 4G 51
Cae'r Fferm CF83: Caer 4D 74
CAERFFILI 4G 75
Cae Rhedyn NP44: C'iog 5H 55
Cae Rhos CF83: Caer 2G 75
Caerleon Ct. CF83: Caer 3B 74
Caerleon Rd. NP18: P'hir 1E 65
NP44: Llanf 1E 65
Cae'r-llwyn Ter. NP11: Yny 4C 58
Caernarvon Cl. NP44: Llan 6G 55
Caernarvon Ct. CF83: Caer 3C 74
Caernarvon Cres. NP44: Llan . . .6G 55
Caernarvon Pl.
NP12: B'wood 6H 41
Cae Robin NP7: Cly 5G 13
Cae'r-Odyn NP13: Blai 4C 18
CAERPHILLY 4G 75
Caerphilly Bus. Pk.
CF83: Caer 5H 75
Caerphilly By-Pass
CF83: Caer 6C 74
Caerphilly Castle 4G 75
CAERPHILLY DISTRICT MINERS
HOSPITAL 6E 75
Caerphilly Enterprise Cen.
CF83: B'ws 1A 76
Caerphilly Leisure Cen. 3G 75
CAERPHILLY PARC ESTATE 2G 75
Caerphilly Rd. CF15: N'grw 6B 74
(not continuous)
CF82: Ystrad 4E 57
CF83: Sen 3C 66
Caerphilly Station (Rail) 5G 75
Caerphilly Vis. Cen. *5G 75*
(off Castle St.)
Caerwent Rd. NP4: C'avn 4A 38
NP44: C'iog 2F 55
Cae Uwchllyn CF83: Caer 6D 74
Cae-yr-Ebol NP44: Pnwd 4E 55
Cae Ysgubor CF82: Cefn H 4D 48
CF83: Caer 6H 67
Caldicot Cl. NP12: B'wood 6A 42
Caldicot Ct. CF83: Caer 3C 74
Caldicot Way NP44: Pnwd 3F 55
Caledfryn Way CF83: Caer 1C 74
Cambrian St. CF81: Deri 5A 30
NP22: Rhym 4B 14
Cambria St. NP4: Grif 5E 47
Cambridge Gdns.
NP23: B'fort 4E 11
Cam Ct. NP44: G'mdw 4A 54
Camellia Dr. NP10: Roger 6G 73
Camnant CF82: Ystrad 4D 56
Campanula Dr. NP10: Roger 6G 73
Campbell St. NP4: P'pool 6F 37
Campion Cl. NP44: H'lys 3F 63
Camrose Wlk. NP44: G'mdw 1H 63
Canal Cl. NP4: Grif 5E 47
Canal Ter. NP11: Aberc 1B 60
Canberra Cl. NP12: Oakd 1C 50
NP44: C'brn, G'mdw 1A 64
Candwr Pk. NP18: P'hir 4H 65
Canford Cl. NP4: C'avn 3G 37
Canning St. NP23: Cwm 3H 25
Canterbury Rd. NP23: B'fort 4G 11
CANTREF 3E 7
Cantref Rd. NP7: A'gvnny 3E 7
Capel Ct. NP4: P'nydd 4F 37
Capel Newydd Av. NP4: B'avn . . .3G 21
(not continuous)
Capel Newydd Rd.
NP4: B'avn 3G 21
Capel St. CF81: Barg 3F 41
NP4: P'pool 1C 46
Capital Valley Ind. Pk.
NP22: Rhym 1B 22
Caradoc Rd. NP44: C'brn 5E 55
Caradoc St. NP4: Abers 2E 37
NP11: C'crn 3C 60
Cardiff Rd. CF81: Barg 4F 41
CF81: Gilf 2F 49
CF83: Caer 5G 75
NP12: Peng 2F 49
Cardigan Cl. NP44: C'iog 3F 55
Cardigan Cres. NP44: C'iog 3F 55
Cardigan Way NP12: B'wood 6A 42
Cardoc Wlk. NP4: B'avn 2G 21
Carfax Path NP44: F'wtr 2G 63
Carlin Rd. NP23: N'glo 1C 18
Carlton Ct. NP4: P'nydd 4F 37
Carlton Dr. NP11: Crum 4G 43
Carlton Pl. NP11: C'keys 6D 60
Carlton Ter. NP11: C'keys 6D 60
Carlyle St. NP13: A'lery 6F 27
Carlyon Rd. NP11: Newb 1C 52
Carmarthen Ct. CF83: Caer 3C 74
Carmel Cl. NP23: G lydan 2D 10
Carmel St. NP13: A'lery 6G 27
NP22: Tred 6H 9
CARMELTOWN 3E 11
Carne St. NP23: Cwm 3H 25
Carno Cl. NP23: G lydan 2D 10
Carno St. NP22: Rhym 4A 14
Caroline Rd. NP4: New I 3G 47
Caroline Way NP4: New I 3G 47
Carter Pl. NP12: B'wood 3B 50
Cart Rd. NP23: N'glo 6A 12
Casaba Ter. NP7: L'fst 6D 6
Castell Meredith CF83: Caer 2H 75
Castell Morgraig CF83: Caer 2H 75
Castell-y-Bwch NP44: H'lys 6F 63
Castell-y-Fan CF83: Caer 2H 75
Castle Av. CF83: Caer 2F 75
Castle Cl. NP11: P'waun 5D 60
Castle Ct. NP11: P'waun 5C 60
NP44: H'lys 3E 63
Castle Ct. Shop. Cen.
CF83: Caer 4G 75
Castle Flds. NP22: Rhym 5B 14
Castle Hill CF82: G'gaer 3C 48
Castle La. NP11: P'waun 5C 60
Castlellwyd CF82: Ystrad 4E 57
Castle Mdws. Pk.
NP7: A'gvnny 4E 7
CASTLE PARK 4G 75
Castle St. NP4: B'avn 2F 21
NP7: A'gvnny 4F 7
NP12: Fleur 4G 49
NP13: A'lery 6G 27
NP22: Tred 3H 15
Castle Vw. CF83: Caer 1E 75
Castle Walks NP7: A'gvnny 5F 7
Castle Wood Rd. NP4: Tal 6C 28
Catholic Rd. NP23: B mawr 3B 12
Cat's La. CF83: B'ws 6F 69
Cedar Cl. NP12: P'fraith 6A 50
NP23: Rassa 2D 10
Cedar Rd. NP11: Pent C 2A 44
Cedars, The NP7: L'fst 6D 6
Cedar Wlk. NP44: Up Cwm 4B 54
Cedar Way CF82: Ystrad 3D 56
Cedar Wood Cl.
NP10: Roger 6G 73
Cedar Wood Dr.
NP10: Roger 6G 73
Cefn Cl. NP44: C'iog 3G 55
Cefn Ct. NP11: Newb 1C 52
NP12: B'wood 2B 50
(off Oak St.)
Cefn Cres. NP13: C'lery 5G 27
CEFN-CRIB 4F 45
Cefn Crib Rd. NP4: P'seg 4E 45
NP11: Crum, P'seg 4E 45
CEFN FFOREST 1H 49
Cefn-Fforest Av. NP12: Cefn F . . .2H 49
(not continuous)
Cefn Fforest Sports Cen. 2H 49
Cefn Glas NP22: Tred 1G 15
CEFN GOLAU 4G 15
CEFN HENGOED 4E 49
Cefn Ilan CF83: Abert 6C 66
Cefn Llwynau St.
CF82: G'gaer 5B 48
Cefn Milwr NP44: F'wtr 3A 64
Cefn Parc NP22: Tred 4H 15
Cefn Rhos NP22: Tred 3G 15
Cefn-Rhychdir Rd
NP24: New T 1D 30
Cefn Rd. CF81: Deri 5A 30
CF82: Heng 6F 49
NP10: Roger 6H 73
NP12: B'wood 1A 50
Cefn-y-Lon CF83: Caer 1C 74
Cefn Y Mynydd
NP24: New T 2C 30
Ceiriog Dr. CF83: Caer 3F 75
Celandine Ct. NP44: F'wtr 1E 63
Celtic Way CF83: B'ws 1B 76
Celyn Av. CF83: Caer 3F 75
Celyn Ct. NP44: Pnwd 3C 54
Celynen Rd. NP11: Aberc 5B 52
Celyn Gro. CF83: Caer 3F 75
Cemaes Rd. NP11: C'maen 5G 43
Cemetery Rd. NP11: Aberc 6C 52
NP13: A'beeg, S Bells 5B 34
NP23: B mawr 3A 12
NP23: Cwm, W lwyd 2G 25
NP23: E Vale 5D 10
Cendl Cres. NP23: Rassa 3D 10
Cendl Ter. NP23: Cwm 3A 26
Cenotaph La. NP4: B'avn 3F 21
Central Av. NP4: P'pool 4E 39
NP11: Newb 3B 52
NP12: Cefn F 1H 49
NP12: Oakd 6D 42
NP12: Oakd 6D 42
Central Bldgs. *CF83: Tret 1D 76*
(off Newport Rd.)
Central Dr. NP4: C'avn 3G 37
Central M. NP4: P'pool 1C 46

Central St. CF82: Ystrad .2D 56
CF83: Caer, L'brad .6A 68
Central Way NP44: Pnwd .4C 54
Cenydd Ter. CF83: Sen .2B 66
Ceredig Ct. NP44: Llan .1E 65
Chain Cl. NP7: A'gvnny .2E 7
Chain Rd. NP7: A'gvnny .2E 7
Chandlers Rd. NP23: B'fort .3F 11
Channel Vw. NP4: P'pool .5A 38
NP11: Ris .4E 73
NP44: Pnwd .4C 54
Channel View Ct. NP11: Ris .4E 73
Chapel Cl. NP4: Var .5D 28
NP12: P'fraith .4D 50
Chapel Ct. CF83: Tret .6H 69
Chapel Farm Ind. Est.
NP11: C'crn .3C 60
Chapel Farm Ter. NP11: C'crn .3C 60
Chapel La. NP7: A'gvnny .2E 7
NP44: C'iog, Pnwd .2F 55
Chapel Orchard NP7: A'gvnny .2E 7
Chapel Rd. NP4: P'nydd .5E 37
NP7: A'gvnny .2E 7
NP13: Blai .4C 18
NP13: S Bells .2D 34
NP23: N'glo .4B 12
NP24: New T .6E 23
Chapel St. CF81: A'goed .2F 41
CF81: Deri .5A 30
CF81: P'tyn .2C 22
NP11: Aberc .5D 52
NP13: A'lery .6G 27
NP23: B mawr .3A 12
NP24: New T .2D 30
NP44: Pnwd .5E 55
Chapel Ter. CF82: Cefn H .6E 49
NP4: P'nydd .5F 37
Chapel Vw. NP11: C'fch .2A 70
Charles Cl. NP7: A'gvnny .1G 7
Charles Ct. *NP23: E Vale .6C 10*
(off Elizabeth Way)
Charles Cres. NP7: A'gvnny .1G 7
Charles Edwards Cl. NP7: L'fst .6E 7
Charles St. CF83: Caer .4G 75
NP4: B'avn .3G 21
NP4: Grif .4E 47
NP11: Pent C .1H 43
NP22: A'swg .3F 23
NP22: Tred .6G 9
NP24: Brith .5F 31
NP44: Pnwd .3E 55
CHARLESVILLE .4E 37
Charlesville NP4: P'nydd .5F 37
Charston NP44: G'mdw .6B 54
Chartist Ct. NP11: Ris .4E 73
Chartist Way NP12: B'wood .2A 50
NP22: Tred .6H 9
CHATHAM .6F 71
Chatham CF83: Mac .6F 71
Chatham Pl. *CF83: Mac .6G 71*
(off Chatham St.)
Chatham St. CF83: Mac .6G 71
Chave Ter. *CF82: Maes C .1G 57*
(off North Av.)
CHELTENHAM .1H 13
Chepstow Cl.
NP12: B'wood .6A 42
NP44: C'iog .3G 55
Chepstow Ct. CF83: Caer .3C 74
Chepstow Ri. NP44: C'iog .3G 55
Cheriton Av. CF82: Cefn H .4E 49
Cheriton Path NP44: F'wtr .1G 63
Cherry Cl. NP23: E Vale .5E 11
Cherry Gro. NP11: C'maen .6G 43
Cherry Tree Cl. CF83: B'ws .6D 68
NP44: C'iog .4H 55
Cherry Tree Rd.
NP12: P'fraith .6A 50
Cherry Trees NP12: Mark .6A 32
Chester Cl. NP4: New I .2H 47
Chester Ct. CF83: Caer .2C 74
Chestnut Cl. CF83: Mac .6F 71
NP4: New I .2H 47
NP23: Rassa .2D 10
Chestnut Ct. NP7: A'gvnny .3H 7
Chestnut Dr. NP7: A'gvnny .4H 7
Chestnut Gro. NP12: P'fraith .6B 50
NP44: Up Cwm .4B 54
Cheviot Cl. NP11: Ris .3F 73
Chiltern Cl. NP11: Ris .4G 73
Christchurch Rd.
NP12: Oakd .1C 50
Church Av. NP4: C'avn .4H 37
Church Cl. NP4: C'avn .4H 37
NP4: New I .5G 47
NP44: C'iog .4G 55
Church Ct. NP22: Tred .2H 15
Church Cres. NP23: E Vale .3E 17
Churchfield Cl. CF82: Tir B .3E 49
CHURCHILL PARK .2F 75
Church La.
NP4: C'avn, P'nydd .5G 37
NP4: New I .4H 47
NP7: Gov .5G 5
NP7: L'fst .6D 6
NP13: C'lery .2G 27
NP23: B mawr .2B 12
Church Mdw. CF82: P'heol .2C 48
Church Pl. CF81: Barg .3F 41
Church Rd. CF82: G'gaer .2B 48
CF83: Abert .6C 66
NP4: Abers, Tal .1D 36
NP4: B'avn .3E 21
NP7: Gov .5H 5
NP11: Newb .2A 52
NP11: Ris .2C 72
NP13: A'beeg .5B 34
NP44: Llanf .3G 65
NP44: Pnwd .4D 54
Church Rd. Ter. NP11: Ris .2C 72
Church Row NP4: Tal .1D 36
Church St. CF81: A'goed .3G 41
CF81: Barg .3E 41
CF81: P'tyn .2C 22
CF82: Ystrad .2D 56
CF83: B'ws .1B 76
CF83: L'brad .4A 68
CF83: Mac .6F 71
NP13: A'lery .6G 27
NP13: Blai .4D 18
NP22: Rhym .4B 14
NP23: E Vale .2E 17
Church Ter. NP4: P'nydd .4F 37
NP24: New T .2D 30
Church Vw. NP12: Oakd .3D 50
NP23: B'fort .4E 11
Churchwood Cl. NP4: P'pool .6H 37
Chu. Wood Rd. NP44: Pnwd .4D 54
Cibi Wlk. NP7: A'gvnny .4F 7
Cilgerran Ct. NP44: Llan .6H 55
Cilgerran Way NP12: B'wood .6B 42
Circle, The NP12: P'fraith .6B 50
NP22: Tred .3H 15
NP44: C'brn .2A 64
Citadel Cl. *NP22: Tred .2G 15*
(off Earl St.)
Claerwen CF82: G'gaer .3B 48
Clairwain NP4: New I .4G 47
Clapham Ter. NP4: B'avn .4E 21
Clare Drew Way NP44: C'iog .4H 55
Claremont Rd. NP11: Newb .1C 52
Clarence Cnr. NP4: P'pool .1C 46
Clarence Pl. NP4: P'pool .2C 46
NP11: Ris .3C 72
Clarence Rd. NP4: P'pool .2C 46
Clarence St NP23: B mawr .3B 12
Clarence St. NP4: P'pool .1C 46
NP13: A'lery .5H 27
Clark Av. NP44: Pnwd .3D 54
Claude Rd. CF83: Caer .5F 75
Cleaves Ter. NP4: Abers .2E 37
Cleveland Dr. NP11: Ris .4F 73
Cliff Rd. NP12: B'wood .2C 50
Clifton Rd. NP7: A'gvnny .3H 7
Clifton Sq. NP4: Grif .4E 47
Clifton St. CF83: Caer .5G 75
NP10: Roger .5G 73
Clifton Ter. *NP4: B'avn .2F 21*
(off Maxworthy Rd.)
Clive St. CF83: Caer .5F 75
CF83: Sen .3C 66
Clomendy Rd. NP44: C'brn .1B 64
(Cwmbran)
NP44: C'brn .5C 54
(Forge Hammer)
Clos Afon Tywi NP12: Cefn F .3H 49
Clos Bryn Celyn
CF82: Ystrad .6D 48
Clos Bury Capel
NP7: A'gvnny .3H 7
Clos Cae Mawr CF82: P'heol .3E 49
Clos Cae Rhos CF82: P'heol .3E 49
Clos Cae'r Wern CF83: Caer .6D 74
Clos Carolyn NP12: Cefn F .3H 49
Clos Ceirw NP12: Cefn F .3H 49
Clos Claerwen NP12: Cefn F .3H 49
Clos Coed Duon
NP12: B'wood .3A 50
Clos Cwm Garw CF83: Caer .4C 74
Clos Cyncoed CF83: Caer .1C 74
Clos Durand NP7: A'gvnny .3H 7
Clos Dwyerw CF83: Caer .6D 74
Clos Enfys CF83: Caer .6D 74
Close, The CF81: Gilf .6F 41
CF82: Cefn H .5E 49
NP44: Oakf .3C 64
Closeways NP11: Newb .2C 52
Clos Golwyg yr Hafod
NP23: B mawr .3C 12
Clos Graddfa CF82: Ystrad .4D 56
Clos Gronw NP12: Cefn F .3H 49
Clos Guto CF83: Caer .3A 76
Clos Gwastir CF83: Caer .6D 74
Clos Gwaun Gledyr
CF83: Caer .4C 74
Clos Gwendraeth
NP12: Cefn F .3H 49
Clos Gwernydd CF83: Caer .3C 74
Clos Gwynle CF83: Caer .6C 74
Clos Llwyn y Pwll
NP23: B mawr .3C 12
Clos Llyswen CF82: P'heol .2D 48
Clos Maes Brag CF83: Caer .4G 75
Clos Morgan Gruffydd
CF83: Abert .6C 66
Clos Mynach CF82: P'heol .2E 49
Clos Nant yr Aber CF83: Caer .3E 75
Clos Pandy CF83: B'ws .1A 76
Clos Pant Glas CF83: Tret .1C 76
Clos Tir Twyn CF82: Ystrad .4E 57
Clos Tir-y-Pwll NP11: Newb .2C 52
Clos Trefin NP12: P'fraith .6C 50
Clos Tyrywen CF83: B'ws .1H 75
Clos Waun Fach CF83: Caer .6C 74
Clos-y-Cedr CF83: Caer .1F 75
Clos y Crydd NP23: B mawr .3C 12
Clos-y-Pant CF83: Caer .6D 74
Clos yr Arad CF83: Caer .6C 74
Clos Ysbyty CF83: Caer .6E 75
Clovelly Av. NP23: E Vale .4F 17
Clover Ct. NP44: F'wtr .2E 63
Club Rd. NP4: P'pool .1A 46
Club Row NP4: Abers .3E 37
NP7: Cly .6G 13
NP13: Blai .4D 18
Clwyd-y-Clap La.
NP4: Mamh .1F 39
CLYDACH .6H 13
Clydach Av. NP23: Rassa .2C 10
Clydach Dingle
NP23: B mawr .1A 12
Clydach St. NP23: B mawr .3A 12
Clyde Cl. NP12: P'fraith .5A 50
Clyde St. NP11: Ris .4D 72
Clyffes NP44: G'mdw .6B 54
Clyne Rd. CF82: Cefn H .4E 49
Clynmawr St. NP13: A'lery .6F 27
Clytha Sq. NP11: Aberc .6D 52
Coach Bach NP22: Tred .6G 9
Coalbrook Vale Ct.
NP23: N'glo .2B 18
Cobden Pl. NP11: C'keys .1G 71
Cobden St. NP11: C'keys .1H 71
Cobner Cl. NP4: C'avn .4H 37
Coch-y-North Rd.
NP4: P'seg, P'nydd, P'pool
.1A 46
Cocker Av. NP44: C'brn .2A 64
COEDCAE .1C 18
Coedcae CF82: Ystrad .3D 56
Coed Cae CF83: Caer .3H 75
Coedcae NP23: Rassa .3C 10
Coed Cae NP24: New T .3D 30
NP44: Pnwd .4C 54
Coed-Cae-Ddu Rd.
NP12: P'fraith .5C 50
COEDCAE MAWR .3D 56
Coedcae Pl. NP4: P'pool .1B 46
Coedcae Rd. CF83: Abert .6D 66
Coedcae Ter. NP4: P'pool .1B 46
Coed Camlas NP4: New I .2F 47
COED-DUON .2B 50
Coed Duon Vw. NP11: Newb .4G 51
COED EVA .3G 63
Coedeva Mill NP44: C'brn .3H 63
Coed Garw NP44: C'iog .3G 55
Coed Gelli Parc
NP12: B'wood .6B 42
Coed Gethin CF83: Caer .1E 75
Coed Glas NP44: C'brn .2A 64
Coed Glas La. NP7: A'gvnny .4G 7
Coed Leddyn CF83: Caer .1E 75
Coed Lee NP44: C'brn .2H 63
Coed Llydd NP4: B'avn .3G 21
Coed Main CF83: Caer .3A 76
Coed Mawr CF82: Ystrad .4D 56
Coed Moelfa Rd.
NP11: Aberc .6C 52
Coed Pwll CF83: Caer .3H 75
Coed Rd. NP4: B'avn .4G 21
Coed Ter. *NP4: B'avn .3G 21*
(off Trem-y-Mynydd)
NP4: Tal .1D 36
Coed Uchel NP7: Gilw .3D 4
Coed-y-Brain Ct. CF83: L'brad .5A 68
Coed-y-Brain Rd.
CF83: L'brad .5A 68
Coed y Bryn NP12: B'wood .3A 50
Coed-y-Canddo Rd.
NP4: New I .2F 47
Coed-y-Garn NP23: W lwyd .1G 25
Coed-y-Graig CF82: Ystrad .4D 56
Coedygric Rd. NP4: Grif .3E 47
Coed-y-Llinos CF83: Caer .4D 74
Coedymoeth Rd.
CF81: A'goed .1G 41
Coed y Pandy CF83: B'ws .1A 76
Coed-y-Pia CF83: L'brad .6F 57
Coed-y-Pica CF83: Abert .6D 66
Coed-yr-Eos CF83: Caer .4D 74
Coed-yr-Haf CF82: Ystrad .2C 56
Coed-y-Wennol CF83: Caer .5D 74
Coggins Cl. CF83: Caer .6C 74
Coity Ter. NP4: B'avn .4D 20
Coldstream Cl. NP44: C'iog .4G 55
Cole Ct. CF83: Caer .3A 76
Coleford Path NP44: G'mdw .6C 54
Colenso Ter. NP22: Rhym .4B 14
NP22: Tred .3A 16
Coleridge Gdns. CF83: Mac .1F 77
Coleridge Grn.
NP44: G'mdw .1H 63
College Rd. NP4: P'pool .6H 37
NP23: E Vale .4D 10
College Ter. NP4: P'nydd .4F 37
Colliers Row NP23: E Vale .6E 11
NP24: New T .2C 30
Colliery Rd. CF83: B'ws, Tret .6F 69
CF83: L'brad .6D 56
Collins Cl. NP23: B mawr .3C 12
Collins Row NP22: Rhym .2A 14
Commercial Bldgs.
NP11: C'fch .6D 58
Commercial Cl. NP4: Tal .6D 28
Commercial Rd. CF83: Mac .6G 71
(Royal Oak)
CF83: Mac .6E 71
(Wesley Hill)
NP4: Tal .6D 28
NP11: Aberc .1C 60
NP11: C'fch .6D 58
NP11: Crum .6B 44
NP13: A'beeg .5A 34
Commercial St.
CF81: A'goed .2F 41
CF81: Gilf .5F 41
CF82: P'heol .2C 48
CF82: Ystrad .2E 57
CF83: Sen .3B 66
NP4: B'avn .3F 21
NP4: Grif .4E 47
NP4: P'pool .6H 37
NP7: A'gvnny .4E 7
NP11: Ris .4C 72
NP11: Yny .5D 58
NP12: P'fraith .5C 50
NP12: Peng .3F 49
NP13: A'lery .6G 27
NP22: Tred .2H 15
NP23: E Vale .3E 17
NP24: New T .2D 30
NP44: C'brn .1B 64
NP44: Pnwd .4E 55
Commercial St. Cvn. Site
NP11: Ris .5D 72
Commin Cl. NP12: Mark .6A 32
Commin Rd. CF81: A'goed .1G 41
Common Rd. NP7: Gilw .3D 4
Commonwealth Rd.
NP23: G lydan .1E 11
Congress Theatre .5E 55
(off Gwent Sq.)
Conway Cl. NP44: C'brn .5E 55
Conway Ct. CF83: Caer .3C 74
NP12: B'wood .6A 42
Conway Rd. NP4: P'pool .6G 37
NP11: Pent C .1A 44
Conway Ter. NP44: C'iog .4F 55
Cools Cl. NP23: Cwm .3A 26
Co-operative Ter. NP4: Tal .6D 28
Coopers Pl. CF83: Caer .6C 74
Coopers Ter. CF82: Ystrad .4E 57
Corbett Cres. CF83: Caer .6G 75
Corbett Gro. CF83: Caer .6D 74

Corbetts La. CF83: Caer 1F **75**
Cornfield Ri. CF83: B'ws 1A **76**
Coronation Bldgs.
NP11: C'fch 1H 69
(off Commercial Rd.)
Coronation Cres. CF81: Foch 4A **22**
NP11: Newb 1C **52**
Coronation Pl.
NP11: P'waun 4D **60**
Coronation Rd.
NP12: B'wood 2B **50**
Coronation St. CF83: Tret 1D **76**
NP11: Ris 4D **72**
NP13: Blai 5D **18**
NP13: S Bells 2D **34**
NP22: Tred 3H **15**
Coronation Ter. CF83: Sen 2C **66**
NP4: P'nydd 5E 37
(off Hanbury Rd.)
NP4: Tal 1E **37**
NP22: Rhym 4A **14**
Corris NP44: C'iog 3F **55**
Cory Pk. NP44: Oakf 5E **65**
Cotswold Way NP11: Ris 4F **73**
Council St. NP23: E Vale 6D **10**
Coundley Cl. NP12: Fleur 4G **49**
COUNTY HOSPITAL 3E **47**
Courtabella
NP12: Argoed, Oakd 3D **42**
Court Farm Cl. NP44: Oakf 3D **64**
Court Farm Rd. NP44: Oakf 3D **64**
Court Gdns. NP10: Roger 6H **73**
Courtlands, The
NP44: G'mdw 6B **54**
Court Ri. NP4: B'avn 2G **21**
Court Rd. CF83: Caer 2E **75**
NP44: C'brn, Oakf 2C **64**
Court Rd. Ind. Est.
NP44: Oakf 2C **64**
Court St. NP23: E Vale 6E **11**
Covert Wlk. NP44: F'wtr 2G **63**
Craig-Ceiliog La.
NP44: H'lys 6F **63**
Craigddu Vw. NP4: Var 4D **28**
Craiglas Cres. NP12: Cefn F 1H **49**
Craig Rhymney
NP24: New T 1B **30**
CRAIGYFEDW **6E 67**
Crane St. NP4: P'pool 1C **46**
Crescent Ct. NP22: Tred 6F **9**
Crescent Rd. CF83: Caer 4F **75**
NP11: Ris 2B **72**
Crescent, The CF82: Maes C 2F **57**
CF83: B'ws 1B **76**
CF83: Caer 4D **74**
CF83: Mac 6E **71**
NP22: Tred 6F **9**
NP23: E Vale 1E **17**
NP23: N'glo 2C **18**
NP44: C'brn 2A **64**
Cresswell Wlk.
NP44: G'mdw 6C **54**
Cresta Rd. NP7: A'gvnny 2D **6**
Criccieth Cl. NP12: B'wood 6A **42**
Crickhowell Rd. NP7: Gilw 1A **4**
Cripps Av. NP22: Tred 3G **15**
Croesonen Parc NP7: A'gvnny 2H **7**
Croesonen Rd. NP7: A'gvnny 2G **7**
Croeso Sq. NP12: B'wood 2A **50**
CROES-PEN-MAEN **5G 43**
Croespenmaen Ind. Est.
NP11: C'maen 6G **43**
Croeswen NP44: Oakf 3C **64**
CROESYCEILIOG **5G 55**
Croesyceiliog By-Pass
NP44: C'iog 3H **55**
CROES-Y-MWYALCH **6D 64**
Croes-y-Pant La.
NP4: Mamh 1F **39**
Croft Ct. NP23: B mawr 3H **11**
Crofton Mede NP44: F'wtr 2G **63**
Crofts Cnr. NP44: G'mdw 6B **54**
Croft St. NP24: New T 1D **30**
Cromwell Pl. NP44: Pnwd 4E **55**
Cromwell Rd. NP11: Ris 1A **72**
Cromwell Rd. Bungs.
NP11: Ris 1A **72**
Cromwell St. NP13: A'lery 6G **27**
Cronin Ct. NP22: Tred 2G **15**
Crook Hill NP13: C'lery 4G **27**
Crosscombe Ter. NP23: Cwm . . .4A **26**
Crossfields NP11: C'maen 6G **43**
CROSS KEYS **1H 71**
Crosskeys R.U.F.C. (Pandy Pk.)
. . . . .1G **71**
Cross Roads NP7: Gilw 3E **5**
Cross St. CF81: Barg 3F **41**
CF81: Deri 5A **30**
CF81: Gilf 5F **41**
CF83: Abert 6D **66**
CF83: B'ws 1B **76**
CF83: Sen 3C **66**
NP4: B'avn 3F **21**
NP4: Var 5D **28**
NP7: A'gvnny 4F **7**
NP13: A'lery 6G **27**
NP13: Blai 4D **18**
NP22: Rhym 5B **14**
NP24: New T 3E **31**
Cross Way NP22: Tred 6G **9**
Crossways Bus. Pk.
CF83: Caer 1G **75**
Crossways Retail Pk.
CF83: Caer 1H **75**
C Row NP4: B'avn 3D **20**
Crown Av. NP22: Tred 5G **9**
Crown Bus. Pk. NP22: Tred 4H **9**
Crown Cl. NP44: Pnwd 3D **54**
Crown Est. NP12: P'fraith 6A **50**
Crown La. NP12: P'fraith 6A **50**
Crown Ri. NP44: Llanf 1E **65**
Crown Rd. NP44: Llanf 3E **65**
Crown st. NP11: Crum 6B **44**
NP13: A'lery 5F **27**
Crown Wlk. CF83: Mac 6G **71**
CRUMLIN **6B 44**
Crumlin Rd.
NP4: P'seg, P'nydd, P'pool
. . . . .5H **45** & 2A **46**
NP11: Crum 5B **44**
(not continuous)
Crumlin St. NP4: P'pool 1B **46**
CRYMLYN **6B 44**
Currie Pl. NP23: Cwm 3H **25**
Currie St. NP23: Cwm 3H **25**
CURWOOD **3F 21**
Curzon St. NP23: B mawr 3B **12**
Cutting, The NP7: L'fst 6D **6**
CWM **4A 26**
Cwm-Aberbeeg By-Pass
NP23: Cwm 2H **25**
Cwmalsie Cres.
NP12: P'fraith 6D **50**
Cwmalsie La. NP12: P'fraith 6D **50**
CWMAVON **2E 29**
Cwmavon Rd.
NP4: Abers, B'avn, Trev
. . . . .3F **21** & 1E **29**
CWMBRAN **5E 55**
Cwmbran Dr.
NP44: C'brn, Oakf, Pnwd . . .5E **55**
Cwmbran F.C. (Cwmbran Stadium)
. . . . .2C **64**
Cwmbran Retail Pk.
NP44: C'brn 6D **54**
Cwmbran Stadium 2C **64**
Cwmbran Station (Rail) 5F **55**
CWMBRÂN **5E 55**
CWMCARN **3C 60**
Cwmcarn Forest Dr.
NP11: C'crn, P'waun 4D **60**
NP11: C'keys 4E **61**
Cwmcarn Forest Vis. Cen. 3E **61**
Cwmcarn Leisure Cen. 3C **60**
CWM-CELYN **3E 19**
Cwmcelyn Newydd
NP13: Blai 3D **18**
Cwm-Celyn Rd. NP13: Blai 4D **18**
Cwm Cottage Rd.
NP13: A'lery 1D **34**
Cwm Darran Pl. CF81: Deri 4A **30**
Cwmdows Ter. *NP11: Newb 3H 51*
(off Cwmtorlais Rd.)
Cwm Draw Ct. NP12: P'fraith . . .6D **50**
Cwm Draw Ind. Est.
NP23: E Vale 1F **17**
Cwm Farm Cl. NP4: P'pool 2C **46**
Cwm Farm Rd.
NP13: A'lery, S Bells 1D **34**
Cwm Fedw CF83: Mac 5F **71**
CWMFELINFACH **1H 69**
CWM FFRWD-OER **5E 37**
CWM FIELDS **2C 46**
CWMGELLI **6C 42**
Cwmgelli Vs. NP12: B'wood 6C **42**
Cwm Glas NP22: Tred 1G **15**
Cwm Hir NP23: B'fort 4E **11**
Cwmhir Rd.
NP4: Glas, Lit M, New I 6F **39**
Cwm-Nant Flds. NP44: C'brn 1A **64**
Cwmnant Vs. NP44: C'brn 1A **64**
CWM-NANT-YR-ODYN **5D 50**
Cwmnofydd La.
CF83: Mac . . . . . . .1H **77** & 6E **71**
Cwm Rhos Vw. NP22: Tred 3G **15**
Cwm Rd. CF81: A'goed 2F **41**
NP7: Gov 5H **5**
NP12: Argoed 3C **42**
NP23: W Iwyd 1G **25**
Cwmsor Cl. NP4: New I 3H **47**
CWMSYFIOG **4F 31**
Cwmsyfiog Rd. CF81: A'goed 1F **41**
Cwmsyfiog Road
NP24: A'goed, Brith 5G **31**
Cwm Ter. NP23: Cwm 4A **26**
CWMTILLERY **3G 27**
Cwmtillery Ind. Est.
NP13: C'lery 3G **27**
Cwmtorlais Rd. NP11: Newb 3H **51**
CWMTYLERI **3G 27**
Cwm-y-Nant NP11: Ris 5D **72**
Cwmynyscoy Rd.
NP4: P'pool 3C **46**
Cwmyrdderch Ct. NP23: Cwm . . .3H **25**
Cwrdy Cl. NP4: Grif 5D **46**
Cwrdy La. NP4: Grif, Up R 5C **46**
Cwrdy Rd. NP4: Grif 5D **46**
Cwrdy Wlk. NP4: Grif 5D **46**
Cwrt Bleddyn NP44: C'brn 2A **64**
Cwrt-Coch St. CF81: A'goed 3G **41**
Cwrt Dowlas NP44: C'brn 3B **64**
(Ty-Coch La.)
NP44: C'brn, Oakf 4B **64**
(Cwmbran Dr.)
Cwrt Draw Llyn CF83: Caer 6E **75**
Cwrtglas NP44: C'iog 5G **55**
Cwrt Hendre NP12: Cefn F 2H **49**
Cwrt Llanfabon CF83: Caer 2E **75**
Cwrt Llechryd NP22: Rhym 1A **14**
Cwrt Nant y Felin CF83: Caer 6C **74**
Cwrt Neuadd Wen
CF81: A'goed 2G **41**
Cwrt Rhyd NP23: B'fort 3D **10**
Cwrt-Ty-Fferm CF83: L'brad 5A **68**
Cwrt Ty Mawr CF83: Caer 5A **76**
Cwrt Tynewydd NP11: Newb 3A **52**
Cwrt y Castell CF83: Caer 4G **75**
Cwrt Y Coed NP12: B'wood 3A **50**
Cwrt yr Gollen *NP23: E Vale 3E 17*
(off Farm Flds. Rd.)
Cwrt-yr-Ysgol NP11: Ris 2C **72**
Cwrt Y Waun NP12: Cefn F 2H **49**
Cylla St. CF82: G'gaer 4C **48**
Cynan Cl. NP23: G lydan 2E **11**
Cyril Pl. NP13: A'lery 5E **27**

D

Daffodil Ct. NP44: F'wtr 1E **63**
Daffodil La. NP10: Roger 6G **73**
Daffyn Ct. NP4: Var 5D **28**
Dafolog Ter. NP24: New T 1E **31**
Daisy Vw. NP4: P'pool 2D **46**
Dale Path NP44: F'wtr 1G **63**
Dale Vw. NP23: N'glo 1C **18**
Dan-y-Bont NP7: Gilw 3D **4**
Dan-y-Bryn NP7: Gilw 3D **4**
Dan Y Bryn NP12: P'fraith 6B **50**
DANYCOED **6G 13**
Dan-y-Coed CF82: Cefn H 5E **49**
Danycoed CF83: Caer 6G **75**
Dan-y-Darren CF83: L'brad 6F **57**
Dan-y-Der CF83: B'ws 6D **68**
Dan-y-Deri NP7: A'gvnny 1G **7**
Dan-y-Gaer Rd.
CF82: G'gaer 3B **48**
DANYGRAIG **3C 72**
Dan y Graig CF81: P'tyn 3D **22**
Dan-y-Graig CF83: Abert 6D **66**
Danygraig CF83: Mac 1E **77**
Dan y Graig NP11: Ris 3C **72**
Danygraig NP44: C'iog 2G **55**
Dan y Graig Bungs. NP11: Ris . . .4B **72**
Dan-y-Graig Rd. NP11: Ris 3C **72**
Dan yr Ardd CF83: Caer 6D **74**
Dan-y-Rhiw Ter.
NP11: Aberc 6B **52**
Darby Cres. NP23: E Vale 1B **16**
DARENFELEN **2G 13**
Darenfelen Rd.
NP23: B mawr 3B **12**
Darran Rd.
NP11: C'keys, Ris 6G **61**
Darren Cl. CF83: Caer 2A **76**
Darren Ct. NP11: Aberc 2C **60**
NP12: Oakd 6E **43**
Darren Dr. NP11: Aberc 2B **60**
Darren Rd. NP13: A'lery 6H **27**
Darwyn Las CF83: B'ws 6D **68**
David St. NP12: B'wood 3C **50**
NP23: E Vale 1D **16**
Davies Dr. CF83: Caer 1E **75**
Davies St. CF82: Ystrad 1E **57**
NP12: Cefn F 2H **49**
NP23: B mawr 3B **12**
Davis Cl. NP4: P'pool 6G **37**
Dean Ct. NP44: H'lys 3E **63**
De Ballon Cl. NP7: A'gvnny 6G **7**
De Braose Cl. NP7: A'gvnny 6G **7**
De Cantelupe Cl.
NP7: A'gvnny 6G **7**
Deerbrook NP44: G'mdw 1G **63**
De Grosmont Cl. NP7: A'gvnny . . .6G **7**
Deighton Cl. NP22: Tred 1G **15**
Delafield Rd. NP7: A'gvnny 2C **6**
Delphinium Rd. NP10: Roger . . .6G **73**
Denbigh Cl. NP12: B'wood 6B **42**
Denbigh Ct. CF83: Caer 3B **74**
Dene Ct. NP4: P'nydd 4F **37**
Denleigh Cl. CF81: Barg 4E **41**
DENSCOMBE **5E 75**
DERI **5A 30**
Deri-Newydd CF81: Deri 4A **30**
Deri Rd. NP7: A'gvnny 3F **7**
(Park Cres.)
NP7: A'gvnny 1F **7**
(Pen-y-Pound Hill Rd.)
Derlwyn St. NP24: New T 2D **30**
Derwen Cl. CF82: Ystrad 2C **56**
NP12: B'wood 1B **50**
Derwendeg Av. CF82: Cefn H 4E **49**
NP12: Cefn F 1H **49**
Derwen Deg Cl. NP7: Gov 5H **5**
Derwen Way NP7: A'gvnny 2G **7**
De Wallingford Cl.
NP7: A'gvnny 6G **7**
Dewberry Gro. NP10: Roger 5G **73**
Dewinton Ter. CF83: L'brad 5A **68**
Diamond Cl. CF83: Caer 3E **75**
Diamond Jubilee Ter.
NP13: A'lery 6G **27**
Dickens Ct. CF83: Mac 1F **77**
Dilwyn Av. CF82: Heng 1E **57**
Dinas Path NP44: F'wtr 1G **63**
Dingle La. NP44: Pnwd 3C **54**
Dingle Rd. NP4: P'pool 2D **46**
NP7: A'gvnny 2C **6**
Dingle, The NP23: E Vale 1F **17**
Division St. NP13: A'lery 6G **27**
Dixon Pl. NP11: Ris 3D **72**
Dol Fran CF83: Caer 3A **76**
Dolwyddelan Cl.
NP12: B'wood 6B **42**
Dolyfelin CF83: B'ws 6D **68**
Dol-y-Felin St. CF83: Caer 4F **75**
Dol-y-Garn Ter. NP13: Blai 3D **18**
Dol-y-Pandy CF83: B'ws 6D **68**
Dol-y-Paun CF83: Caer 5D **74**
Dol-yr-Eos CF83: Caer 3H **75**
Dorallt Cl. NP44: H'lys 2D **62**
Dorallt Way NP44: H'lys 3D **62**
Dorleigh Ct. NP44: G'mdw 4B **54**
Dorstone Wlk. NP44: Llan 6G **55**
Downey Gro. CF82: P'heol 3D **48**
Dragon La. NP7: Gov 4H **5**
Dranllwyn Cl. CF83: Mac 6E **71**
Dranllwyn La. CF83: Mac 6E **71**
Drayton Ct. NP44: G'mdw 6C **54**
Drenewydd Mus. 2A **14**
Drive, The CF81: Gilf 6F **41**
D Row NP4: B'avn 3D **20**
Drybrook Cl. NP44: C'brn 6F **55**
Duffryn Bus. Pk. CF82: Ystrad . . .5E **57**
Duffryn Cl. CF82: P'heol 1C **48**
Duffryn Rd. NP11: W'vle 2C **70**
NP13: A'lery 5G **27**
Duffryn St. CF81: P'tyn 3C **22**
CF82: Tir B 3F **49**
CF82: Ystrad 6D **48**
Duffryn Ter. NP11: W'vle 2E **71**
NP24: New T 2D **30**
Duffryn Vw. NP22: Rhym 6C **14**
DUKE'S MEADOW **6G 9**
DUKESTOWN **5G 9**
Dukestown Rd NP22: Tred 5H **9**
Duke St. NP4: B'avn 3F **21**
NP13: A'lery 1C **34**
NP22: Tred 3H **15**
Dumfries Cl. NP7: L'fst 6D **6**
Dumfries Pl. NP23: B mawr 2B **12**
Dunnet Gdns. NP4: New I 4H **47**
Dunraven Ct. CF83: Caer 3B **74**

Dunraven Rd. NP44: Llan 1E **65**
Dyfed Dr. CF83: Caer 2E **75**
Dyffryn Pl. NP23: Cwm 5A **26**
Dyffryn Rd. NP23: W Iwyd 6G **17**
Dyffryn St. CF81: A'goed 3G **41**
Dylan Av. NP12: Cefn F 2H **49**
Dylan Dr. CF83: Caer 2F **75**
Dynevor Cl. NP44: Llan 6H **55**
Dynevor St. CF81: Foch 4A **22**

E

Earl Cl. NP4: Var 5D **28**
Earlsmede NP44: G'mdw 6B **54**
Earl St. NP4: Var 6D **28**
NP13: A'lery 1D **34**
NP22: Tred 2G **15**
East Av. CF83: B'ws 1B **76**
CF83: Caer 3E **75**
NP4: Grif 6E **47**
East Pen-Twyn NP13: Blai 5D **18**
East Pen-Twyn Bungs.
NP13: Blai 5E **19**
East Pentwyn Rd. NP13: Blai 4D **18**
East Rd. CF82: G'gaer 4C **48**
NP44: Oakf 3C **64**
East Roedin NP44: F'wtr 3H **63**
East Side Row NP13: C'lery 3G **27**
East Vw. CF83: Caer 5G **75**
NP4: Grif 5E **47**
NP4: P'pool 1B **46**
NP24: Brith 4F **31**
Eastview Ter. CF81: Barg 4F **41**
Eastville Rd. NP13: S Bells 2D **34**
NP23: E Vale 3F **17**
Eastway NP4: Lit M, P'pool 3E **39**
Ebbw Ct. NP11: C'keys 1H **71**
Ebbw Pl. NP23: Rassa 3C **10**
Ebbw St. NP11: Ris 3C **72**
EBBW VALE 2E **17**
EBBW VALE HOSPITAL 2E 17
Ebbw Vale Leisure Cen. 6E 11
Ebbw Vw. NP23: B'fort 4E **11**
Ebbw Vw. Ter. NP11: Newb 3A **52**
Ebenezer Ct. NP22: Tred 6H **9**
Ebenezer St. NP22: Tred 6H **9**
Edgcort NP44: F'wtr 2G **63**
Edgehill NP12: P'fraith 4A **50**
NP44: Llanf 2E **65**
Edinburgh Cl. NP44: G'mdw 6A **54**
Edlogan Sq. NP44: C'iog 3G **55**
Edlogan Way NP44: C'brn 5F **55**
Edmund Pl. NP11: Newb 4F **51**
Edmunds Cl. NP13: Blai 4C **18**
Edmund St. CF81: P'tyn 3C **22**
Edwards Ct. NP23: E Vale 6D **10**
Edwards Row CF81: Deri 5A **30**
Edward's Ter. NP11: Newb 3G **51**
Edward St. CF82: Ystrad 4D **56**
NP4: Grif 4E **47**
NP4: P'pool 6G **37**
NP11: C'crn 3D **60**
NP12: Cefn F 2G **49**
NP13: A'lery 5G **27**
Edwardsville NP11: C'crn 3C **60**
Edward Ter. CF83: Abert 5D **66**
NP22: Tred 3A **16**
Edward Thomas Cl.
CF83: Rud 3E **77**
Eglwys Fan NP22: Rhym 6C **14**
Eglwysilan Rd.
CF15: Caer 5A **74**
CF37: P'prdd, R'fln 6A **66**
CF83: Abert 6A **66**
Eglwysilan Way CF83: Abert 6C **66**
Elan Wlk. NP44: G'mdw 1H **63**
Elgam Av. NP4: B'avn 2G **21**
Elgam Grn. *NP4: B'avn 2G **21***
(off Up. Woodland St.)
Elgar Cl. NP12: Cefn F 2H **49**
Elidyr Cres. NP11: Newb 1A **52**
Elidyr Rd. NP11: Newb 1A **52**
Elim Way NP12: P'fraith 4D **50**
Elizabeth Row NP4: Abers 2B **36**
Elizabeth Way NP23: E Vale 6C **10**
Elled Rd.
NP4: P'nydd, P'pool 5F **37**
Ellesmere Ct. NP11: Newb 1C **52**
Ellick St. NP4: B'avn 2F **21**
Elliot Colliery Winding House
3E 31
ELLIOT'S TOWN 3E **31**
Elliot St. NP24: New T 3E **31**
Ellipse, The NP4: Grif 6D **46**
Ellwood Path NP44: G'mdw 6B **54**
Elm Cl. NP4: C'avn 3F **37**
Elm Ct. NP11: Newb 6C **44**
NP12: Oakd 3C **50**
Elm Dr. NP11: Ris 3D **72**
Elm Gro. CF83: Caer 2H **75**
Elmgrove CF83: Tret 1C **76**
Elm Gro. NP4: Grif 6E **47**
NP7: Gilw 2D **4**
Elmhurst Cl. NP4: C'avn 4G **37**
Elms Rd. NP7: Gov 5H **5**
Elms, The NP12: Oakd 6F **43**
Elm St. CF81: A'goed 3G **41**
NP23: Cwm 3H **25**
Elmwood NP22: Tred 4A **16**
Elmwood Gro. NP22: Tred 4A **16**
Emanuel Cl. CF83: Caer 6C **74**
Emlyn Av. NP23: E Vale 4D **10**
Emlyn Dr. CF83: Caer 3F **75**
Emlyn Rd. NP4: Tal 5C **28**
NP23: Cwm 3H **25**
Endyngs NP44: F'wtr 2G **63**
ENERGLYN 2E **75**
Energlyn Cl. CF83: Caer 3E **75**
Energlyn Ct. *CF83: Caer 3E **75***
(off Energlyn Cl.)
Energlyn Cres. CF83: Caer 2E **75**
Energlyn Row CF83: Caer 1E **75**
Energlyn Ter. CF83: Caer 2D **74**
Eppynt Cl. NP11: Ris 3F **73**
Erasmus Ter. *CF82: Maes C 1G **57***
(off Jenkin St.)
Eridge Rd. NP4: Var 6E **29**
E Row NP4: B'avn 3D **20**
Estate Rd. NP4: B'avn 1D **20**
NP4: P'nydd 5E **37**
Eureka Pl. NP23: E Vale 1E **17**
Evelyn St. NP13: A'lery 6G **27**
Excelsior St. NP23: W Iwyd 6G **17**
Exchange Ct. NP11: Ris 2C **72**
Exchange Rd. NP11: Ris 2C **72**
Exeter Cl. NP44: G'mdw 6A **54**
Exeter Pl. NP4: Abers 2E **37**
Exford Gro. NP7: Gilw 3C **4**

F

Factory Cotts. NP11: Ris 4E **73**
Factory La. NP4: Abers 2E **37**
Factory Pk. Factory Shopping Village
NP23: W Iwyd 2G **25**
Factory Rd. CF81: Barg 1D **40**
NP23: B mawr 3B **12**
FAIRFIELD 1D **36**
Fairfield NP4: P'pool 6F **37**
NP4: Tal 1D **36**
NP22: Tred 1A **16**
Fairfield Cl. NP12: B'wood 3B **50**
Fairhill NP44: F'wtr, G'mdw 1G **63**
Fairhill Wlk. NP44: F'wtr 1G **63**
(Fairwater Cl., not continuous)
NP44: F'wtr 1F **63**
(Oaksford)
Fairhome NP7: Gilw 2D **4**
Fairoak La. NP44: C'iog 5G **55**
Fair Vw. CF81: P'tyn 3C **22**
NP12: Cefn F 2G **49**
NP22: Tred 6F **9**
Fairview NP23: E Vale 1D **16**
Fairview Av. NP11: Ris 3D **72**
Fairview Ct. NP4: P'nydd 5F **37**
Fairview Ter. NP4: Tal 6D **28**
FAIRWATER 2G **63**
Fairwater Cl. NP44: F'wtr 1G **63**
Fairwater Leisure Cen. 1F 63
Fairwater Sq. Shops
NP44: F'wtr 1F **63**
Fairwater Way NP44: F'wtr 2G **63**
Fairway Dr. CF83: Caer 1E **75**
Fairways CF81: Barg 2D **40**
Fairways, The NP12: B'wood 1B **50**
Fairway, The NP4: New I 3H **47**
Falcon Ter. NP11: W'vle 2D **70**
NP23: Cwm 4A **26**
Fallowfields NP44: F'wtr 2G **63**
Farlays NP44: F'wtr 2F **63**
Farlow Wlk. NP44: G'mdw 1H **63**
(not continuous)
Farm Cl. CF83: Abert 6D **66**
NP12: Oakd 6D **42**
Farmers La. NP23: B'fort 2G **11**
Farm Flds. Rd. NP23: E Vale 3E **17**
Farm Hill NP4: C'avn 4G **37**
Farm La. NP44: C'brn 5F **55**
Farm Rd. CF81: P'tyn 2C **22**
CF83: Caer 4H **75**
NP4: P'pool 2C **46**
NP4: Tal 6C **28**
NP11: Crum 5C **44**
NP23: N'glo 6B **12**
Farm Ter. NP24: New T 1E **31**
Farm Vw. NP12: Peng 5G **41**
Farraday Dr. CF82: P'heol 2D **48**
Feeder Bank NP22: Tred 6G **9**
Feeder Row NP11: C'crn 4D **60**
Fernbank NP44: G'mdw 1G **63**
Fernbrook Cl. NP23: G Iydan 1E **11**
Fern Cl. NP11: Crum 4G **43**
Ferncroft Way NP4: C'avn 3G **37**
Ferndale Cl. NP23: Rassa 2C **10**
Fernfield Ter. NP13: A'lery 6G **27**
Fernhill Ter. NP24: New T 2E **31**
FERNLEA 2C **72**
Fernlea NP11: Ris 2C **72**
Festival Cres. NP4: New I 3H **47**
Festival Dr. NP23: E Vale 4F **17**
Festival Pk. NP23: W Iwyd 2G **25**
Fetty Pl. NP44: C'brn 2A **64**
Fferm-y-Bryn CF82: Ystrad 2D **56**
Fflorens Rd. NP11: Newb 6A **44**
(not continuous)
Ffordd Erw CF83: Caer 6D **74**
Ffordd Eynon Evans
CF83: Caer 1C **74**
Ffordd Las CF83: Abert 5D **66**
Ffordd Penrhos CF83: Caer 4C **74**
Ffordd Traws Cwm
CF83: Caer 6D **74**
Fford Traws Cwm CF83: Caer 6C **74**
Ffos-yr-Hebog CF83: L'brad 6F **57**
Ffrosmaen Rd. NP23: N'glo 1C **18**
Ffrwd Rd. NP4: Abers 1E **37**
Ffrwd Ter. CF83: L'brad 3A **68**
Ffwrwm Rd. CF83: Mac 6E **71**
Ffynnon Coed NP7: Cly 1H **13**
Ffynnon Ct. *NP23: B mawr 3A **12***
(off Orchard St.)
Fieldings *NP44: F'wtr 2G **63***
(off Fairwater Way)
Fields Av. NP44: Pnwd 3D **54**
Field's Pk. Rd. NP11: Newb 2H **51**
Fields Pk.Ter. NP11: C'keys 6C **60**
Fields Rd. NP11: Ris 5E **73**
NP22: Tred 4A **16**
NP44: Oakf 2B **64**
Field St. NP22: Rhym 5C **14**
Field Ter. NP24: New T 1D **30**
Field Vw. Rd. NP44: C'iog 4G **55**
Firbank Ter. NP11: C'fch 6D **58**
Firs Rd. NP7: A'gvnny 4G **7**
NP7: Mardy 1H **7**
First Av. CF83: Caer 4D **74**
Firs, The NP4: B'avn 3H **21**
Firth Rd. NP23: E Vale 1C **16**
Fitzroy Av. NP23: E Vale 5E **11**
Fitzroy Lodge NP12: Cefn F 2H **49**
Fitzroy St. NP23: B mawr 2A **12**
Five Ho's. NP4: Up R 3B **46**
FIVE LOCKS 3C **54**
Five Locks Cl. NP44: Pnwd 2D **54**
Five Locks Rd. NP44: Pnwd 3D **54**
Five Oaks La. NP44: C'iog 4G **55**
Flannel St. NP7: A'gvnny 4F **7**
FLEUR-DE-LIS 3G 49
Fleur-de-Lys Av.
NP12: P'fraith 4A **50**
Floral Av. NP12: Cefn F 3G **49**
Florence Cl. NP13: A'lery 6H **27**
Florence Gro. CF83: Caer 5F **75**
Florence Pl. NP4: Grif 5E **47**
Flyno n-Wen Ter.
NP12: Peng 6G **41**
FOCHRIW 4A 22
Fochriw Rd. CF81: P'tyn 3B **22**
Folly La. NP4: C'avn 4H **37**
(not continuous)
NP4: Mamh, P'pool 3C **38**
Folly Rd. NP4: C'avn 4H **37**
Folly Vw. NP4: P'pool 6A **38**
Ford Rd. NP12: Fleur 3F **49**
Forest Av. CF82: Cefn H 4E **49**
Forest Cl. NP44: F'wtr 3G **63**
Forest Hill NP7: Gilw 3C **4**
NP12: P'fraith 6A **50**
Forest Vw. NP11: C'crn 3E **61**
NP44: H'lys 3D **62**
Forge Cres. NP22: Rhym 1C **22**
FORGE HAMMER 5D **54**
Forge Hammer Ind. Est.
NP44: C'brn 5D **54**
Forge Rd. CF83: Mac 6F **71**
NP4: B'avn 3D **20**
Forge Row 1F 29
Forge Row *NP4: P'nydd 5E **37***
(off Hanbury Rd.)
NP7: Gilw 5A **4**
FORGE SIDE 3C **20**
Forgeside NP13: Blai 4C **18**
NP44: C'brn 5E **55**
Forge Side Rd. NP4: B'avn 3E **21**
Forsythia Cl. NP11: Ris 4F **73**
Fosterville Cres. NP7: A'gvnny 5G **7**
Fothergills Rd. NP24: New T 2D **30**
Foundry Bri. NP13: A'lery 6G **27**
Foundry Rd. NP4: Abers 2D **36**
Fountain Ct. NP13: C'lery 4G **27**
Fountain Rd. NP4: P'pool 2E **47**
Fowler St. NP4: P'pool 5F **37**
Fox Av. NP11: Newb 4F **51**
Frances St. CF83: Abert 6C **66**
Francis Morris Est.
NP4: B'avn 3G **21**
Francis St. CF81: Barg 3F **41**
NP11: Ris 4D **72**
NP12: Fleur 3G **49**
Francombe Way NP7: Mardy 1H **7**
Freehold Land Rd.
NP4: P'nydd 3F **37**
Friars Gdn. NP44: Llan 2E **65**
Frogmore Cen. NP7: A'gvnny 4F **7**
Frogmore St. NP7: A'gvnny 4F **7**
Frondeg NP22: Tred 4G **15**
Fron Wen NP12: Cefn F 3H **49**
Frost Pl. NP12: B'wood 2A **50**
Frost Rd. NP23: B'fort 3E **11**
Full Moon Ind. Est.
NP11: W'vle 2F **71**
Furnace St. NP23: B'fort 4E **11**
Fuscia Way NP10: Roger 6G **73**

G

Gaen St. NP13: A'lery 5G **27**
Gaer Pl. CF82: G'gaer 3B **48**
Gainsborough Cl. NP44: Oakf 3D **64**
Gainsborough Rd.
NP22: Tred 3F **15**
GALLOWSGREEN 1E **29**
Gantre Cl. NP23: G Iydan 2D **10**
Gantref Way NP23: B'fort 4E **11**
Gardd Jolyon NP12: Cefn F 3H **49**
GARDEN CITY 5E **17**
Garden City NP22: Rhym 1C **22**
Garden Cl. CF83: L'brad 3B **68**
Gardens, The NP7: Gilw 2D **4**
NP11: Yny 5C **58**
Garden St. CF83: L'brad 4A **68**
NP23: E Vale 1E **17**
Garden Suburbs
NP11: P'waun 5D **60**
Garden Village CF83: Caer 3G **75**
Garfield Rd. NP12: B'wood 3B **50**
Garfield Ter. NP23: E Vale 6D **10**
Garn Cross NP23: N'glo 6B **12**
GARNDIFFAITH 5D **28**
Garndyrus Ter. NP4: B'avn 2G **21**
GARN FACH 6C **12**
GARNLYDAN 2D **10**
Garn Rd. NP7: B'avn, G Erw 4G **13**
NP23: N'glo 6B **12**
Garn St. NP11: Aberc 6C **52**
Garn Ter. NP23: W Iwyd 6G **17**
GARN YR ERW 1C **20**
Garreg Wen CF82: P'heol 1C **48**
Garth Cl. CF83: Rud 4E **77**
NP4: C'avn 3G **37**
Garth Dan-y-Bryn
NP23: B'fort 3E **11**
Garth Est. CF83: Abert 6B **66**
Garth La. CF83: Rud 4E **77**
Garth Lwyd CF83: Caer 2A **76**
GARTH PLACE 4E **77**
Garth Rd. NP44: C'brn 2A **64**
Garth St. CF81: P'tyn 3C **22**
Garth Vw. CF83: B'ws 6E **69**
Garw Row NP44: C'iog 4H **55**
Garw, The NP44: C'iog 4H **55**
Garw Wood Dr. NP44: C'iog 3G **55**
Gavenny Way NP7: A'gvnny 4G **7**
Gaynors *NP44: F'wtr 2G **63***
(off Pace Rd.)
Gelliargwellt Rd.
CF82: G'gaer 4B **48**
(not continuous)

Gelli Av. NP11: Ris 4D 72
Gelli Cl. NP11: Ris 3D 72
NP22: Tred 2H 15
Gelli Cres. NP11: Ris 3D 72
Gelli Crug NP23: Rassa 2C 10
Gelli-Crug Rd. NP13: A'lery 5G 27
Gelli Dawel CF83: Caer 3E 75
Gelli Deg CF83: Caer 2E 75
Gellideg Cl. CF82: Maes C 1G 57
Gellideg Hgts. CF82: Maes C 1G 57
Gellideg Ind. Est.
CF82: Maes C 1H 57
Gellideg La. CF82: Maes C 1H 57
Gelli Deg St. CF82: Maes C 1G 57
Gelli Fawr Ct. NP44: H'lys 3E 63
GELLIFELEN 2G 13
GELLIGAER 3C 48
Gelligaer Rd. CF46: T'lewis 2A 48
CF82: Cefn H 4E 49
Gelligroes Rd. NP12: P'fraith 6C 50
GELLI-HAF 5G 49
Gellihaf Rd. NP12: Fleur 3G 49
Gelli La. NP12: P'fraith 6B 50
Gelli Pl. *NP4: Abers 2D 36*
(off High St.)
Gelli Rhwy Rd. NP4: Var 5D 28
Gelli Rd. NP22: Tred 2G 15
Gelli-Ron CF82: P'heol 1C 48
Gelli Ter. CF83: Sen 4C 66
Gelli-Unig Pl. NP11: P'waun 5D 60
Gelli Unig Rd. NP11: P'waun 5D 60
Gelli-Unig Ter. NP11: P'waun 5D 60
Gelliwen St. CF82: G'gaer 4C 48
Gelynos Av. NP12: Argoed 2C 42
George Daggar's Av.
NP13: A'lery 4E 27
George Hill NP24: Brith 5F 31
George St. CF81: A'goed 3G 41
CF82: Ystrad 1D 56
NP4: B'avn 3F 21
NP4: P'nydd 5F 37
NP4: P'pool 6G 37
(not continuous)
NP11: C'crn 3D 60
NP11: W'vle 1E 71
NP12: Argoed 2C 42
NP12: B'wood 2C 50
NP13: A'lery 5G 27
NP23: B mawr 3A 12
NP24: New T 2D 30
NP44: Pnwd 5E 55
GEORGETOWN 4A 16
Georgetown Hill NP22: Tred 3A 16
Gerbera Dr. NP10: Roger 6G 73
Ger Nant CF82: Ystrad 4D 56
Ger-y-Felin NP12: P'fraith 1C 58
Gethering Ter. NP4: B'avn 3D 20
Gibbs Cl. NP12: B'wood 2A 50
Gifford Cl. NP44: C'brn 2A 64
Gilbert Ter. NP7: Mardy 1H 7
Gilboa Rd. NP11: Newb 3H 51
Gilchrist Thomas Ct.
NP4: B'avn 2E 21
Gilchrist-Thomas Ind. Est.
NP4: B'avn 2D 20
Gilchrist Wlk. NP4: B'avn 2G 21
Giles Rd. NP4: B'avn 3H 21
Gileston Wlk. NP44: G'mdw 1H 63
GILFACH 6F 41
Gilfach Fargoed Station (Rail)
4F 41
Gilfach St. CF81: Barg 4F 41
GILWERN 3D 4
Gilwern Farm Cl. NP18: P'hir 4H 65
Gilwern Pk. Ind. Site NP7: Gilw 3F 5
Gilwern Pl. NP44: Pnwd 4D 54
Gipsy La. NP7: L'fst 6D 6
Glade Cl. NP44: F'wtr 3F 63
Gladstone Pl. NP4: Grif 1E 55
Gladstone Rd. NP11: Crum 5B 44
Gladstone St. NP11: C'keys 1G 71
NP13: A'lery 5F 27
NP13: Blai 5D 18
NP23: B mawr 3B 12
Gladstone Ter. NP4: B'avn 3G 21
NP4: Var 3D 28
NP22: Rhym 4A 14
Gladys Ter. NP7: L'fst 6D 6
Glamor Gan St.
NP23: B mawr 3A 12
Glanbaiden NP7: Gov 4G 5
Glanbrynna *NP11: Newb 4F 51*
(off High St.)
Glanddu Rd. NP12: Fleur 3F 49
Glan-Ddu Ter. CF82: Tir B 3F 49
Glandovey Ter. NP22: Tred 2G 15
GLANDWR 6B 34
Glandwr Ind. Est.
NP13: A'beeg 6A 34
Glandwr St. NP13: A'beeg 6A 34
NP13: A'lery 5F 27
Glan Ebbw Ter. NP13: A'lery 6G 27
NP23: W Iwyd 6F 17
Glan Ffrwd CF83: Caer 1C 74
Glanffrwd Av. NP23: E Vale 5D 10
Glanffrwd Ct. NP23: E Vale 5D 10
Glanffrwd Ter. NP23: E Vale 5D 10
Glan Gavenny NP7: A'gvnny 3H 7
GLANGRWYNEY 1C 4
Glangrwyney Rd. NP7: Gilw 1C 4
Glanheulog NP23: B mawr 2A 12
Glanhowy Rd. NP12: Yny 3C 58
Glanhowy St. NP22: Tred 5G 9
Glan Islwyn NP12: P'fraith 5B 50
Glanmoor NP7: Gilw 3D 4
Glan Nant Cl. CF83: Caer 6F 75
Glannant St. NP11: C'fch 2H 69
Glan Rhyd CF83: Caer 3E 75
Glanrhyd NP7: Gilw 3D 4
Glan Rhyd NP44: F'wtr 3F 63
Glanrhyd Cl. NP22: Tred 5G 9
Glanshon Ct. NP11: Newb 6D 44
Glantorvaen Rd. NP4: P'pool 1C 46
Glanwern Ho. NP4: P'pool 1B 46
Glanwern Ter. NP4: P'pool 1B 46
GLAN-Y-NANT 2E 49
Glan-y-Nant CF81: Foch 4A 22
NP22: Rhym 3B 14
Glan-y-Nant Cl. NP44: C'brn 2A 64
Glan-yr-Afon CF83: Mac 6E 71
NP22: Rhym 4A 14
Glanyrafon NP23: B'fort 4E 11
Glanyrafon Ter. NP13: Blai 1D 26
Glan-yr-avon NP24: New T 2D 30
Glanystruth NP13: Blai 3D 18
Glascoed La. NP4: Glas 6H 39
Glascoed Rd. NP4: New I 3H 47
Glas Fryn CF82: P'heol 2D 48
Glasfryn NP12: B'wood 3A 50
Glaslyn Ct. NP44: C'iog 4F 55
Glebe Rd. CF83: Tret 1D 76
Glebe St. CF83: B'ws 1B 76
Glen Coed CF82: Maes C 2F 57
Glencourt NP4: Grif 6E 47
Glendale Gdns. NP12: Fleur 4F 49
Glenfields Est. CF83: Caer 4D 74
Glengariff Ct. NP4: Grif 5D 46
Glenroy NP4: Up R 4A 46
GLENSIDE 2H 71
Glenside NP44: Pnwd 3D 54
Glen Vw. CF82: Maes C 2F 57
CF82: Ystrad 1D 56
Glenview NP11: Crum 6B 44
Glen Vw. NP12: Holly B 3H 31
NP44: C'brn 5D 54
Glen Vw. Bungs. NP23: N'glo 5A 12
Glen View Ct. NP11: Newb 4G 51
Glen Vw. Rd. NP4: C'avn 3G 37
Glen Vw. Ter. CF81: Deri 6A 22
Glenview Ter. CF83: L'brad 3B 68
NP11: Yny 5C 58
Globe Hill NP23: E Vale 3E 17
Gloster's Pde. NP4: New I 4H 47
Gloucester Cl. NP44: Llan 6H 55
Glyn Bedw CF83: L'brad 1B 68
GLYNCOED 5E 11
Glyn Collen CF83: L'brad 1B 68
Glyn Deri CF81: Deri 4A 30
Glyn Derw CF83: Caer 3F 75
Glyn Derwen CF83: L'brad 2B 68
Glyndwr Rd. NP23: Rassa 2C 10
NP44: C'brn 5F 55
Glyndwyr Gdns. NP7: A'gvnny 6G 7
GLYN EBWY 2E 17
Glyn Eiddew CF83: L'brad 1B 68
Glyn-Gaer Rd. CF82: P'heol 2C 48
Glyn Llwyfen CF83: L'brad 1B 68
Glynmarch St. CF81: Deri 5A 30
Glyn St. NP22: A'swg 3E 23
Glyn Ter. CF81: Foch 4A 22
NP11: Yny 5D 58
NP22: Tred 4A 16
Glyntirion NP44: C'brn 2A 64
Glyn Vw. *NP4: P'pool 2A 46*
(off Crumlin Rd.)
Gobanniun Way NP7: A'gvnny 6G 7
Godfrey Rd. NP44: Pnwd 4D 54
Godrer Coed CF82: P'heol 2E 49
Gold Cliff Ct. NP44: C'brn 6F 55
Golden Gro. *NP11: Newb 3A 52*
(off Torlais St.)
Golf Rd. NP4: New I 3G 47
Golwg y Coed CF83: Caer 2C 74
Golwg-y-Mynydd NP22: Tred 4F 9
Golwg-yr-Eglwys CF83: B'ws 1A 76
Golwyg-y-Mynydd
NP22: Rhym 4B 14
GOLYNOS
NP4 6C 28
NP10 4H 73
Goodrich Av. CF83: Caer 5H 75
Goodrich Ct. NP44: Llan 1E 65
Goodrich St. CF83: Caer 5G 75
Gordings NP44: G'mdw 6B 54
Gordon Av. NP11: Crum 4C 44
Gordon Cl. NP12: B'wood 3A 50
Gordon Rd. NP4: Tal 1D 36
NP12: B'wood 3A 50
(not continuous)
Gorsedd Cl. NP23: G lydan 2E 11
Gorse Ter. NP24: New T 2E 31
Goshen St. NP22: Rhym 5B 14
GOVILON 5H 5
Govilon Pl. NP44: Pnwd 4D 54
Gower Grn. NP44: C'iog 3G 55
Goy Pl. CF82: Heng 1E 57
Graddfa Ind. Est. CF83: L'brad 3A 68
Graddfa Vs. CF83: L'brad 2A 68
Graham Ct. CF83: Caer 4H 75
Grahams's Yd. NP22: Tred 6H 9
Graig Ebbw NP23: Rassa 3C 10
Graig Rd. CF82: Heng 1E 57
NP11: Newb 3B 52
NP13: S Bells 3D 34
NP44: G'mdw, Up Cwm 5A 54
Graig Ter. CF81: Barg 2E 41
CF83: Sen 2B 66
NP23: Cwm 5A 26
Graig Vw. CF83: Mac 6G 71
NP11: Ris 4C 72
NP11: Yny 6D 58
NP13: B'thel 6B 34
NP44: Up Cwm 3B 54
Graig Vw. Ter. NP4: Tal 5C 28
Graigwen Cres. CF83: Abert 6E 67
Graig-y-Bedw NP24: New T 2E 31
Graig y nos NP22: Tred 6H 9
GRAIG-Y-RHACCA 1F 77
Graig-y-Rhacca CF83: Mac 6C 70
Graig-yr-Wylan CF83: Caer 5D 74
Graig Ysguthan CF83: L'brad 6F 57
Grange Cl. CF83: Caer 4E 75
Grange Ct. NP4: P'nydd 4F 37
Grange Hill NP12: Cefn F 3H 49
Grange Ind. Est. NP44: C'brn 1C 64
Grange La. NP44: C'brn 5E 55
Grange Path NP44: Llanf 2E 65
Grange Rd. NP44: C'brn 5F 55
(not continuous)
Grange, The CF83: Caer 4E 75
Granston Ho. NP44: F'wtr 1G 63
Granston Sq. NP44: F'wtr 1G 63
Granville St. NP13: A'lery 5F 27
Gravel La. NP12: B'wood 3B 50
Grays Gdns. CF83: Mac 1F 77
Gray St. NP13: A'lery 6G 27
Greater Gwent Crematorium
NP44: C'iog 2H 55
Gt. Oaks Pk. NP10: Roger 6H 73
Gt. Western Cotts.
NP12: Holly B 4H 31
Green Acre NP44: C'brn 2A 64
Greenacre Dr. CF83: B'ws 6E 69
Greenacre Gdns. CF83: Tret 1C 76
Greencourt NP44: C'iog 3G 55
Greenfield NP11: Newb 2B 52
Greenfield Av. NP11: Newb 2B 52
Greenfield Cl. NP44: Pnwd 3D 54
Greenfield Cres. NP23: B'fort 3D 10
Greenfield Pl. CF83: Abert 6B 66
NP4: B'avn 3G 21
Greenfield St. CF81: P'tyn 3C 22
NP24: New T 1C 30
Greenfield Ter *NP22: Tred 3A 16*
(off Georgetown Hill)
Greenfield Ter. NP4: Var 3D 28
NP11: Pent C 3A 44
NP11: Yny 5C 58
NP12: Argoed 3C 42
NP23: E Vale 3F 17
Greenforge Way
NP44: C'brn 6C 54
Greenhill Cl. NP4: Grif 6E 47
Greenhill Pl. CF82: G'gaer 3B 48
Greenhill Rd. NP4: Grif 5E 47
NP44: C'brn 5D 54
Greenland Rd. NP4: C'avn 4G 37
NP23: B mawr 3B 12
Greenlands NP11: Newb 2B 52
Greenland St. CF81: Barg 3E 41
GREENMEADOW 6A 54
Greenmeadow CF83: Mac 2G 77
Green Mdw. NP22: Tred 6A 10
Greenmeadow Bungs.
NP12: Peng 2F 49
Greenmeadow Cl. NP44: C'brn 1A 64
Greenmeadow Community Farm
5B 54
Greenmeadow Cres.
NP4: Lit M 2H 39
Greenmeadow Dr.
NP11: C'keys 1A 72
Greenmeadow Rd.
NP11: C'fch 2A 70
Greenmeadow Sq.
NP44: C'brn 1A 64
(off Greenmeadow Way)
Greenmeadow Ter.
NP13: C'lery 4G 27
Greenmeadow Way
NP44: C'brn, G'mdw 6C 54
Green Row CF83: Mac 6E 71
Green St. NP23: W Iwyd 2G 25
(Augusta Pk.)
NP23: W Iwyd 6F 17
(Augusta St.)
Greensway NP22: A'swg 3F 23
Green, The NP12: P'fraith 4A 50
NP22: A'swg 3F 23
Greenway CF83: B'ws 1H 75
Green Way NP4: Tal, Var 6D 28
Greenway Cl. NP4: Grif 5D 46
Greenway Dr. NP4: Grif 5D 46
Greenways NP23: E Vale 1C 16
Greenway Wlk. NP4: Grif 5D 46
Greenway Workshops
CF83: B'ws 1A 76
Green Willows NP44: Oakf 3C 64
Greenwood Av. NP22: Tred 6F 9
NP44: Pnwd, Up Cwm 3B 54
Greenwood Ct. CF83: Caer 4H 75
NP24: New T 2C 30
Greenwood Dr. NP44: H'lys 3D 62
Greenwood Pl. NP7: Gilw 3E 5
Greenwood Rd. NP4: Abers 6E 29
NP12: B'wood 6H 41
Grey Cres. CF82: Tir B 3F 49
Greys Rd. NP4: P'pool 3C 46
Greystones Av. NP7: Mardy 1H 7
Greystones Cres. NP7: Mardy 1H 7
Grey Waters NP44: Llan 6G 55
Griffin Av. NP4: B'avn 3G 21
Griffiths Ct. NP4: B'avn 3D 20
Griffiths Gdns. NP22: Tred 6F 9
Griffiths Sq. NP22: Tred 6F 9
Griffiths St. CF82: Ystrad 1D 56
GRIFFITHSTOWN 4E 47
Griffithstown Railway Mus. 5F 47
Griffiths Way NP4: Var 6D 28
Groesonen Rd.
NP7: A'gvnny 2H 7
Groeswen Dr. CF83: Caer 3C 74
Groeswen Rd. CF15: Caer 5A 74
CF83: Caer 5A 74
GROFIELD 4E 7
Gros-Faen Ter. CF81: Deri 1B 40
Grosmont NP44: C'iog 3G 55
Grosmont Cl. NP12: B'wood 6B 42
Grosmont Rd. NP4: New I 3H 47
Grosvenor Pl. NP4: Grif 6E 47
Grosvenor Rd. NP7: A'gvnny 3H 7
Grosvenor St. NP13: A'lery 5F 27
Grove Av. NP7: L'fst 6D 6
Grove Cl. NP4: P'nydd 4E 37
Grove Cres. NP4: C'avn 4G 37
Grove Est. CF83: Tret 6H 69
NP4: P'nydd 4E 37
Grove Mans. NP7: L'fst 6D 6
Grove Pk. NP44: Pnwd 3E 55
Gro. Park Av. NP44: Pnwd 3E 55
Grove Pl. NP4: Grif 5E 47
Grove Rd. NP4: P'nydd 5E 37
NP11: Ris 2B 72
Groveside Rd. NP12: Oakd 1D 50
Grove St. CF83: L'brad 4A 68
NP11: Newb 3A 52
Grove Ter. CF83: Sen 2B 66
NP4: P'nydd 4F 37
Grove, The NP12: P'fraith 5B 50
Grove Wlk. NP11: C'maen 6G 43
Gruffyd Dr. CF83: Caer 2F 75
Grwyne Pl. NP12: Argoed 3C 42
Guest St. CF81: Foch 4A 22
Gurnos Est. NP23: B mawr 2H 11

Gwalia Ter. NP13: Blai 3D **18**
Gwaun Delyn Cl.
NP23: N'glo 2C **18**
Gwaunfelin Wlk. NP4: B'avn 2G **21**
Gwaun-Fro CF82: P'heol 1C **48**
Gwaun Helyg NP23: E Vale 1C **16**
Gwaun Helyg Rd.
NP23: E Vale 6C **10**
Gwaun Hyfryd CF83: Caer 3A **76**
Gwaun Newydd CF83: Caer 3A **76**
Gwaun y Cwrt CF83: Caer 6C **74**
Gwendoline Rd. NP11: Ris 4C **72**
Gwent Ct. NP12: Fleur 3F **49**
NP22: Tred 1G **15**
Gwent Pl. NP7: Mardy 1H **7**
Gwent Rd. NP7: Mardy 1H **7**
Gwent Shopping Cen.
NP22: Tred 2H **15**
Gwent Sq. NP44: C'brn 5E **55**
Gwent St. NP4: P'pool 1B **46**
Gwent Ter. NP13: Blai 3D **18**
NP23: N'glo 6C **12**
Gwent Way NP22: Tred 1G **15**
Gwerna Cres. CF82: Maes C 2F **57**
Gwern Av. CF83: Sen 3B **66**
Gwern Berthi Rd.
NP13: C'lery 4G **27**
Gwern Las NP13: C'lery 5G **27**
Gwerthonor La. CF81: Gilf 6E **41**
Gwerthonor Pl. CF81: Gilf 6F **41**
Gwerthonor Rd. CF81: Gilf 1F **49**
Gwladys Av. CF81: Barg 2E **41**
GWRHAY . . . . **.3D 42**
Gwyddon Rd. NP11: Aberc 1C **60**
Gwyn Cres. NP4: Var 4D **28**
Gwyn Dr. CF83: Caer 3F **75**
Gwynllyw NP44: Pnwd 3C **54**
Gypsy Cres. NP7: L'fst 6D **6**
Gypsy La. CF15: Caer 6B **74**
NP4: Abers, P'nydd 4D **36**

H

Haden St. NP4: P'pool 1B **46**
Hadrian's Cl. CF82: G'gaer 2B **48**
Hafan-Werdd CF83: Caer 2A **76**
Hafod-Art NP13: L'hth 1C **44**
Hafodarthen NP13: B'thel 6C **34**
Hafod Cl. NP12: Peng 3G **49**
NP18: P'hir 5H **65**
Hafod Ct. Rd. NP44: G'mdw 4A **54**
Hafod-fan Rd.
NP13: S Bells 2D **34**
Hafod La. NP23: W Iwyd 1F **25**
Hafod Rd. NP18: P'hir 5H **65**
Hafod Tudor Ter.
NP11: W'vle 1D **70**
Hafod-y-Bryn NP11: Ris 4E **73**
Hafod-y-Mynydd
NP22: Rhym 6C **14**
Hafod-yr-Ynys Rd.
NP11: Crum 6B **44**
(not continuous)
Hafren Rd. NP44: G'mdw 5A **54**
Haines Cl. CF83: Caer 6D **74**
Haldane Ct. CF83: Caer 4A **76**
Haldens, The NP44: F'wtr 2G **63**
Halfpennys, The NP7: Gilw 2D **4**
Halls Crossing NP12: Oakd 2C **50**
Halls Rd.
NP11: C'keys, P'waun 5D **60**
NP11: Newb 3H **51**
Halls Rd. Ter. NP11: C'keys 6D **60**
Hall St. NP12: B'wood 2B **50**
NP23: W Iwyd 6F **17**
Haman Pl. CF82: G'gaer 3B **48**
Hampton Cl. CF82: G'gaer 3C **48**
Hanbury Cl. NP44: C'brn 5E **55**
Hanbury Gdns. NP4: P'nydd 5F **37**
Hanbury Rd. CF81: Barg 3F **41**
NP4: P'nydd 5E **37**
NP4: P'pool 1C **46**
Hanbury Sq. CF81: Barg 3F **41**
Hanbury St. NP12: Peng 2F **49**
Hand Farm Rd. NP4: New I 2F **47**
Hanley Path NP44: G'mdw 1H **63**
Harcourt Pl. NP22: Rhym 4A **14**
Harcourt Rd. NP23: B mawr 3A **12**
Harcourt St. NP23: E Vale 6E **11**
Harcourt Ter. NP22: Tred 3H **15**
NP24: Brith 4F **31**
Hardy Ct. NP4: P'nydd 4F **37**
Harford Gdns. NP22: Tred 1A **16**
Harford Sq. NP23: E Vale 6F **11**
Harford St. NP22: Tred 1A **16**
Harlech Cl. NP12: B'wood 6A **42**
NP44: C'iog 3G **55**
Harlech Ct. CF83: Caer 3C **74**
Harold Rd. NP7: A'gvnny 3E **7**
Harold St. NP44: Pnwd 4E **55**
Harper's Rd. NP4: Var 6E **29**
Hartshorn Ct. CF83: Caer 4A **76**
Harvard Rd. CF83: Abert 6C **66**
Hassocks Lea NP44: F'wtr 2G **63**
Hastings Cl. NP7: A'gvnny 6G **7**
Hatherleigh Pl. NP7: A'gvnny 4E **7**
Hatherleigh Rd. NP7: A'gvnny 3E **7**
Hatter St. NP23: B mawr 3A **12**
Haulfryn NP7: Cly 6G **13**
Haulwen Rd. CF82: P'heol 1D **48**
Havard's Rw. NP22: Rhym 5C **14**
Haven way NP7: A'gvnny 2D **6**
Hawarden Grn. NP44: Llan 1E **65**
Hawkes Ridge NP44: F'wtr 1E **63**
Hawthorn Av. CF82: Heng 6E **49**
Hawthorn Dr. NP12: P'fraith 6A **50**
Hawthorne Glade
NP13: Blai 4E **19**
Hawthorn Pl. NP11: P'waun 5D **60**
Hawthorn Rd. NP4: Grif 6D **46**
NP23: B'fort 3E **11**
Hawthorns, The
NP44: Up Cwm 3B **54**
Hawtin Pk. Ind. Est.
NP12: P'fraith 5H **49**
Hayswayn NP44: F'wtr 2G **63**
Hazel Cl. NP4: New I 2H **47**
Hazel Ct. NP23: Rassa 2D **10**
Hazel Gro. CF83: Caer 2H **75**
CF83: Tret 6G **69**
Hazel Wlk. NP44: C'iog 3G **55**
Hazelwood Rd. NP11: Newb 1C **52**
Head of the Hill Ct.
NP22: Tred 5G **9**
Heads of the Valleys Ind. Est.
NP22: Rhym 5A **14**
Heads of the Valleys Rd.
NP7: A'gvnny, Gov, L'fst 4F **5**
NP7: B mawr 6G **13**
NP7: Gilw 5A **4**
NP22: Rhym, Tred 1A **14**
NP22: Tred 6D **8**
NP23: B'fort, B mawr, Rassa
.4A **10**
NP23: B mawr 2C **12**
Heather Cl. NP22: Tred 5A **10**
Heather Ct. NP44: F'wtr 2E **63**
Heathfield Cl. NP23: G lydan 2E **11**
Heathfield Wlk.
CF81: A'goed 2F **41**
Heathlands CF82: Ystrad 1D **56**
Heath Rd. NP12: P'fraith 5A **50**
Hector Av. NP11: Crum 4C **44**
Helpstone Ter. NP4: P'pool 6F **37**
Henderson Rd.
NP23: B mawr 3H **11**
Hendre CF83: Caer 6H **67**
NP23: E Vale 6F **11**
Hendre Ct. NP44: H'lys 3E **63**
Hendredenny Dr. CF83: Caer 3B **74**
HENDREDENNY PARK . . . . **.3C 74**
Hendre Rd. CF83: Abert 6B **66**
Henfron CF83: Caer 1D **74**
HENGOED . . . . **.6F 49**
Hengoed Av.
CF82: Cefn H, Heng 4E **49**
Hengoed Cres. CF82: Cefn H 5E **49**
Hengoed Hall Cl.
CF82: Cefn H 6E **49**
Hengoed Hall Dr.
CF82: Cefn H 5E **49**
Hengoed Hall Gdns.
CF82: Cefn H 5E **49**
Hengoed Parc CF82: Heng 6F **49**
Hengoed Rd.
CF82: Cefn H, Heng 6E **49**
(Hengoed)
CF82: Cefn H, P'heol 2D **48**
(Pen-pendair-heol)
Hengoed Station (Rail) 1F **57**
HENLLYS . . . . **.3E 63**
Henllys La. NP44: H'lys 3D **62**
HENLLYS VALE . . . . **.6G 63**
Henllys Village Rd.
NP44: H'lys 3E **63**
Henllys Way NP44: C'brn 2B **64**
NP44: F'wtr, H'lys 3E **63**
Hen Rd. NP13: L'hth 6C **34**
Henry St. CF81: Barg 3E **41**
Hensol Cl. NP44: Llan 6G **55**
Henwaun St. NP13: Blai 6D **18**
Henwaun St. Sth. NP13: Blai 6D **18**
Heol Adam CF82: G'gaer 6A **40**
Heol-Ael-y-Bryn NP23: E Vale . . .4D **10**
Heol Aneurin CF83: Caer 1C **74**
Heol Aneurin Bevan
NP22: Rhym 4B 14
(off Queen's Cr.)
Heol Ap Gethin NP23: N'glo 2D **18**
Heol Arthur Fear NP13: Blai 4D **18**
Heol Barri CF83: Caer 2E **75**
Heol Bedd-Dyn-Hir
NP7: Gilw, Gov 5C **4**
Heol Berllan CF83: Caer 2G **75**
Heol Beulah CF83: L'brad 5A **68**
Heol Beuno NP4: New I 2G **47**
Heol Bro Wen CF83: Caer 3G **75**
Heol Brychan CF81: Barg 4D **40**
Heol Brynteg CF82: Ystrad 3D **56**
Heol Caeau-Meinion
NP12: B'wood 3A **42**
Heol Cae Bach CF83: Caer 1G **75**
Heol Cae Celynnen
CF83: Caer 1G **75**
Heol Cae-Derwen CF81: Barg . . .4D **40**
Heol Cae Fan Heulog
CF83: Caer 2G **75**
Heol Cae Gwyn CF83: Caer 6D **74**
Heol Cae Maen CF83: Caer 2G **75**
Heol Caradoc CF81: Barg 4D **40**
Heol Cattwg CF82: G'gaer 3B **48**
Heol Celyn CF82: Heng 1E **57**
Heol Clyd CF83: Caer 2C **74**
Heol Coedcae CF81: Barg 4D **40**
Heol Cwarrel Clark
CF83: Caer 6G **67**
Heol Cwm Ifor CF83: Caer 1C **74**
Heolddu Av. CF81: Barg 3D **40**
Heolddu Cres. CF81: Barg 3D **40**
Heolddu Dr. CF81: Barg 3D **40**
Heolddu Grn. CF81: Barg 3D **40**
Heolddu Gro. CF81: Barg 2E **41**
Heolddu Leisure Cen. 3D **40**
Heolddu Rd. CF81: Barg 3E **41**
NP12: P'fraith 1C **58**
Heol Deiniol NP4: New I 2G **47**
Heol Derw CF82: Heng 1E **57**
NP23: B mawr 2H **11**
Heol Derwen NP4: New I 2G **47**
Heol Dewi CF82: Heng 1E **57**
Heol Edward Lewis
CF82: G'gaer 2B **48**
Heol Erw-y-Rhos CF83: Caer 2G **75**
Heol Evan Wynne CF81: P'tyn . . .2C **22**
Heol Fach CF81: Barg 5E **41**
CF83: Caer 3D **74**
Heol Fargoed CF81: Barg 5E **41**
Heol Fawr CF46: Nels, Ystrad . . .2A **56**
CF83: Caer 1C **74**
Heol Fer CF83: Caer 1D **74**
Heol Ganol CF83: Caer 4E **75**
NP23: B mawr 3A **12**
Heol Gerrig NP13: A'lery 6G **27**
Heol Gethin CF82: Cefn H 5E **49**
Heol Gledyr CF83: Caer 5F **75**
Heol Glyn CF83: Caer 2E **75**
Heol Graig Wen CF83: Caer 2C **74**
Heol Gwaun Rhos
CF83: Caer 2G **75**
Heol Gwyn Lliw NP23: B'fort 4G **11**
Heol Hamlin NP7: A'gvnny 3H **7**
Heol Helig NP23: B mawr 3H **11**
Heol Iago CF81: Foch 4A **22**
Heol Isaf NP4: New I 2G **47**
NP23: B mawr 3A **12**
Heol Klockner NP22: Rhym 5A **14**
Heol Las CF83: Caer 6H **67**
Heol Lewis CF83: Caer 2A **76**
Heol Maddoc NP4: New I 2G **47**
Heol Maerdy CF83: Caer 3A **76**
Heol Newydd NP44: Up Cwm . . .3C **54**
Heol Onen NP23: B mawr 3H **11**
Heol Padarn NP4: New I 2G **47**
Heol Pees CF82: Heng 1F **57**
Heol Penallta CF82: G'gaer 3C **48**
Heol Pencarreg CF81: Barg 4D **40**
Heol Pen-Rhiws-Eglws
NP12: Argoed 1A **42**
Heol Pen-y-Cae NP23: E Vale . . .5D **10**
Heol Pit-y-Ceiliogod
NP12: B'wood 6H **41**
(not continuous)
Heol Pont y Seison
CF46: Nels, Ystrad 1B **56**
Heol Pwllypant CF83: Caer 2E **75**
Heol Rhos CF83: Caer 4C **74**
Heol Serth CF83: Caer 1C **74**
Heol Siloam NP23: B'fort 3F **11**
Heol Teilo NP4: New I 2G **47**
Heol Thomas CF83: Caer 5E **75**
Heol Tir Bach CF83: Caer 1C **74**
Heol Tir Gibbon CF83: Caer 2D **74**
Heol Tir Ton NP11: C'fch 2A **70**
Heol Tir-y-Llan CF81: A'goed 3G **41**
Heol Trecastell CF83: Caer 5E **75**
Heol Trelyn Rd.
NP12: P'fraith 5A **50**
Heol Ty Crwn CF83: Caer 2G **75**
Heol Tyddyn CF83: Caer 6C **74**
Heol-ty-Gwyn CF83: L'brad 2B **68**
Heol Ty Merchant CF83: Caer . . .2G **75**
Heol Tynewydd
NP12: Argoed, B'wood 2A **42**
Heol Uchaf CF82: Heng 6E **49**
Heol-Uchaf NP22: Rhym 3B **14**
Heol Waen NP23: Rassa 3C **10**
Heol Waun NP4: Tal 6D **28**
Heol Waun Fawr CF83: Caer 6D **74**
Heol Waun Waelod
CF83: Caer 6E **75**
Heol y Beddau CF83: Caer 5E **75**
Heol y Bedw-Hirion
NP12: A'goed 3A **42**
Heol y Berth CF83: Caer 6D **74**
Heol-y-Bryn CF81: Foch 3A **22**
Heol-y-Carnau CF83: Caer 2G **75**
Heol y Cefn
NP12: A'goed, B'wood 6H **41**
Heol-y-Coed NP12: Yny 2C **58**
Heol-y-Cwm CF83: Caer 6E **75**
Heol-y-Ddol CF83: Caer 2G **75**
Heol y Derwen NP12: Cefn F 2H **49**
Heol-y-Dreflan CF83: Caer 2G **75**
Heol-y-Felin CF82: Cefn H 4D **48**
CF83: Caer 4E **75**
Heol y Garth CF83: Rud 4E **77**
Heol-y-Gogledd CF83: Caer 1D **74**
Heol-y-Gors CF83: Caer 2G **75**
Heol-y-Graig CF82: Ystrad 3D **56**
Heol y Mynyd CF81: Barg 4D **40**
Heol-y-Nant CF83: Caer 4E **75**
Heol Ynys Ddu CF83: Caer 6D **74**
Heol-y-Parc CF83: Caer 4E **75**
Heol-y-Pia CF83: Caer 4D **74**
Heol y Pwca NP44: Pnwd 3C **54**
Heol-yr-Onen CF83: Caer 4E **75**
Heol-yr-Ysbyty CF83: Caer 6D **74**
Heol yr Ysgol CF83: Tret 1D **76**
Heol-yr-Ysgol NP23: E Vale 1C **16**
Heol Ysgol Newydd
CF81: A'goed 2F **41**
Heol Ysgubor CF83: Caer 6D **74**
Heol-y-Twyn NP22: Rhym 3B **14**
Heol-y-Waun CF81: P'tyn 3D **22**
CF82: G'gaer 3B **48**
Heol-y-Wern CF83: Caer 2G **75**
Herbert Av. NP10: Roger 5F **73**
NP11: Ris 5F **73**
Herbert Dr. CF83: Caer 2E **75**
Herbert's Cl. NP4: Var 5D **28**
Herbert's Rd. NP4: Var 4D **28**
Herbert St. NP11: Crum 5E **45**
NP24: Brith 4F **31**
Herbert Ter. NP11: Crum 5E **45**
Hereford Rd.
NP7: A'gvnny, Mardy 4G **7**
NP23: B'fort 4F **11**
Herons Way CF83: Caer 6D **74**
Herrick Pl. CF83: Mac 6C **70**
Highbury Dr. NP12: B'wood 3B **50**
High Cl. NP44: Llanf 2E **65**
Highfield Cl. NP4: P'nydd 4E **37**
NP11: Ris 3C **72**
NP22: Tred 5F **9**
NP44: Llanf 3E **65**
Highfield Ct. NP11: Newb 3A **52**
Highfield Cres.
CF81: A'goed 2G **41**
NP7: A'gvnny 2G **7**
NP12: P'fraith 6B **50**
Highfield Rd. NP12: P'fraith 6B **50**
Highfields Way
NP12: B'wood 4A **50**
Highland Cres.
NP12: P'fraith 5E **50**
Highland Gro. NP44: Pnwd 3E **55**
Highlands Cres.
NP23: B'fort 3F **11**
Highlands Rd. NP23: B'fort 3F **11**
Highland Ter. NP12: B'wood 2B **50**
Highmead NP12: P'fraith 5A **50**
High Meadows NP11: Aberc 5C **52**

High St. CF81: Barg 3F 41
CF81: P'tyn 2C 22
CF82: Ystrad 2E 57
CF83: Abert 5D 66
CF83: L'brad 4A 68
CF83: Sen 2C 66
CF83: Tret 6H 69
NP4: Abers 2D 36
NP4: B'avn 3F 21
NP4: Grif 4E 47
NP4: P'pool 1B 46
NP4: Var 5D 28
NP7: A'gvnny 4F 7
NP11: Aberc 6C 52
NP11: Newb 3A 52
(Bryngwyn Rd.)
NP11: Newb, P'fraith 4F 51
(Newbridge Rd.)
NP11: P'waun 6D 60
NP11: Yny 5C 58
NP12: Argoed 2C 42
NP12: B'wood 6B 42
(Tredegar Rd.)
NP12: B'wood 2B 50
(Wesley Rd.)
NP12: Peng 3F 49
NP12: Peng 1F 49
NP13: A'lery 6G 27
NP13: Blai 2C 18
NP13: L'hth 1C 44
NP13: S Bells 2D 34
NP22: Rhym 5B 14
NP23: E Vale 4E 17
NP24: New T 5F 23
Hightree Ri. NP12: Oakd 1D 50
High Trees Rd. NP7: Gilw 3D 4
High Way, The
NP4: New I, P'pool 2F 47
Highway, The
NP44: C'iog 3H 55
NP44: Oakf 2C 64
Hilary Rd. NP11: Newb 1C 52
Hiley Av. NP7: Gilw 3C 4
Hileys Row NP7: Cly 6A 4
Hillary Ri. NP11: P'waun 4D 60
Hill Cres. NP23: B mawr 3A 12
Hillcrest NP4: New I 3H 47
NP4: Var 5D 28
NP7: A'gvnny 2G 7
Hill Crest NP23: B mawr 3A 12
Hillcrest Rd. NP4: New I 2F 47
Hillcrest Vw. NP13: C'lery 4G 27
Hillgrove Av. NP7: Mardy 1H 7
Hill Ri. NP4: Abers 6E 29
Hill Rd. CF81: Deri 5A 30
CF81: P'tyn 2B 22
NP7: A'gvnny 2E 7
NP22: A'swg 3F 23
Hillside CF81: Foch 3A 22
CF83: Caer 6G 75
NP4: B'avn 2G 21
NP7: A'gvnny 2F 7
NP11: Crum 6B 44
NP11: Ris 4D 72
(not continuous)
NP23: E Vale 2E 17
Hillside Av. CF83: Abert 6B 66
NP4: B'avn 2G 21
NP12: Mark 5A 32
Hillside Ct. NP44: Pnwd 4D 54
Hillside Dr. NP4: P'pool 3C 46
Hillside Gdns. CF81: Gilf 5E 41
Hillside Pk. CF81: Barg 5E 41
Hillside Rd. NP4: Grif 4D 46
Hillside Ter. CF81: Deri 3A 30
CF82: Ystrad 2C 56
CF83: B'ws 1B 76
NP12: B'wood 2B 50
NP13: L'hth 1D 44
NP23: W Iwyd 6G 17
Hillside Vw. CF81: Barg 5E 41
Hill St. CF81: Barg 2E 41
CF82: Ystrad 1D 56
NP4: B'avn 3F 21
NP4: Grif 4E 47
NP4: P'nydd 5F 37
NP11: Aberc 5C 52
NP11: Newb 3A 52
NP11: Ris 4D 72
NP13: A'lery 1C 34
NP22: Rhym 6C 14
NP23: B mawr 3A 12
NP23: E Vale 3F 17
NP44: Oakf 2B 64
HILLTOP 2D 16
Hill Top NP44: C'brn 1A 64
Hilltop Cres. NP11: Newb 2B 52
Hilltop Grn. NP44: Pnwd 4C 54
Hilltop Shopping Cen.
NP23: E Vale 1D 16
Hill Vw. CF82: Heng 1F 57
CF82: Maes C 2G 57
NP7: Gilw 2D 4
NP11: C'fch 1A 70
NP12: P'fraith 5B 50
NP22: Tred 4A 16
Hinter Path *NP44: F'wtr 2G 63*
(off Jule Rd.)
Hodges Cres. NP12: Peng 5G 41
Hogarth Cl. NP44: Oakf 3D 64
Holland St. NP23: E Vale 2E 17
Hollies, The NP11: C'maen 6G 43
HOLLYBUSH
NP44 3H 63
NP12 2H 31
Hollybush NP44: C'brn 2A 64
Hollybush Cl. NP44: C'brn 2H 63
Hollybush Ter. NP4: P'nydd 5F 37
Hollybush Vw. NP44: F'wtr 3A 64
Hollybush Way
NP44: C'brn, F'wtr, Oakf 3G 63
Holly Cl. NP23: Rassa 2D 10
Holly Lodge Cl. NP44: C'iog 3H 55
Holly Lodge Gdns.
NP44: C'iog 3H 55
Holly Lodge Grn. NP44: C'iog 3H 55
Holly Lodge Rd. NP44: C'iog 3G 55
Holly Pl. NP12: B'wood 2B 50
Holly Rd. NP11: Ris 3D 72
Holly Ter. NP11: Newb 3A 52
Hollywell Cres. NP7: A'gvnny 5G 7
Hollywell Rd. E.
NP7: A'gvnny 5G 7
Holmdale NP44: G'mdw 1G 63
Holyhead Ct. CF83: Caer 3B 74
Holyoake Ter. NP4: P'nydd 4F 37
Holywell Cl. NP7: A'gvnny 4G 7
Holywell Rd. NP7: A'gvnny 5G 7
Homeland Pl. NP12: B'wood 3C 50
Homeleigh NP11: Newb 2H 51
Honeyfield Rd. NP23: Rassa 2C 10
Honeysuckle Cl. NP23: Rassa 2D 10
Hope St. NP13: Blai 4D 18
Horace Ter. CF83: L'brad 5A 68
Horeb Ct. NP11: Pent C 2A 44
Horner St. CF82: Tir B 3F 49
Hospital Rd. CF82: P'heol 1D 48
NP4: C'avn, P'nydd 4F 37
NP23: N'glo 1C 18
Howard Dr. CF83: Caer 2F 75
Howards Way NP23: W Iwyd 6F 17
Howy Rd. NP23: Rassa 2C 10
Hughes Av. NP23: E Vale 1D 16
Huntingdon Cl. NP44: G'mdw 6A 54
Hyde St. NP13: L'hth 1D 44
Hynam Pl. NP4: Var 6E 29

I

Idris Davies Pl. *NP22: Rhym 1C 22*
(off Plantation Pl.)
Ilan Rd. CF83: Abert 6C 66
Incline Rd. NP4: Abers 1E 37
Ingles *NP44: F'wtr 2G 63*
(off Henllys Way)
Inkerman Row NP13: Blai 3C 18
Inkerman Ter. NP22: Tred 4G 15
Institution Ter. NP23: E Vale 3E 17
Intermediate Rd.
NP23: B mawr 2B 12
Iris Rd. NP10: Roger 6G 73
Iron Row NP22: Tred 3H 15
Iron St. NP22: Tred 3H 15
Isaf Rd. NP11: Ris 4E 73
Isca Cl. NP44: C'brn 5F 55
Is-Fryn NP22: Rhym 3B 14
Islwyn NP11: Yny 5C 58
Islwyn Cl. NP12: Peng 2G 49
NP23: E Vale 1D 16
Islwyn Ct. NP11: Ris 4E 73
Islwyn Dr. CF83: Caer 3F 75
Islwyn Indoor Bowls Cen. 6B 50
Islwyn Rd. NP11: W'vle 1F 71
Islwyn St. NP11: Aberc 6B 52
NP11: C'fch 2A 70
Islwyn Ter. NP12: P'fraith 5D 50
Islwyn Workshops
NP11: Ris 5D 72
Itton St. NP23: Cwm 4H 25
Ivor Gdns. NP4: B'avn 3F 21
Ivor St. NP4: B'avn 3F 21
NP11: C'crn 4D 60
NP12: Peng 3F 49
(not continuous)
Ivy Cl. NP23: Rassa 3B 10
Ivy Dene Cl. NP4: C'avn 4G 37
Ivy Row NP24: Brith 5F 31

J

James Cl. NP12: Fleur 3F 49
James's Row NP23: B'fort 3D 10
James St. CF81: A'goed 3G 41
CF83: L'brad 4A 68
CF83: Tret 6H 69
NP4: B'avn 3F 21
NP4: P'pool 6H 37
NP12: Mark 6A 32
NP13: A'lery 6G 27
NP22: Tred 4A 16
NP23: E Vale 1E 17
NP24: Brith 4F 31
NP24: New T 2D 30
James Ter. CF82: Heng 6F 49
NP7: Cly 1H 13
Jamesville NP11: C'crn 3C 60
Jasmine Cl. NP10: Roger 6G 73
Jenkins Row CF81: Deri 5A 30
NP22: Rhym 6C 14
Jenkin St. CF82: Maes C 1G 57
Jerry's La. CF83: B'ws 6E 69
Jerusalem Cl. NP4: New I 4H 47
Jerusalem La.
NP4: Glas, New I 4H 47
Jerusalem St. NP22: Rhym 6C 14
John Baker Cl. NP44: Oakf 3C 64
John St. CF81: Barg 4E 41
NP4: P'pool 1C 46
NP11: C'crn 3D 60
NP11: Yny 6C 58
NP12: Mark 6B 32
NP23: E Vale 6D 10
Jones St. NP24: New T 2D 30
Jubilee Ct. NP7: Mardy 1H 7
Jubilee Rd. NP13: S Bells 2D 34
NP24: New T 3F 31
Jubilee Ter. NP4: P'pool 5F 37
Jule Rd. NP44: F'wtr 2G 63
Julian's Cl. CF82: G'gaer 2B 48
Junction Cottage Mus. 2E 47
Juniper Cres. NP44: H'lys 3F 63

K

Kays & Kears Ind. Est.
NP4: B'avn 2D 20
Kear's Row NP4: Var 2E 29
Keats Cl. NP44: C'brn 1A 64
Keble Ct. CF83: Mac 6C 70
Keir Hardie Cl. NP23: G lydan 1E 11
Keir Hardie Ter. NP11: Crum 4B 44
Kemeys Fawr Cl. NP4: Grif 6D 46
Kemys St. NP4: Grif 5E 47
Kemys Wlk. NP44: C'brn 2A 64
KENDON 5G 43
Kendon Rd. NP11: Crum 5H 43
Kenfig Pl. NP44: Llan 6G 55
Kenilworth Pl. NP44: C'brn 1H 63
Kennard Ct. NP4: B'avn 3E 21
Kennard Cres. NP4: B'avn 3E 21
Kennard Pl. *NP4: B'avn 2E 21*
(off North St.)
Kennard Ter. NP11: Crum 6A 44
Kestrel Vw. CF82: Heng 6E 49
Kidwelly Cl. NP12: B'wood 5B 42
NP44: Llan 1D 64
(not continuous)
Kidwelly Ct. CF83: Caer 3C 74
Kidwelly Rd. NP44: Llan 1D 64
Kiln Rd. NP7: L'fst 6D 6
Kimberley Rd. NP13: S Bells 2D 34
Kimberley Ter. NP22: Tred 4A 16
Kincoed Rd. NP12: Oakd 6E 43
King Charles Rd.
NP11: Newb 4G 51
King Edward Av. CF83: Caer 5G 75
King Edward Rd.
NP23: B mawr 2B 12
King Edward Ter.
NP22: Rhym 4B 14
Kings Av. NP22: Rhym 4B 14
Kings Cl. CF83: Abert 6D 66
Kingsfield NP23: E Vale 6E 11
King's Hill CF82: Heng 6E 49
Kingsland Wlk. NP44: G'mdw 6B 54
Kingslea *NP44: F'wtr 2G 63*
(off Jule Rd.)
Kingsley Pl. CF83: Sen 3B 66
King St. CF81: P'tyn 2C 22
CF83: Abert 6D 66
NP4: B'avn 2F 21
NP4: P'pool 6G 37
NP7: A'gvnny 4F 7
NP11: C'fch 1H 69
NP13: A'lery 1C 34
NP22: Tred 6A 10
NP23: B mawr 3H 11
(not continuous)
NP23: Cwm 4A 26
NP23: N'glo 6B 12
Kingswood Cl. CF82: Heng 6F 49
Kinnock Ct. NP44: C'iog 3G 55
Kitchener St. NP4: P'nydd 5D 36
Knoll Rd. NP7: A'gvnny 3D 6

L

Laburnam Av. NP22: Tred 6G 9
Laburnum Cl. NP10: Roger 6G 73
NP23: Rassa 2D 10
Laburnum Dr. NP4: New I 2H 47
NP44: H'lys 3F 63
Laburnum Gro. NP12: P'fraith 6B 50
Laburnum Ter. NP11: Aberc 5D 52
Laburnum Wlk. NP7: A'gvnny 3H 7
(not continuous)
Ladybench NP44: F'wtr 2G 63
Ladysmith Rd. NP12: B'wood 3B 50
Ladysmith Ter. NP22: Tred 3A 16
Lady Tyler Ter. NP22: Rhym 6C 14
Ladywell NP44: Pnwd 4E 55
Lake Rd. NP23: B mawr 3B 12
Lakeside NP13: C'lery 2G 27
NP22: Tred 6E 9
Lakeside Cl. NP22: Tred 6E 9
NP44: Oakf 5D 64
Lakeview NP44: Oakf 5D 64
Lamb Cl. NP7: A'gvnny 4E 7
Lamb La. NP18: P'hir 4H 65
Lamb's Sq. NP23: B'fort 3D 10
Lancaster Dr. NP7: Gilw 3E 5
Lancaster Rd. NP4: New I 5G 47
Lancaster St. NP13: Blai 6D 18
NP13: S Bells 2C 34
Langstone Ct. NP44: C'brn 2H 63
Lansbury Av. CF82: Cefn H 5E 49
Lansbury Cl. CF83: Caer 2E 75
LANSBURY PARK 3A 76
Lansbury Rd. NP23: B mawr 3H 11
Lansbury Ter. NP23: B'fort 3G 11
Lansdown Dr. NP7: A'gvnny 2G 7
Lansdowne NP4: Grif 6E 47
Lansdowne Rd.
NP23: G lydan 2E 11
Lansdown Rd. NP7 A'gvnny 2G 7
Larch Cl. NP4: New I 3G 47
Larch Gro. CF83: Caer 2H 75
Lasgarn La. NP4: C'avn, Trev 1H 37
Lasgarn Pl.
NP4: Abers, P'nydd 2F 37
Lasgarn Vw. NP4: Tal, Var 6D 28
NP4: Var 4D 28
Laundry Pl. NP7: A'gvnny 4E 7
Laural Wlk. NP44: Up Cwm 3C 54
Laurel Ct. CF83: B'ws 1B 76
Laurel Dr. NP12: P'fraith 6B 50
Laurel Grn. NP44: Up Cwm 3B 54
Lavender Way NP10: Roger 6G 73
Lawn Ter. NP22: Rhym 5B 14
Lawrence Av. NP12: Mark 6A 32
NP13: A'lery 4E 27
Lawrence St. CF83: Caer 4G 75
Lawrence Ter. NP24: New T 6E 23
Laybourne Cl. NP44: Pnwd 5E 55
Lea Ct. NP12: P'fraith 6D 50
Leadon Ct. NP44: G'mdw 5A 54
Leas, The NP44: Pnwd 4C 54
Ledbrooke Cl. NP44: C'brn 2H 63
Legion's Way CF82: G'gaer 2A 48
Leicester Dr. NP44: G'mdw 6A 54
Leicester Sq. CF82: P'heol 2D 48
Leigh Rd.
NP4: C'avn, P'nydd 4F 37
Leighton Ct. NP44: G'mdw 1H 63
Leonard St. NP12: Fleur 3G 49
Letchworth Rd. NP23: E Vale 6D 10

Lethbridge Ter. *NP4: Abers* 2E **37**
(off Pentwyn Rd.)
Lewis Av. NP12: B'wood 1B **50**
Lewis Cl. NP4: Var 5D **28**
NP11: Crum 5C **44**
Lewis Cres. CF81: Gilf 6F **41**
Lewis Dr. CF83: Caer 2E **75**
Lewis's La. NP7: A'gvnny 4F **7**
Lewis St. CF81: A'goed 1G **41**
CF82: Ystrad 2D **56**
CF83: Mac 6F **71**
NP4: Abers 1E **37**
NP11: Crum 5B **44**
NP12: B'wood 2B **50**
Lewis's Wlk. *NP7: A'gvnny* 4F **7**
(off Lewis's La.)
Lewis Ter. *CF83: L'brad* 4A **68**
(off De Winton Ter.)
NP4: P'nydd 5F **37**
Lewis Wood NP4: P'nydd 4E **37**
Leydene Cl. NP11: Ris 2C **72**
Libanus Rd. NP12: B'wood 4C **50**
NP23: E Vale 6E **11**
Library Sq. NP7: A'gvnny 4F **7**
Lilac Gro. NP10: Roger 6G **73**
Lilian Gro. NP23: E Vale 5E **11**
Lilian Rd. NP12: B'wood 3B **50**
Lily Way NP10: Roger 6H **73**
Lime Ct. CF81: Barg 4D **40**
NP11: Newb 1C **52**
Lime Gro. NP12: P'fraith 6B **50**
Limekiln Rd. NP4: P'nydd 3F **37**
Limestone Rd. NP23: N'glo 4B **12**
Limestone Rd. E.
NP23: N'glo 4B **12**
Limetree Ct. NP7: A'gvnny 5G **7**
Linden Av. NP7: A'gvnny 2E **7**
Linden Ct. NP11: Newb 1D **52**
Linden Gro. CF83: Caer 2H **75**
NP7: Gov 5H **5**
Linden Lea Dr. NP12: B'wood 3A **50**
Lindsay Gdns. NP22: Tred 6G **9**
Link Rd. NP4: New I 3G **47**
Links, The NP4: C'avn 4H **37**
Linton Ct. NP4: Abers 2F **37**
Lion St. NP4: B'avn 3F **21**
NP7: A'gvnny 4F **7**
Lion Ter. NP7: Gilw 4C **4**
Lisburn Rd. CF82: Ystrad 2D **56**
Liswerry Cl. NP44: Llan 1E **65**
(not continuous)
Liswerry Dr. NP44: Llan 6H **55**
Littledene NP44: G'mdw 6B **54**
Little La. NP23: B'fort 3G **11**
LITTLE MILL 2H **39**
Llanarth Cl. CF83: Mac 6G **71**
Llanarth Rd. NP11: Newb 1A **52**
NP12: P'fraith 5D **50**
Llanarth Sq. NP11: Ris 4D **72**
Llanarth St. CF83: Mac 6G **71**
NP11: W'vle 2C **70**
Llanarth Vs. NP11: W'vle 2C **70**
LLANBRADACH 4A **68**
Llanbradach Station (Rail) 4A **68**
Llancayo Pk. CF81: Barg 2E **41**
Llancayo St. CF81: Barg 2E **41**
Llandaff Grn. NP44: C'brn 5E **55**
Llandaff Rd. NP23: B'fort 4F **11**
Llandegefedd Way
NP4: New I 4G **47**
Llandegveth Cl. NP44: C'iog 3H **55**
Llandenny Wlk. NP44: C'brn 6E **55**
Llanderfel Ct. NP44: G'mdw 5A **54**
Llandowlais St.
NP44: C'brn, Oakf 2B **64**
Llanelen Rd. NP7: L'fst 6D **6**
LLANELLI 3A **4**
LLANELLY 3A **4**
Llanelly Chu. Rd. NP7: Gilw 5A **4**
LLANELLY HILL 3H **13**
Llanelly Hill Cvn. Site
NP7: Gilw 5A **4**
Llanelly Hill Rd.
NP7: Cly, Gilw 6A **4**
Llanerch La. NP11: Pent C 3A **44**
Llanerch Path NP44: G'mdw 1G **63**
Llanerch Rd. NP11: Pent C 2A **44**
Llanfabon Dr.
CF83: B'ws, Tret 6G **69**
LLANFACH 6C **52**
Llanfach Rd. NP11: Aberc 6C **52**
Llanfedw Cl. CF83: Caer 2B **76**
LLAN-FFWYST 6D **6**
LLANFOIST 6D **6**
Llanfoist Cres. NP4: B'avn 2G **21**
LLANFRECHFA 3G **65**
LLANFRECHFA GRANGE HOSPITAL 1F **65**
Llanfrechfa Way
NP44: C'brn, Llan 1C **64**
Llangattock Ct. NP44: C'iog 4H **55**
Llangattwg Cl. NP23: B'fort 3F **11**
Llangorse Path NP44: Llan 2D **64**
Llangorse Rd. NP44: Llan 1D **64**
Llangynidr Rd. NP23: G lydan 1E **11**
LLANHILEDD 1C **44**
LLANHILLETH 1C **44**
Llanhilleth Ind. Est.
NP13: L'hth 2C **44**
Llanon NP44: C'iog 3F **55**
Llanover Av. NP12: P'fraith 5B **50**
Llanover Cl. NP4: B'avn 3H **21**
Llanover Rd. NP4: B'avn 3G **21**
NP4: Trev 2E **29**
Llanover Rd. Est. NP4: B'avn 3H **21**
Llanover St. NP11: Aberc 6B **52**
LLANTARNAM 4E **65**
Llantarnam By-Pass
NP44: Llanf, Oakf 6E **65**
Llantarnam Cl. NP44: C'brn 1C **64**
(not continuous)
Llantarnam Gdns. NP44: Oakf 4E **65**
Llantarnam Grange Arts Cen. 5F **55**
Llantarnam Ind. Est.
NP44: Oakf 4D **64**
Llantarnam Ind. Pk.
NP44: Oakf 4C **64**
Llantarnam Leisure Cen. 4E **65**
Llantarnam Pk. Way
NP44: Oakf 4C **64**
Llantarnam Rd.
NP44: C'brn, Oakf 1C **64**
Llanthewy Cl. NP44: C'iog 4H **55**
LLANVIHANGEL PONTYMOEL 6D **38**
LLANWENARTH 3B **6**
Llan Wenarth NP7: Gov 5H **5**
Llanwe Narth Rd. NP7: Gov 5H **5**
Llanwenarth Vw. NP7: Gilw 3D **4**
LLANYRAFON 1D **64**
Llanyrafon Farm Mus. 1D **64**
Llanyrafon Mill 1D **64**
Llan-yr-Avon Sq. NP44: Llan 1D **64**
Llan-yr-Avon Way
NP44: C'iog, Llan 1D **64**
LLECHRYD 2A **14**
Llewallyn's Row NP7: L Hill 2H **13**
Llewellyn Av. NP11: C'maen 5G **43**
Llewellyn Dr. CF83: Caer 3F **75**
Llewellyn St. CF81: Gilf 6F **41**
Lloyd Av. NP11: Crum 4C **44**
Llwyd-y-Berth CF83: Caer 5D **74**
Llwynbach Ter.
NP12: Holly B 3H **31**
Llwyn Celyn NP23: E Vale 1C **16**
NP44: C'brn 2A **64**
Llwyncelyn Ter. NP13: A'beeg 1H **43**
Llwyn Coed NP12: B'wood 3A **50**
Llwyn Eithan CF83: Caer 2A **76**
Llwyn Helyg NP22: Tred 4F **9**
Llwynon NP11: Ris 3D **72**
Llwyn-on Cl. CF83: Caer 3E **75**
Llwynon Cres. NP12: Oakd 6E **43**
Llwyn-on La. NP12: Oakd 6D **42**
Llwyn Onn CF82: P'heol 2D **48**
NP44: C'iog 5H **55**
Llwynon Rd. NP12: Oakd 6E **43**
Llwyn-on Rd. NP13: S Bells 2D **34**
Llwyn-on St. CF83: Caer 3E **75**
Llwynu Cl. NP7: A'gvnny 2G **7**
Llwynu La. NP7: A'gvnny 1G **7**
Llwynu Rd. NP7: A'gvnny 3G **7**
Llys Cambria CF83: L'brad 5A **68**
Llys Cwm Llwydrhew
NP13: S Bells 3D **34**
Llys Gwyrdd NP44: H'lys 4F **63**
Llys Joseph Parry
NP22: Rhym 4A **14**
Llys Mabon NP22: Rhym 4A **14**
Llys Nant Pandy CF83: Caer 3F **75**
Llys Onnen NP23: E Vale 1C **16**
Llyswen CF82: P'heol 2D **48**
CF83: Mac 6E **71**
Llyswen Wlk. NP44: Llan 2D **64**
Llys-y-Celyn CF83: Caer 2H **75**
Llys y Coed CF82: Ystrad 4D **56**
Llys-y-Fedwen CF83: Caer 3H **75**
Llys yr Efail NP13: Blai 4C **18**
Llywelyn Rd. NP44: C'brn 5E **55**
Load of Hay Rd. NP11: Crum 5A **44**
Lock Up La. NP4: Abers 2E **37**
Lodge Rd. NP4: Abers 1D **36**
Lodge Wood
NP4: New I, P'pool 2E **47**
Lon Fach CF83: Caer 5E **75**
Lon Fawr CF83: Caer 5E **75**
Long Acre NP44: F'wtr 2G **63**
Longbridge NP18: P'hir 5H **65**
Longbridge Ct. *NP11: Ris* 2C **72**
(off St Mary St.)
Lon Gellideg NP12: Oakd 3F **43**
Longfellow Gdns.
CF83: Mac 6B **70**
Long Hollow NP44: C'brn 5E **55**
Longhouse Gro. NP44: H'lys 3E **63**
Long Row NP4: Up R 3B **46**
NP24: New T 3E **31**
Lon Hafren CF83: Caer 6E **75**
Lon Helyg NP44: C'iog 5H **55**
Lon Isaf CF83: Caer 5E **75**
Lon Nant NP44: Pnwd 4F **55**
Lon Pennant NP12: B'wood 6B **42**
Lon Robin Goch CF83: Caer 4D **74**
Lon Uchaf CF83: Caer 5E **75**
Lon-y-Barri CF83: Caer 2E **75**
(not continuous)
Lon-y-Ddraenen CF83: Caer 5E **75**
Lon-y-Deri CF83: Caer 5E **75**
Lon-y-Fran CF83: Caer 4D **74**
Lon-y-Garwa CF83: Caer 6E **75**
Lon-y-Gors CF83: Caer 5D **74**
Lon-y-Llyn CF83: Caer 5E **75**
Lon-yr-Afon CF83: L'brad 3B **68**
Lon-y-Rhedyn CF83: Caer 5D **74**
(not continuous)
Lon-y-Rheydyn CF83: Caer 5E **75**
Lon yr Odyn CF83: Caer 4H **75**
Lon yr Ysgol CF83: B'ws 1A **76**
Lon y Tresglen CF83: Caer 4D **74**
Lon y Twyn CF83: Caer 5G **75**
Lon-y-Waun CF83: Caer 5D **74**
Lon-y-Wern CF83: Caer 5E **75**
Louvain Ter. NP23: E Vale 1F **17**
Lwr. Bailey St. NP23: B mawr 3B **12**
Lwr. Bridge St. NP4: P'pool 1C **46**
Lwr. Brynhyfryd Ter.
CF83: Sen 2C **66**
Lwr. Castle St. NP7: A'gvnny 4F **7**
NP13: A'lery 1C **34**
Lwr. Coronation St.
NP22: Tred 3H **15**
Lwr. Court Ter. NP13: L'hth 1C **44**
Lwr. Cross St. *NP24: New T* 2C **30**
(off Railway Ter.)
Lwr. Garn Ter. NP4: G Erw 1B **20**
Lwr. Glantorvaen Ter.
NP4: B'avn 3E **21**
Lwr. Glyn Gwyn St. CF83: Tret 1D **76**
Lwr. Gwastod Ter.
NP13: C'lery 3G **27**
Lwr. Harper's Rd. NP4: Abers 6E **29**
Lwr. Hill St. NP4: B'avn 3F **21**
Lwr. Lancaster St.
NP13: S Bells 3C **34**
Lwr. Leigh Rd.
NP4: C'avn, P'nydd 3F **37**
Lwr. Monk St. NP7: A'gvnny 4G **7**
LOWER NEW INN 4G **47**
LOWER OCHRWYTH 5D **72**
Lwr. Park Gdns. NP4: P'pool 6H **37**
Lwr. Park Ter. NP4: P'pool 1C **46**
Lwr. Rhymney Valley Relief Rd.
CF83: Caer, L'brad 6A **68**
Lower Rd. NP24: New T 4F **31**
Lower Row NP22: Rhym 2A **14**
Lwr. Royal La. NP13: A'lery 5F **27**
Lwr. St James St.
NP12: Argoed 3C **42**
Lwr. Salisbury St. NP22: Tred 3H **15**
Lwr. Square NP23: B'fort 3D **10**
Lwr. Stanley Ter.
NP24: New T 3E **31**
Lwr. Stoney Rd. NP4: Var 6E **29**
Lwr. Ty-Gwyn Rd. NP4: Var 5D **28**
Lwr. Viaduct Ter. NP11: Crum 5B **44**
Lwr. Waun St. NP4: B'avn 2F **21**
Lwr. Woodland St.
NP4: B'avn 2G **21**
Lwr. Wyndham Ter. NP11: Ris 4E **73**
LOWLANDS 3D **54**
Lowlands Cres. NP44: Pnwd 3D **54**
Lowlands Rd. NP44: Pnwd 3E **55**
Lowlands, The CF83: L'brad 2B **68**
Ludlow Cl. NP44: Llan 2E **65**
(not continuous)
Ludlow St. CF83: Caer 5F **75**
Lydwood Cl. CF83: Mac 6F **71**
Lyncroft NP44: G'mdw 6B **54**
Lyne Rd. NP11: Ris 4D **72**
Lyn Pac Trad. Est.
NP44: Pnwd 3E **55**

M

McDonnell Rd. CF81: Barg 3E **41**
MACHEN 6E **71**
Machen Cl. NP11: Ris 4E **73**
Machen St. NP11: Ris 3C **72**
Machine Mdw. NP4: P'nydd 4F **37**
Mclaren Cotts. NP22: A'swg 3F **23**
Maendy Pl. NP44: Pnwd 3C **54**
Maendy Sq. NP44: Pnwd 4C **54**
Maendy Way
NP44: C'brn, Pnwd, Up Cwm 3C **54**
Maendy Wood Ri.
NP44: Pnwd 4C **54**
Maerdy Vw. NP22: Rhym 2D **22**
Maes Briallu CF83: Caer 3A **76**
Maesderwen Cres.
NP4: P'pool 2D **46**
Maesderwen Ri. NP4: P'pool 2D **46**
Maesderwen Rd. NP4: P'pool 2D **46**
Maes Glas CF83: Caer 5H **75**
NP22: Tred 1H **15**
NP23: Rassa 3C **10**
Maes Gwyn CF83: Caer 5G **75**
Maesgwyn NP11: Newb 4F **51**
NP44: Pnwd 3D **54**
Maeshafod NP13: Blai 6D **18**
Maes Hir CF83: Caer 2E **75**
Maeshyfryd NP7: Gov 5H **5**
Maesruddud La.
NP12: B'wood 5B **42**
Maesteg NP11: Newb 4F **51**
Maes Watford CF83: Caer 6E **75**
Maes-y-Celyn NP4: P'pool 3D **46**
Maes-y-Cnyw Ter.
NP13: L'hth 1D **44**
Maes y Coed NP12: B'wood 3A **50**
Maes-y-Coed Ter.
CF82: Ystrad 2C **56**
MAESYCWMMER 1G **57**
Maes-y-Dderwen
CF82: P'heol 1C **48**
Maes-y-Drudwen CF83: Caer 5D **74**
Maes-y-Felin CF83: Caer 4G **75**
Maes-y-Garn Rd. NP12: Oakd 5E **43**
Maes-y-Garreg NP23: Rassa 3B **10**
MAESYGWARTHA 4B **4**
Maesygwartha Rd. NP7: Gilw 5A **4**
Maes-y-Haf NP22: Rhym 1D **22**
Maes y Pandy CF83: B'ws 6D **68**
Maes-yr-Afon CF83: Caer 2A **76**
Maes y Rhiw Ct.
NP44: G'mdw 6A **54**
Maes-y-Siglen CF83: Caer 4D **74**
Mafeking Ter. NP22: Tred 4A **16**
Magna Porta Gdns.
NP44: Oakf 5E **65**
Magnolia Dr. NP12: B'wood 4B **50**
Maindee Rd. NP11: C'fch 6D **58**
Maindee Ter. NP44: Pnwd 4D **54**
Main Rd. CF82: Maes C 2E **57**
NP7: Cly 1G **13**
NP7: Gilw 3D **4**
NP11: Newb 4C **52**
Main St. NP11: Crum 6B **44**
NP11: Newb 3A **52**
Majora Cl. NP7: A'gvnny 2F **7**
Major Cl. NP44: F'wtr 1E **63**
Malford Gro. NP7: Gilw 3C **4**
Mall, The NP44: C'brn 6F **55**
Malpas Rd. NP20: Malp, Oakf 6D **64**
Malpas St. NP44: C'brn 1B **64**
Malthouse La. NP4: P'pool 6G **37**
Malthouse Rd. NP18: C'ln 6H **65**
NP44: C'ln, Oakf 6D **64**
Malvern Cl. NP11: Ris 4G **73**
Malvern Ter. NP11: Ris 4D **72**
MAMHILAD 2D **38**
Mamhilad Pk. Est.
NP4: P'pool 3E **39**
Mandeville Rd.
NP12: Cefn F 3H **49**
Manest St. NP22: Rhym 5B **14**
MANMOEL 2C **32**
Manmoel Ct. NP12: Oakd 6F **43**
Manmoel Rd.
NP11: C'maen, Oakd 5F **43**
NP12: A'beeg, Argoed, Crum,
Man M, Oakd 6E **33**

Man-Moel Rd.
NP12: Man M 1D 24
NP23: E Vale, Tred 6B 10
Manorbier Cl. NP12: B'wood 6A 42
Manorbier Dr. NP44: Llan 6G 55
Manor Cl. NP11: Ris 4E 73
Manor Ct. NP11: Ris 3E 73
Manor Ga. NP44: G'mdw 6B 54
Manor Pk. NP11: Newb 1B 52
Manor Rd.
NP4: Abers, Tal, Var 6E 29
NP11: Ris 4E 73
NP12: P'fraith 6B 50
Manor Way NP4: Abers, Tal 1E 37
NP11: Ris 4E 73
Mansfield Rd. NP11: Pent C 2A 44
Maple Av. NP11: Ris 3E 73
NP22: Tred 6G 9
Maple Cl. NP7: A'gvnny 3H 7
NP12: P'fraith 6A 50
Maple Cres. NP4: Grif 6D 46
Maple Gdns. NP11: Ris 5F 73
Maple Rd. NP4: Grif 5D 46
Maple Rd. Sth. NP4: Grif 6D 46
Maple Ter. NP11: Aberc 6C 52
Maple Way NP23: Rassa 2C 10
MARDY 1H 7
Mardy Cl. CF83: Caer 4H 75
Mardy Cres. CF83: Caer 4H 75
Margaret St. CF81: Gilf 6F 41
Marian-Wen St. NP12: Cefn F 1H 49
Marigold Cl. NP10: Roger 6G 73
Marine Ind. Est. NP23: Cwm 5A 26
Marine St. NP23: Cwm 4H 25
Marion Jones Ct. NP12: Yny 2C 58
Maritime Ct. CF83: B'ws 1H 75
Market Arc. *NP4: P'pool 1C 46 (off Crane St.)*
Market Pl. NP11: Aberc 1C 60
Market Pl., The
NP12: B'wood 2B 50
Market Rd. NP23: N'glo 5B 12
Market Sq. NP23: B mawr 3B 12
NP23: E Vale 1E 17
Market St. CF83: Caer 5G 75
NP4: B'avn 3F 21
NP4: P'pool 1C 46
NP13: A'lery 6G 27
NP22: Tred 3H 15
NP23: E Vale 1E 17
MARKHAM 6A 32
Markham Cres. NP12: Oakd 5E 43
Markham Ter. NP12: Mark 5A 32
Marlborough Rd.
NP13: S Bells 2D 34
NP44: G'mdw 6A 54
Marl Ct. NP44: G'mdw 4B 54
Marloes Path NP44: G'mdw 6B 54
Marne St. NP11: C'crn 3C 60
Marsh Ct. NP7: A'gvnny 5G 7
Marshfield Ct. NP12: P'fraith 1C 58
Marston Path NP44: G'mdw 1H 63
Martindale Cl. NP22: Tred 1G 15
Martindale Rd. NP4: Grif 5E 47
Martin's Fld. NP11: Newb 3H 51
Martins Rd. CF81: Foch 3A 22
Martin Ter. NP4: B'avn 3D 20
Marwyn Gdns. CF81: Barg 5E 41
Maryland Rd. NP11: Ris 4D 72
Mary St. CF83: Tret 1D 76
NP4: B'avn 3F 21
Matthew Ter. *NP4: P'nydd 5E 37 (off Chapel Rd.)*
Maxton Ct. CF83: Caer 4H 75
Maxworthy Rd. NP4: B'avn 2F 21
Mayfield Ter. NP23: B'fort 3E 11
Maynes NP44: F'wtr 2G 63
Mead La. NP44: C'brn 5E 55
Meadowbrook Av.
NP44: Pnwd 3D 54
Meadow Cl. NP4: Grif 1E 55
NP11: Ris 1A 72
NP12: Peng 2G 49
Meadow Cres. CF83: Caer 5G 75
NP11: Ris 5F 73
NP22: Tred 5G 9
Meadowgate NP12: P'fraith 1A 58
Meadowland Dr. NP10: Roger 6F 73
Meadow La. NP7: A'gvnny 2C 6
NP44: C'iog 4H 55
Meadow Rd. NP12: P'fraith 5D 50
Meadows, The NP11: Ris 1A 72
Meadow St. NP13: L'hth 1C 44
Meadow Ter. NP24: New T 1E 31
Meadow Vw. CF83: B'ws 6D 68
Meadow Wlk. NP11: C'maen 6G 43
Meadow Way CF83: Caer 6C 74
Meadway Rd. NP7: A'gvnny 2G 7
Mechanic's Sq. NP22: Tred 6H 9
Medart Pl. NP11: C'keys, Ris 1A 72
Medart St. NP11: C'keys 1A 72
Melbourne Ct. NP12: Cefn F 3H 49
NP44: G'mdw 6D 54
Melbourne Rd. NP13: A'lery 6G 27
Melin Gwlan CF83: Caer 3E 75
Melin St. NP11: C'fch 2A 70
Melville Ter. CF83: Caer 3G 75
Melyn Bach NP4: Lit M 2H 39
Mendip Cl. NP11: Ris 4G 73
Merchants Hill
NP4: P'nydd, P'pool 5F 37
Merchants Hill Cl.
NP4: P'nydd 5F 37
Merchant St. CF81: P'tyn 2C 22
Meredith Ter. NP11: Newb 3A 52
Mere Path NP44: G'mdw 6B 54
Mersey Cl. NP12: P'fraith 6A 50
Merthyr NP22: Rhym 1A 14
Merthyr Rd. NP7: A'gvnny 4E 7
NP7: Gilw, Gov, L'fst 4F 5
NP22: Tred 1A 14
Mews, The NP11: C'crn 4D 60
Meyricks NP44: F'wtr 3G 63
Michael Way NP4: P'pool 6G 37
MIDDLE COEDCAE 3G 21
Middle Coedcae Rd.
NP4: B'avn 3G 21
Middle Row NP22: Rhym 2A 14
Midway NP4: P'pool 3E 39
Midway Cl. NP7: Mardy 1H 7
Midway La. NP7: Mardy 1H 7
Milfraen Av. NP23: N'glo 6C 12
Millbrook Ct. NP4: Lit M 2H 39
Millbrook Pl. NP4: Lit M 3H 39
Millbrook Rd. NP12: P'fraith 5D 50
Mill Cl. CF83: Caer 3E 75
NP7: A'gvnny 5G 7
Mill Cres. NP7: Gov 4H 5
Millers Ride NP44: Llan 6G 55
Mill La. CF82: L'brad, Ystrad 5D 56
NP7: Gov 5H 5
NP44: Llan 1E 65
Mill Rd. CF81: Deri 5A 30
CF83: Caer 3F 75
NP4: P'nydd 5F 37
NP12: P'fraith 6D 50
Mill St. NP11: C'fch 1H 69
NP11: Ris 5E 73
NP13: Blai 5D 18
Mill St. Ind. Est.
NP7: A'gvnny 5F 7
Mill Ter. NP11: Ris 4E 73
NP23: Cwm 4H 25
Milton Cl. *CF81: A'goed 3G 41 (off Ty Fry Rd.)*
NP23: E Vale 1C 16
NP44: C'brn 1A 64
Milton Pl. CF83: Mac 6B 70
Milton Ter. NP24: Brith 4E 31
Miners Row NP7: L Hill 2H 13
Mining School Hill
NP11: Crum 6B 44
Minories *NP44: F'wtr 2G 63 (off Rede Rd.)*
Min yr Afon CF83: Mac 6F 71
Miskin Grn. NP44: Llan 6G 55
Mitchell Rd. NP44: Llanf 2E 65
Mitchell Ter. NP4: P'nydd 4F 37
Mitre St. NP13: A'lery 6G 27
Moel Fryn CF83: Caer 2C 74
Molescombe NP44: F'wtr 2G 63
Mona Cl. NP44: Pnwd 4F 55
Monk St. NP7: A'gvnny 4G 7
Monmouth Cl. NP4: New I 4G 47
Monmouth Ct. CF83: Caer 3C 74
Monmouth Cres. Cl.
NP4: New I 5G 47
Monmouth Ho. NP44: C'brn 6E 55
Monmouth Rd. NP7: A'gvnny 5G 7
Monmouth Vw. CF83: L'brad 4B 68
Monmouth Wlk. NP12: Mark 6A 32
NP44: C'brn 6E 55
Monnow Ct. NP44: G'mdw 5A 54
Montague St. NP13: A'lery 5F 27
Montclaire Av. NP12: B'wood 3B 50
Montresor Ct. NP44: Oakf 4E 65
Moores Row CF81: Foch 4A 22
Moorings, The NP4: P'pool 2E 47
Moorland Rd. CF81: Barg 3D 40
NP23: E Vale 2D 16
Moor Vw. NP23: E Vale 1D 16
NP23: Rassa 3B 10
Moreton St. NP4: P'pool 1B 46
Morgan Jones Flats
CF83: Caer 4F 75
Morgan Ri. NP4: B'avn 2F 21
Morgan St. CF83: Caer 3F 75
CF83: L'brad 3A 68
NP4: B'avn 3F 21
NP13: A'lery 5G 27
NP22: Tred 3H 15
NP24: New T 2D 30
Morgan Ter. CF81: Deri 4A 30
NP22: Tred 4G 15
Moriah Hill NP11: Ris 3D 72
Moriah St. NP22: Rhym 1C 22
Morlais Ct. CF83: Caer 3C 74
Morley Rd. NP13: A'lery 5F 27
MORNINGTON MEADOWS 2B 76
Morrison St. NP12: B'wood 2B 50
Morris Ri. NP4: B'avn 2F 21
Morrisville NP11: W'vle 2C 70
Morton's Farm NP23: B mawr 3H 11
Moseley Ter. NP44: Pnwd 2E 55
Moss Rd. NP44: G'mdw 6B 54
Mostyn Thomas Cl.
NP13: Blai 4C 18
MOUNTAIN AIR 1C 16
Mountain La. NP4: Grif 4D 46
Mountain Rd. CF81: Barg 3C 40
CF83: B'ws 5E 69
CF83: Caer 5G 75
NP4: Up Cwm, Up R 3A 54
NP10: Roger 2F 73
NP11: Ris 2F 73
NP23: Rassa 3C 10
NP44: Up Cwm 3A 54
Mountain Vw. CF83: Abert 6E 67
CF83: Caer 1F 75
CF83: Mac 6E 71
NP4: P'nydd 5E 37 (off Mountain Vw. Rd.)
NP7: L'fst 6D 6
NP12: Mark 6A 32
Mountain Vw. Rd.
NP4: P'nydd 5E 37
Mountbatten NP22: Rhym 6C 14
MOUNT PLEASANT 5E 37
Mt. Pleasant CF81: Barg 2E 41
CF82: Maes C 1G 57
NP7: L Hill 2H 13
NP11: Aberc 6B 52
NP11: Yny 5C 58
NP12: B'wood 2B 50
NP12: Fleur 3G 49
NP13: Blai 4C 18
Mt. Pleasant Cl. NP44: Pnwd 4D 54
Mt. Pleasant Ct. NP13: B'thel 6B 34
Mt. Pleasant Est. NP13: B'thel 6C 34
Mt. Pleasant Rd. NP4: P'nydd 5F 37
NP11: Ris 3D 72
NP23: E Vale 6D 10
NP44: Pnwd 3D 54
Mt. Pleasant Sq. NP23: E Vale 6D 10
Mt. Pleasant St. CF81: A'goed 2F 41
Mt. Pleasant Ter.
NP11: P'waun 5D 60
Mount Rd. NP4: C'avn 4A 38
NP11: Ris 3D 72
Mountside NP11: Ris 4G 73
Mount St. CF81: P'tyn 2C 22
NP7: A'gvnny 3E 7
NP22: Tred 2H 15
NP23: E Vale 3E 17
Mount Vw. NP12: Fleur 3G 49
Moyle Gro. NP18: P'hir 5H 65
Mozart Cotts. CF81: P'tyn 3C 22
Mulberry Cl. NP10: Roger 6H 73
Museum Ct. NP4: Grif 5E 47
Musselwhite Ct. NP12: P'fraith 5D 50
Mydriam Pl. NP22: Tred 6H 9
Mynydd Ct. NP4: P'pool 3C 46
MYNYDDISLWYN 3F 59
Mynydd Islwyn Cl.
NP12: P'fraith 5A 50
Mynydd Maen Rd.
NP44: Pnwd, Up Cwm 3C 54
Mynydd Vw. NP4: P'pool 3B 46
Myrtle Gro. CF82: Heng 1E 57

N

Nant Celyn NP22: Rhym 6C 14
Nant Celyn Cl. NP44: Pnwd 3C 54
Nantcorn Rd. NP11: C'crn 3D 60
Nant Ddu CF83: Caer 5F 75
Nant-Ffyddlon CF82: P'heol 2C 48
Nantgarw Rd. CF83: Caer 6C 74
Nant-Gau NP12: Oakd 5E 43
Nantgavenny La. NP7: Mardy 1H 7
Nant Melyn NP23: Rassa 3B 10
Nant Twyn Harris
CF82: Ystrad 4D 56
NANT-Y-BWCH 5F 9
Nant-y-Cwm NP13: L'hth 1D 44
NANTYGLO 5B 12
Nantyglo Leisure Cen. 5A 12
Nant-y-Hwyad CF83: Caer 4D 74
Nant-y-Milwr Cl. NP44: H'lys 4E 63
Nant-y-Rhos NP12: P'fraith 6C 50
Napier St. CF83: Mac 6E 71
Narberth Ct. CF83: Caer 3B 74
Narberth Cres. NP44: Llan 6H 55
Navigation Rd. NP11: Ris 2C 72
Navigation St. CF83: Tret 6H 69
Neath Ct. NP44: G'mdw 5A 54
Neerings NP44: F'wtr 1F 63
Nelson Rd. CF82: Ystrad 1C 56
Nelson St. NP23: B'fort 3E 11
Nelson Ter. NP24: Brith 4E 31
Nethercourt NP44: G'mdw 6B 54
Neuadd St. NP13: A'lery 5F 27
Neuaddwen St.
CF81: A'goed 2G 41
Nevern Wlk. NP44: Llan 1E 65
Neville St. NP4: Var 5D 28
Neville Ter. NP4: B'avn 2G 21
NEVILL HALL HOSPITAL 4D 6
Nevill St. NP7: A'gvnny 4F 7
Newall St. NP13: A'lery 6G 27
Newbarn Path NP44: Llanf 2E 65
NEWBRIDGE 3A 52
Newbridge Leisure Cen. 3B 52
Newbridge Rd. NP12: P'fraith 5D 50
Newbridge Rd. Ind. Est.
NP12: P'fraith 4E 51
New Bryngwyn Rd.
NP11: Newb 3H 51
New Bryngwyn St.
NP12: Fleur 3G 49
NEWCHURCH 5F 11
Newchurch Ct. NP44: G'mdw 6C 54
Newchurch Rd. NP23: E Vale 5E 11
New Cwm Ter. NP23: Cwm 4A 26
Newfoundland Way
NP12: B'wood 3A 50
Newgale Row NP44: C'brn 6F 55
New Gladstone St. NP13: Blai 5D 18
New High St. NP13: S Bells 3D 34
NEW INN 3G 47
New James St. NP4: B'avn 3G 21
Newlands Ct. NP4: P'nydd 4F 37
Newlands, The NP7: Mardy 1H 7
Newlyn Rd. NP11: Newb 2C 52
Newman Rd. NP4: C'avn 4G 37
Newnham Pl. NP44: C'brn 6E 55
New Pk. Rd. NP11: Ris 2A 72
Newport Rd.
CF83: B'ws, Mac, Tret 2H 75
NP4: New I 6G 47
NP11: C'crn 3C 60
NP11: Ris 5E 73
NP12: Argoed, Holly B, Mark 1B 24
NP12: P'fraith 1C 58
NP22: Tred 4H 15
NP44: C'iog 3H 55
NP44: Llanf, Llan, Oakf 5D 64
New Queen St. NP4: B'avn 3F 21
New Rank NP7: L Hill 2H 13
New Rd. CF81: Deri 5A 30
CF82: Heng, Peng, Tir B 3F 49
NP4: Grif, New I 4E 47
NP4: Tal 6C 28
NP4: Var 5D 28
NP11: C'fch 1A 70
NP12: Argoed 2C 42
NP12: Cefn F 3G 49
NP12: Oakd 3D 50
NP12: Peng 3F 49
NP23: N'glo 5B 12
New Row CF83: Mac 6E 71
NP44: H'lys 2D 62
New St. CF83: Caer 1E 75
NP44: Pnwd 4E 55
Newton Cl. CF82: P'heol 2D 48
Newton Ind. Est.
NP11: C'keys 2H 71
Newton Wynd NP44: F'wtr 2G 63
NEWTOWN 6F 11
NEW TREDEGAR 2D 30
New Tredegar Sports Hall 1C 30

New William St. NP4: B'avn 3F 21
Neyland Path NP44: F'wtr 1G 63
Nicholas St. NP4: P'pool 1C 46
Nightingale Ter. NP4: P'nydd 5E 37
Nine Mile Point Ct.
NP11: C'fch 1A 70
Nine Mile Point Ind. Est.
NP11: C'fch 2A 70
Nine Mile Point Rd.
NP11: W'vle 2D 70
Nobel Sq. Ind. Est.
NP23: B mawr 3C 12
Nolton Pl. NP44: C'brn 2H 63
Nookfield, The NP7: Gov 6G 5
Norfolk Cl. NP44: G'mdw 6A 54
Norman St. NP13: A'lery 5G 27
North Av. CF82: Maes C 1G 57
NP22: Tred 6F 9
Nth. Blackvein Ind. Est.
NP11: W'vle 1F 71
North Ct. NP4: P'nydd 4F 37
North Rd. CF81: Barg 2E 41
CF82: G'gaer 3C 48
NP4: Abers 2E 37
NP4: P'pool 1B 46
NP11: C'crn, P'waun 5D 60
NP11: Newb 2B 52
NP44: C'iog 4G 55
North St. NP4: B'avn 2E 21
NP7: A'gvnny 3E 7
NP23: B'fort 3F 11
North Vw. NP4: P'nydd 4F 37
North Vw. Ter. CF83: Caer 4G 75
NORTHVILLE 5F 55
North Wlk. NP44: C'brn 5E 55
Northway NP4: P'pool 3E 39
Noth Vw. NP7: Gov 5H 5
Nursery Cr. NP22: Rhym 1D 22
Nursery Ri. CF83: B'ws 6D 68
Nursery Ter. NP22: Tred 1H 15
Nydfa Rd. NP12: Peng 2F 49

O

Oak Ct. NP4: P'nydd 4F 37
NP12: Oakd 3C 50
(off Vale Vw. Rd.)
OAKDALE 5E 43
OAKDALE HOSPITAL 6D 42
Oakdale Path NP44: G'mdw 1H 63
Oakdale Pl. NP4: P'nydd 5E 37
Oakdale Ter. NP12: Oakd 2C 50
Oakdene Way NP7: Gilw 3C 4
OAKFIELD 3C 64
Oakfield NP12: P'fraith 5D 50
Oakfield Gdns. CF83: Mac 6G 71
Oakfield Rd. NP22: Tred 4A 16
NP44: Oakf 2C 64
Oakfield St. CF82: Ystrad 2E 57
CF83: L'brad 2B 68
Oakfield Ter. NP23: E Vale 3F 17
Oakland Gdns. CF81: Barg 4E 41
Oaklands CF81: Barg 5E 41
NP18: P'hir 5H 65
Oaklands Rd. NP4: Grif 6D 46
Oaklands Vw. NP44: G'mdw 6A 54
Oakland Ter. NP11: Crum 6B 44
NP22: Rhym 4B 14
NP44: C'brn, Oakf 3B 64
Oak La. CF83: Mac 6G 71
Oakleigh Ct. NP44: H'lys 3E 63
Oak Pl. CF81: Barg 5D 40
Oaks Ct. NP4: Abers 2E 37
Oaks End Cl. CF82: P'heol 2D 48
Oaksford NP44: F'wtr 1F 63
Oaks Rd. NP4: Abers 2E 37
Oaks, The CF83: Mac 6G 71
NP12: Oakd 6F 43
NP44: C'iog 4H 55
Oak St. NP11: Aberc 5C 52
NP12: B'wood 2B 50
NP13: A'lery 5F 27
NP23: Cwm 4H 25
NP44: C'brn 1B 64
Oak Ter. CF83: L'brad 4A 68
NP11: C'keys 6D 60
NP12: Fleur 3G 49
Oak Tree Cl. NP4: New I 2G 47
Oak Tree Ct. NP11: Newb 6D 44
NP44: Oakf 2B 64
Oak Tree Dr. CF82: Cefn H 4D 48
NP10: Roger 6G 73
Oak Tree La. NP7: Gilw 2E 5
Oak Vw. NP4: B'avn 3H 21
Oakwood Cl. NP11: Crum 3G 43
Offway NP44: F'wtr 3H 63
Ogilvie Ter.
CF81: Deri . . . . . . .5A 22 & 3A 30
Ogmore Ct. CF83: Caer 3C 74
Ogmore Pl. NP44: Llan 1E 65
Old Abergavenny Rd.
NP4: Lit M, Mamh, P'pool
. . . . .2E 39
Old Barn Way NP7: A'gvnny 2G 7
NP13: A'lery 1D 34
Old Blaen-Afon Rd.
NP23: B mawr 3B 12
Old Blaina Rd. NP13: A'lery 5E 27
Old Brewery La. NP22: Rhym . . .5A 14
Old Bri. Ct. NP44: G'mdw 4A 54
Oldbury Rd. NP44: C'brn 1B 64
Old Church La. CF82: Maes C . . .6G 49
Old Duke Rd. NP22: Tred 5H 9
Old Est. Yd. NP4: P'pool 2E 47
OLD FURNACE 2A 46
Old Hereford Rd.
NP7: A'gvnny, Mardy 3F 7
Old James St. NP4: B'avn 3F 21
Old La. NP4: Abers 1E 37
Old Monmouth Rd.
NP7: A'gvnny 4G 7
Old Nantgawr Rd.
CF15: N'grw 6A 74
Old Pant Rd. NP11: Newb 3B 52
Old Parish Rd. CF82: Heng 6F 49
OLD PENYGARN 5H 37
Old Queen St. NP4: B'avn 2F 21
Old Rectory Cl. NP7: Gilw 4A 4
Old Rd. NP4: Abers 2F 37
Old Row NP44: H'lys 2D 62
Old School Ct. NP11: C'keys 6D 60
Old School Grange
CF82: Heng 1E 57
Old School Pl. NP4: P'nydd 5E 37
Old Station Yd. CF83: B'ws 6E 69
Old Trap Rd. NP7: Gilw 4B 4
Old Vicarage Cl. NP12: Peng 2F 49
Old William St. NP4: B'avn 3F 21
Oliver Jones Cres.
NP22: Tred 2G 15
Olway Cl. NP44: Llan 2D 64
(not continuous)
Open Hearth Cl. NP4: Grif 5E 47
Orchard Cl. NP4: C'avn 3G 37
NP7: A'gvnny 3E 7
NP7: Gilw 4C 4
Orchard Ct. NP12: P'fraith 5E 51
Orchard Farm Est.
NP4: C'avn 4H 37
Orchard La. NP12: Peng 5G 41
NP44: C'brn 4E 55
Orchard M. NP7: A'gvnny 4E 7
Orchard Pl. NP44: C'brn 1A 64
Orchard St. NP7: A'gvnny 3E 7
NP23: B mawr 3A 12
NP24: New T 1D 30
Orchid Cl. CF82: Tir B 3E 49
Orchid Ct. NP44: F'wtr 2F 63
Osborne Rd.
NP4: P'nydd, P'pool 5G 37
NP11: Pent C 2A 44
NP23: B mawr 3H 11
Ostringen Cl. NP7: A'gvnny 4G 7
Overdale Wlk.
NP11: C'maen 6G 43
Overdene NP12: P'fraith 6C 50
Owendale Ter. NP4: Abers 3E 37
Oxford Pl. NP13: L'hth 1D 44
Oxford St. CF82: G'gaer 2C 48
NP4: Grif 4E 47
NP7: A'gvnny 3G 7
NP13: A'lery 5G 27
Oxford Ter. NP4: B'avn 4D 20
Oxtens NP44: F'wtr 3G 63
Oxwich Cl. CF82: Cefn H 4E 49

P

Pace Rd. NP44: F'wtr 2G 63
Padarn Pl. NP44: Pnwd 4E 55
Paddock Cl. NP44: Pnwd 4D 54
Paddock Ri. NP44: Llan 2E 65
Paddocks, The NP12: B'wood . . .6B 42
NP44: Llan 2E 65
Pag Lan Rd. CF82: Heng 6F 49
Palm Cl. NP4: New I 2H 47
Palmer Pl. NP12: B'wood 2A 50
Pandy NP44: G'mdw 6C 54
Pandy La. CF83: Mac 6F 71
Pandy-Mawr Rd. CF83: B'ws 6D 68
Pandy Pk. 1G 71
Pandy Rd. CF83: B'ws 6B 68
NP11: C'maen 5G 43
Pandy Vw. NP11: C'keys 6C 60
Pantddu Fld. NP13: A'beeg 6A 34
Pantddu Rd. NP13: A'beeg 5A 34
PANTEG 4H 47
Panteg NP23: E Vale 5E 11
Panteg Ind. Est. NP4: Grif 5E 47
Panteg Ter. NP11: Newb 3A 52
Panteg Way NP4: New I 4F 47
Pant Farm Cl. NP11: Newb 3B 52
Pant Farm Est. NP11: Newb 3B 52
PANT-GLAS 2C 36
Pant Glas CF83: L'brad 2B 68
NP22: Tred 3G 15
Pant Glas Ind. Est.
CF83: B'ws 2C 76
Pant Glas Rd. NP44: Oakf 5A 64
Pant Gwyn Cl. NP44: H'lys 3E 63
Pant La. NP7: A'gvnny 4E 7
Pant Llygodfa CF83: Caer 6D 74
Pant Rd. NP11: Newb 3B 52
PANTSIDE 2C 52
Pant St. CF81: A'goed 2F 41
Pant Vw. NP11: Newb 2B 52
NP23: N'glo 2D 18
Pantycefn Rd. NP12: Mark 6A 32
Pantycelyn Dr. CF83: Caer 2E 75
Pantycelyn St. CF82: Ystrad 1D 56
Pant-y-Dwr NP22: Tred 5F 9
Pant-y-Fforest NP23: E Vale 6F 11
Pantyfid Rd. CF81: A'goed 1G 41
Pant y Glan NP23: B'fort 3G 11
Pant y Mynydd NP23: B'fort 3G 11
Pant-y-pwdyn NP13: A'lery 1D 34
Pant-y-Pwdyn Rd.
NP13: A'lery 6G 27
Pant-yr-Eos NP44: Pnwd 5D 54
Pant-y-Resk Rd.
NP11: Aberc, Myn 5H 51
Pant-yr-Heol Cl. NP44: H'lys 4E 63
Parade, The NP44: C'brn 6E 55
Parc Av. CF83: Caer 2H 75
NP44: Pnwd 3D 54
Parc Bryn NP12: P'fraith 6A 50
Parc Bychan NP23: E Vale 6F 11
Parc Cenedlaethol Bannau Brycheiniog
NP7 .5C 4
NP23 . . . . .1D 12
NP4 . . . . .1B 38
Parc Cotts. CF83: Sen 3C 66
Parc Derwen CF82: Cefn H 4E 49
Parc Gwledig Cwm Sirhywi 3C 70
Parc Plas NP12: B'wood 3A 50
(not continuous)
Parc Ponty Pandy
CF83: Caer 2H 75
Parc Ter. CF83: Sen 2B 66
Parc-y-Felin St. CF83: Caer 3G 75
Parfitt Pl. NP12: B'wood 2A 50
Parfitt Ter. NP44: Pnwd 4D 54
Park Av. CF83: B'ws 1B 76
NP7: A'gvnny 3F 7
Park Cl. NP7: A'gvnny 3G 7
NP44: H'lys 3E 63
Park Ct. NP4: P'pool 6H 37
NP7: A'gvnny 3G 7
NP11: C'crn 3C 60
(off Caradoc St.)
Park Cres. CF81: Barg 4E 41
NP4: P'pool 6A 38
NP7: A'gvnny 3F 7
NP7: Cly 5G 13
NP23: B mawr 3A 12
Park Dr. CF81: Barg 4D 40
Parke's La. NP4: P'pool 2A 46
Park Gdns. NP4: B'avn 2F 21
NP4: P'pool 6H 37
Park Hill NP11: Newb 2A 52
NP22: Tred 5G 15
Parkhill Cres. NP23: B'fort 4F 11
Park Ho. Flats NP4: P'pool 6H 37
Parklands NP12: B'wood 1B 50
Parklands Cl. NP44: Pnwd 4E 55
Park La. CF82: Ystrad 2C 56
CF83: Caer 5F 75
NP7: A'gvnny 3G 7
Parklawn Cl. NP44: Pnwd 3E 55
Park Pl. CF81: Gilf 5F 41
NP11: C'keys 6D 60
NP11: Newb 3A 52
NP11: Ris 4D 72
NP13: A'lery 6G 27
Park Pl. NP22: Tred 3A 16
(not continuous)
NP23: W Iwyd 1G 25
Park Rd. CF81: Barg 3E 41
CF82: Heng 1E 57
CF82: Maes C 3F 57
NP4: P'pool 6H 37
(not continuous)
NP7: A'gvnny 3F 7
NP11: Newb 3A 52
NP11: Ris 4C 72
NP23: E Vale 4E 17
(Festival Dr.)
NP23: E Vale 5E 17
(Prince Edward Cres.)
NP23: W Iwyd 6F 17
Park Rd. Ind. Est. NP11: Ris 4D 72
Park Row NP22: Tred 3H 15
Parkside NP44: C'brn 1B 64
Parkside Ct. NP4: P'nydd 4F 37
Park St. NP4: B'avn 3F 21
NP4: Grif 4E 47
NP7: A'gvnny 4E 7
NP11: C'crn 3C 60
NP11: C'keys 6C 60
Park Ter. NP4: P'nydd 4F 37
NP12: Oakd 3C 50
Park, The NP4: B'avn 2F 21
Park Vw. CF81: Barg 4D 40
NP4: P'pool 2D 46
NP11: C'keys 6C 60
NP13: Blai 2C 18
NP22: Tred 4G 15
NP23: B mawr 3H 11
NP23: B'fort 3D 10
NP44: Pnwd 3E 55
Park Vw. Bungs.
NP12: Oakd 2D 50
Park Vw. St. NP23: W Iwyd 6G 17
Park Vw. Ter. NP4: P'nydd 5E 37
Parkville NP22: Tred 4H 15
Parkway NP11: Crum 1G 43
NP13: A'beeg, Crum, Pent C
. . . . .1G 43
Parrish Pl. CF83: Sen 3C 66
(off Commercial St.)
Parrot Row NP13: N'glo 2C 18
Parry Bldgs. NP11: Newb 3A 52
Parry Jones Cl. NP13: Blai 4C 18
Parry Ter. NP11: Crum 6A 44
Parson's Row NP13: Blai 4C 18
Partridge Rd. NP13: L'hth 1B 44
Partridge Row NP23: B'fort 4D 10
Part St. NP13: Blai 6D 18
Pastures, The NP44: Llan 6H 55
Paxton Cl. CF82: P'heol 2D 48
PEACEHAVEN 6B 16
Peacehaven NP22: Tred 6B 16
Peacehaven Ct. NP22: Tred 6B 16
Pegasus Ct. NP7: A'gvnny 5G 7
Pembrey Gdns NP12: P'fraith . . .5D 50
Pembrey Path NP44: G'mdw 6C 54
Pembroke Cl. NP12: B'wood 6A 42
Pembroke Ct. CF83: Caer 3B 74
Pembroke Pl. NP4: Var 2D 28
NP44: Llan 6H 55
Pembroke St. NP22: Tred 6F 9
Pembroke Ter. NP4: Var 2D 28
Penallt NP7: L Hill 2H 13
Penallta Community Pk. 5B 48
Penallta Ind. Est.
CF82: G'gaer 4C 48
Penallta Rd.
CF82: G'gaer, Ystrad 3C 48
Penarth Ct. NP44: Llan 2E 65
(not continuous)
Penbedw NP44: C'iog 5H 55
Pencerrig St. CF83: L'brad 4A 68
Pen Clawdd CF83: Caer 2A 76
Pencoed NP22: Tred 3G 15
Pencoed Av. NP12: Cefn F 1H 49
Pencoed Pl. NP44: C'iog 3F 55
Pendarren Rd. NP13: A'beeg 5A 34
Pendarren St. CF82: P'heol 1D 48
Pen-Deri Cl. NP12: Oakd 6F 43
Pendinas Av. NP11: C'maen 5G 43
Pendine Wlk. NP44: G'mdw 1H 63
Pendoylan Wlk. NP44: C'brn 1H 63
PENGAM 2G 49
Pengam Rd.
CF81: A'goed, Peng 4G 41
CF81: Peng 1E 49
CF82: Peng, P'heol 1D 48
CF82: Ystrad 2E 57
NP12: Peng 2G 49
NP12: Peng 4G 41

Pengam Station (Rail) 1F 49
Pengam St. NP12: Peng 2F 49
Pen Heol-Shenkyn
NP12: B'wood 2A 42
Penlas NP23: E Vale 1C 16
PENLLWYN
NP12 . . . . 5B 50
NP7 . . . . 2H 13
Penllwyn Av. NP12: P'fraith 5C 50
Penllwyn Est. NP7: L Hill 2H 13
Penllwyn La. CF83: Mac 6C 70
NP12: P'fraith 5B 50
Penllwyn St. NP11: C'fch 1H 69
Penllwyn Wlk. CF83: Mac 6B 70
Penllyn Av. NP44: Pnwd 3E 55
Penmaen NP12: Oakd 5E 43
Penmaen Cl. CF82: Cefn H 4E 49
Penmaen Cnr. NP12: Oakd 6D 42
Penmaen Est. NP12: Oakd 1D 50
Penmaen Ind. Est.
NP12: P'fraith 4C 50
Penmaen Rd. NP12: P'fraith . . . 3D 50
Penmaen Small Bus. Cen.
NP12: P'fraith 4C 50
Penmaen Vs. NP12: Oakd 1D 50
Penmaes Rd. NP44: G'mdw . . . 6A 54
Pen Mynydd NP4: B'avn 2G 21
Pennant St. NP23: E Vale 1D 16
Pennar Cl. NP11: Newb 3G 51
Pennar Crossing
NP12: Newb 4F 51
Pennar La. NP11: Newb 3F 51
Pennar St. NP11: Newb 3A 52
Pennine Cl. NP11: Ris 4G 73
Pennyfields NP44: G'mdw 6B 54
Pen Padrig NP7: Gov 5G 5
PEN-PEDAIR-HEOL 1D 48
PENRHIW 3D 72
Pen Rhiw NP12: Oakd 5E 43
Penrhiw Av. NP12: Oakd 6D 42
Penrhiwbicca NP11: Newb 3A 52
Pen-Rhiw Est. NP13: B'thel 6B 34
PENRHIWGARREG 1D 34
Pen-Rhiw-Garreg Rd.
NP13: A'lery 6H 27
Penrhiw La. CF83: Mac 5F 71
Penrhiw Rd. NP11: Ris 3D 72
Penrhiw Ter. NP11: Aberc 6C 52
NP12: Oakd 5D 42
Pen-Rhiw Vs. NP12: Oakd 6D 42
Penrhyn Ter. NP24: New T 2E 31
Penrice Grn. NP44: Llan 1E 65
Pensarn Way NP44: H'lys 3E 63
Pentland Cl. NP11: Ris 4G 73
PENTRAPEOD 6G 33
Pentrebane St. CF83: Caer 5F 75
Pentre Cl. NP44: F'wtr 3G 63
Pentre La. NP4: Mamh 1E 39
NP7: A'gvnny 1C 6
NP44: Bet, H'lys, Oakf 6F 63
PENTRE-PIOD 4D 36
Pentrepiod Rd.
NP4: Abers, P'nydd 4D 36
NP4: P'nydd 5F 37
Pentre Rd. NP7: A'gvnny 2C 6
PENTWYN 6A 22
PEN-TWYN
NP11 . . . . 2A 44
NP4 . . . . 2E 37
Pentwyn CF83: Caer 1D 74
NP23: E Vale 2C 16
Pentwyn Av. NP12: B'wood 1B 50
Pentwyn Ct. NP12: B'wood 1B 50
Pentwyngwyn Rd.
CF83: Caer, Rud 2A 76
Pentwyn Hgts. NP4: Abers 2E 37
Pentwyn Isaf CF83: Caer 1E 75
Pentwyn La. NP7: Gov 6G 5
PENTWYN-MAWR 4G 51
Pentwyn Rd. NP4: Abers 2D 36
NP11: Pent C 2A 44
NP12: B'wood 1B 50
Pentwyn Ter. NP4: Abers 2E 37
NP11: Pent C 2A 44
PEN-Y-BONT 4G 27
Pen-y-Bont CF82: P'heol 1C 48
Pen y Bont NP7: Gov 5H 5
Pen-y-Bont NP22: Tred 5F 9
Pen-y-Bont Rd. NP13: C'lery . . . 4G 27
Pen-y-Bont Ter. NP7: Gilw 3C 4
PENYBRYN 4C 48
Pen-y-Bryn CF83: Caer 1C 74
NP4: P'pool 6A 38
Penybryn Av. NP12: Cefn F 6H 41
Pen-y-Bryn Ct. NP11: C'maen . . 5G 43
Penybryn Ter. CF82: G'gaer 4C 48
Pen-y-Bryn Ter. NP12: P'fraith . . . 6A 50
NP23: E Vale 3E 17
Pen-y-Cae CF82: Ystrad 3D 56
CF83: Caer 2A 76
Pen-y-Caeau Ct. NP11: Newb . . . 6D 44
Pen-y-Cae Cl. NP11: C'maen . . . 6H 43
Pen-y-Craig CF82: P'heol 2D 48
Pen-y-Crug NP23: Rassa 2C 10
Pen-y-Cwarel NP12: Yny 3C 58
Pen-y-Cwm NP22: A'swg 2D 22
Pen-y-Dre CF83: Caer 6H 67
NP22: Rhym 3B 14
NP23: E Vale 4D 10
Pen-y-Fal Rd. NP7: A'gvnny 3F 7
Penyfan Cvn. and Leisure Pk.
NP12: Man M 6E 33
Penyfan Cl. NP11: Pent C 1A 44
Pen-y-Fan Ind. Est.
NP11: Crum 3G 43
Pen-y-fan Pond Country Pk. 1G 43
Pen-y-Fan Way NP12: Oakd 6E 43
Penyffordd CF83: Caer 3E 75
PENYGARN 6A 38
Penygarn Rd.
NP4: C'avn, P'pool 5H 37
Penygraig Row CF81: P'tyn 2B 22
Pen-y-Graig Ter. NP4: P'pool . . . 2C 46
NP13: B'thel 6B 34
Pen-y-Groes CF83: Caer 1D 74
NP12: Oakd 5F 43
Pen-y-Lan NP23: E Vale 4E 11
Penylan Cl. NP4: New I 3H 47
Penylan Ct. NP44: F'wtr 3G 63
Penylan Flds. NP4: Var 4E 29
Penylan Rd. NP4: Var 4D 28
NP12: Argoed 1C 42
NP44: F'wtr 2F 63
Penylan Ter. NP11: Newb 2A 52
Pen-y-Llan La.
NP4: Lit M, New I 5E 39
Pen-y-Mead NP12: P'fraith 5A 50
Pen y Parc NP23: E Vale 1C 16
Penyparc NP44: Pnwd 3D 54
PEN-Y-POUND 3F 7
Pen-y-Pound NP7: A'gvnny 2E 7
(not continuous)
Pen-y-Pound Ct. NP7: A'gvnny . . . 2E 7
Pen-yr-Allt CF83: Caer 6E 75
PENYRHEOL
CF83 . . . . 2D 74
NP4 . . . . 4C 46
Penyrheol Rd.
NP4: P'pool, Up R 3C 46
Pen-yr-Heol Rd. NP4: P'seg 2F 45
NP13: P'seg 2F 45
Pen-y-Rhiw NP7: L'narth 1H 5
Penywain La. NP4: P'pool 1A 46
Penywain Rd. NP4: P'pool 6F 37
Penywain St. NP4: P'pool 6G 37
Penywain Ter. NP4: P'pool 6G 37
Pen-y-Waun Cl. NP44: C'brn . . . 1A 64
Pen-y-Waun Rd.
NP11: Pent C 2A 44
Penywaun Rd. NP44: F'wtr 2H 63
(not continuous)
Pen-y-Waun Rd.
NP44: G'mdw 1A 64
(not continuous)
Pen-y-Werlod NP12: Mark 5A 32
Pen-y-Werlod Ter.
NP12: Mark 5A 32
Penywrlod CF82: G'gaer 2A 48
Pergoed La. NP4: Glas 6H 39
Perry Ct. NP44: G'mdw 5A 54
PERSONDY 5D 52
Persondy Ter. NP11: Aberc 6D 52
Perth Ct. NP12: Cefn F 3H 49
Perthy Cl. NP44: F'wtr 3G 63
Pettingale Rd. NP44: C'iog 3H 55
Petunia Wlk. NP10: Roger 6G 73
Philanthropic Cotts.
NP44: H'lys 3E 63
(off Dorallt Way)
Philip St. NP11: Pent C 1A 44
Phillips Cl. NP23: Rassa 2C 10
Phillips St. NP4: B'avn 2F 21
NP24: New T 3E 31
Phillips Ter. CF83: Sen 2B 66
PHILLIP'S TOWN 1D 30
Phillip St. NP11: Ris 3C 72
Phillips Wlk. NP22: Rhym 4B 14
Piccadilly Sq. CF83: Caer 4G 75
Picton Rd. NP4: Tal 1D 36
NP22: Tred 5H 9
Picton St. CF81: P'tyn 2C 22
NP4: Grif 4E 47
Picton Ter. CF81: P'tyn 2C 22
Picton Wlk. NP44: F'wtr 1G 63
Picwic Grn. NP44: G'mdw 1G 63
(off Byways)
Pine Cl. NP11: Ris 3D 72
Pine Gdns. NP4: P'pool 1A 46
Pine Gro. CF82: Ystrad 2D 56
Pines, The NP7: Mardy 1H 7
Pine Tree Rd. NP4: New I 3G 47
Pinewood Ct. NP12: P'fraith . . . 4B 50
Pioneer Ter. NP11: C'fch 1H 69
Pisgah Cl. NP4: Tal 6D 28
Pisgah Rd. NP4: Tal 6D 28
Plantation Dr. NP44: C'iog 5H 55
Plantation Pl. NP22: Rhym 1C 22
Plantation Row NP23: E Vale . . . 3E 17
Plantation Ter. CF81: Foch 4A 22
NP22: Rhym 1C 22
Plas Bryn Gomer NP44: C'iog . . . 3G 55
Plas Cae Llwyd CF83: L'brad . . . 4A 68
Plas Craig NP44: C'brn 5F 55
Plas Cwim Parc CF83: Sen 3B 66
Plas Cwrt NP44: Oakf 3C 64
Plas Derwen NP44: C'iog 5H 55
Plas Derwen Cl. NP7: A'gvnny . . . 6G 7
Plas Derwen Vw. NP7: A'gvnny . . 6G 7
Plas Derwen Way NP7: A'gvnny . . 6G 7
Plas Ebbw NP44: C'brn 5E 55
Plas Grug CF83: Caer 6E 75
Plasgwyn Ter. NP12: Fleur 3G 49
Plas Islwyn NP44: C'brn 5E 55
Plas Nant CF83: Abert 6D 66
Plas Newydd NP23: E Vale 3E 17
(off Farm Flds. Rd.)
Plas Phillips CF83: Caer 4E 75
Plas Rd. NP12: Fleur 3G 49
Plas Ter. NP12: Fleur 3G 49
Plas Thomas CF83: Caer 5E 75
Plas Trosnant NP44: C'brn 4E 55
Plasturtwyn Ter. CF83: L'brad . . 2B 68
Plas Twyn NP44: C'brn 4F 55
Plas Ty-Coch NP44: Oakf 3C 64
Plas Vw. NP12: B'wood 3B 50
Plasycoed Rd. NP4: P'nydd 6C 36
Pleasant Ct. NP4: P'nydd 3E 37
Pleasant Pl. CF83: Caer 2D 74
Pleasant Vw. CF81: Foch 4A 22
CF82: Maes C 2F 57
NP11: C'maen 5G 43
NP12: B'wood 1B 50
NP13: L'hth 1C 44
NP23: B mawr 2A 12
NP23: E Vale 1E 17
NP24: New T 2C 30
Plinlimon Cl. NP11: C'maen 5H 43
Plynlimon Av. NP11: C'maen 5H 43
Pochin Cres. NP22: Tred 5A 16
Polo Ground Ind. Est.
NP4: New I 3F 47
(High Way, The)
NP4: New I 4F 47
(Pont-y-Felin Rd.)
Pond Rd. NP23: N'glo 4A 12
Pond Row NP11: C'crn 4D 60
Pont Ap Hywell NP4: P'pool 6H 37
Pontbryn Rd. NP11: Crum 4E 45
Pontgam Ter. NP11: Yny 3C 58
PONTHIR 5H 65
PONTLLANFRAITH 4B 50
Pontllanfraith Leisure Cen. 5B 50
PONTLOTTYN 2C 22
Pontlottyn Rd. CF81: Foch 3A 22
Pontlottyn Station (Rail) 2C 22
PONTNEWYDD 4E 55
Pontnewydd Wlk. NP44: C'brn . . 4E 55
PONTNEWYNYDD 5G 37
Pontnewynydd Small Bus. Cen.
NP4: P'nydd 5E 37
PONTRHYDYRUN 3F 55
Pontrhydyrun Rd.
NP44: Pnwd 2E 55
PONT-Y-FELIN 5G 47
Pontyfelin Av. NP4: New I 4F 47
Pont-y-Felin La. NP4: New I 5G 47
Pont-y-Felin Rd. NP4: New I 4F 47
PONT-Y-GOF 6F 11
Pontygof NP23: B mawr 2C 12
Pont-y-Gof NP23: E Vale 6E 11
Pontygwindy Ind. Est.
CF83: Caer 1F 75
Pontygwindy Rd. CF83: Caer . . . 1F 75
Pontymason Cl. NP10: Roger . . . 6H 73
Pontymason Ct. NP10: Roger . . . 6H 73
Pontymason La. NP10: Roger . . . 4G 73
NP11: Ris, Roger 4G 73
PONTYMISTER 4C 72
Pontymister Ind. Est.
NP11: Ris 5D 72
PONTYMOEL 2D 46
Ponty Pandy La. CF83: Caer 2F 75
Ponty Pandy Vw. CF83: Caer 2F 75
PONTYPOOL 6H 37
Pontypool & Blaenavon Steam Railway
. . . . 1B 20
Pontypool & New Inn Station (Rail)
. . . . 2G 47
Pontypool Leisure Cen. 1D 46
Pontypool Mus. 6H 37
Pontypool Nth. Ind. Est.
NP4: P'nydd 5F 37
Pontypool Pk. 1D 46
Pontypool R.F.C. (Pontypool Pk.)
. . . . 1D 46
Pontypool Ski & Leisure Cen.
. . . . 6A 38
Pontypool Western By-Pass
NP4: P'nydd, P'pool 5G 37
PONTYPWL 6H 37
PONTYWAUN 5D 60
Poplar Av. NP4: New I 2G 47
Poplar Rd. CF83: Caer 5H 75
NP22: Tred 4A 16
NP44: C'iog 4G 55
Poplars Cl. NP7: Mardy 1H 7
Poplars Rd. NP7: Mardy 1H 7
Poplars, The NP11: Ris 2A 72
Poppy Pl. NP10: Roger 6G 73
Porset Cl. CF83: Caer 4H 75
Porset Dr. CF83: Caer 4G 75
Porset Pk. CF83: Caer 3H 75
Porset Row CF83: Caer 2A 76
Porters Rd. NP23: N'glo 5B 12
Porth Mawr Rd. NP44: C'brn 5E 55
Portland Pl. NP12: Cefn F 3A 50
Portland St. NP13: A'lery 5G 27
Postern NP44: F'wtr 2H 63
(off Henllys Way)
Post Office Ter. NP18: P'hir 5H 65
Pottery Rd.
CF82: Cefn H, P'heol 3D 48
Powell's Ter. NP24: New T 1D 30
Powell St. CF82: Tir B 3F 49
NP13: A'lery 6G 27
Powis Cl. NP12: B'wood 6A 42
Presceli Cl. NP11: Ris 3F 73
Prescoch La. NP4: P'pool 3D 46
Presteigne Wlk.
NP44: C'brn 1H 63
Preston St. NP13: A'lery 5G 27
Pretoria Rd. NP13: S Bells 2D 34
Pretoria Ter. NP22: Tred 3A 16
Price Av. NP4: C'avn 4H 37
(off Church Av.)
Price Cl. NP4: C'avn 4H 37
Prices Av. NP4: C'avn 4H 37
Price St. NP22: Rhym 4B 14
Primitive Pl. NP23: B'fort 3E 11
Primrose Ct. NP44: F'wtr 2E 63
Primrose Way
NP10: Roger 6G 73
Prince Andrew Rd.
NP11: Pent C 2A 44
Prince Edward Cres.
NP23: E Vale 5E 17
Prince of Wales Ind. Est.
NP11: Aberc 1B 60
Prince Philip Av.
NP23: G lydan 2D 10
Princes Av. CF83: Caer 6G 75
Princes Ct. NP23: E Vale 6F 11
Princes Ri. CF83: Caer 6G 75
Princess Ct. NP22: Tred 1H 15
Princess Cres.
NP11: Pent C 1H 43
Princess St. NP13: A'lery 1C 34
Prince's St. NP7: A'gvnny 4F 7
Prince St. NP4: B'avn 3F 21
NP4: P'pool 6G 37
NP11: W'vle 1D 70
NP23: N'glo 6B 12
Prince's Wlk. NP4: New I 3H 47
PRINCETOWN 6B 8
Priorsgate NP12: Oakd 6F 43
Priory Ct. NP11: C'crn 3C 60
Priory Gdns. NP7: A'gvnny 4G 7
Priory La. NP7: A'gvnny 4F 7
Priory Rd. NP7: A'gvnny 3G 7
Priory St. NP11: Ris 4D 72
Pritchards Ter. NP12: Fleur 5G 49
Pritchard Ter. NP24: New T 1D 30
Promenade, The NP4: Abers 2D 36
NP22: Tred 3H 15

Prospect Pl. NP4: New I 4G **47**
NP22: A'swg 3E **23**
NP22: Tred 3A **16**
NP44: C'brn 1A **64**
Prospect Rd. NP7: A'gvnny 4E **7**
Provident Cotts.
CF82: Maes C 1G 57
(off North Av.)
Pwllglas Rd. NP12: Cefn F 2H **49**
PWLLYPANT **1F 75**

Q

Quantock Cl. NP11: Ris 4F **73**
Quarry Row NP13: Blai 3E **19**
Queen's Cr. NP22: Rhym 4B **14**
Queen Sq. NP22: Tred 3H **15**
NP23: E Vale 1E **17**
Queens Rd. NP11: Newb 2B **52**
Queen's Rd. NP24: New T 3E **31**
Queen St. CF81: P'tyn 2B **22**
NP4: Grif 4E **47**
NP4: P'pool 6G **37**
NP7: A'gvnny 4F **7**
NP13: A'lery 1C **34**
NP13: Blai 4D **18**
NP13: Blai 1C **18**
NP23: B mawr 3A **12**
(Bailey St.)
NP23: B mawr 2B **12**
(Clydach St.)
NP23: N'glo 1C **18**
NP23: W lwyd 1F **25**
Queens Vs. NP23: E Vale 5E **11**
Queensway NP23: G lydan 2E **11**
Queen Victoria St.
NP22: Tred 3G **15**

R

Radford Ter. NP23: B'fort 3E **11**
Radnor Way NP44: C'brn 1B **64**
Radstock Ct. NP7: A'gvnny 4F **7**
Raglan Cl. NP4: Tal 1D **36**
NP12: B'wood 6A **42**
Raglan Ct. CF83: Caer 3C **74**
NP44: C'iog 3F **55**
Raglan St. NP11: Ris 2B **72**
Raglan Ter. NP7: A'gvnny 6H **7**
NP23: B'fort 4E **11**
Railway Pl. NP11: Crum 6B **44**
Railway St. NP11: Ris 2C **72**
NP13: L'hth 1C **44**
Railway Ter. CF81: Foch 3A **22**
CF81: Gilf 5F **41**
CF83: Caer 5G **75**
NP4: Grif 1E **55**
NP11: Aberc 6B **52**
NP12: Holly B 1A **32**
NP13: A'beeg 5A **34**
NP13: Blai 4C **18**
NP23: Cwm 4A **26**
NP24: Brith 4F 31
(off Station Rd.)
NP24: New T 1C **30**
Railway Vw. NP12: Fleur 4G **49**
NP22: Tred 1H **15**
NP23: E Vale 3E **17**
Ramping Rd. NP11: C'crn 3D **60**
Ramsden st. NP22: Rhym 6C **14**
Ramsey Wlk. NP44: Pnwd 4C **54**
Ramson Cl. CF82: P'heol 3D **48**
Ranks, The NP11: Aberc 1C **60**
RASSAU **3C 10**
Rassau Ind. Est.
NP23: Rassa 2H **9**
Rassau Rd. NP23: Rassa 3A **10**
Ravenscourt NP44: G'mdw 6B **54**
Ravenswood Ct. NP11: Ris 2B **72**
Rawlinson Ter. NP22: Tred 4A **16**
Rectory Cl. CF83: Caer 6F **75**
Rectory Gdns. CF83: Mac 6F **71**
Rectory Rd. CF82: G'gaer 2B **48**
CF83: B'ws 6F **69**
CF83: Caer 5F **75**
NP11: Crum 5C **44**
Redbrook Av. CF83: Tret 1D **76**
Redbrook Ct. CF83: Caer 6F **75**
Redbrook La. CF83: Mac 1E **77**
Redbrook Way NP44: C'brn 6F **55**
Rede Rd. NP44: F'wtr 2G **63**
Red Lion Sq. NP22: Tred 2H **15**
Redwick Ct. NP44: C'brn 1C **64**
REDWOOD MEMORIAL HOSPITAL
....5B **14**
Rees St. NP23: E Vale 1E **17**
Rees Ter. CF83: L'brad 3A **68**
Reform St. CF81: P'tyn 3C **22**
Regent St. NP7: A'gvnny 4F **7**
NP13: L'hth 1D **44**
Reservoir Rd. NP23: B'fort 3D **10**
NP23: Rassa 2D **10**
RHISGA **2B 72**
RHIW **5A 44**
Rhiwamoth St. CF81: A'goed 2G **41**
CF82: G'gaer 3C **48**
Rhiw Cantcrion
CF81: Deri, Foch 4B **22**
Rhiw Fach CF83: Caer 2D **74**
Rhiw Farm Cres.
NP11: Crum 5A **44**
Rhiw Frank NP4: Abers 3D **36**
Rhiw Melin NP44: Up Cwm 3B **54**
RHIW-PARC **6G 27**
RHIW-PARK **6G 27**
Rhiw Pk. Rd. NP13: A'lery 6G **27**
Rhiw Pk. Ter NP13: A'lery 6G **27**
Rhiw Syr Dafydd Hill
NP12: Oakd 6D **42**
Rhiw Wen NP23: E Vale 5D **10**
Rhodfa Ganol CF81: Foch 4A **22**
Rhodfa Glascoed
NP12: B'wood 3A **50**
Rhodri Pl. NP44: Llan 1E **65**
Rholben Rd. NP7: A'gvnny 2G **7**
Rhondda Cl. NP23: Rassa 3C **10**
Rhonos Rd. NP7: Cly 5G **13**
Rhos Av. CF82: P'heol 1D **48**
Rhos Helyg CF83: Caer 3A **76**
Rhosili Rd. CF82: Cefn H 4E **49**
Rhoslan NP22: Tred 6A **10**
Rhos St. CF83: Caer 2F **75**
Rhos, The CF83: Caer 3H **75**
Rhos-y-Bettws CF82: P'heol 2C **48**
Rhos y Dderwen
NP12: B'wood 3A **50**
Rhosyn Gwyn NP24: New T 3E **31**
Rhuddlan Ct. CF83: Caer 2B **74**
Rhyd Clydach NP23: B mawr 2B **12**
Rhyd Ter. NP22: Tred 5B **16**
Rhyd, The NP22: Tred 5B **16**
Rhyd Tre Derwen
NP4: P'nydd 4E **37**
Rhyd-y-Cae NP23: Rassa 3C **10**
Rhyd-y-Gwern Cl.
CF83: Caer 2A **76**
Rhyd y Gwern Isaf
CF83: Mac 6F **71**
Rhyd-y-Gwern La.
CF83: Mac 6E **71**
Rhydynos St. NP4: B'avn 3F **21**
RHYMNEY **5B 14**
RHYMNEY BRIDGE **2A 14**
Rhymney Cl. NP12: P'fraith 5A **50**
NP23: Rassa 3C **10**
Rhymney Ct. NP44: G'mdw 5A **54**
Rhymney Row NP22: Tref 1C **8**
Rhymney Station (Rail) **6B 14**
Rhymney Ter. CF83: Caer 5F **75**
RHYMNI **5B 14**
Rhys Rd. NP12: Cefn F 3H **49**
Rhyswg Rd. NP11: Aberc 1C **60**
Richmond Cl. CF83: L'brad 4A **68**
NP44: Pnwd 4E **55**
Richmond Pl. NP44: Pnwd 4E **55**
Richmond Rd. NP4: Grif 1E **55**
NP7: A'gvnny 3G **7**
NP13: A'lery, S Bells 1D **34**
NP44: Pnwd 3E **55**
Richmond St. NP44: Pnwd 4E **55**
Richmond Ter. NP22: Tred 4A **16**
Ridgeway CF83: Mac 1E **77**
NP4: C'avn 4A **38**
RIFLE GREEN **2F 21**
Rifle Grn. NP4: B'avn 2F **21**
Rifleman St. NP11: Ris 3C **72**
Rifle St. NP4: B'avn 2F **21**
RISCA **2B 72**
RISCA DAY HOSPITAL **2B 72**
Risca Leisure Cen. **4H 73**
Risca Rd. NP10: Roger 5G **73**
NP11: C'keys 6C **60**
Rise, The NP12: Cefn F 2G **49**
NP23: N'glo 2C **18**
NP44: Pnwd 4C **54**
Rising Sun Cl. NP12: Oakd 5D **42**
Rising Sun Ind. Est.
NP13: Blai 3C **18**
Riverbank Ho.
CF82: Maes C 5F **57**
Rivermead Way
NP10: Roger 6G **73**
River Rd. CF81: P'tyn 2C **22**
NP23: Cwm 4H **25**
River Row NP4: P'nydd 4F **37**
NP13: Blai 5D **18**
Riverside NP4: P'pool 5G **37**
NP13: Blai 4D **18**
NP23: B'fort 3D **10**
Riverside Ct. CF83: Sen 3C **66**
NP4: P'pool 6H **37**
NP12: Oakd 2C **50**
Riverside Dr. NP4: B'avn 3F **21**
Riverside Pk. CF83: B'ws 6D **68**
Riverside Ter. CF83: Mac 6E **71**
NP11: Newb 3B **52**
Riversmead NP44: Llan 1D **64**
River Ter. NP12: Peng 2F **49**
River Vw. NP12: Oakd 6D **42**
Roath Ct. NP44: Llan 6G **55**
Roberts Row NP13: C'lery 3G **27**
Roberts Ter. NP22: Tred 3A **16**
Rochdale Ter. NP4: P'nydd 4E **37**
Roch St. NP13: A'lery 5H **27**
ROCK **5C 42**
Rock Fach
NP12: Argoed, B'wood 5C **42**
Rockfield Ho. NP4: P'pool 6G **37**
Rockhill Rd. NP4: P'pool 1D **46**
Rockleigh Av. CF81: A'goed 2G **41**
Rock Villa Cl. NP4: Var 4D **28**
Rock Vs. NP12: Argoed 4D **42**
Roderick Hill Ct.
NP22: Tred 5F **9**
Roderick Pl. NP23: E Vale 3E **17**
Rolls Av. CF82: P'heol 2D **48**
Rolls Cl. NP44: F'wtr 1F **63**
Roman Ridge CF82: G'gaer 2A **48**
Romsley Ct. NP44: G'mdw 1H **63**
Rosary, The NP4: C'avn 5H **37**
Roseberry St. NP4: Grif 4E **47**
Roseberry Ter. NP13: A'lery 6F **27**
Rose Ct. NP11: Newb 1C **52**
NP44: F'wtr 1E **63**
Rose Gdns. NP44: C'iog 5H **55**
Rose Heyworth Bus. Pk.
NP13: A'lery 3E **27**
Rose Heyworth Est.
NP13: A'lery 4F **27**
Rose Heyworth Rd.
NP13: A'lery, Blai 2D **26**
Rosemary La.
NP4: P'pool 6H **37**
Rosemead NP44: G'mdw 6A **54**
Rosemont Av. NP11: Ris 3D **72**
Rose Ter. *NP4: P'nydd 5E 37*
(off Chapel Rd.)
Rose Wlk. NP10: Roger 6G **73**
Rosnewydd Ter.
NP12: B'wood 3B **50**
Rosser St. NP4: P'pool 6F **37**
Ross Rd. NP7: A'gvnny 4G **7**
(not continuous)
Rother Av. NP7: A'gvnny 1F **7**
Roundhouse Cl.
NP23: N'glo 5B **12**
Roundstables NP4: Abers 2D **36**
Rowan Cres. NP4: Grif 5D **46**
Rowan Pl. NP22: Rhym 4B **14**
Rowan Rd. NP11: Ris 3E **73**
Rowan Way NP23: Rassa 2D **10**
Rowland Dr. CF83: Caer 6D **74**
Royal Cl. NP11: Aberc 6B **52**
Royal Cres. NP11: Newb 1A **52**
Royal Oak CF83: Mac 6G **71**
Royal Oak Cl. CF83: Mac 6G **71**
Royal Oak Grn.
NP44: C'iog 5H **55**
Royce Cl. CF82: P'heol 2D **48**
RUDRY **5F 77**
Rudry Cl. CF83: Caer 2B **76**
Rudry Rd. CF83: Caer 2A **76**
CF83: Rud 6H **77**
Rumney Wlk. NP44: Llan 6H **55**
Ruperra St. NP24: New T 2D **30**
Rushbrook NP44: G'mdw 6B **54**
Rush Dr. NP11: Crum 2G **43**
Rushmere Rd.
NP12: P'fraith 6B **50**
Ruskin Cl. NP44: F'wtr 1F **63**
Russel Cl. NP4: New I 3H **47**
NP23: Rassa 3B **10**
Russell St. NP24: Brith 4F **31**
NP44: Pnwd 4E **55**
Ruth Rd. NP4: New I 2F **47**
Ruth St. CF81: Barg 3E **41**

S

Saffron Ct. NP44: F'wtr 2E **63**
St Andrews Cl. NP44: Pnwd 2F **55**
St Andrews Cres.
NP7: A'gvnny 2G **7**
St Andrews Dr. NP12: P'fraith 4B **50**
St Anne's Cl. NP11: Newb 4G **51**
NP44: Pnwd 4E **55**
St Annes Cres. CF81: Gilf 5F **41**
St Anne's Gdns.
CF82: Maes C 2G **57**
St Annes Gdns. CF83: Abert 6D **66**
St Annes Rd. NP12: Cefn F 3H **49**
St Anne St. CF81: Gilf 5E **41**
St Anthony's Cl. NP4: Grif 5D **46**
St Arvans Rd. NP44: C'brn 6F **55**
St Asaph's Way CF83: Caer 6F **75**
St Athan's Ct. CF83: Caer 5E **75**
St Augustine Rd. NP4: Grif 5D **46**
St Benedicts Cl. NP4: Grif 5D **46**
St Bleddian Cl. NP12: P'fraith 5B **50**
St Brides Cl. NP44: Llan 1D **64**
(not continuous)
St Cadoc's Rd. NP4: C'avn 5A **38**
St Catherines Cl. CF83: B'ws 1A **76**
St Catherine's Ct.
NP11: C'keys 1G **71**
St Cattwg's Av. CF82: G'gaer 3B **48**
St Cenydd Cl. CF83: Caer 3D **74**
NP12: P'fraith 4B **50**
St Cenydd Rd. CF83: Caer 3D **74**
St Christopher's Dr.
CF83: Caer 5E **75**
St Clares NP22: Rhym 2C **22**
St Clears Cl. CF83: Caer 5F **75**
St Clears Pl. *NP22: Tred 6H 9*
(off Dukestown Rd.)
St Cynidr Cl. NP23: E Vale 1D **16**
St David's Av. NP12: Oakd 2C **50**
St David's Cl. CF82: P'heol 2D **48**
NP4: P'pool 6H **37**
St Davids Cl. NP7: Mardy 1H **7**
NP12: P'fraith 4B **50**
NP22: Rhym 5B **14**
ST David's Cl. NP23: E Vale 1D **16**
St David's Dr. CF83: Mac 1E **77**
St David's Ind. Est.
NP12: Peng 2G **49**
St David's Pk. NP24: New T 3D **30**
St David's Pl. NP7: A'gvnny 1G **7**
St David's Rd. CF82: Maes C 2G **57**
NP7: A'gvnny, Mardy 1G **7**
NP12: Peng 2F **49**
NP44: C'brn, Pnwd 4F **55**
St David's Way CF83: Caer 6E **75**
St Deinols Cl. NP12: Peng 3G **49**
ST DIALS **1H 63**
St Dials Ct. NP44: C'brn 1B **64**
St Dials Rd.
NP44: C'brn, G'mdw 6B **54**
(not continuous)
St Dominics Retreat
NP4: P'pool 1B **46**
St Donat's Ct. CF83: Caer 5E **75**
St Donats Pl. NP44: Llan 1E **65**
St Fagans St. CF83: Caer 5F **75**
St Faith's Cl. NP7: L'fst 6E **7**
St Francis Cl. NP7: A'gvnny 2H **7**
St George's Ct. NP22: Tred 1H **15**
(not continuous)
St George's Cres.
NP7: A'gvnny 2H **7**
(not continuous)
St Gwladys Av. CF81: Barg 3E **41**
St Gwladys Ct. CF81: Barg 3E **41**
St Helen's Cl. NP7: A'gvnny 4E **7**
St Helen's Ct. CF83: Caer 5E **75**
St Helen's Rd. NP7: A'gvnny 4E **7**
St Hilda's Rd. NP4: Grif 5E **47**
St Ilan's Way CF83: Caer 6F **75**
ST ILLTYD **4C 34**
St James Cl. CF82: Maes C 2G **57**
CF83: Caer 2B **76**
St James' Fld. NP4: P'pool 1C **46**
St James Pk. NP22: Tred 4B **16**
St James Way NP22: Tred 2A **16**
(not continuous)
St Johns Cl. NP4: P'pool 6F **37**
St John's Cres. NP4: P'pool 6F **37**
NP10: Roger 6H **73**

St Johns Dr. NP12: P'fraith 4B 50
St John's La. NP7: A'gvnny 4F 7
St John's Sq. *NP7: A'gvnny 4F 7*
(off St John's St.)
St John's St. NP7: A'gvnny 4F 7
St Joseph Pl. NP44: Oakf 5E 65
St Julian's Ct. CF83: Caer 5E 75
St Julians Hgts. NP12: Fleur 5F 49
St Lukes Rd. NP4: P'nydd 4F 37
St Luke's Rd. NP22: Tred 5F 9
St Madoc Cl. NP12: P'fraith 4B 50
St Maelog Cl. NP12: P'fraith 4B 50
St Margaret's Av.
NP12: Cefn F 2H 49
St Margarets Cl. CF83: Tret 1C 76
St Margaret's Rd.
CF83: Caer 5E 75
ST MARTINS 5F 75
St Martin's Cres. CF83: Caer 6F 75
NP22: Tred 6F 9
St Martin's Rd. CF83: Caer 6E 75
St Mary's Cl. NP4: Grif 4D 46
St Mary's Ct. NP11: Ris 2C 72
St Marys Rd. NP7: A'gvnny 3G 7
St Mary's Rd. NP12: P'fraith 5B 50
NP44: C'iog 4G 55
St Mary St. CF81: Gilf 5F 41
CF83: B'ws 1A 76
NP4: Grif 4D 46
NP11: Ris 2B 72
St Matthew's Rd.
NP4: P'pool 2D 46
St Mellons Ct. CF83: Caer 5E 75
St Michael Gro. NP44: Oakf 4E 65
St Michael's Rd.
NP7: A'gvnny 3E 7
St Nicholas Ct. CF83: Caer 5E 75
St Oswalds Cl. NP4: Grif 6E 47
St Peter's Cl. NP11: Newb 2C 52
St Peters Cl. NP44: F'wtr 1G 63
St Peters Dr. NP12: P'fraith 4B 50
St Rhidian Cl. NP12: P'fraith 4B 50
St Ronans NP7: A'gvnny 6G 7
St Sannan rd. NP12: P'fraith 5A 50
St Teilo's Cl. NP23: E Vale 1D 16
St Teilo's Rd. NP7: A'gvnny 2H 7
St Teilo's Way CF83: Caer 6E 75
St Telio's Cl. NP12: P'fraith 4B 50
St Thomas Ct. NP4: Tal 6D 28
St Tudor's Vw NP12: B'wood 3B 50
St Woolos Grn. NP44: C'brn 5E 55
Salisbury Ct. NP44: C'brn 6C 54
Salisbury St. NP11: C'keys 1H 71
Salisbury Ter. NP4: Var 2D 28
NP24: Brith 4E 31
Sally, The NP4: P'pool 1A 46
Salop St. CF83: Caer 5G 75
Salway Av. NP12: Peng 6G 41
Samson's Av. NP4: Var 4D 28
Samuel Salter Cl. NP7: L'fst 6E 7
Sandybrook Cl. NP44: C'brn 2H 63
Sannan St. CF81: A'goed 1G 41
Sansom St. NP11: Ris 2C 72
Sarno Sq. NP7: A'gvnny 4H 7
Sarn Pl. NP11: Ris 2C 72
Saron Pl. NP23: E Vale 3E 17
Sawtells Ter. NP4: P'nydd 5E 37
Saxon Ct. *NP23: B mawr 3A 12*
(off Orchard St.)
Scala Cinema 6H 37
School Av. NP23: N'glo 6C 12
School Cl. NP4: P'pool 1B 46
School Ct. NP44: C'brn 1B 64
School Cres. NP4: Grif 6E 47
School La. NP4: Abers 1E 37
NP4: P'pool 6G 37
NP7: Gilw 3D 4
NP7: Gov 5G 5
NP11: Pent C 2A 44
NP23: Rassa 3C 10
School Rd. NP4: P'nydd 5E 37
NP23: B'fort, Rassa 3C 10
School St. CF81: A'goed 2F 41
CF81: Deri 5A 30
CF81: P'tyn 2C 22
CF83: L'brad 5A 68
NP12: Fleur 4G 49
NP24: Brith 4F 31
NP24: New T 3E 31
(Elliot's Town)
NP24: New T 1C 30
(Tir-Phil)
School Ter. CF83: Sen 2C 66
NP4: P'nydd 5E 37
(off Old School Pl.)
NP23: Cwm 3H 25
School Vw. NP4: P'pool 2D 46
NP23: N'glo 5A 12
SCWRFA 6G 9
Scwrfa Rd. NP22: Tred 5G 9
SEBASTOPOL 6E 47
Second Av. CF83: Caer 4D 74
Selby Cl. NP44: Llanf 1E 65
SENGHENYDD 3C 66
Severn Cl. NP11: Ris 4E 73
Severn Rd. NP12: P'fraith 5A 50
Severn Vw. NP4: Var 5E 29
NP44: Up Cwm 3B 54
Severn Vw. Ter. *NP4: Abers 2E 37*
(off Pentwyn Hgts.)
Sevins *NP44: F'wtr 2H 63*
(off Henllys Way)
Shakespeare Cres.
NP23: E Vale 1D 16
Shakespeare Rd.
NP44: C'brn, G'mdw 1H 63
Shannon Cl. NP12: P'fraith 5A 50
Shaw Cl. NP23: E Vale 1B 16
Shawley Ct. NP44: G'mdw 1H 63
Shelley Cl. *CF81: A'goed 3G 41*
(off Ty Fry Rd.)
NP11: C'maen 6G 43
Shelley Ct. CF83: Mac 6B 70
Shelley Grn. NP44: G'mdw 1H 63
Shepherds Cl. NP22: Tred 5H 9
Sherbourne Ct. NP4: Grif 6E 47
Sherbourne Rd. NP4: Grif 6E 47
Shirdale Cl. CF82: Maes C 1G 57
Shires, The NP7: Gilw 1D 4
Shop Rd. NP4: Trev, Var 3E 29
Shop Row NP13: Blai 4C 18
NP22: Tred 3H 15
NP22: Tref 1D 8
Shop Ter. NP7: Cly 6H 13
Short Path *NP44: F'wtr 2G 63*
(off Jule Rd.)
Sid Griffiths Ct. NP4: Var 5D 28
Siloam Hill CF83: Mac 6E 71
Silver St. NP11: P'waun 5D 60
Sir Alfred Owen Way
CF83: Caer 1F 75
SIRHOWY 6A 10
Sirhowy Ct. NP22: Tred 6A 10
NP44: G'mdw 5B 54
Sirhowy Hill Ind. Est.
NP22: Tred 2H 15
Sirhowy Valley Country Pk. 3C 70
Sirhowy Vw. NP12: P'fraith 6D 50
SIRHYWI 6A 10
Sir Ivor's Rd. NP12: P'fraith 6C 50
Sir Stafford Cl. CF83: Caer 2H 75
SIX BELLS 2D 34
Six Bells Rd. NP13: S Bells 3C 34
Skenfrith Cl. NP12: B'wood 6B 42
Skirrid Rd. NP7: A'gvnny 3F 7
Ski Slope 1D 46
Sluvad Rd. NP4: New I 4H 47
Smallbrook Cl. NP44: C'brn 6F 55
Smith Rd. NP13: A'lery 5F 27
Smiths Ter. NP12: Oakd 3D 50
Snail Creep NP4: Trev, Var 2E 29
SNATCHWOOD 3E 37
Snatchwood Ct. NP4: P'nydd 4E 37
Snatchwood Rd.
NP4: Abers, P'nydd 3E 37
Snatchwood Ter. NP4: Abers 3E 37
Snowden Ct. CF83: Caer 4H 75
Snowdon Cl. NP11: Ris 3E 73
Snowdon Ct. NP44: C'iog 4G 55
Snowdrop La. NP10: Roger 6G 73
Soar Cl. NP44: C'iog 3H 55
SOFRYDD 5C 44
Sofrydd Rd. NP11: Crum 4C 44
Solent Cl. NP12: P'fraith 5A 50
Somerset Ind. Est.
NP44: C'brn 5F 55
Somerset Rd.
NP44: C'brn, Pnwd 5F 55
Somerset St. NP13: A'lery 6G 27
NP23: B mawr 2B 12
Somerset Ter. NP23: B'fort 3E 11
Sorrel Dr. CF82: P'heol 2D 48
South Av. NP4: Grif 1D 54
South Bank NP23: B'fort 3G 11
South Cl. NP44: Llanf 2E 65
Southend NP22: Tred 5B 16
Southend Ter. CF81: P'tyn 3C 22
Southern St. CF83: Caer 5G 75
Southlands NP13: Blai 4D 18
Sth. Pandy Rd. CF83: Caer 2F 75
Sth. Pontypool Ind. Pk.
NP4: New I 3F 47
South Rd. CF82: G'gaer 4C 48
NP44: Oakf 3C 64
South St. CF81: Barg 3E 41
NP4: Grif 6E 47
NP23: B'fort 3F 11
South Vw. NP4: P'pool 6G 37
South Vw. Ho's.
CF82: G'gaer 3C 48
South Vw. Rd.
NP12: B'wood 1B 50
Southview Ter. NP4: B'avn 3F 21
Sth. Vw. Ter. NP24: New T 1D 30
SOUTHVILLE 1B 64
South Wlk. NP44: C'brn 6E 55
Southway NP4: Lit M, P'pool 4E 39
SOWHILL 1B 46
Spencer Sq. NP22: Tred 3H 15
Spencer St. NP23: E Vale 3E 17
Spinks Ct. NP7: A'gvnny 2G 7
Spinney, The NP12: P'fraith 6A 50
Spring Bank NP13: A'lery 5F 27
SPRINGFIELD 5D 50
Springfield Cl. NP44: C'iog 3G 55
Springfield Ct.
NP12: P'fraith 6D 50
Springfield Rd.
CF82: Maes C 2F 57
NP4: Grif 6D 46
NP7: A'gvnny 3G 7
NP11: Ris 5E 73
Springfields NP11: C'maen 6G 43
Springfield Ter. NP4: New I 3G 47
NP4: P'nydd 6D 36
NP11: Newb 4F 51
NP12: Holly B 3H 31
NP13: L'hth 1C 44
Springfield Vw.
CF82: Maes C 2F 57
Spring Gro. NP44: G'mdw 6A 54
Spring La. NP44: C'iog 4G 55
Spring Ter. NP4: Grif 5D 46
Springvale NP44: C'brn 5C 54
Springvale Ind. Est.
NP44: C'brn 5C 54
Springvale Way NP44: C'brn 5D 54
Springwells NP7: A'gvnny 3H 7
Square, The CF81: P'tyn 2C 22
CF82: P'heol 2D 48
CF82: Ystrad 2E 57
CF83: Abert 6C 66
CF83: B'ws 1B 76
NP12: B'wood 2B 50
(off High St.)
NP12: Peng 1F 49
NP24: New T 2C 30
Stable Lane NP22: Tred 4H 15
Stable Row NP4: B'avn 2F 21
Stafford Rd.
NP4: Grif, P'pool 3E 47
Standard St. CF83: Tret 1D 76
Stanfield St. NP23: Cwm 4H 25
Stanhope St. NP7: A'gvnny 3E 7
Stanley Dr. CF83: Caer 2E 75
Stanley Pl. NP44: Pnwd 4E 55
Stanley Rd. NP4: Var 5D 28
Stanley St. CF83: Sen 2C 66
NP11: C'fch 1H 69
NP12: B'wood 2B 50
Starbuck St. CF83: Rud 4E 77
Star La. NP4: C'avn 5G 37
Star St. NP22: Tred 5G 9
NP44: C'brn 1B 64
Station App. NP23: E Vale 6E 11
Station Av. NP11: Yny 6C 58
Station Enterprises
NP7: A'gvnny 5H 7
Station Farm NP44: C'iog 4F 55
Station Pl. NP11: Ris 3C 72
Station Rd. CF81: Barg 2F 41
CF82: Ystrad 2D 56
CF83: L'brad 4A 68
NP4: Grif 4E 47
NP7: A'gvnny 5G 7
NP7: Cly 5G 13
(not continuous)
NP7: Gilw 5C 4
NP7: Gov 6G 5
NP11: Crum 6B 44
NP11: Ris 4C 72
NP12: Peng 1F 49
NP13: Blai 4C 18
NP18: P'hir 5H 65
NP22: A'swg 3F 23
NP22: Tred 5F 9
NP23: B mawr 3B 12
NP23: E Vale 1E 17
Station Rd. NP23: W Iwyd 6G 17
NP24: Brith 4E 31
NP44: Pnwd 4E 55
Station Row NP24: New T 2D 30
Station St. CF81: P'tyn 2C 22
CF83: Mac 6F 71
NP4: Abers 2E 37
NP11: Newb 4F 51
Station Ter. CF81: Foch 4A 22
CF83: Caer 5G 75
(Bartlett St.)
CF83: Caer 3D 74
(Ty-Isaf)
CF83: Sen 3B 66
NP23: Cwm 4A 26
NP44: Pnwd 4E 55
Steel Works Road
NP23: E Vale 3F 17
Steepfield NP44: C'iog 3G 55
Stephens Cres. NP7: Gov 5H 5
Stevelee NP44: F'wtr 2H 63
Stewart St. NP23: Cwm 5A 26
Steynton Path NP44: F'wtr 1H 63
Stiels NP44: F'wtr 3G 63
Stockland St. CF83: Caer 5F 75
Stocktonville NP22: Tred 1G 15
Stockton Way NP22: Tred 1G 15
Stonebridge Rd. NP23: Rassa 3B 10
Stonerwood Vw. NP11: Newb . . .1C 52
Stone's Ho's NP13: Blai 3C 18
Stoney Rd. NP4: Var 6E 29
Stour Ct. NP44: G'mdw 5A 54
Stowepath NP44: Llan 1E 65
Strand, The NP44: C'brn 5E 55
Strathview NP11: Newb 4F 51
Stryd Hywel Harris
CF82: Ystrad 4D 56
Stuart St. CF81: P'tyn 2C 22
Sufflex Est. NP11: Ris 5E 73
Summerfield Hall La.
CF82: Maes C 1G 57
Summerfield La. CF83: Mac 1F 77
Summerfield Rd. NP7: A'gvnny . . .3G 7
NP23: Rassa 2C 10
Summerfield Ter. NP12: Fleur . . .4G 49
Sunlea Cres.
NP4: New I, P'pool 1F 47
Sunningdale CF83: Caer 5D 74
Sunnybank CF83: Abert 6E 67
Sunny Bank NP7: A'gvnny 4E 7
Sunnybank NP23: B mawr 2A 12
NP24: New T 2D 30
Sunnybank Ct. NP4: Grif 4E 47
NP23: B mawr 2A 12
(off Sunnybank)
Sunnybank Rd. NP4: Grif 4D 46
NP12: B'wood 1A 50
Sunny Bank Ter. CF83: Mac 6E 71
Sunnybank Ter. NP13: A'beeg . . .6A 34
Sunnybank Way NP4: Grif 5D 46
Sunny Crest NP11: Newb 2B 52
Sunny Hill NP22: Rhym 1D 22
Sunny Pl. NP18: P'hir 4H 65
Sunny Vw. CF81: P'tyn 3C 22
NP12: Argoed 3C 42
Surgery Rd. NP13: Blai 2C 18
Swan Cres. NP23: B'fort 3F 11
Swan Sq. NP4: Abers 2E 37
SWFFRYD 5C 44
Swn-yr-Nant CF82: P'heol 2C 48
Sycamore Av. NP7: A'gvnny 4G 7
NP22: Tred 6G 9
Sycamore Ct. CF81: Barg 5D 40
NP12: Oakd 3C 50
NP44: H'lys 3E 63
Sycamore Cres. NP11: Ris 4E 73
Sycamore Pl. NP44: Up Cwm . . .4B 54
(not continuous)
Sycamore Rd. NP4: Grif 6D 46
Sycamore Rd. S. NP4: Grif 6D 46
Sycamore Ter. NP11: Aberc 6C 52
Sychan Ter. NP4: Abers 2E 37
Sydney Ct. NP12: Cefn F 3H 49
Syndicate Ter. NP11: C'fch 1H 69
Syr Dafydd Av. NP12: Oakd 5E 43

T

Tabor Rd. CF82: Maes C 1G 57
TAFARNAUBACH 6D 8
Tafarnaubach Ind. Est.
NP22: Tred 5C 8
Taff Cl. NP23: Rassa 3D 10
Taff Ct. NP44: G'mdw 4A 54

Tafwy's Wlk. CF83: Caer 4F 75
Tai'r-Heol CF82: P'heol 1C 48
Talfaen Cl. NP4: C'avn 4H 37
Talgarth Cl. NP44: C'brn 1B 64
Taliesin NP44: C'brn 5E 55
TALLISTOWN 5A 26
TALYWAIN 6D 28
Talywain Ho. NP4: Tal 6D 28
Tamar Cl. NP12: P'fraith 6A 50
Tanglewood Cl. NP7: A'gvnny 4G 7
Tanglewood Dr. NP13: Blai 4E 19
Tanlan Sq. NP24: New T 3E 31
Tansy Cl. CF82: P'heol 3D 48
Tan-y-Bryn CF83: Sen 4C 66
Tanybryn NP11: Ris 5F 73
Tan-y-Bryn NP22: Rhym 1D 22
Tan-y-Coed NP4: P'nydd 4E 37
Tan-y-Llan Ter. NP22: Rhym 4B 14
Taylor St. NP11: Ris 2C 72
Teel Works Rd. NP23: E Vale 6E 11
Tegfan CF83: Caer 4D 74
Tegfan Ct. NP44: H'lys 3E 63
Telford Cl. CF82: P'heol 2D 48
Telor-y-Goed CF83: L'brad 6F 57
Temperance Hill NP11: Ris 2C 72
Tenby Cl. NP44: Llan 6G 55
Tenby Ct. CF83: Caer 3C 74
Tenison Rd. NP4: C'avn 4A 38
Tennyson Ter. NP24: Brith 4E 31
Tern Ct. NP44: G'mdw 4A 54
Terrace, The NP22: Rhym 5B 14
Tewdric Ct. NP44: C'iog 4H 55
Tewends NP44: F'wtr 2G 63
Teynes NP44: F'wtr 2G 63
Thames Cl. NP12: P'fraith 5A 50
The Glyn NP11: Crum 5E 45
The Lawns Ind. Est.
NP22: Rhym 6B 14
Third Av. CF83: Caer 4D 74
Thistle Ct. NP44: F'wtr 1E 63
Thistle Way NP11: Ris 4E 73
Thomas Ellis Way
NP22: Tred 1A 16
Thomas Flds NP22: Rhym 5C 14
Thomas St. CF81: A'goed 1G 41
CF81: Gilf 5F 41
CF82: Maes C 1G 57
CF83: Abert, Caer 6D 66
CF83: L'brad 4A 68
CF83: Tret 1D 76
NP24: New T 2D 30
Thomasville CF83: Caer 3D 74
Thorncliff Ct. NP44: G'mdw 1H 63
Thorncombe Rd.
NP12: B'wood 3C 50
Thorne Av. NP11: Newb 2A 52
THORNHILL 5B 54
Thornhill Cl. NP23: B mawr 2B 12
NP44: Up Cwm 3B 54
Thornhill Gdns. NP10: Roger 6H 73
Thornhill Rd.
NP44: G'mdw, Up Cwm 5B 54
Thornhill Way NP10: Roger 6H 73
Thornleigh Rd. NP11: Pent C . . .2A 44
Three Elms Cl. CF82: Cefn H 5E 49
Three Oaks Cl. CF83: B'ws 6D 68
Tillery Rd. NP13: C'lery 4G 27
(Crook Hill)
NP13: C'lery 5G 27
(Tillery St.)
Tillery St. NP13: A'lery 6G 27
Tillsland NP44: F'wtr 3H 63
Tintern Cl. NP44: C'brn 1B 64
Tir Bach Rd. NP12: Yny 2C 58
Tir-Berllan NP12: Oakd 5E 43
Tir Coed CF83: Caer 2D 74
Tirpentwys Ter. NP4: P'nydd 5E 37
TIR-PHIL 2D 30
Tir-Philkins
NP12: Oakd, P'fraith 3D 50
Tirphil Station (Rail) 2D 30
TIR-Y-BERTH 3F 49
Tir-y-Berth NP23: E Vale 4D 10
Tir-y-Berth St. CF82: Tir B 3F 49
Tir-y-Cwm La. NP11: Ris 4C 72
Tir-y-Cwm Rd. NP11: Ris 3C 72
Tir-y-Pwll Ter. NP11: Newb 2C 52
Tollgate Cl. CF83: Caer 2A 76
Tolpath NP44: F'wtr 2F 63
Ton-Mawr Av. NP4: B'avn 3F 21
Ton-Mawr Rd. NP4: B'avn 3F 21
Ton Rd. NP44: C'brn 2H 63
NP44: F'wtr 1F 63
Ton-y-Felin Rd. CF83: Caer 4G 75
Tonypistyll Rd. NP11: Newb 4G 51
Top Rd. NP4: Var 5D 28
Torfaen Bus. Cen. NP4: New I . . .3F 47
TORFAEN COMMUNITY HOSPITAL
(TALYGARN) 3E 47
Torfaen Ter. *NP4: P'nydd 4F 37*
(off Freehold Land Rd.)
Torlais St. NP11: Newb 3A 52
Toronto Cl. NP12: Oakd 1C 50
Tor Vw. CF83: B'ws 6D 68
Tor-y-Crug NP23: Rassa 2C 10
Tothill St. NP23: E Vale 6D 10
Tourist Info. Cen.
Abergavenny 4G 7
Caerphilly 5F 75
Towers, The NP44: C'brn 6F 55
Trafalgar Cl. NP23: B mawr 3B 12
Trafalgar Rd. NP23: B mawr 2B 12
Trafalgar St. NP11: Ris 5D 72
Tram La. NP44: Llanf 4F 65
Tram Rd. NP12: P'fraith 6C 50
NP44: Up Cwm 3B 54
Tram Rd. Ind. Est.
NP12: P'fraith 6C 50
Tramroadside NP11: Newb 3A 52
Tramway Cl. NP44: F'wtr 2F 63
TRANCH 1A 46
Tranch Rd. NP4: P'pool 1A 46
Trannon Ct. NP44: G'mdw 5B 54
Tranquil Pl. NP44: Oakf 2B 64
Tranters Ter. *NP44: Up Cwm 3C 54*
(off Ty Pwca Rd.)
Trap Well CF83: Caer 2A 76
Traws Mawr La. NP44: Oakf 6B 64
TRECENYDD 4D 74
Trecenydd Ind. Est.
CF83: Caer 4D 74
TREDEGAR 3H 15
Tredegar Av. NP23: E Vale 2D 16
Tredegar Bus. Pk. NP22: Tred . . .2H 15
Tredegar Ct. NP11: C'keys 2G 71
TREDEGAR GENERAL HOSPITAL
. . . . .3H 15
Tredegar Gap NP23: E Vale 1D 16
Tredegar Leisure Cen. 4H 15
Tredegar Rd. NP12: B'wood 6C 42
NP23: E Vale 2C 16
NP24: New T 1D 30
Tredegar St. NP11: C'keys 1G 71
NP11: Ris 3C 72
Tredegar Ter. CF81: A'goed 3F 41
NP11: C'keys 1G 71
NP11: Ris 4C 72
Trederwen NP23: E Vale 1C 16
TREDOMEN 2C 56
Tredomen Athletic Stadium 4E 57
Tredomen Ind. Pk.
CF82: Ystrad 1C 56
Tredomen Ter. CF82: Ystrad 2C 56
Tredomen Vs. CF82: Ystrad 1C 56
Tre Edwards NP22: Rhym 4A 14
Tree Tops Av. NP12: B'wood 1B 50
TREFIL 1D 8
Trefil Rd. NP22: Tred, Tref 1C 8
Tre-Herbert Rd. NP44: C'iog 2H 55
Trelech Cl. NP44: C'brn 1C 64
Trelyn La. NP12: Fleur 3F 49
Trelys Cl. NP12: Fleur 4F 49
Trem Penallta CF82: Cefn H 6E 49
Trem Twynbarlwm
NP44: C'brn 2B 64
Trem y Castell CF83: Caer 6C 74
Trem-y-Mynydd NP4: B'avn 3G 21
Trem-yr-Efail CF82: Ystrad 4D 56
Trenant NP23: E Vale 1D 16
Tre Newydd NP23: E Vale 6F 11
TREOWEN 1A 52
Treowen Av. NP12: P'fraith 5B 50
Treowen Rd. NP11: Newb 6A 44
TRETHOMAS 1D 76
Tretower Ct. NP44: Llan 6H 55
Trevelyan Ct. CF83: Caer 4H 75
TREVETHIN 4G 37
Trevine Path NP44: F'wtr 1H 63
Tre York NP22: Rhym 6B 14
Tribute Av. NP11: C'crn 3D 60
Tridwr Rd. CF83: Abert 6C 66
TRINANT 3A 44
Trinant Ter. NP11: Pent C 2A 44
Trinity Cl. CF82: Ystrad 2D 56
Trinity Ct. NP11: Ris 3C 72
Trinity Rd. NP44: Pnwd 4D 54
Trinity Sq. NP7: A'gvnny 4F 7
Trinity St. NP7: A'gvnny 4F 7
Trinity Ter. NP7: A'gvnny 4F 7
Troed-y-Bryn CF83: Caer 2D 74
Troed y Rhiw CF82: Ystrad 3D 56
Troed-y-Rhiw NP11: Aberc 6B 52
Troed-y-Rhiw Rd.
NP11: W'vle 1D 70
TROSNANT 2C 46
Trosnant Cres. CF82: G'gaer 5C 48
Trosnant St. NP4: P'pool 1C 46
(not continuous)
Trostrey NP44: F'wtr 3H 63
Trostrey Cl. NP4: New I 3H 47
Troy Rd. NP13: L'hth 6C 34
Trussel Rd. NP44: C'brn 5E 55
Tuckers Vs. NP12: B'wood 2B 50
Tudor Cl. NP23: Rassa 2C 10
Tudor Cres. NP23: B mawr 3A 12
Tudor Gdns. CF83: Mac 6E 71
Tudor Rd. NP44: C'brn 6E 55
Tudor St. NP7: A'gvnny 4E 7
Tudor Woods NP44: Llan 1E 65
Tulip Wlk. NP10: Roger 6G 73
Tunnel Ter. NP11: Newb 3H 51
Turberville Rd. NP44: C'brn 5F 55
Turners End NP44: F'wtr 2G 63
Turnpike Cl. NP4: P'pool 1F 47
Turnpike Rd.
NP44: C'iog, Llanf 5H 55
Twinings, The NP44: G'mdw 6B 54
Twissell's Rd. NP4: P'pool 1A 46
Twm Barlwm Cl. NP11: Ris 3F 73
Twmbarlwm Ri. NP44: H'lys 2D 62
Twm Barlwm Vw.
NP44: Llanf 1E 65
Twmpath Gdns. NP4: P'pool 1B 46
Twmpath Rd. NP4: P'pool 1B 46
TWO LOCKS 2B 64
Two-Locks Rd. NP44: C'brn 2A 64
Twyll Gwyn Ter. NP11: Newb 3H 51
Twyn NP12: Fleur 4F 49
TWYN-ALLWS 5E 5
Twyn Allwys Rd. NP7: Gov 5F 5
Twyn Carno NP22: Rhym 4B 14
Twyncarn Rd.
NP11: C'crn, P'waun 4C 60
Twyncarn Ter. *NP11: C'crn 4C 60*
(off Newport Rd.)
TWYN CYNGHORDY 3H 11
Twyn Cynghordy
NP23: B mawr 3A 12
Twyncynghordy Rd.
NP23: B mawr 3H 11
NP23: B'fort, B mawr 3G 11
Twyn Gdns. NP12: Cefn F 2H 49
Twyn-Gwyn Rd.
NP11: C'fch, Yny 5D 58
Twyn Plas NP11: Aberc 6D 52
Twyn Rd. CF82: Ystrad 4D 56
NP11: Aberc 6C 52
Twyn Star NP22: Tred 5G 9
Twyn, The CF83: Caer 5G 75
TWYN WENALLT 5C 4
Twynyffald Rd. NP12: B'wood . . .1A 50
Ty Bedwellty *NP12: Cefn F 1A 50*
(off Bryn Rd.)
Ty Box Cl. NP44: Pnwd 4D 54
Ty Box Rd. NP44: Pnwd 4D 54
(not continuous)
Ty-Brachty Ter. NP11: C'maen . . .5G 43
Ty Bryn NP22: Tred 2H 15
Ty Bryn Hill NP13: A'lery 5F 27
Ty Bryn Rd. NP13: A'lery 5F 27
Ty-Bwmpyn Rd. NP4: P'nydd 6C 36
Ty-Canol Ct. NP44: F'wtr 2F 63
Ty Canol La. CF83: Mac 6E 71
Ty-Canol La. CF83: Tret 5H 69
Ty-Canol Row NP44: F'wtr 2F 63
Ty-Canol Way
NP44: F'wtr, G'mdw 1E 63
Ty-Clyd Cl. NP7: Gov 4H 5
TY-COCH 3B 64
Ty-Coch NP22: Rhym 3B 14
Ty-Coch Cl. NP44: Oakf 5D 64
Ty-Coch Distribution Cen.
NP44: C'brn 3B 64
Ty-Coch La. NP44: C'brn 3A 64
NP44: Oakf 4C 64
Ty-Coch Way
NP44: C'brn, Oakf 2B 64
Ty Coed NP44: G'mdw 4B 54
Ty-Dan-y-Wal Rd.
NP13: C'lery 2G 27
Tydfil Rd. CF83: B'ws 6E 69
Tydies NP44: F'wtr 3G 63
Tydraw La. NP4: Lit M 2H 39
Ty Fry Cl. NP4: B'avn 2G 21
Ty Fry Rd. CF81: A'goed 3G 41
Ty Gwyn NP4: Lit M 2H 39
Ty-Gwyn Rd. NP4: Var 4D 28
NP7: Gilw 5D 4
Ty Gwyn Rd. NP44: F'wtr 1F 63
NP44: G'mdw 6B 54
Ty Gwyn Way NP44: G'mdw 6A 54
Ty-Heulwen *NP23: N'glo 5B 12*
(off Limestone Rd. E.)
Ty-Isaf CF83: Caer 2C 74
NP11: Ris 5E 73
Ty-Isaf Bungs. CF83: Caer 2C 74
Ty-Isaf Circ. NP11: Ris 5E 73
Ty-Isaf Cres. NP11: Ris 5E 73
Ty-Isaf Pk. Av. NP11: Ris 5E 73
Ty-Isaf Pk. Cres. NP11: Ris 5E 73
Ty-Isaf Pk. Rd. NP11: Ris 5E 73
Ty-Isaf Pk. Vs. NP11: Ris 5E 73
Ty-Isha Ter. NP12: B'wood 1A 50
Tyla Glas CF83: Caer 6E 75
Tyla-Gwyn CF82: P'heol 1C 48
Tyleri Gdns. NP13: A'lery 5G 27
Ty-Llwydd Pl. NP11: Newb 3A 52
Tyllwyd Wlk. CF81: A'goed 2G 41
TY LLWYN 3F 17
Ty-Melin NP11: C'maen 6G 43
Ty Mynydd NP4: B'avn 3G 21
NP44: Pnwd 4E 55
Ty Mynyddislwyn
NP12: P'fraith 6C 50
Ty-Nant CF82: P'heol 1C 48
Ty Nant CF83: Caer 3D 74
Ty Nant Ddu NP4: P'nydd 5G 37
TYNEWYDD 4E 9
Tynewydd Av. NP44: Pnwd 3E 55
Ty-Newydd Ct. NP44: Pnwd 4E 55
Tynewydd Farm Cl.
NP44: Pnwd 3E 55
Tynewydd Grn. NP44: Pnwd 3E 55
Ty-Newydd Ho. NP44: Pnwd 4E 55
Tynewydd Nth. Cl.
NP44: Pnwd 3E 55
Ty-Newydd Rd. NP44: Pnwd 4E 55
Tynewydd Sth. Cl.
NP44: Pnwd 3E 55
Tynewydd St. CF81: P'tyn 3C 22
Tynewydd Ter. NP11: Newb 3A 52
Tyn-y-Coed CF82: Ystrad 2D 56
Ty'n-y-Coedcae CF83: Mac 2G 77
Tynycoed Cres. NP12: Cefn F . . .1H 49
Tyn-y-Cwm Rd. NP11: Ris 5F 73
Ty'n-y-Graig Rd. CF83: L'brad . . .4A 68
Tynygraig Ter. CF83: L'brad 4A 68
Tyn y Parc CF83: Abert 5C 66
Tyn y Waun Rd. CF83: Mac 6F 71
Tynywern Ter. CF83: Tret 6H 69
Ty Pucca Cl. CF83: Mac 6F 71
Ty Pwca Pl.
NP44: Pnwd, Up Cwm 3C 54
Ty Pwca Rd.
NP44: Pnwd, Up Cwm 3C 54
Tyr Comn. NP7: Gilw 2D 4
Ty'r Meddyg NP23: E Vale 4F 11
Ty-Rosser Gwyn NP4: Var 4D 28
Ty Scott NP22: Tred 2G 15
TY-SIGN 3E 73
TY SIRHOWY HOSPITAL 6B 42
Ty Trappa NP44: Pnwd 3C 54
Ty Trappa Pl. NP44: Pnwd 3C 54
Ty Tudor NP44: C'brn 6F 55

U

Ullswater Ct. NP44: G'mdw 6C 54
Under Cardiff Rd. *CF81: Barg . . .4F 41*
(off Cardiff Rd.)
Underhill Cres. NP7: A'gvnny 2F 7
Underwood CF83: Caer 6G 75
Underwood Av. CF82: Maes C . . .2F 57
Underwood Rd. NP12: Oakd 1D 50
Underwood Ter. CF83: Abert 6E 67
Union Rd. E. NP7: A'gvnny 4E 7
Union Rd. Ind. Est.
NP7: A'gvnny 4D 6
Union Rd. W. NP7: A'gvnny 3D 6
Union St. CF81: P'tyn 2C 22
NP4: Abers 2E 37
NP22: Tred 2G 15
Universal Vs. CF83: Sen 2B 66
Upland Dr. NP4: C'avn 4G 37
Upland Rd. NP12: P'fraith 5D 50
Uplands NP11: Newb 2A 52
Uplands Ter. NP44: C'brn 6C 54
UPLANDS, THE 6H 73
Up. Arail St. NP13: S Bells 2C 34
Up. Bridge St. NP4: P'pool 1C 46
Up. Bryhyfryd Ter. CF83: Sen . . .2C 66
Up. Capel St. CF81: Barg 3E 41

Up. Church St. CF81: Barg 3E 41
UPPER COEDCAE 2G 21
Up. Coedcae Rd. NP4: B'avn 2G 21
Up. Court Ter. NP13: L'hth 1C 44
Up. Cross St. *NP24: New T 2C 30*
(off Railway Ter.)
UPPER CWMBRAN 3B 54
Up. Cwmbran Rd.
NP44: Up Cwm 3A 54
Up. Francis St. CF83: Abert 6C 66
Up. Garn Ter. NP4: G Erw 1B 20
Up. Glantorvaen Ter.
NP4: B'avn 3E 21
Up. Glyn Gwyn St. CF83: Tret . . .6H 69
Up. Griffin St. NP13: S Bells 2D 34
Up. Gwastod Ter.
NP13: C'lery 3H 27
Up. Gwyddon Rd.
NP11: Aberc 1C 60
Up. High St. CF81: Barg 3F 41
NP22: Rhym 3B 14
Up. Hill St. NP4: B'avn 3G 21
Up. North Rd. CF81: Barg 2E 41
UPPER OCHRWYTH 6C 72
Up. Park Ter. NP4: P'pool 1C 46
UPPER RACE 3A 46
Upper Rd. NP24: New T 4F 31
Up. St James St.
NP12: Argoed 3C 42
Up. Salisbury St. NP22: Tred . . .3H 15
Up. Stanley Ter.
NP24: New T 3E 31
Up. Tribute Av. NP11: C'crn 3D 60
Up. Trosnant St. NP4: P'pool 1C 46
Up. Viaduct Ter. NP11: Crum . . .5B 44
Up. Waun St. NP4: B'avn 2F 21
Up. Woodland St.
NP4: B'avn 2F 21
Up. Wood St. CF81: Barg 4E 41
Usk Ct. NP44: G'mdw 5B 54
Usk Dr. NP7: Gilw 3E 5
Usk Pl. NP23: Rassa 2D 10
Usk Rd. CF81: Barg 2E 41
NP4: Lit M, Mamh 1G 39
NP4: Lit M, New I, P'pool . . .2E 47
Uskvale Ct. NP4: P'pool 1F 47
Usk Vw. NP7: Gov 5H 5

V

Valentine Rd. NP4: Abers 2F 37
Vale Ter. NP22: Tred 4A 16
Vale Vw. CF81: Barg 5E 41
CF82: Maes C 2F 57
NP7: A'gvnny 1G 7
NP11: Ris 3D 72
NP22: Tred 5B 16
NP44: H'lys 3E 63
Vale Vw. Rd. NP12: Oakd 3C 50
Valley Rd. NP23: E Vale 6D 10
Valley Vw. CF82: Cefn H 4E 49
NP11: Pent C 1A 44
NP12: P'fraith 6B 50
Valley Vw. Rd. NP13: C'lery 4G 27
VAN 5H 75
Vancouver Dr. NP12: Oakd 1C 50
Vanfield Cl. CF83: Caer 5H 75
Van Rd. CF83: Caer 5G 75
Van Ter. CF83: Caer 5A 76
VARTEG 3E 29
Varteg Pl. NP22: Tred 6H 9
Varteg Rd.
NP4: B'avn, Trev, Var 3F 21
Venosa Trad. Est. CF83: Caer . . .3G 75
Ventnor Rd. NP44: C'brn 1B 64
Vere Pl. CF81: Gilf 6F 41
Vere St. CF81: Gilf 6F 41
Vernon Pl. NP11: C'maen 6G 43
Verwey Rd. NP23: N'glo 1C 18
Viaduct Ct. NP4: P'pool 2D 46
Viaduct Rd. NP4: Var 6D 28
Vicarage Cl. CF81: Barg 3E 41
Vicarage Gdns.
NP10: Roger 6H 73
NP22: Tred 6G 9
Vicarage La. CF81: Barg 3E 41
CF81: P'tyn 3C 22
NP4: Abers 6E 29
NP12: P'fraith 5E 51
VICTORIA 6F 17
Victoria Bus. Pk.
NP23: W Iwyd 6F 17
Victoria Ct. NP7: A'gvnny 3G 7
Victoria Pl. CF81: Gilf 5F 41
Victoria Rd. CF82: Maes C 6G 49
NP4: Abers 6E 29
NP4: P'pool 2D 46
NP12: Fleur, Maes C 3G 49
NP13: A'beeg 4B 34
Victoria Rd. NP22: Rhym 5B 14
NP23: E Vale 3E 17
Victoria St. CF83: L'brad 2B 68
NP4: Grif 4E 47
NP7: A'gvnny 4E 7
NP13: A'lery 5F 27
NP13: Blai 4C 18
NP44: C'brn 1B 64
Victoria Ter. NP11: Newb 3A 52
NP13: L'hth 1C 44
NP22: Tred 3A 16
VICTORIA VILLAGE 6E 29
Victor Rd. NP13: C'lery 5G 27
Vigar Ter. NP11: Ris 4D 72
Village Ct. NP12: Oakd 6E 43
Village La. NP23: W Iwyd 1F 25
Villas, The *CF81: Foch 4A 22*
(off Brook Row)
NP11: Newb 3H 51
NP12: Mark 5A 32
Vincent Av. NP23: N'glo 6C 12
Vincent St. NP4: B'avn 2F 21
Vine St. NP11: Aberc 6C 52
Violet Wlk. NP10: Roger 6F 73
Virginia Cl. CF83: Caer 3G 75
Virginia Ter. CF83: Caer 3F 75
Virginia Vw. CF83: Caer 3G 75
Vivian St. NP13: A'lery 1C 34

W

Wades, The *NP44: F'wtr 2G 63*
(off Rede Rd.)
Waengron NP13: Blai 4D 18
WAINFELIN 6F 37
Wainfelin Av. NP4: P'pool 6F 37
Wainfelin Rd. NP4: P'pool 5G 37
Walkdens NP44: F'wtr 2G 63
Walk, The CF82: Heng 1E 57
NP4: New I 3G 47
NP13: Blai 1C 18
NP23: E Vale 2E 17
NP23: N'glo 1C 18
Wallis Dr. CF82: P'heol 2D 48
Wall St. NP23: E Vale 1E 17
Walter Conway Av.
NP22: Tred 3G 15
Walters Av. NP11: Crum 5C 44
Walter St. NP13: A'lery 5G 27
NP22: A'swg 3E 23
NP22: Tred 5A 16
Ware Rd. CF83: Caer 6D 74
Warmington Pl. NP22: Rhym 4B 14
Warne St. NP12: Fleur 3G 49
Warn's Ter. NP22: A'swg 3E 23
Warren Ct. NP12: P'fraith 6D 50
Warrendale *NP44: F'wtr 2G 63*
(off Rede Rd.)
Warren Dr. CF83: Caer 6G 75
Warwick Cl. NP4: New I 5G 47
NP44: G'mdw 6A 54
Warwick Rd. NP23: B mawr 3H 11
WATERLOO
NP4 . . . . .1E 37
CF83 . . . . .2G 77
Waterloo NP12: Oakd 4E 43
Waterloo Ct. NP4: Grif 1E 55
Waterloo Pl. CF83: Mac 2G 77
NP4: Tal 1D 36
Waterloo Rd. NP4: Tal 1D 36
Waterloo Ter. CF81: P'tyn 3C 22
Waterloo Terrace Rd.
CF83: Mac 2G 77
Waterside NP7: A'gvnny 4G 7
Waterworks Rd.
NP4: Abers, Trev 6F 29
Watford Cl. CF83: Caer 6E 75
WATFORD PARK 6E 75
Watford Ri. CF83: Caer 6F 75
Watford Rd. CF83: Caer 6E 75
Watson Row CF81: Deri 5A 30
WATTSVILLE 2E 71
Waun Borfa Rd.
NP12: Cefn F, Peng 1G 49
Waunddu NP4: P'nydd 5E 37
WAUNDEG 5E 9
Waundeg NP22: Tred 5E 9
Waun Dew NP23: B'fort 3F 11
Waun Ebbw NP23: N'glo 5A 12
Waun-Ebbw Rd. NP23: N'glo 5A 12
Waun Erw CF83: Caer 2G 75
Waunfach Flats CF83: Caer 3F 75
Waunfach St. CF83: Caer 3F 75
Waun Fain CF83: Caer 1E 75
Waun Fawr NP23: Rassa 3C 10
Waunfawr Gdns.
NP11: C'keys 2A 72
Waunfawr Ho. NP11: C'keys 2H 71
Waunfawr Park Rd.
NP11: C'keys 1H 71
Waunfawr Rd. NP11: C'keys 1H 71
Waunfawr Ter. NP11: C'keys 1H 71
Waunganol St. CF83: Caer 3G 75
Waun Goch CF82: Cefn H 4D 48
Waungoch Rd. NP12: Oakd 6F 43
(not continuous)
Waun Gogh Ter. *NP23: B'fort 3E 11*
(off Nelson St.)
Waunheulog NP23: N'glo 4A 12
Waun Hywel Rd.
NP44: Pnwd 3C 54
WAUNLLAPRIA 2H 13
Waun Llwyn Cres.
NP12: B'wood 2A 50
WAUN-LWYD 1G 25
Waun Rd. NP44: C'brn 2H 63
Waunwern Pk. Cvn. Site
NP4: P'pool 2A 46
Waun-y-Pound Ind. Est.
NP23: E Vale 5B 10
Waun-y-Pound Rd.
NP23: E Vale 5C 10
Wayfield Cres. NP44: Pnwd 4E 55
Wedgewood Ct. CF83: Caer 4A 76
Weir Vw. NP22: Tred 5F 9
Weldon Cl. NP44: C'iog 4H 55
Wellfield Cl. NP7: A'gvnny 2F 7
Wellfield La. NP4: Grif 6D 46
Wellington Dr. NP44: G'mdw 6A 54
Wellington La. NP4: P'pool 1A 46
Wellington Rd. NP4: Tal 1D 36
Wellington Ter. NP24: Brith 4E 31
Wellington Way NP22: Rhym . . .1C 22
Wellspring Ter. NP11: Ris 4D 72
Well St. NP23: B mawr 3A 12
Wentloog Cl. NP44: C'brn 6E 55
Wentsland Cres. NP4: P'pool . . .1A 46
Wentsland Rd. NP4: P'pool 1A 46
Wentwood Cl. NP44: Pnwd 3C 54
Wentwood Pl. NP11: Ris 4F 73
WERN DDU 6C 76
Wernddu Ct. CF83: Caer 5A 76
Wern-ddu Row CF83: Caer 6B 76
Wern Fach Ct. NP44: H'lys 3E 63
Wern Hill NP4: P'pool 1B 46
Wern Rd. NP4: Grif 6E 47
Wern School Cl. NP4: Grif 6E 47
Wern Ter. NP4: P'pool 1B 46
Wesleyan Pl. NP23: B'fort 3E 11
Wesley Cl. NP44: C'brn 1A 64
Wesley Hill CF83: Mac 6D 70
Wesley Pl. NP11: Ris 4C 72
Wesley Rd. CF83: Caer 6C 74
NP12: B'wood 2B 50
Wesley St. NP44: C'brn 1B 64
Wesley Ter. NP4: P'nydd 6C 36
NP7: L Hill 3H 13
NP11: Pent C 3A 44
West Av. CF82: Maes C 1G 57
CF83: Caer 4D 74
NP4: Grif 6D 46
West Bank NP44: Llanf 1E 65
WEST END 6B 52
W. End Av. NP4: P'nydd 4F 37
West End Ter. NP23: E Vale 1E 17
Western Av NP23: B mawr 3H 11
Western Cres. NP22: Tred 2G 15
Western Dr. CF81: Barg 4D 40
CF83: Caer 6D 74
Western Ind. Est. CF83: Caer . . .6D 74
Western Rd. NP7: A'gvnny 3D 6
Western Ter. NP11: C'fch 1H 69
NP11: C'keys 6C 60
NP23: E Vale 6E 11
Westgil Pen Ffordd
NP12: Cefn F 3A 50
West Hill NP22: Tred 2G 15
W. Hill Rd. NP4: C'avn 4G 37
Westley Bldgs. NP23: N'glo 5B 12
West Pl. NP4: P'pool 1C 46
WEST PONTNEWYDD 4C 54
West Rd. CF82: G'gaer 5C 48
West Roedin NP44: F'wtr 3H 63
Westside Rd. CF83: Sen 3B 66
West St. CF81: Barg 3E 41
West Vw. NP11: Newb 3A 52
NP44: C'brn 6C 54
West Vw. Cres. NP12: Oakd 6D 42
Westview Ter. CF83: Caer 2A 76
West Vw. Ter. NP4: B'avn 2E 21
NP23: E Vale 3F 17
West View Vs. CF81: A'goed 3F 41
Westville NP22: A'swg 3E 23
Wheatley Pl. NP12: B'wood 1A 50
Whistle Rd. NP4: G Erw 1A 20
Whitebrook Way
NP44: C'brn 1B 64
White Cross La. CF83: Caer 3C 74
White Hall La. NP44: Llanf 1E 65
White Hart Dr. CF83: Mac 6D 70
Whitehorne St. NP11: Crum 6B 44
Whitehorse La. NP7: A'gvnny 4F 7
Whitehouse Cl. NP44: C'iog 4G 55
White Ho. Ct. NP13: C'lery 4G 27
White House Gdns.
NP4: Lit M 2H 39
Whitehouse Rd. NP44: C'iog 4G 55
White Rose Way
NP24: New T 2D 30
White's Cl. NP7: A'gvnny 5G 7
White St. CF83: Caer 5G 75
Whitworth Flds. NP22: Tred 5A 16
Whitworth Ter. NP22: Tred 4A 16
Wilcrick Way NP44: Pnwd 4F 55
Wilkins Ter. CF83: Caer 1E 75
William Adams Ct.
NP23: E Vale 1E 17
William Brown Cl.
NP44: Oakf 4D 64
William Forbes Bungs.
CF81: A'goed 1F 41
William Harris Bungs.
CF83: Abert 6D 66
William Morris Way
NP23: Rassa 4C 10
Williams St. NP12: B'wood 2C 50
William St. CF81: A'goed 3G 41
CF81: Gilf 5F 41
CF82: Tir B 3F 49
CF83: Abert 6D 66
CF83: Tret 6H 69
NP11: C'fch 2A 70
NP11: Crum 6A 44
NP12: Fleur 4G 49
NP12: Holly B 2A 32
NP23: Cwm 4H 25
NP44: Pnwd 4E 55
Willins NP44: F'wtr 3G 63
Willow Cl. NP7: A'gvnny 5G 7
NP23: E Vale 6D 10
Willow Ct. NP11: Newb 1C 52
NP22: Tred 5F 9
Willow Dr. NP12: Oakd 3C 50
Willow Parc NP11: C'maen 6F 43
Willow Ri. CF82: P'heol 2C 48
Willow Rd. NP11: Crum 4G 43
Willows, The CF83: B'ws 6F 69
NP13: A'lery 1D 34
WILLOWTOWN 1D 16
willow Wlk. NP10: Roger 6G 73
Wimborne Ri. NP44: Pnwd 4C 54
WINCHESTOWN 5A 12
Windermere Ct.
NP44: G'mdw 6C 54
Windsor Av. NP11: Newb 3H 51
Windsor Pl. CF83: Abert 6C 66
CF83: Sen 3C 66
NP13: A'beeg 6A 34
Windsor Rd. NP4: Grif 4E 47
NP7: A'gvnny 2D 6
NP13: S Bells 2D 34
NP23: B mawr 3H 11
NP44: F'wtr, G'mdw 1G 63
Windsor St. CF83: Caer 5G 75
Windsor Ter. NP13: A'beeg 6A 34
Windy Ridge NP12: P'fraith 5E 51
Wine St. CF81: P'tyn 2C 22
Wingfield Cres. CF83: L'brad 2B 68
Wingfield Ter. CF83: L'brad 3B 68
Winifred Ter. NP13: C'lery 3G 27
Winsford Gro. NP7: Gilw 3C 4
Winstone Rd. NP4: C'avn 4G 37
Winterson Cl. NP23: Rassa 2B 10
Wiston Path NP44: F'wtr 1G 63
Woodbine Cotts.
NP4: P'nydd 6D 36
Woodbine Rd. NP12: B'wood 2B 50
Wood Cl. NP44: Llanf 2E 65
Woodfield Cross NP22: Tred 5A 16
Woodfield Pk. Cr.
NP12: Oakd 3C 50

Woodfield Rd. NP4: New I 3G **47**
NP22: Tred 4A **16**
NP23: Cwm 3A **26**
WOODFIELDSIDE 2C **50**
Woodfieldside Bus. Pk.
NP12: P'fraith 4D **50**
Woodfield St. NP12: Oakd 3D **50**
Woodfield Ter. CF82: Tir B 3E **49**
NP12: Oakd 3D **50**
Woodland Ct. NP44: C'iog 5G **55**
Woodland Cres. NP7: L'fst . . . . . .6D **6** (Grove Av.)
NP7: L'fst . . . . .6D **6** (Llanelen Rd.)
Woodland Dr. NP10: Roger 6H **73**
NP11: Newb 3B **52**
NP11: Pent C 2A **44**
Woodland Pl. CF81: Gilf 6F **41**
CF82: Cefn H 5E **49**
NP12: Peng 2G **49**
Woodland Rd. NP7: A'gvnny 3G **7**
NP12: P'fraith 5D **50**
NP44: C'iog 4G **55**
Woodlands NP4: Tal 6D **28**
NP22: Tred 6F **9**
Woodlands, The NP4: P'pool 6A **38**
Woodland St. NP4: B'avn 2G **21**
NP44: C'brn 5C **54**
Woodland Ter. CF83: Abert 6C **66**
CF83: Sen 2C **66**
NP4: P'nydd 5E **37**
NP11: Aberc 6B **52**
NP12: Argoed 3C **42**
Woodland Ter. NP13: A'beeg 4A **34**
NP13: C'lery 3G **27**
NP24: New T 6G **23**
Woodland Vw. NP4: P'pool 5G **37**
NP4: Var 4D **28**
NP11: W'vle 2E **71**
Wood Path NP44: C'iog 3G **55**
Woodside CF82: Tir B 3F **49**
Woodside Cres.
NP23: E Vale 3E **17**
Woodside Rd. NP4: C'avn 3G **37**
NP44: C'brn 5E **55**
Woodside Ter. NP11: Crum 5C **44**
NP13: L'hth 1C **44**
NP44: C'brn 5D **54**
Woodside Way NP44: C'brn 5C **54**
Wood St. CF81: Barg 4E **41**
NP11: C'crn 3C **60**
Woodview Ct. NP4: P'pool 1B **46**
Wood Vw. Cres. NP11: Ris 4D **72**
Wood Vw. Rd. NP11: Ris 3D **72**
Woodview Ter. NP4: P'pool 1B **46**
NP11: Crum 5H **43**
Woodville Ter. NP12: Argoed 2C **42**
Woodward Av. NP11: C'keys 1G **71**
Woodward Rd. NP11: C'keys 1H **71**
Woolpitch NP44: G'mdw 6B **54**
Worcester Cl. NP44: Llan 6G **55**
Worcester Path NP44: Llan 6G **55**
Worcester St. NP23: B mawr 3A **12**
Wordsworth Cl. NP23: E Vale . . .1C **16**
NP44: C'brn 1A **64**
Works La. CF82: Tir B 4F **49**
Wye Ct. NP44: G'mdw 5B **54**
WYLLIE 2C **58**
Wyndham Rd. NP7: A'gvnny 3H **7**
Wyndham St. CF83: Mac 6E **71**
Wyndham Ter. NP11: Ris 4E **73**

Y

Yard Row NP23: B'fort 4E **11**
Y Cedrwydden
NP12: B'wood 4A **50**
Y Cilgant CF83: Caer 1D **74**
Y Dolydd CF83: Caer 6E **75**
Yellow Row *NP4: P'pool . . . . . . .2A* ***46*** *(off Crumlin Rd.)*
Yew Gro. NP12: Oakd 3C **50**
Yew St. CF81: A'goed 2G **41**
Yew Tree Rd. NP11: Newb 2B **52**
Yew Tree Ter. NP44: C'brn 1A **64**
NP44: C'iog 4G **55**
Y Felin Ffrwd CF83: Caer 3D **74**
Y FENNI 4F **7**
Y Glyn CF82: Maes C 2F **57**
Y GROES-WEN 5A **74**
YNYSDDU 6C **58**
Ynys Glyd St. CF82: Ystrad 4E **57**
Ynys Hywel Countryside Cen. .2A **70**
Ynys La. NP44: C'iog 4G **55**
Ynyswen NP12: P'fraith 6D **50**
Ynys-y-Coed NP12: Oakd 1D **50**
York Av. NP12: Oakd 6E **43**
NP23: E Vale 5E **17**
York Cl. NP44: G'mdw 6A **54**
York Pl. NP11: C'crn 3B **60**
NP11: Ris 2C **72**
York St. NP13: A'lery 6F **27**
York Ter. NP22: Tred 3A **16**
NP23: Cwm 4H **25**
YSBYTY'R TRI CHWM 4D **10**
Ysgol Pl. NP44: Up Cwm 3C **54**
Ysgubor Fach CF83: Mac 6E **71**
Ysguborwen NP7: A'gvnny 2G **7**
Ysgubor Wen NP22: Tred 6H **9**
Ystrad Deri NP22: Tred . . . . .5H **9** (not continuous)
Ystrad Drain NP4: B'avn, Var 6D **20**
YSTRAD MYNACH 2E **56**
YSTRAD MYNACH HOSPITAL . . . 3D **56**
Ystrad Mynach Sports Hall 2E **57**
Ystrad Mynach Station (Rail) . . .2D **56**
Ystrad Ter NP11: Aberc 5D **52**

Z

Zephaniah Way NP13: Blai 4C **18**
Zion Hill *NP4: P'nydd . . . . .5F* ***37*** *(off Pentrepiod Rd.)*
Zion Pl. NP23: E Vale 3E **17**
Zion St. NP23: E Vale 3E **17**

The representation on the maps of a road, track or footpath is no evidence of the existence of a right of way.

The Grid on this map is the National Grid taken from Ordnance Survey mapping with the permission of the Controller of Her Majesty's Stationery Office.

Nid yw'r ffaith bod ffordd, trac neu lwybr wedi eu nodi ar y map yn brawf bod hawl tramwyo yn bodoli.

Y grid ar y map hwn yw'r Grid Cenedlaethol a gymerwyd oddi ar Fap yr Arolwg Ordnans gyda chaniatâd Rheolwr Llyfrfa Ei Mawrhydi.